コンプレックス・エイジ

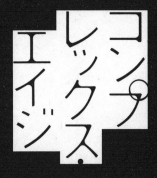

Complex age

Yui Sakuma

5

C O N T E N T S

Complex age

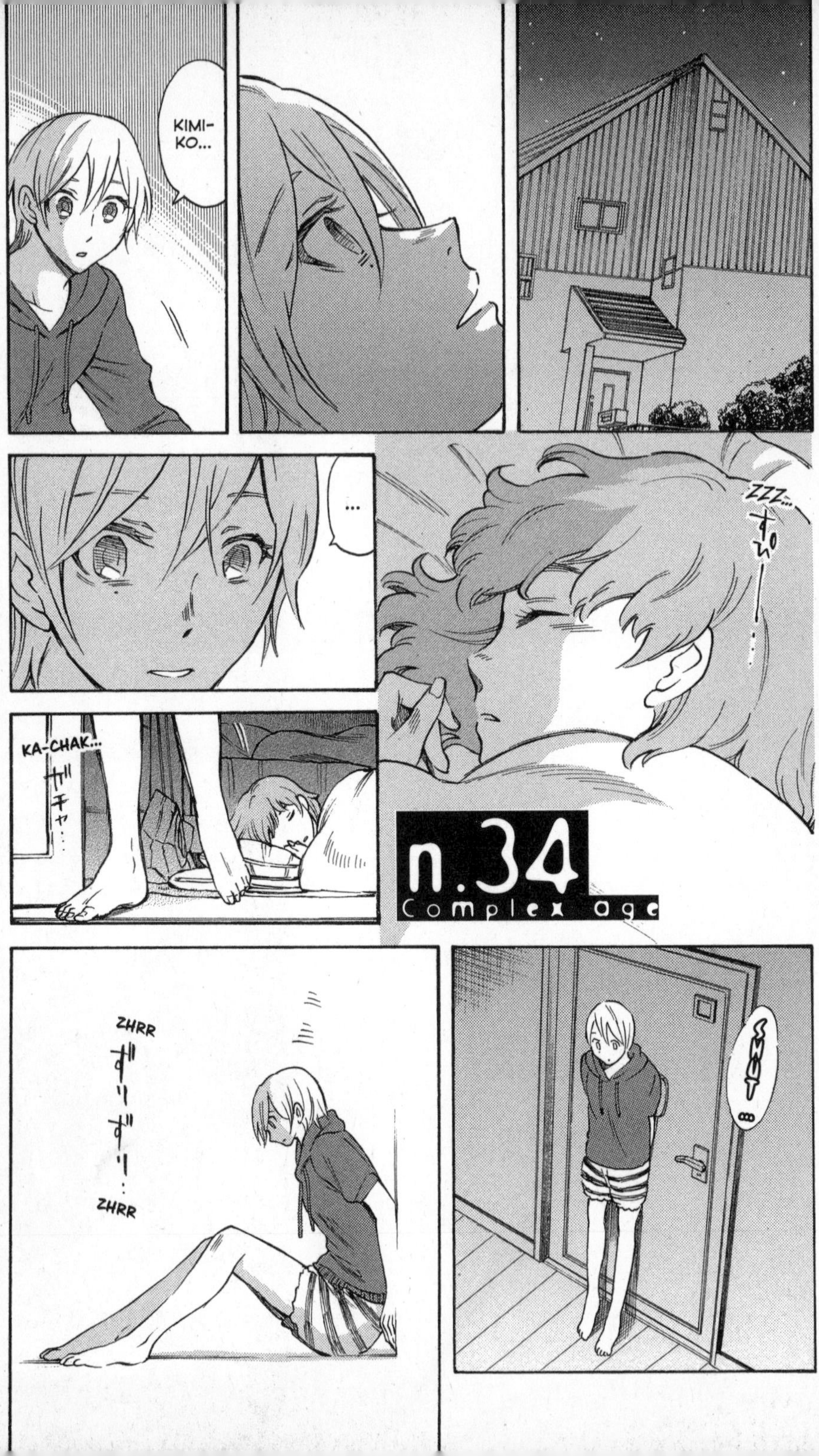
KIMI-
KO...
ZZZ...
すぴー…
n.34
Complex age
...
KA-CHAK...
ガチャ…
SHUT
ZHRR
ずりずり…
ZHRR

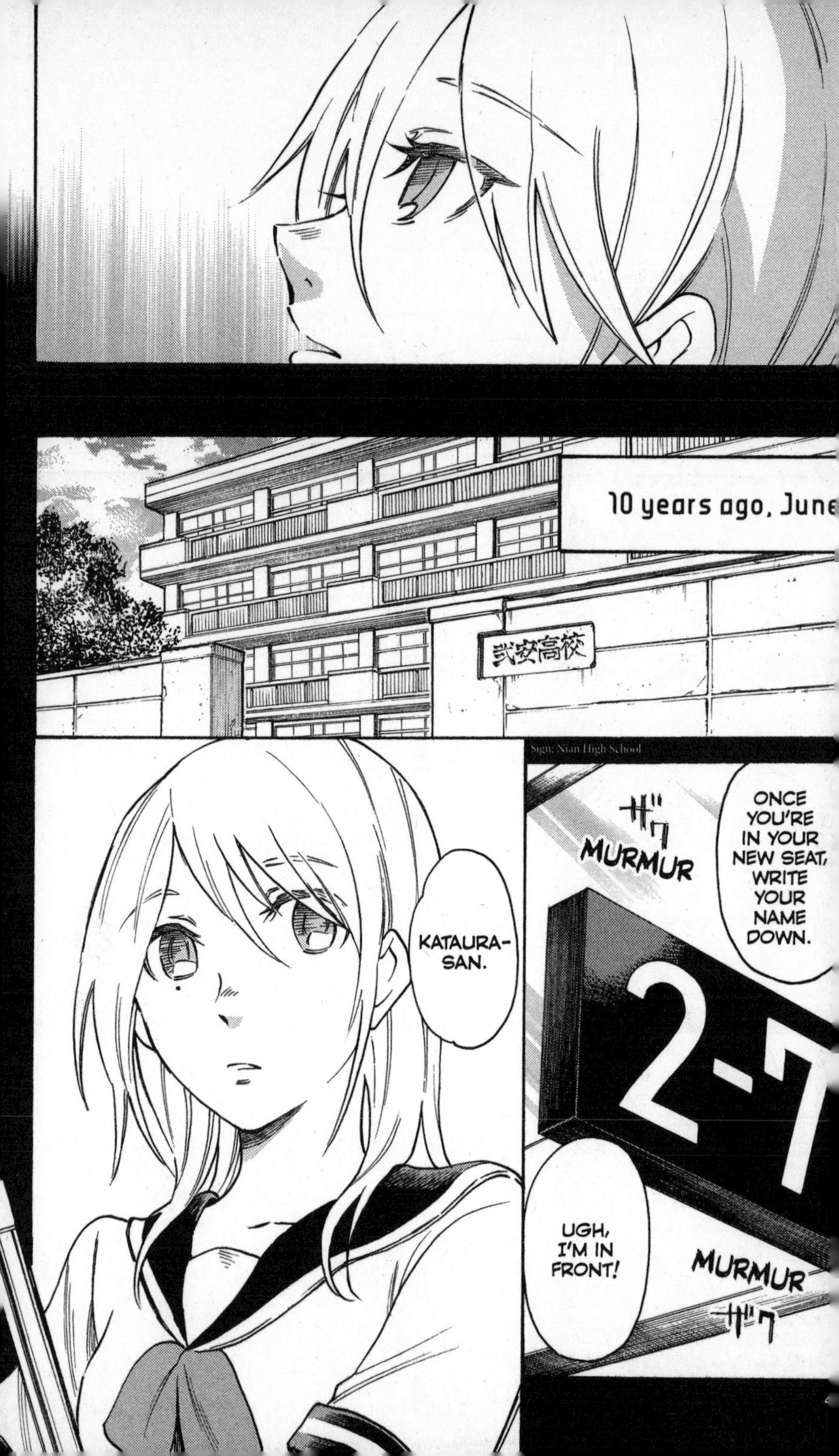
10 years ago, June
弐安高校
Sign: Nian High School
ONCE YOU'RE IN YOUR NEW SEAT, WRITE YOUR NAME DOWN.
ザワ MURMUR
UGH, I'M IN FRONT!
ザワ MURMUR
KATAURA-SAN.

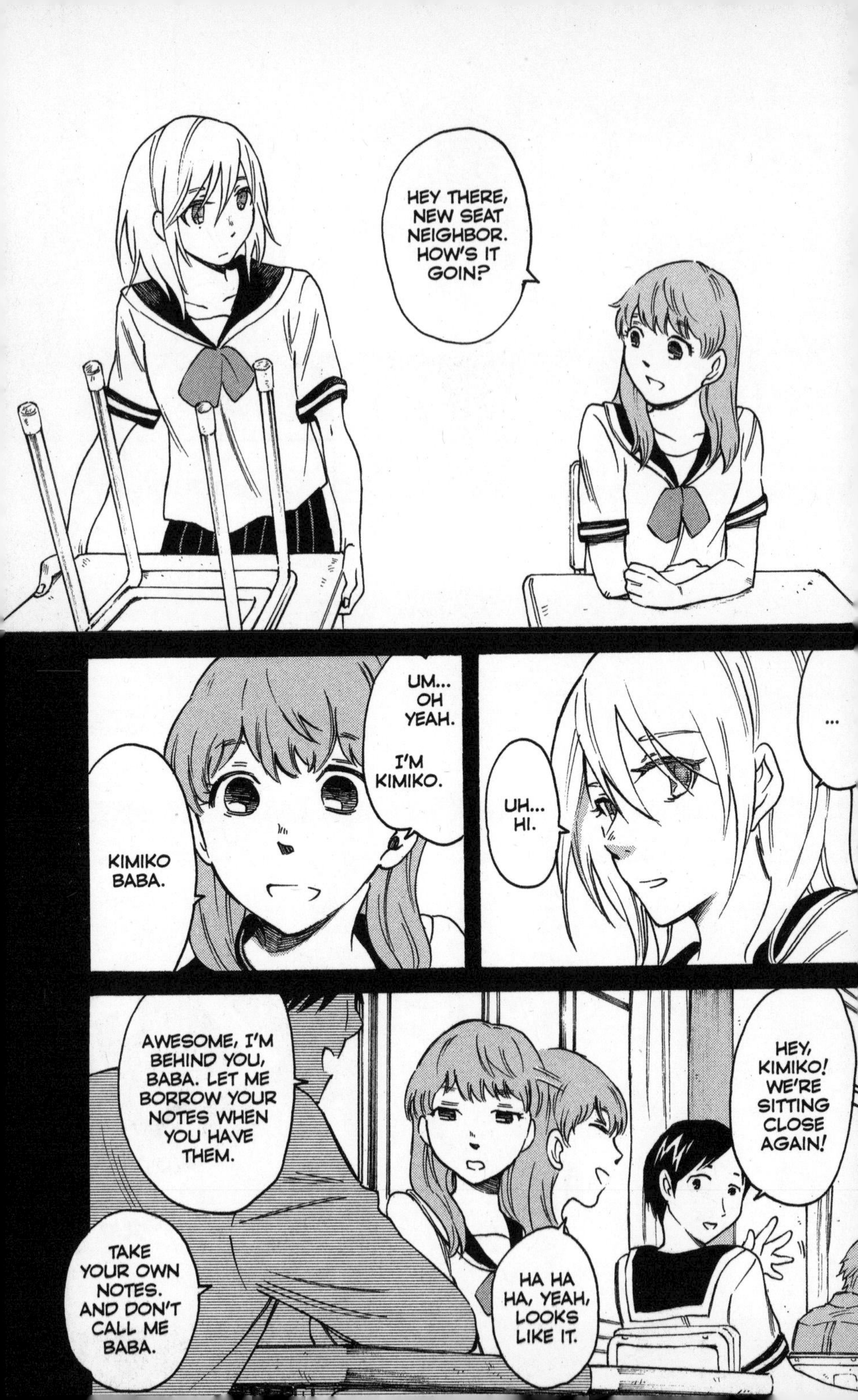
HEY THERE, NEW SEAT NEIGHBOR. HOW'S IT GOIN?
...
UH... HI.
UM... OH YEAH.
I'M KIMIKO.
KIMIKO BABA.
HEY, KIMIKO! WE'RE SITTING CLOSE AGAIN!
HA HA HA, YEAH, LOOKS LIKE IT.
AWESOME, I'M BEHIND YOU, BABA. LET ME BORROW YOUR NOTES WHEN YOU HAVE THEM.
TAKE YOUR OWN NOTES. AND DON'T CALL ME BABA.

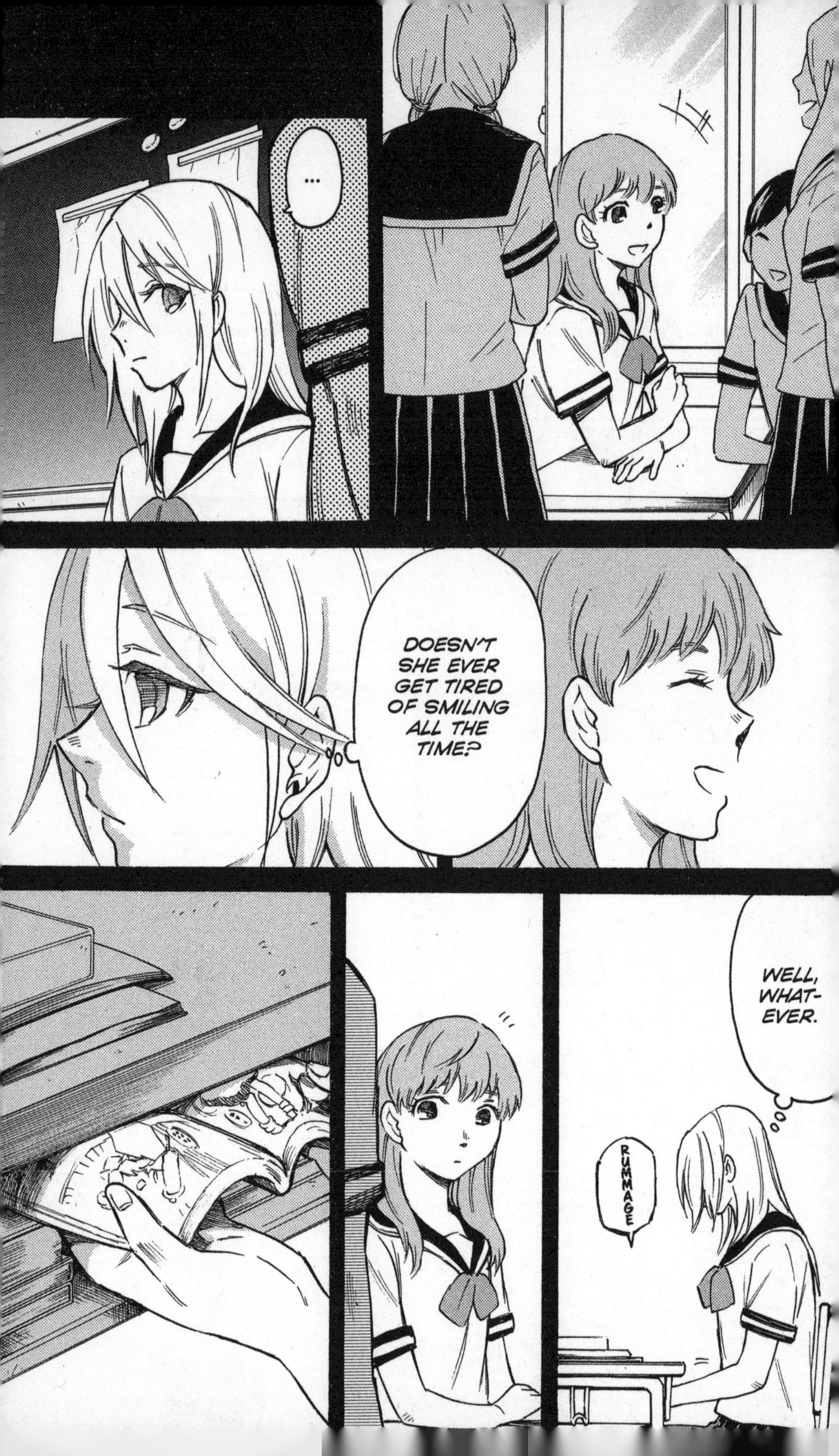
...
DOESN'T SHE EVER GET TIRED OF SMILING ALL THE TIME?
WELL, WHAT-EVER.
RUMMAGE

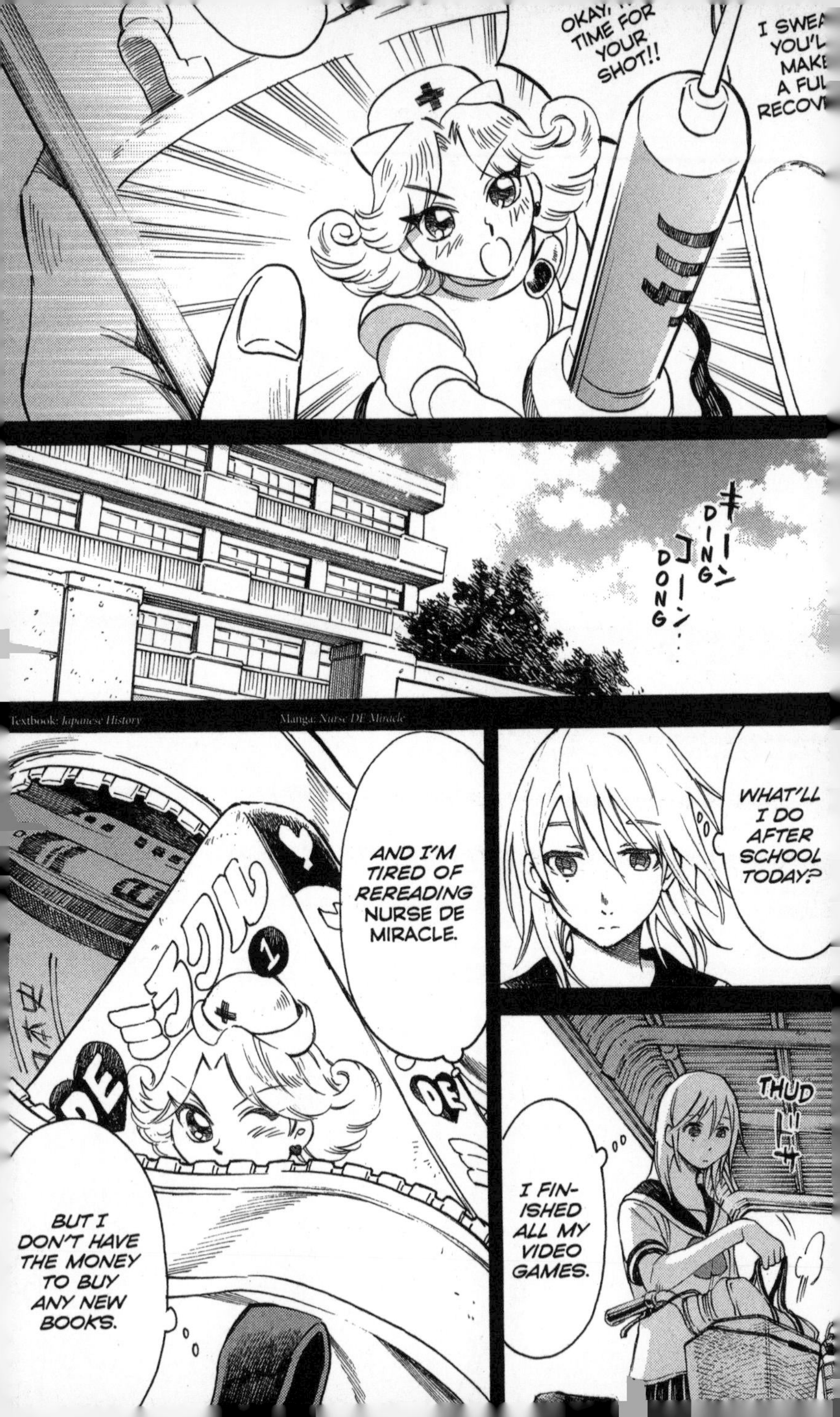
OKAY, TIME FOR YOUR SHOT!!
DING DONG...
Textbook: Japanese History
Manga: Nurse DE Miracle
WHAT'LL I DO AFTER SCHOOL TODAY?
THUD
I FIN-ISHED ALL MY VIDEO GAMES.
AND I'M TIRED OF REREADING NURSE DE MIRACLE.
BUT I DON'T HAVE THE MONEY TO BUY ANY NEW BOOKS.

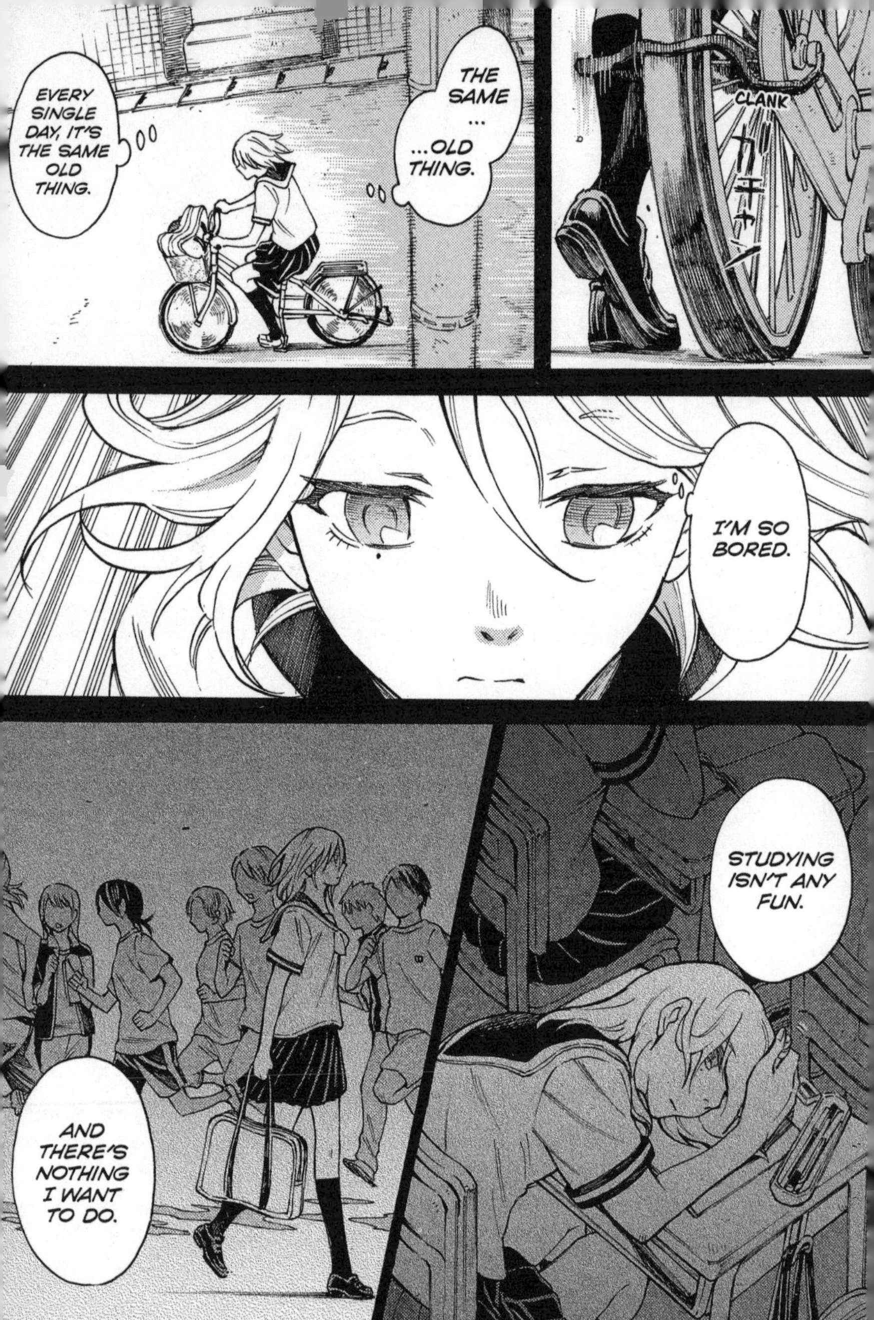
CLANK
THE SAME ... ...OLD THING.
EVERY SINGLE DAY, IT'S THE SAME OLD THING.
I'M SO BORED.
STUDYING ISN'T ANY FUN.
AND THERE'S NOTHING I WANT TO DO.

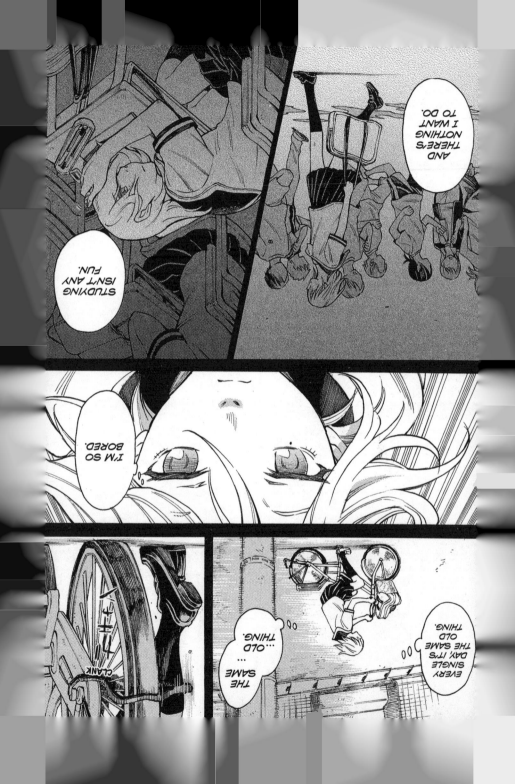

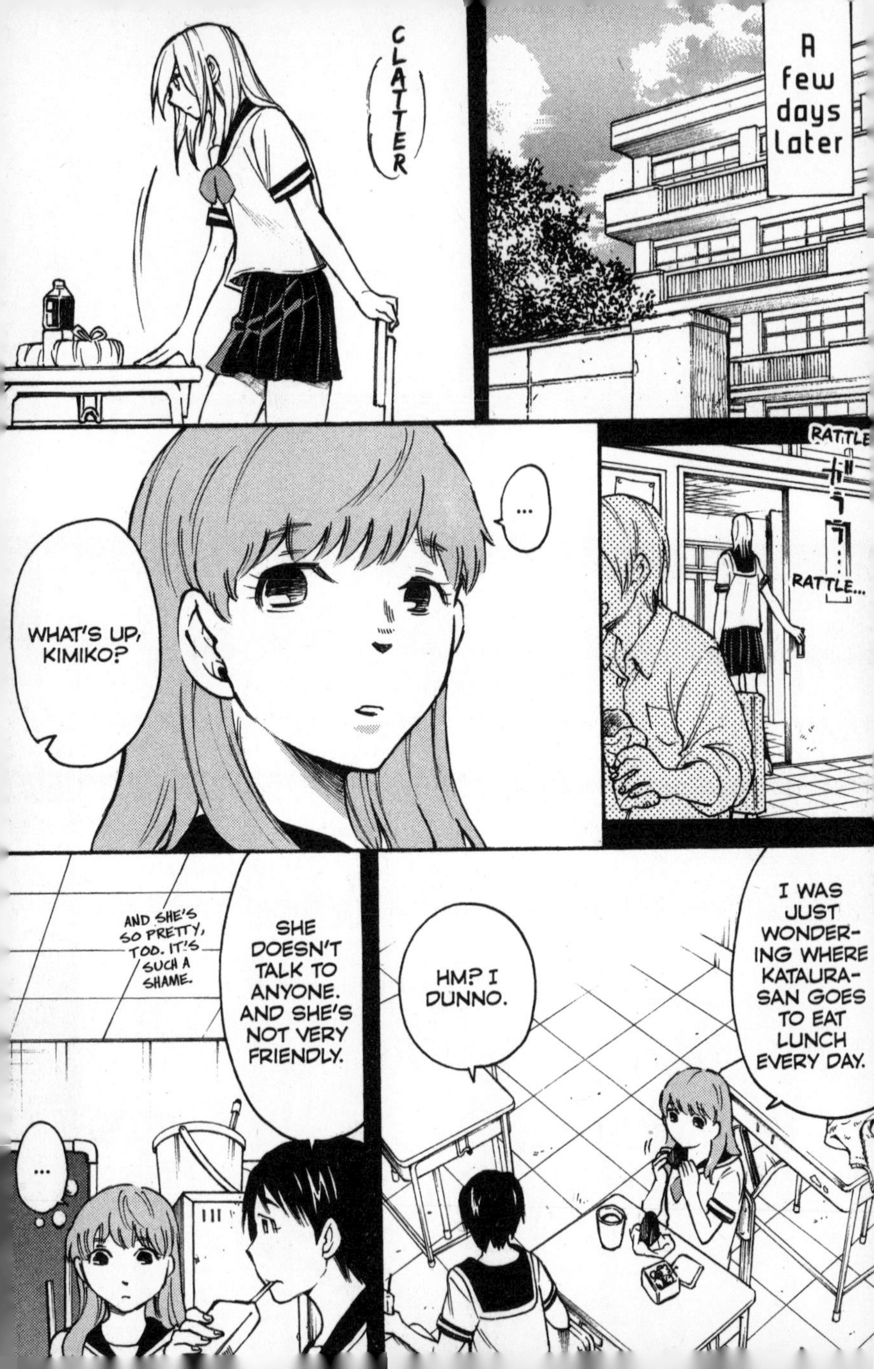
A few days later
CLATTER
RATTLE
RATTLE...
...
WHAT'S UP, KIMIKO?
I WAS JUST WONDERING WHERE KATAURA-SAN GOES TO EAT LUNCH EVERY DAY.
HM? I DUNNO.
SHE DOESN'T TALK TO ANYONE. AND SHE'S NOT VERY FRIENDLY.
AND SHE'S SO PRETTY, TOO. IT'S SUCH A SHAME.
...

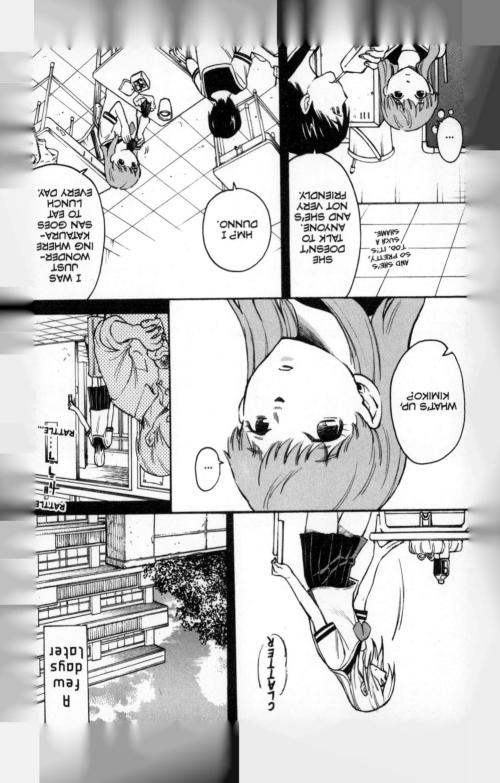

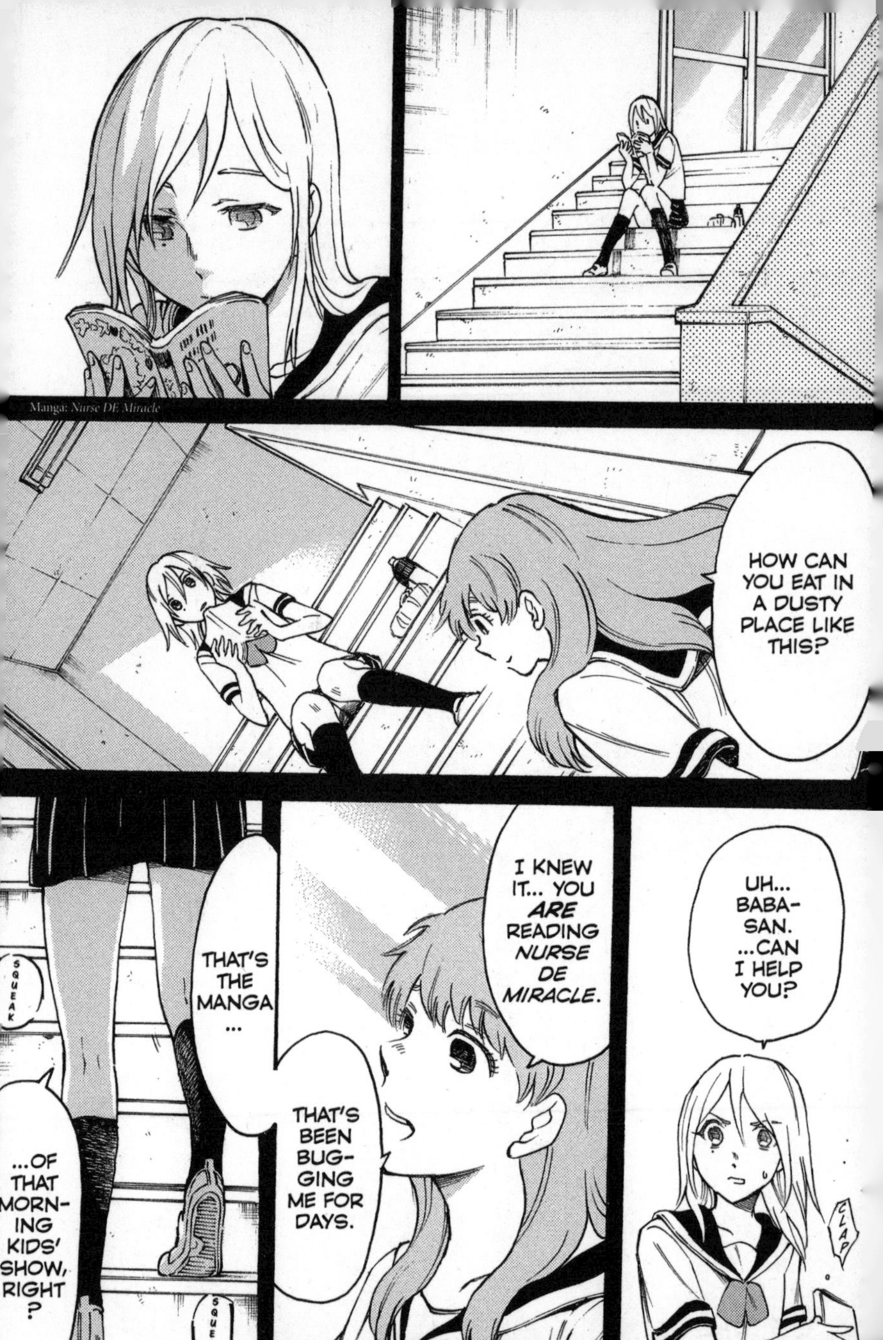
Manga: Nurse DE Miracle
HOW CAN YOU EAT IN A DUSTY PLACE LIKE THIS?
UH... BABA-SAN. ...CAN I HELP YOU?
CLAP
I KNEW IT... YOU *ARE* READING *NURSE DE MIRACLE*.
THAT'S THE MANGA ...
THAT'S BEEN BUG-GING ME FOR DAYS.
SQUEAK
...OF THAT MORN-ING KIDS' SHOW, RIGHT ?

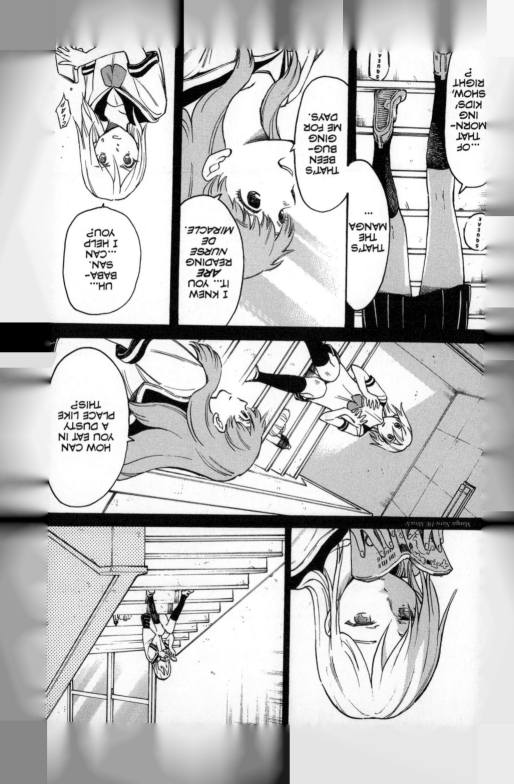

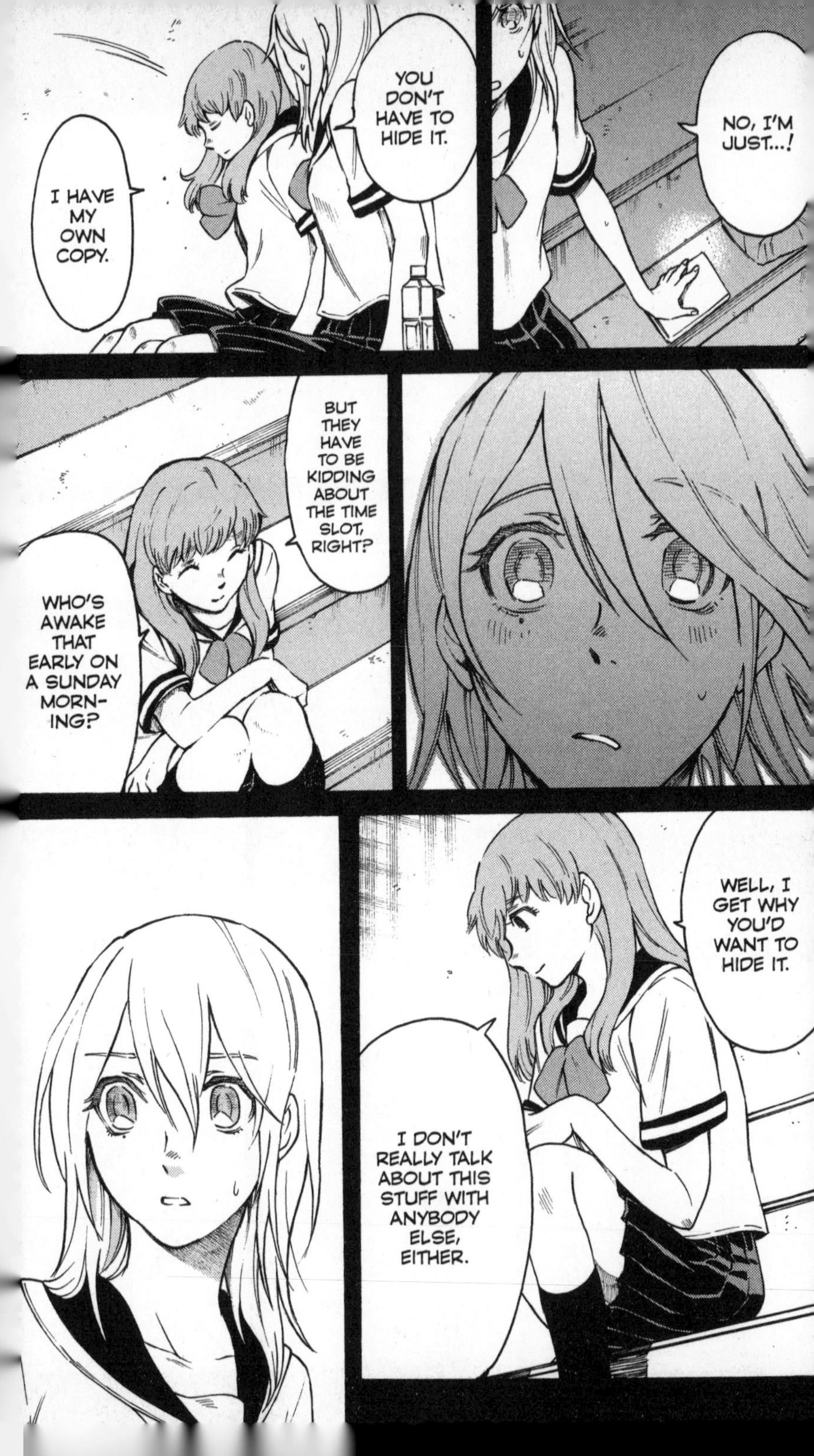
NO, I'M JUST...!
YOU DON'T HAVE TO HIDE IT.
I HAVE MY OWN COPY.
BUT THEY HAVE TO BE KIDDING ABOUT THE TIME SLOT, RIGHT?
WHO'S AWAKE THAT EARLY ON A SUNDAY MORNING?
WELL, I GET WHY YOU'D WANT TO HIDE IT.
I DON'T REALLY TALK ABOUT THIS STUFF WITH ANYBODY ELSE, EITHER.

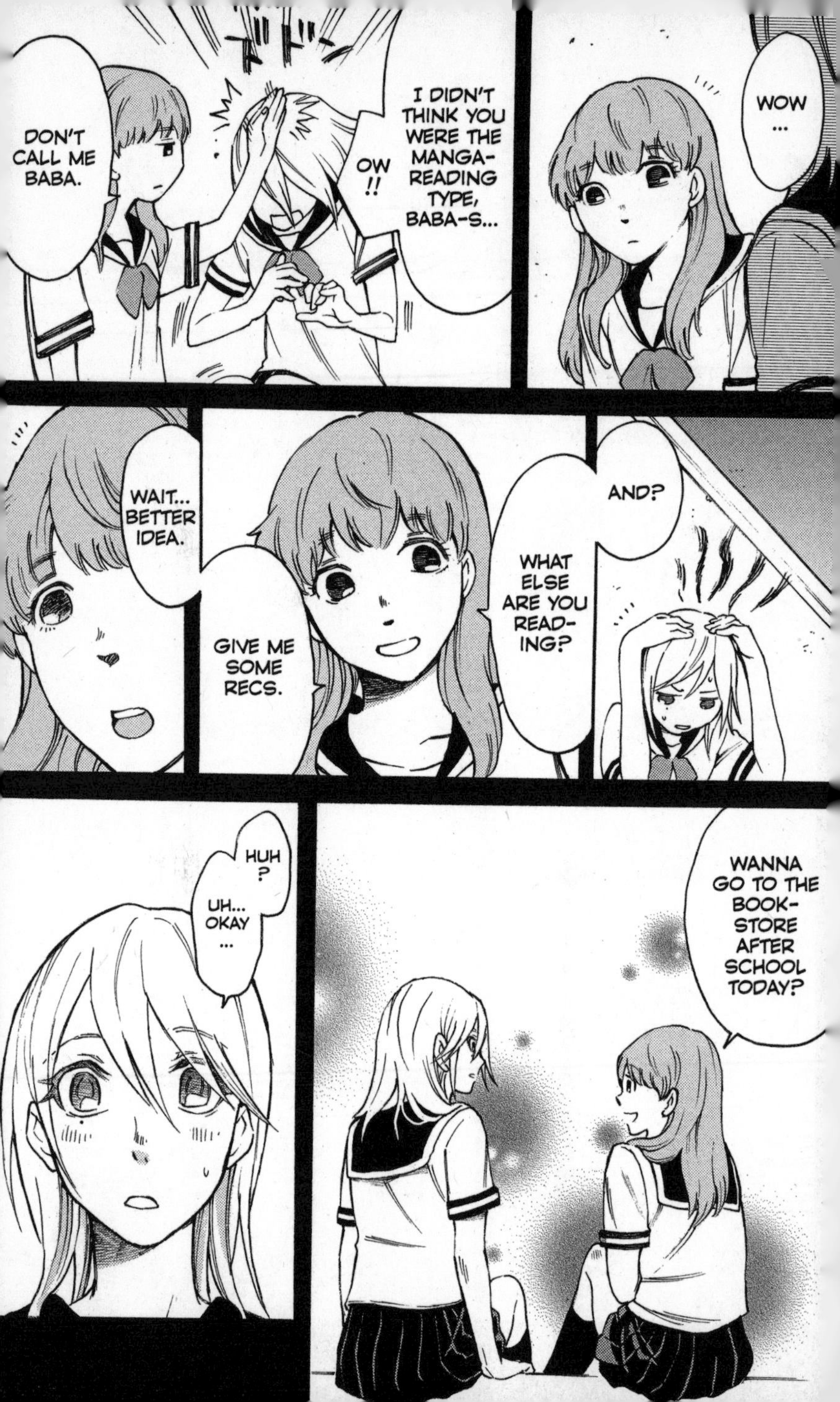
WOW ...
I DIDN'T THINK YOU WERE THE MANGA-READING TYPE, BABA-S...
OW !!
DON'T CALL ME BABA.
AND?
WHAT ELSE ARE YOU READ-ING?
GIVE ME SOME RECS.
WAIT... BETTER IDEA.
WANNA GO TO THE BOOK-STORE AFTER SCHOOL TODAY?
HUH ?
UH... OKAY ...

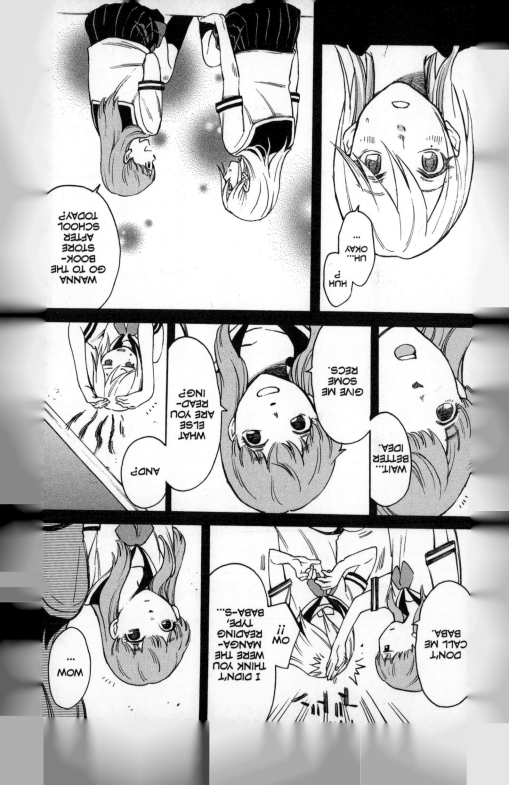

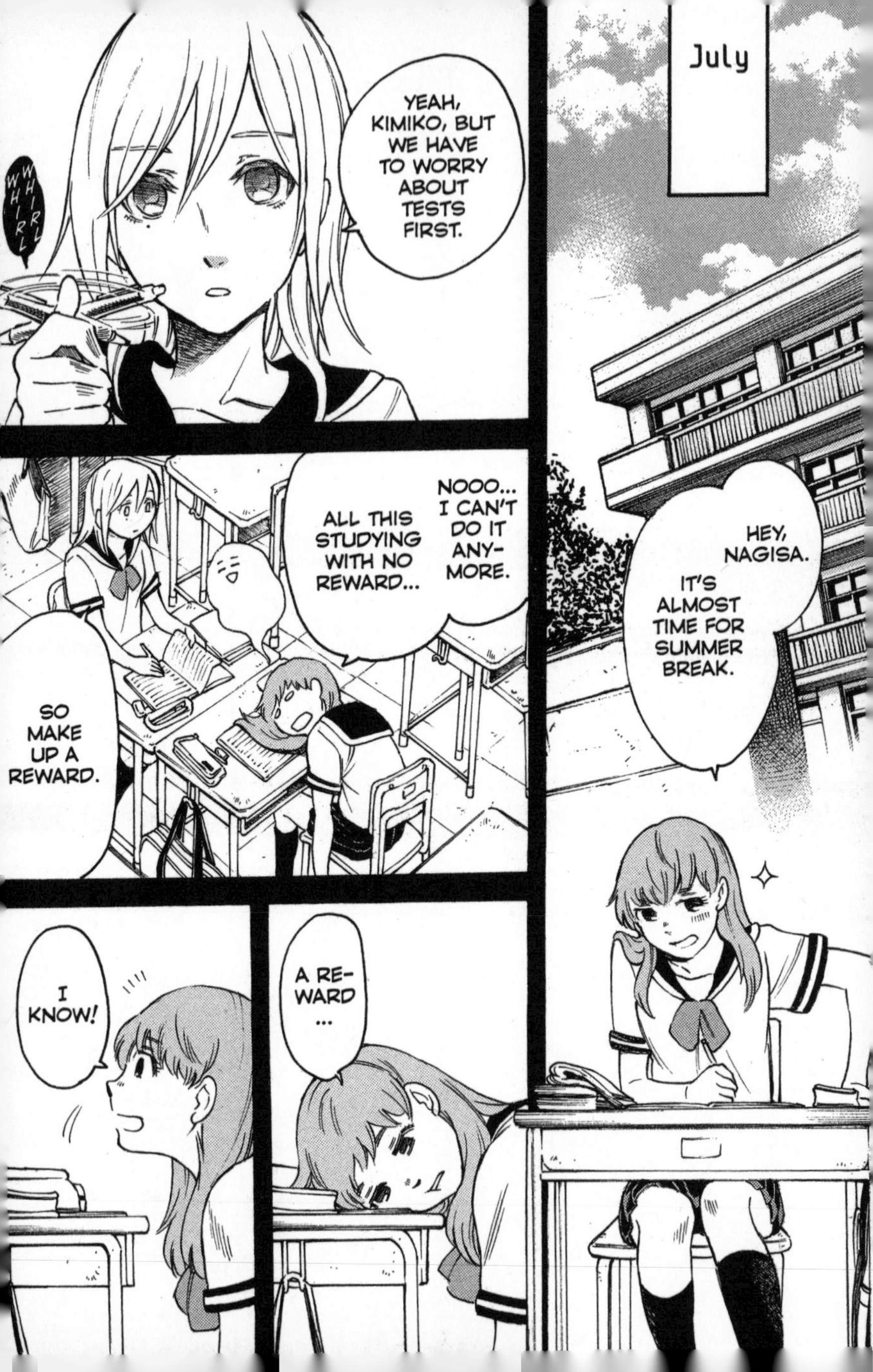
July
HEY, NAGISA.
IT'S ALMOST TIME FOR SUMMER BREAK.
YEAH, KIMIKO, BUT WE HAVE TO WORRY ABOUT TESTS FIRST.
WHIRL WHIRL
NOOO... I CAN'T DO IT ANY-MORE.
ALL THIS STUDYING WITH NO REWARD...
SO MAKE UP A REWARD.
A RE-WARD ...
I KNOW!

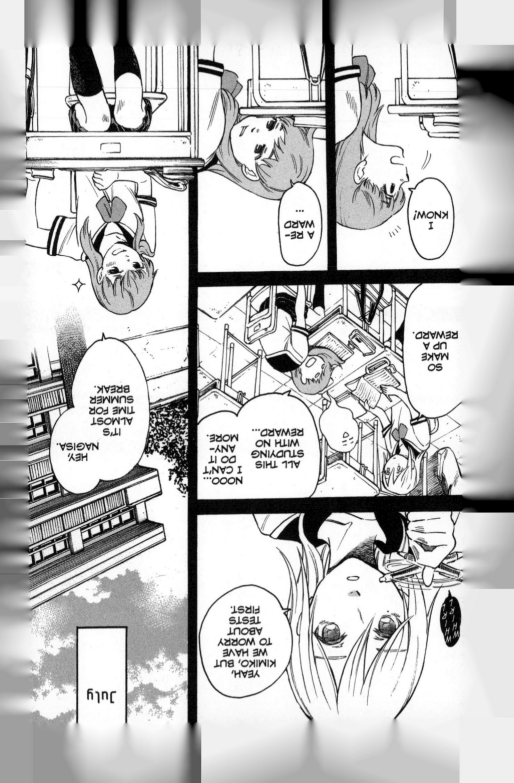

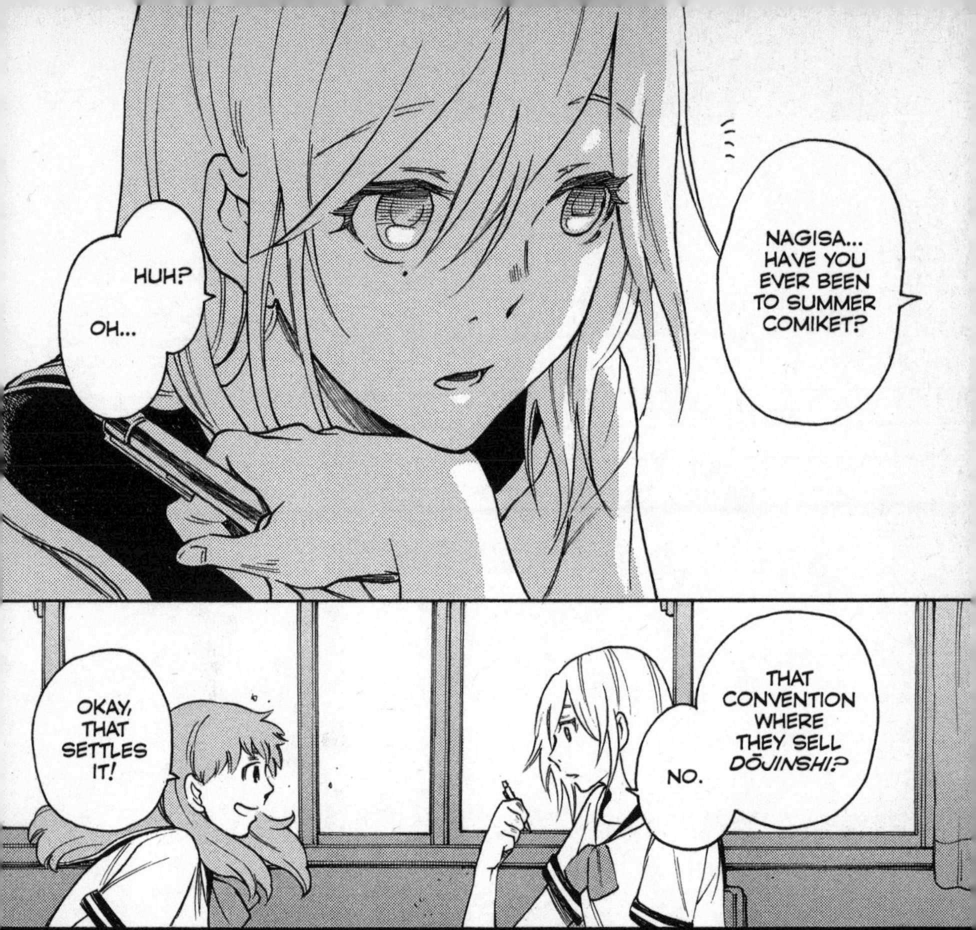
NAGISA... HAVE YOU EVER BEEN TO SUMMER COMIKET?
HUH?
OH...
THAT CONVENTION WHERE THEY SELL *DŌJINSHI*?
NO.
OKAY, THAT SETTLES IT!

Summer Comiket: Short for Summer Comic Market, a large *dōjinshi* fair held in August.

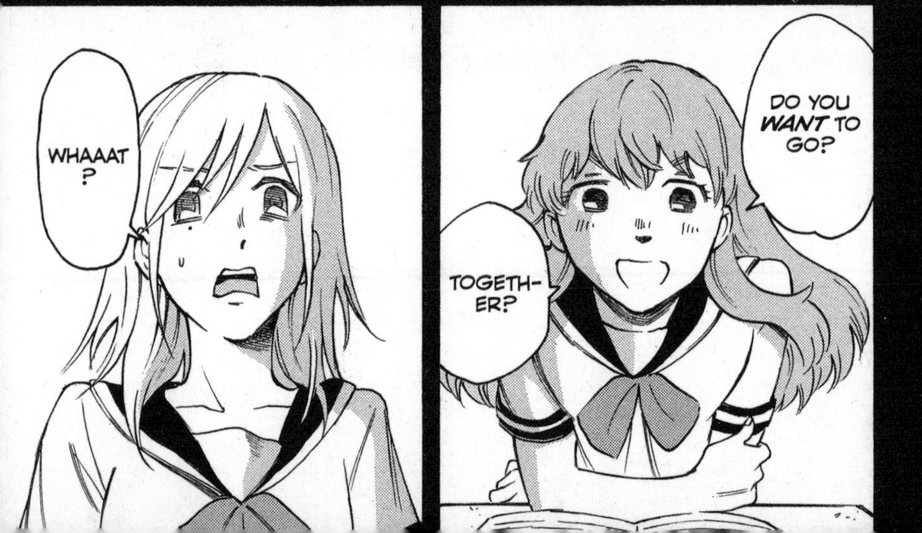
DO YOU ***WANT*** TO GO?
TOGETH-ER?
WHAAAT?

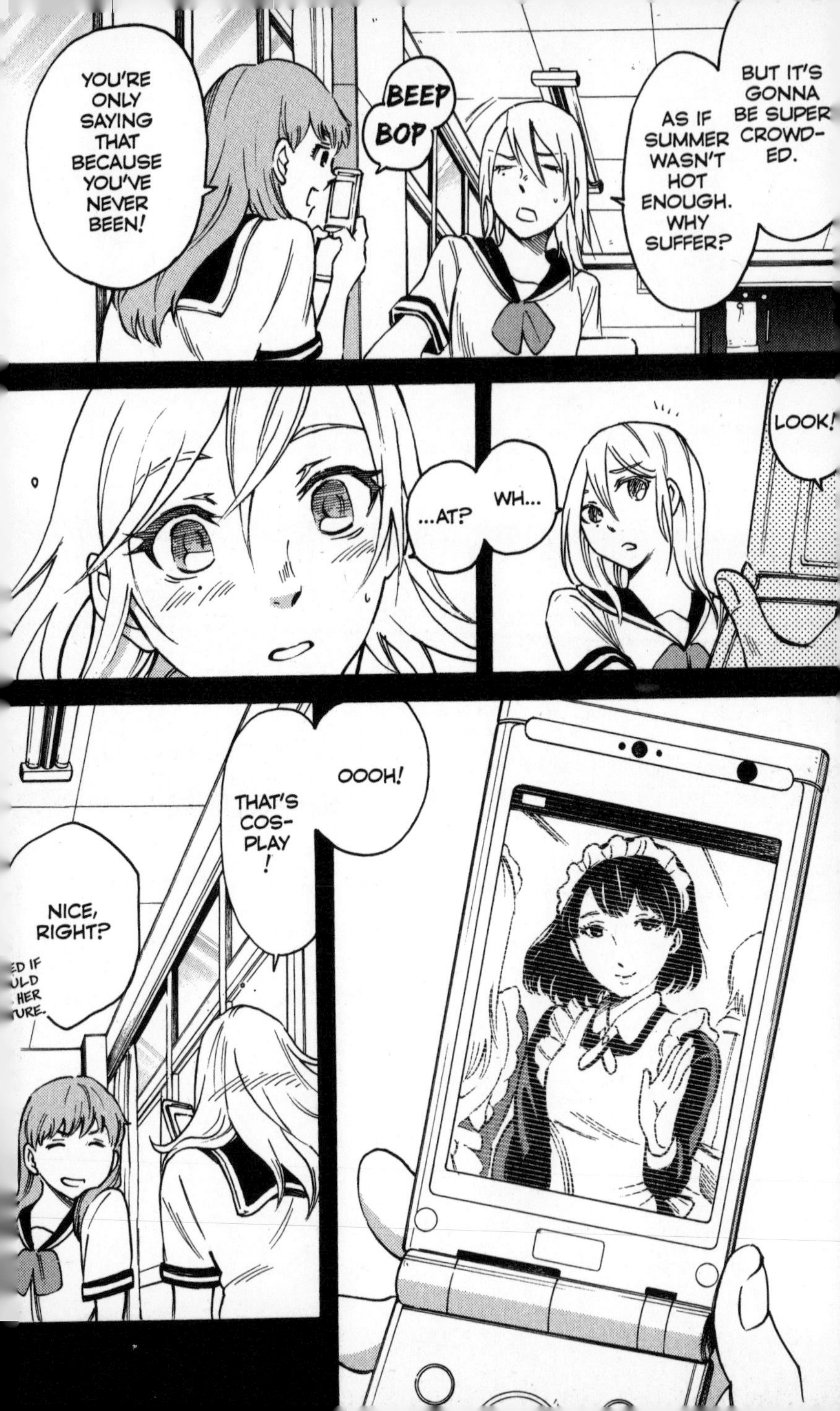
BUT IT'S GONNA BE SUPER CROWD-ED.
AS IF SUMMER WASN'T HOT ENOUGH. WHY SUFFER?
BEEP BOP
YOU'RE ONLY SAYING THAT BECAUSE YOU'VE NEVER BEEN!
LOOK!
WH...
...AT?
OOOH!
THAT'S COS-PLAY!
NICE, RIGHT?

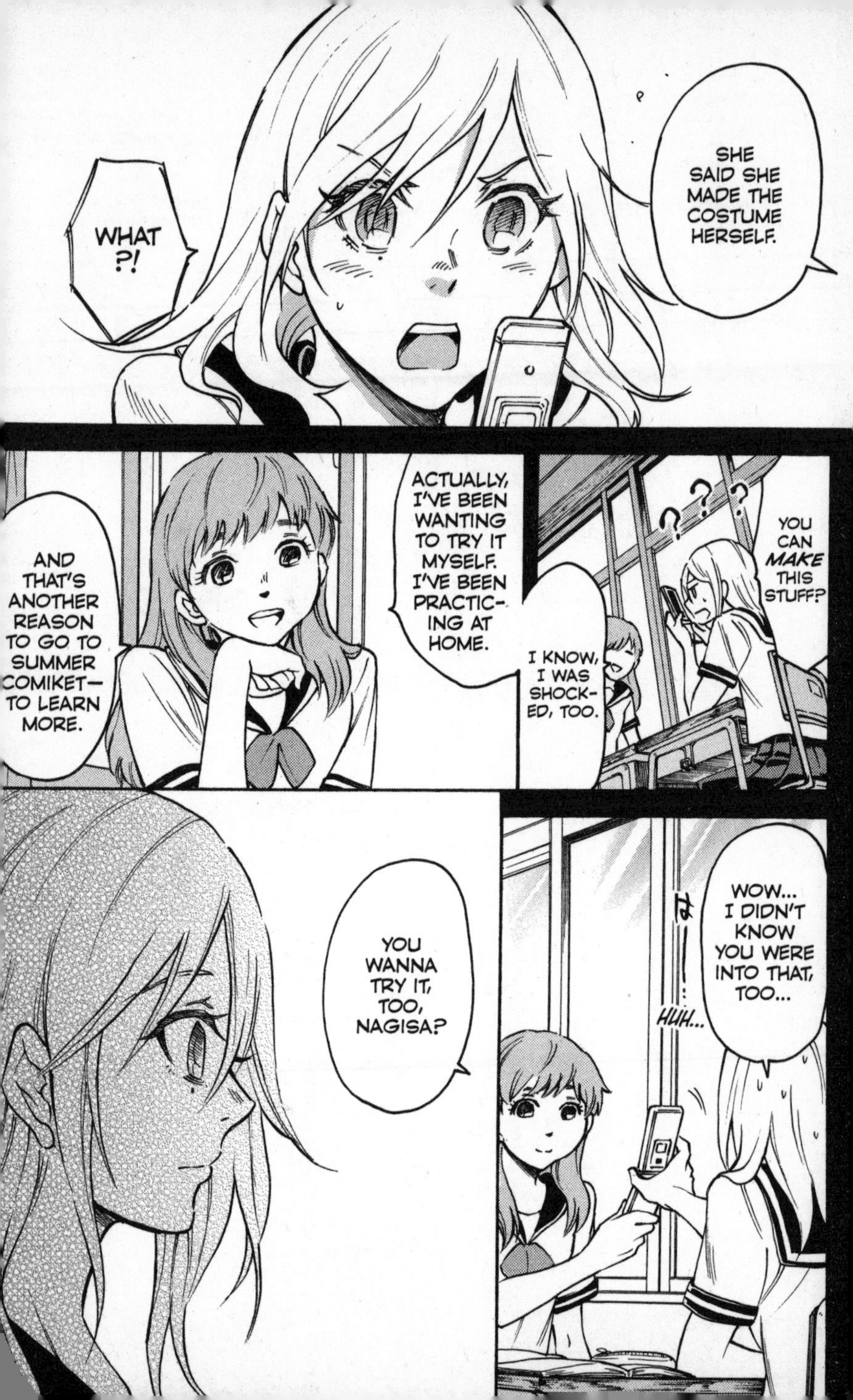
SHE SAID SHE MADE THE COSTUME HERSELF.
WHAT ?!
YOU CAN *MAKE* THIS STUFF?
I KNOW, I WAS SHOCKED, TOO.
ACTUALLY, I'VE BEEN WANTING TO TRY IT MYSELF. I'VE BEEN PRACTICING AT HOME.
AND THAT'S ANOTHER REASON TO GO TO SUMMER COMIKET—TO LEARN MORE.
WOW... I DIDN'T KNOW YOU WERE INTO THAT, TOO...
はー…
HUH...
YOU WANNA TRY IT, TOO, NAGISA?

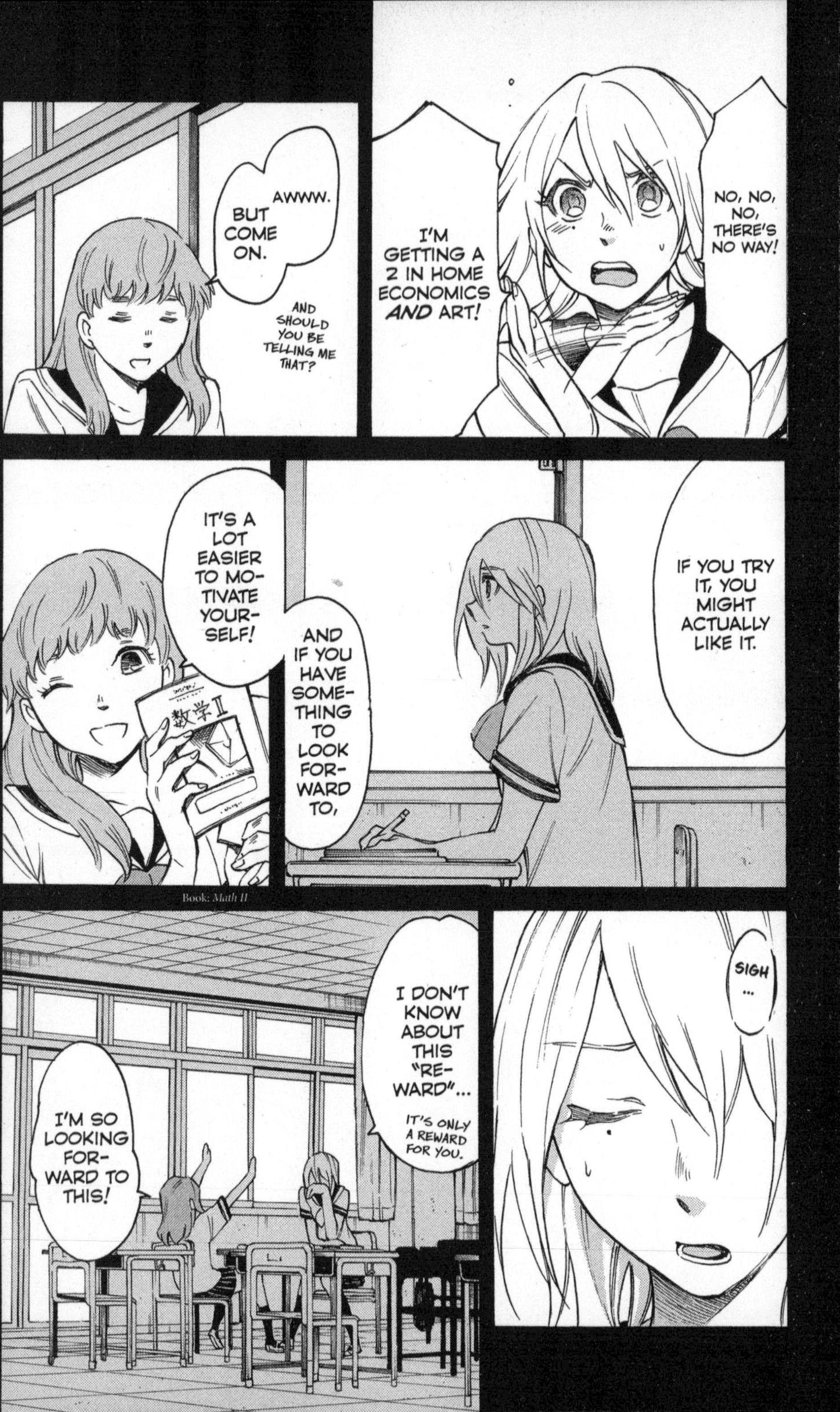
NO, NO, NO, THERE'S NO WAY!
I'M GETTING A 2 IN HOME ECONOMICS *AND* ART!
AWWW. BUT COME ON.
AND SHOULD YOU BE TELLING ME THAT?
IF YOU TRY IT, YOU MIGHT ACTUALLY LIKE IT.
AND IF YOU HAVE SOMETHING TO LOOK FORWARD TO,
IT'S A LOT EASIER TO MOTIVATE YOURSELF!
数学II
SIGH ...
I DON'T KNOW ABOUT THIS "REWARD"...
IT'S ONLY A REWARD FOR YOU.
I'M SO LOOKING FORWARD TO THIS!

Book: *Math II*

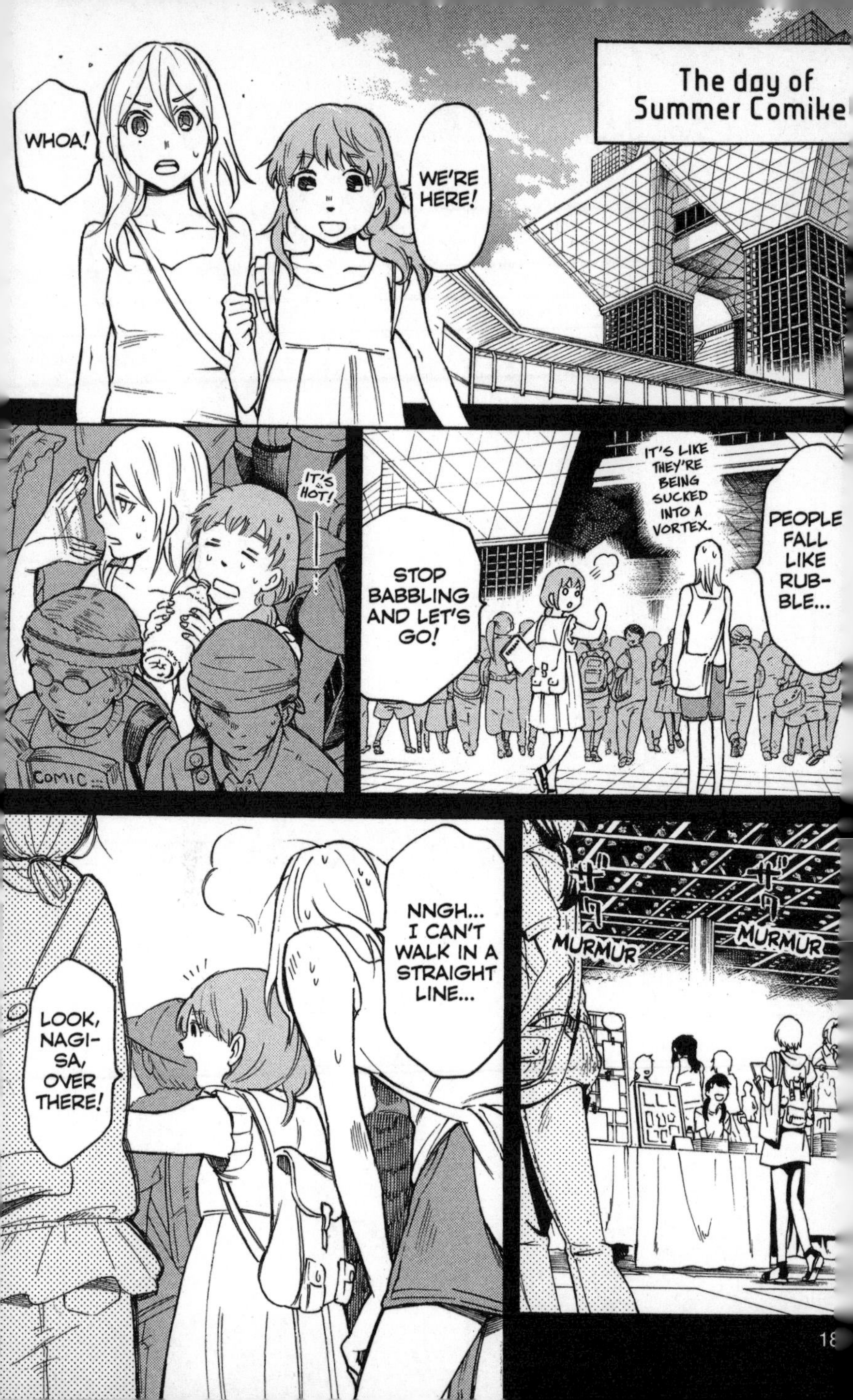
The day of Summer Comike
WE'RE HERE!
WHOA!
PEOPLE FALL LIKE RUB-BLE...
IT'S LIKE THEY'RE BEING SUCKED INTO A VORTEX.
STOP BABBLING AND LET'S GO!
IT'S HOT!
COMIC...
MURMUR
MURMUR
NNGH... I CAN'T WALK IN A STRAIGHT LINE...
LOOK, NAGI-SA, OVER THERE!

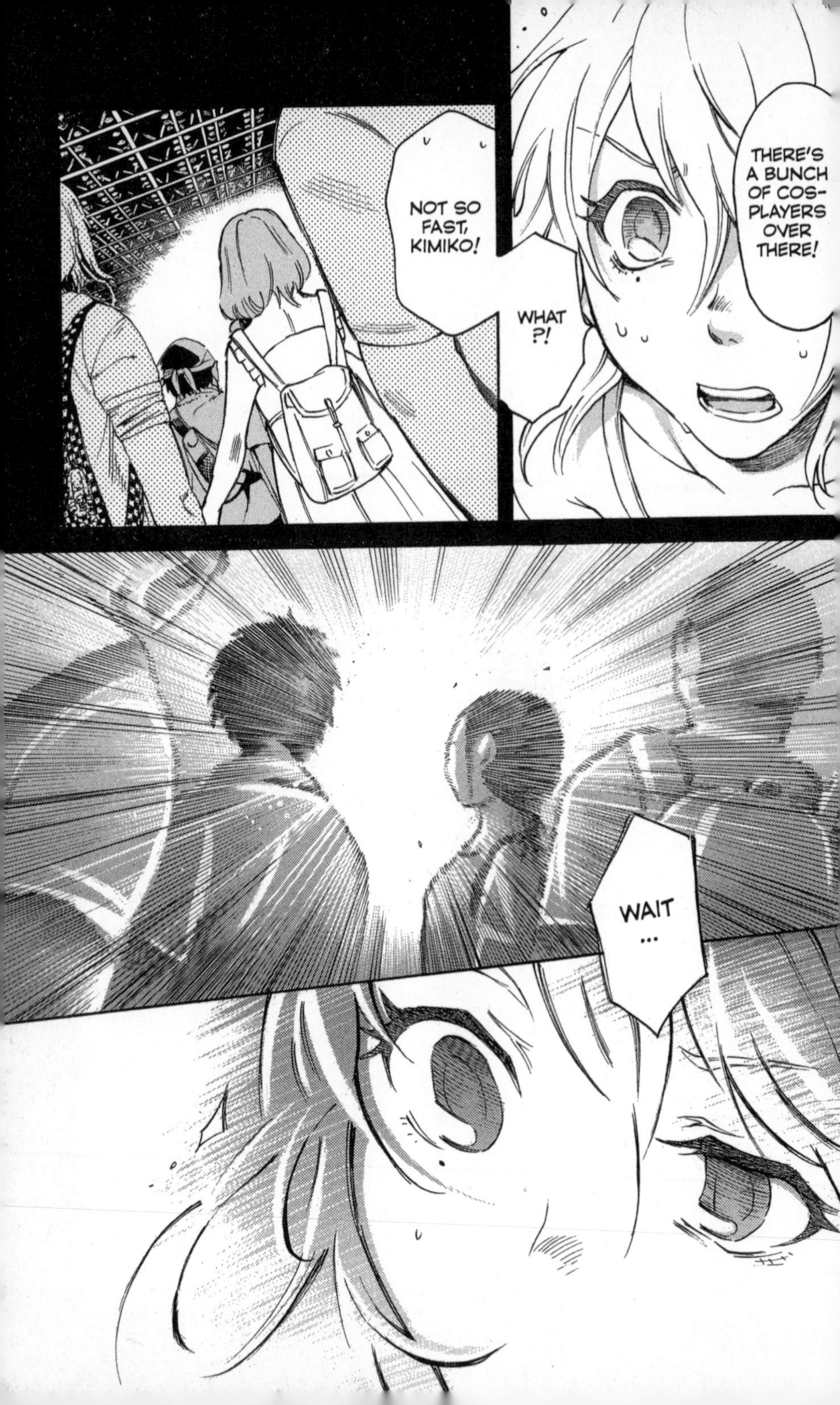
THERE'S A BUNCH OF COS-PLAYERS OVER THERE!
WHAT ?!
NOT SO FAST, KIMIKO!
WAIT ...

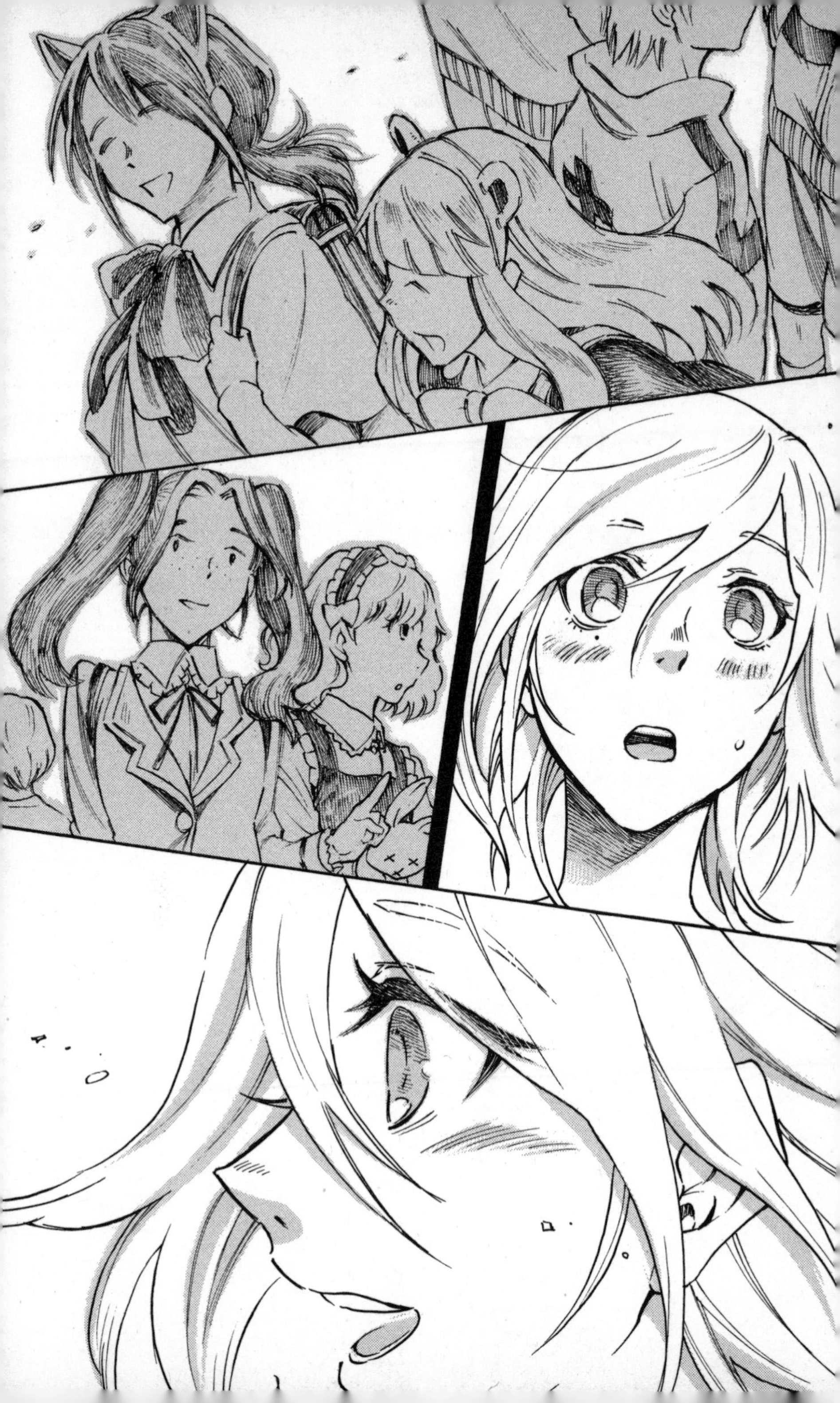

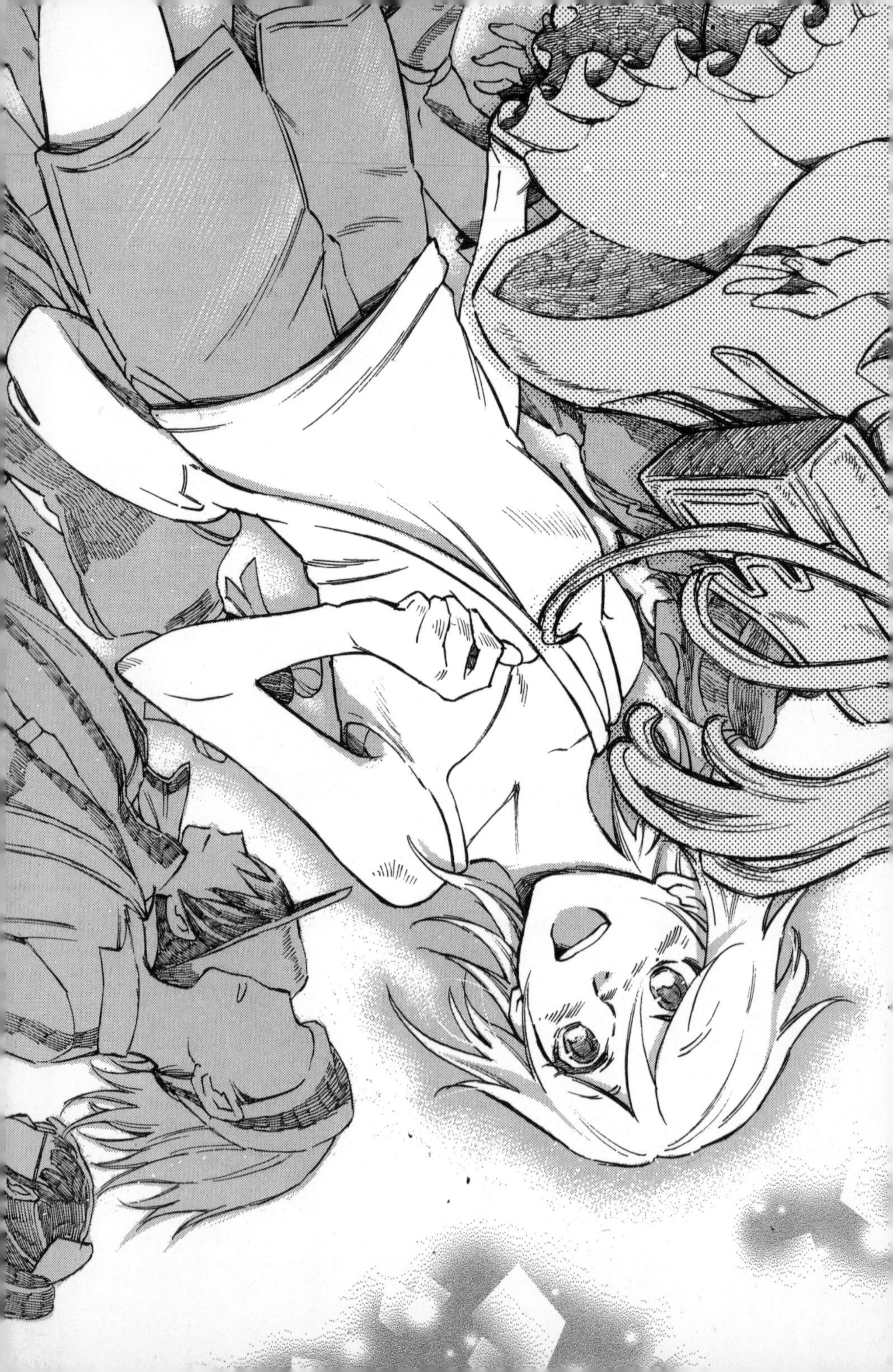

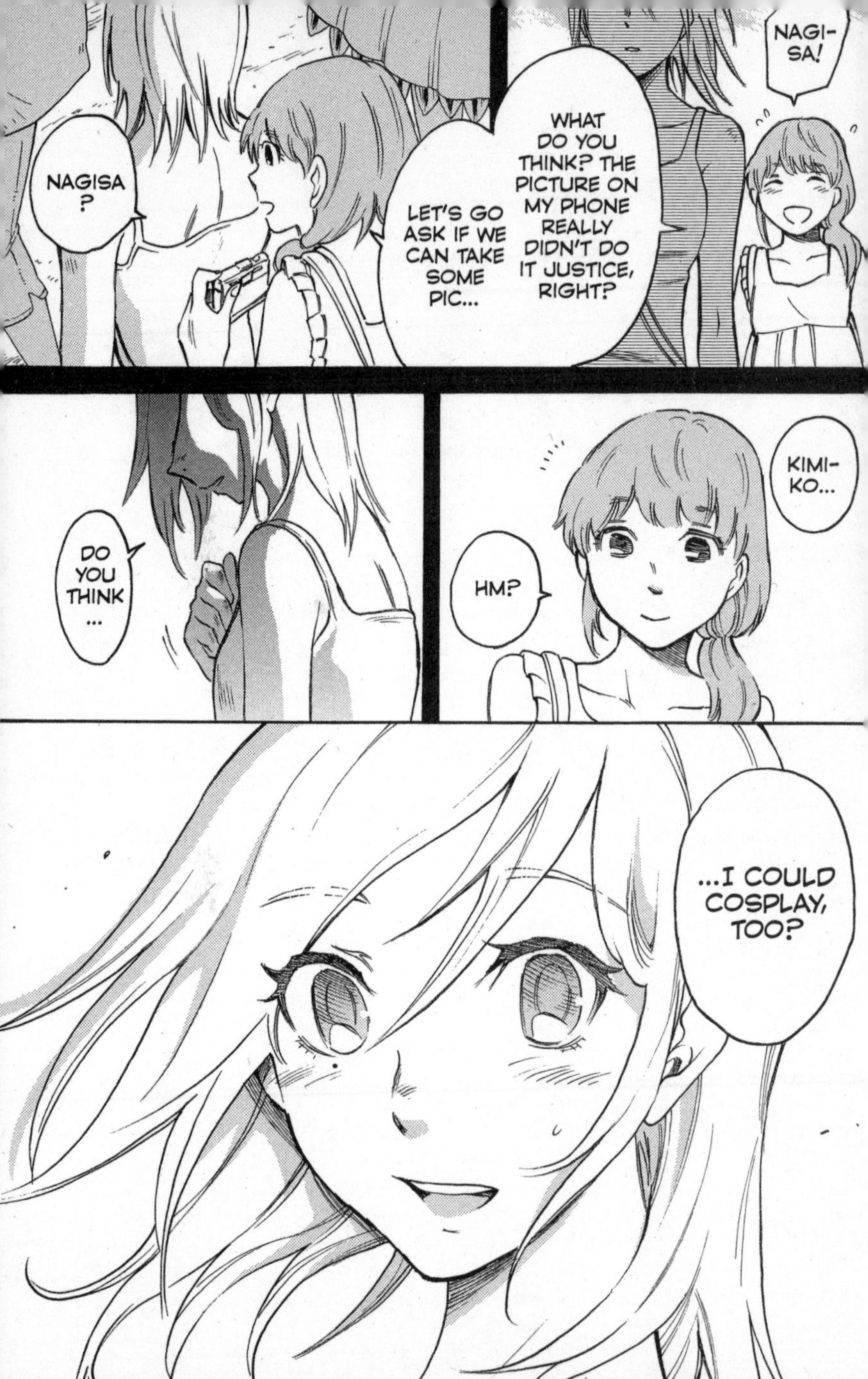
NAGI-SA!
WHAT DO YOU THINK? THE PICTURE ON MY PHONE REALLY DIDN'T DO IT JUSTICE, RIGHT?
LET'S GO ASK IF WE CAN TAKE SOME PIC...
NAGISA ?
KIMI-KO...
HM?
DO YOU THINK ...
...I COULD COSPLAY, TOO?

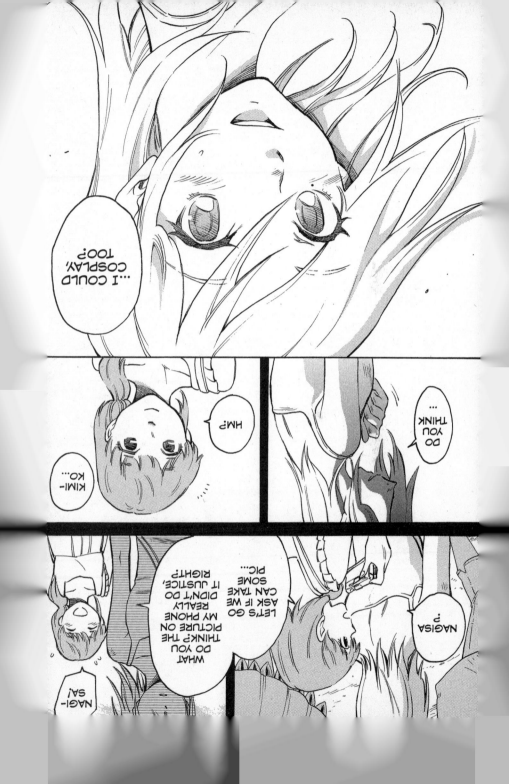

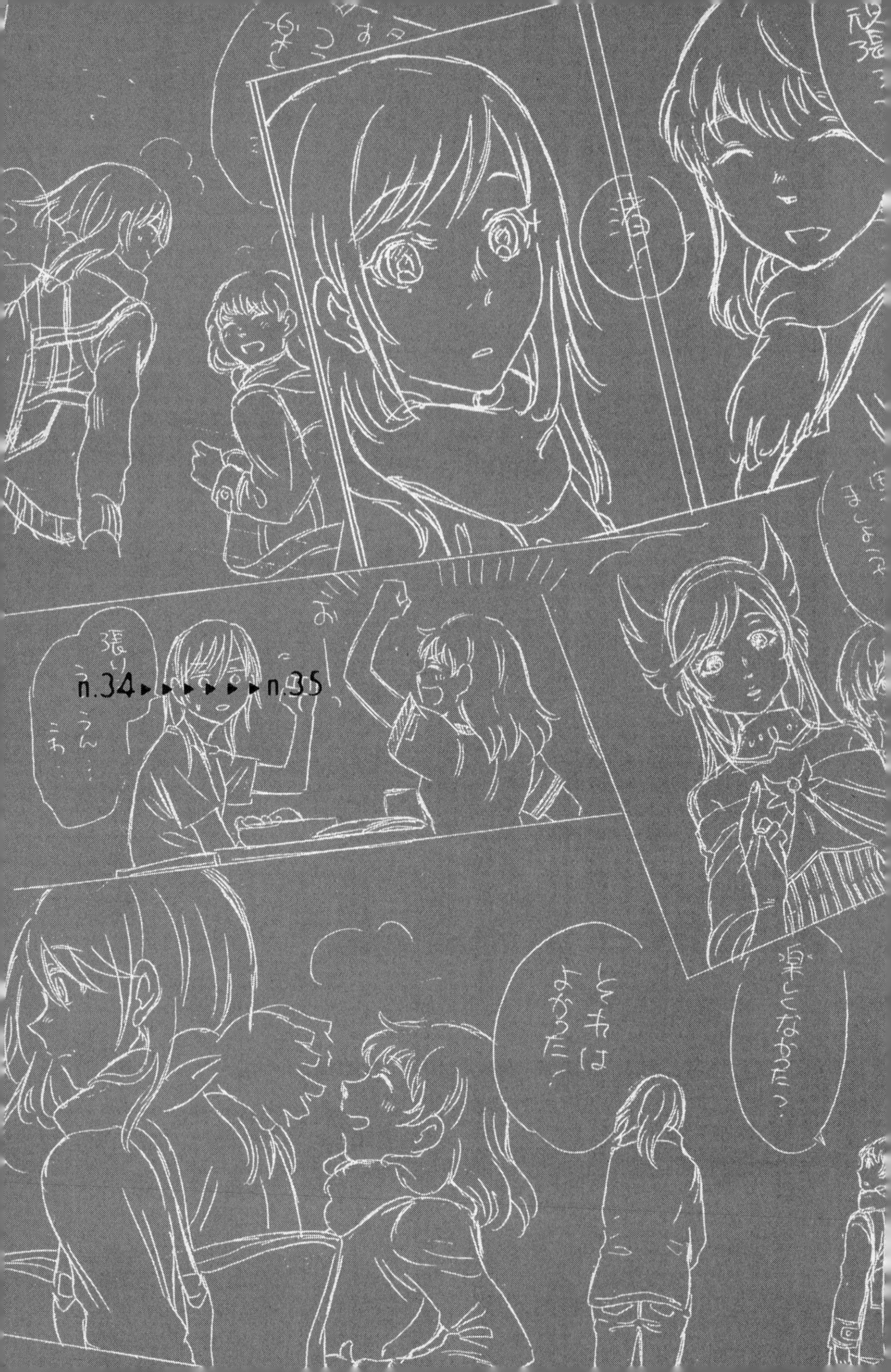
n.34▸▸▸▸▸▸▸n.35
それは よかった

SINCE IT GOT BROUGHT UP...

NOW WE'RE AT VOLUME FIVE. THANK YOU FOR PICKING UP ANOTHER INSTALLMENT.

FOR THE BONUSES IN THIS VOLUME, I THOUGHT I'D TALK ABOUT MY HOME PREFECTURE OF MIYAGI... (ONLY THE FRONT OF THE TRAIN STATION SHOWED UP IN THE MANGA, SO I HAVEN'T GOTTEN IT OUT OF MY SYSTEM YET.)

IT'S BEEN A SHORT 10 YEARS SINCE I MOVED TO THE CAPITAL.

I HOPE I CAN ENJOY ANOTHER 10 YEARS HERE.

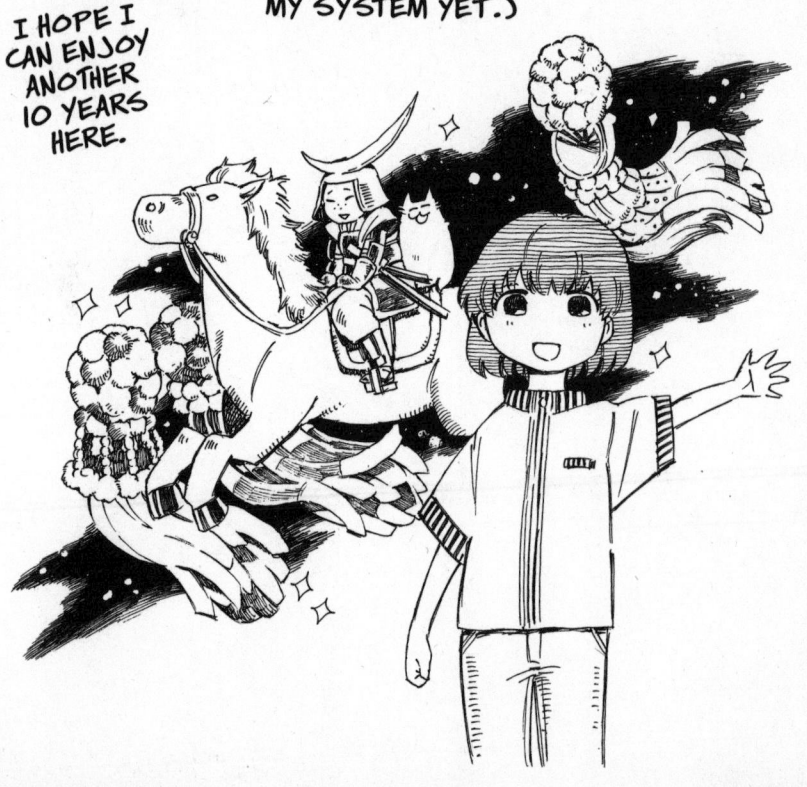

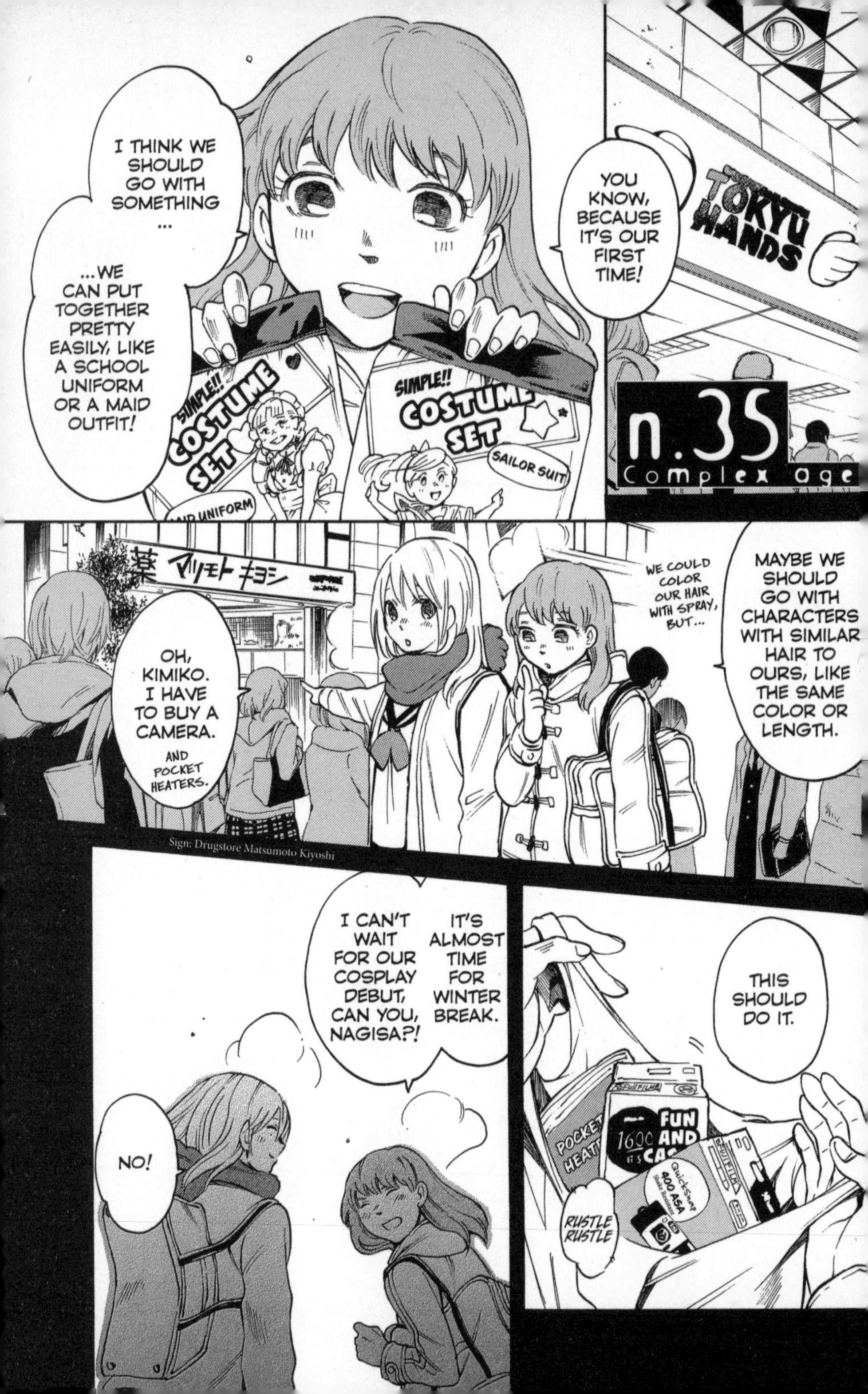
n.35
Complex age
TOKYU HANDS
I THINK WE SHOULD GO WITH SOMETHING ...
...WE CAN PUT TOGETHER PRETTY EASILY, LIKE A SCHOOL UNIFORM OR A MAID OUTFIT!
YOU KNOW, BECAUSE IT'S OUR FIRST TIME!
SIMPLE!! COSTUME SET
SAILOR SUIT
SIMPLE!! COSTUME SET
AID UNIFORM
MAYBE WE SHOULD GO WITH CHARACTERS WITH SIMILAR HAIR TO OURS, LIKE THE SAME COLOR OR LENGTH.
WE COULD COLOR OUR HAIR WITH SPRAY, BUT...
薬 マツモトキヨシ
OH, KIMIKO. I HAVE TO BUY A CAMERA.
AND POCKET HEATERS.
THIS SHOULD DO IT.
FUN AND CA
1600
POCKET HEAT
QuickSnap 400 ASA
RUSTLE RUSTLE
IT'S ALMOST TIME FOR WINTER BREAK.
I CAN'T WAIT FOR OUR COSPLAY DEBUT, CAN YOU, NAGISA?!
NO!
Sign: Drugstore Matsumoto Kiyoshi

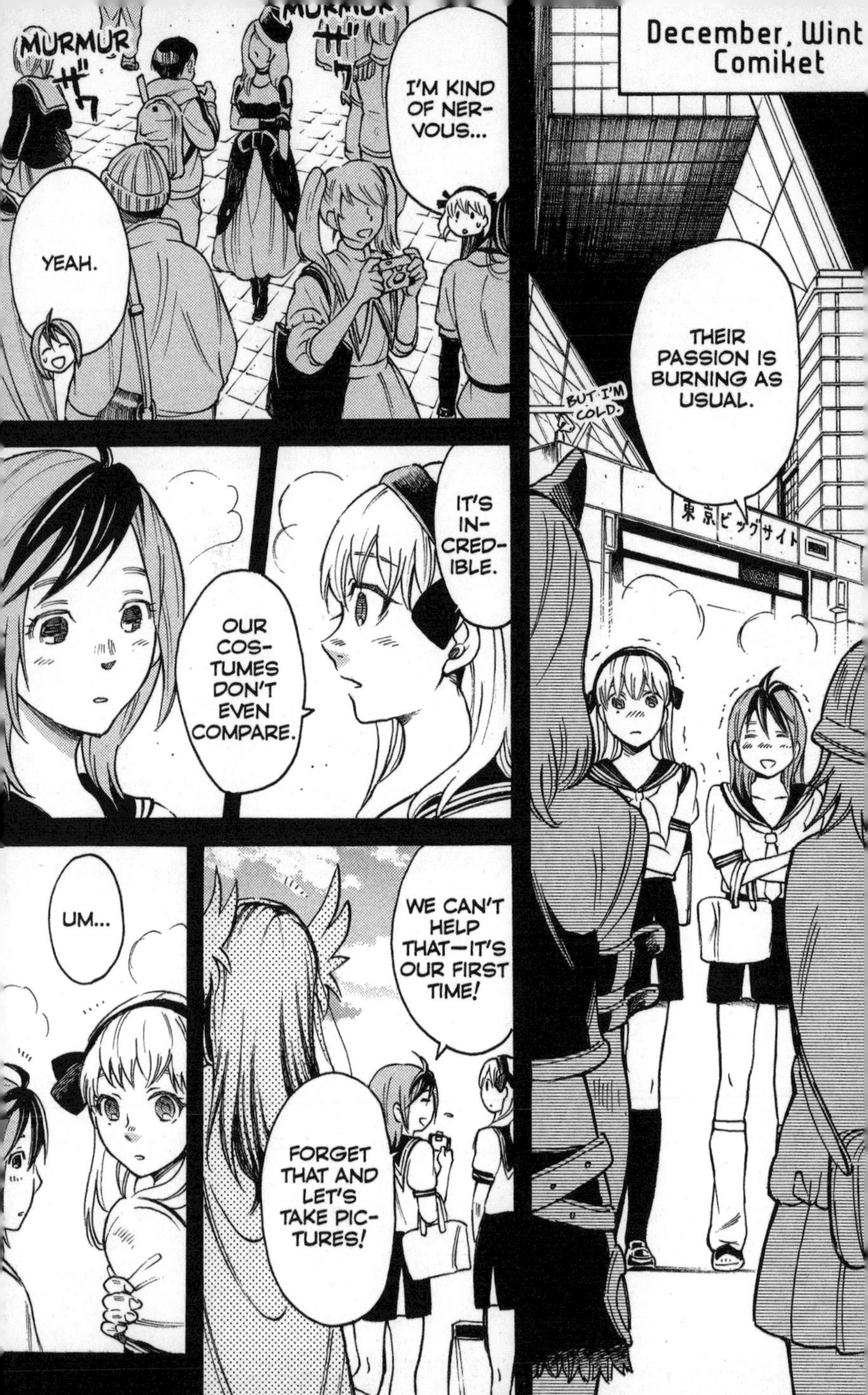
December, Wint
Comiket
THEIR PASSION IS BURNING AS USUAL.
BUT I'M COLD.
東京ビッグサイト
MURMUR ザワ
MURMUR ザワ
I'M KIND OF NER-VOUS...
YEAH.
IT'S IN-CRED-IBLE.
OUR COS-TUMES DON'T EVEN COMPARE.
WE CAN'T HELP THAT—IT'S OUR FIRST TIME!
FORGET THAT AND LET'S TAKE PIC-TURES!
UM...

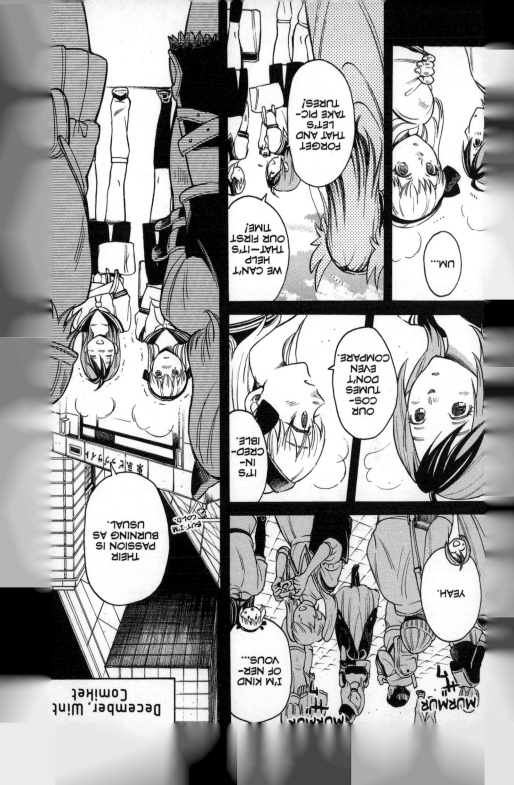

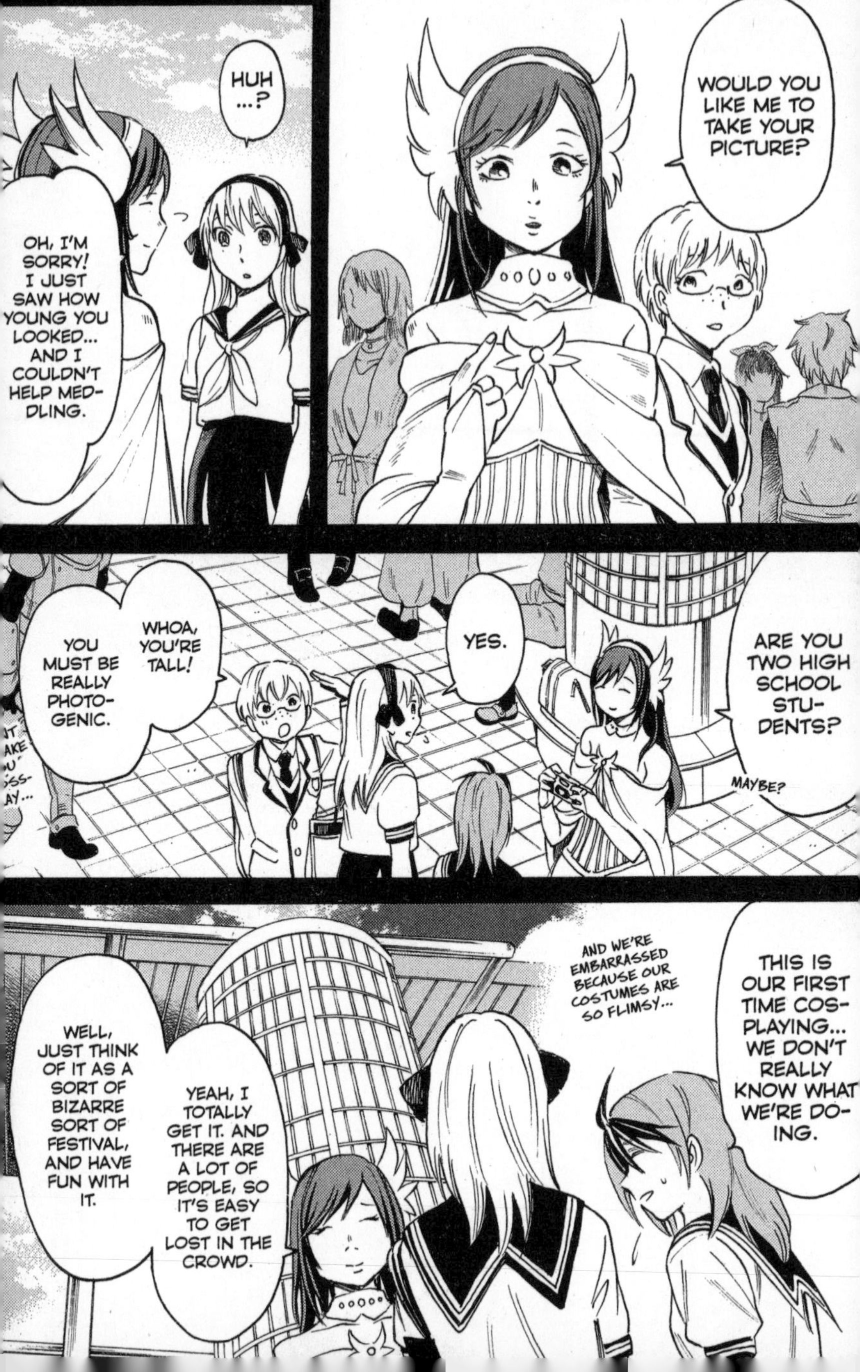
WOULD YOU LIKE ME TO TAKE YOUR PICTURE?
HUH ...?
OH, I'M SORRY! I JUST SAW HOW YOUNG YOU LOOKED... AND I COULDN'T HELP MED-DLING.
ARE YOU TWO HIGH SCHOOL STU-DENTS?
MAYBE?
YES.
WHOA, YOU'RE TALL!
YOU MUST BE REALLY PHOTO-GENIC.
THIS IS OUR FIRST TIME COS-PLAYING... WE DON'T REALLY KNOW WHAT WE'RE DO-ING.
AND WE'RE EMBARRASSED BECAUSE OUR COSTUMES ARE SO FLIMSY...
YEAH, I TOTALLY GET IT. AND THERE ARE A LOT OF PEOPLE, SO IT'S EASY TO GET LOST IN THE CROWD.
WELL, JUST THINK OF IT AS A SORT OF BIZARRE SORT OF FESTIVAL, AND HAVE FUN WITH IT.

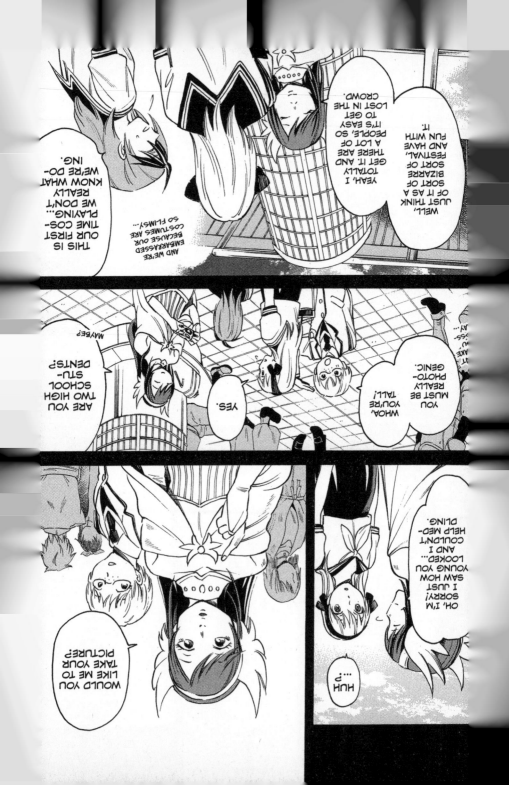

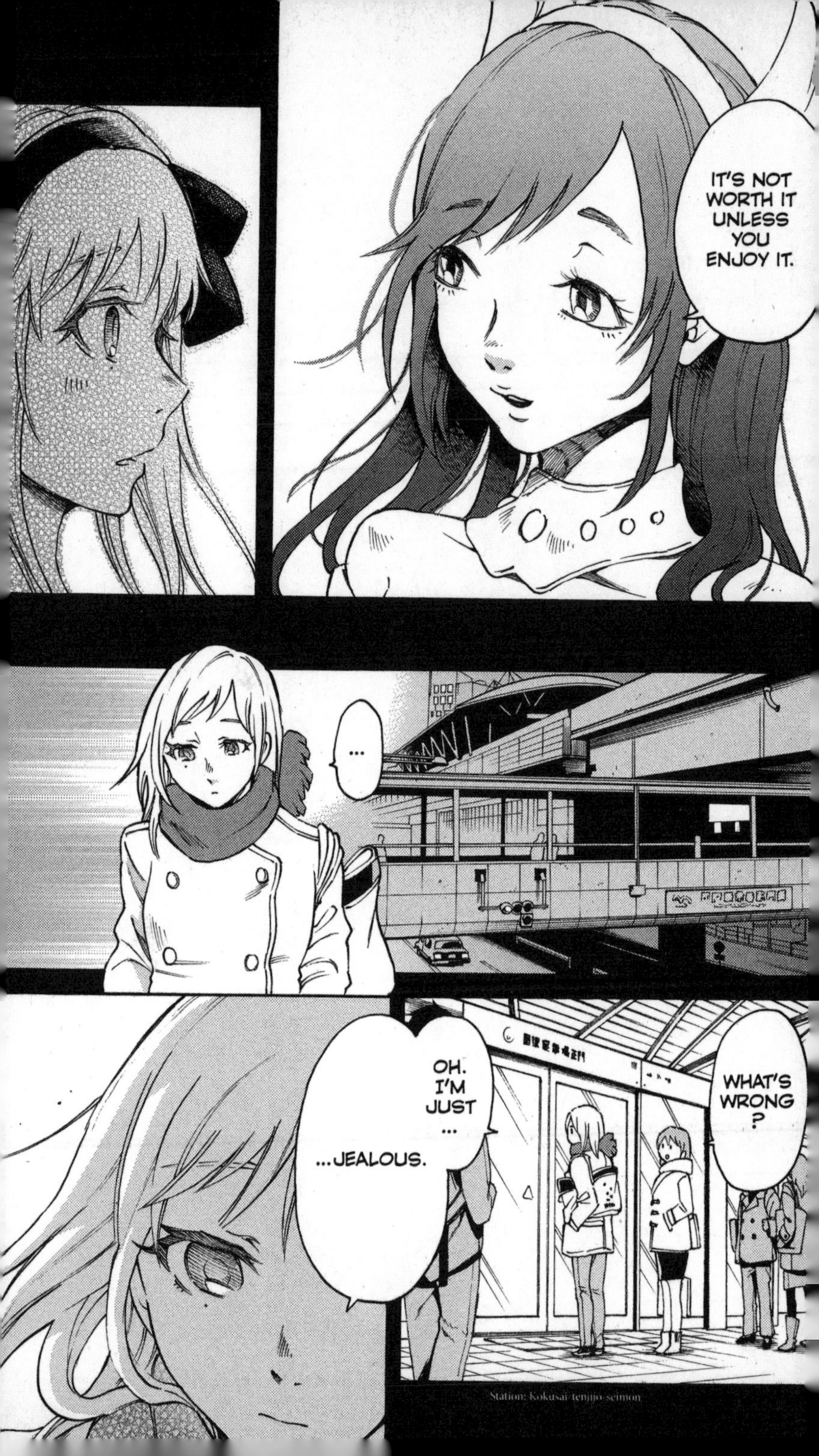
IT'S NOT WORTH IT UNLESS YOU ENJOY IT.
...
WHAT'S WRONG?
OH. I'M JUST...
...JEALOUS.
Station: Kokusai-tenjijo-seimon

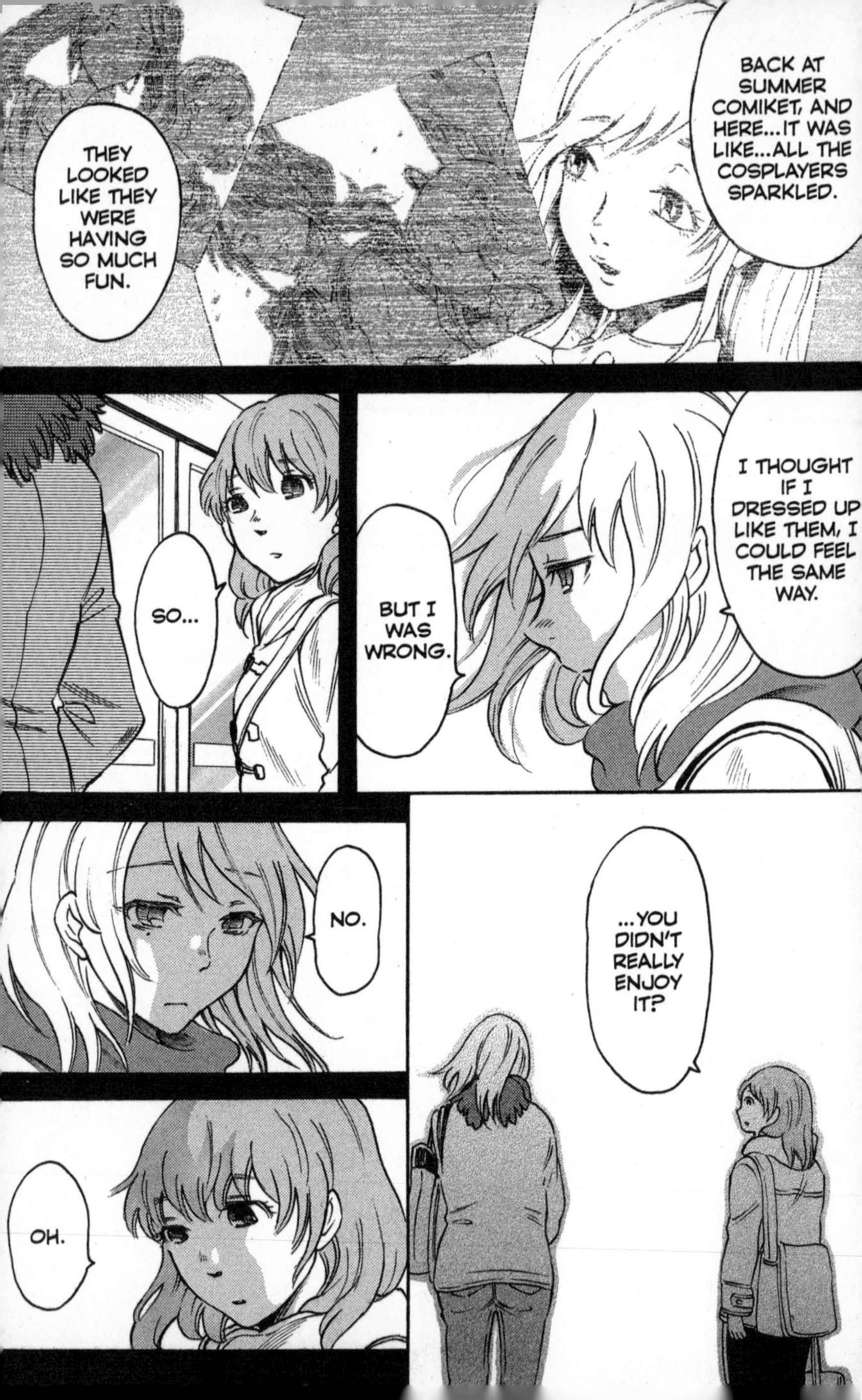
BACK AT SUMMER COMIKET, AND HERE...IT WAS LIKE...ALL THE COSPLAYERS SPARKLED.
THEY LOOKED LIKE THEY WERE HAVING SO MUCH FUN.
I THOUGHT IF I DRESSED UP LIKE THEM, I COULD FEEL THE SAME WAY.
BUT I WAS WRONG.
SO...
...YOU DIDN'T REALLY ENJOY IT?
NO.
OH.

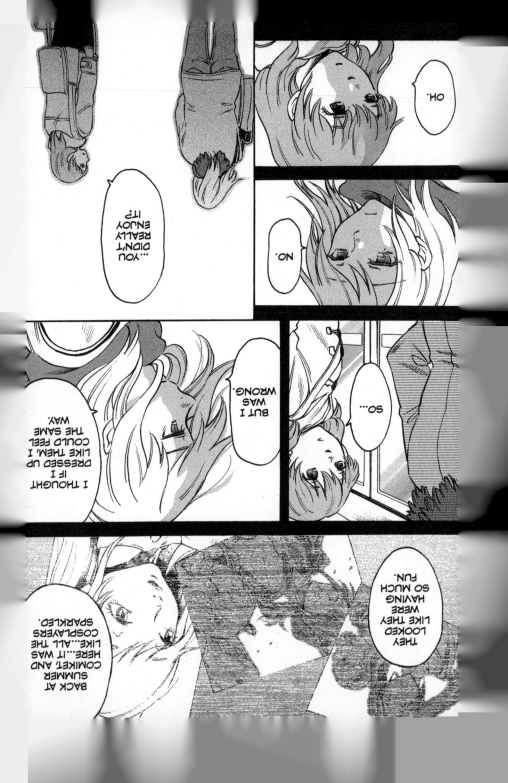

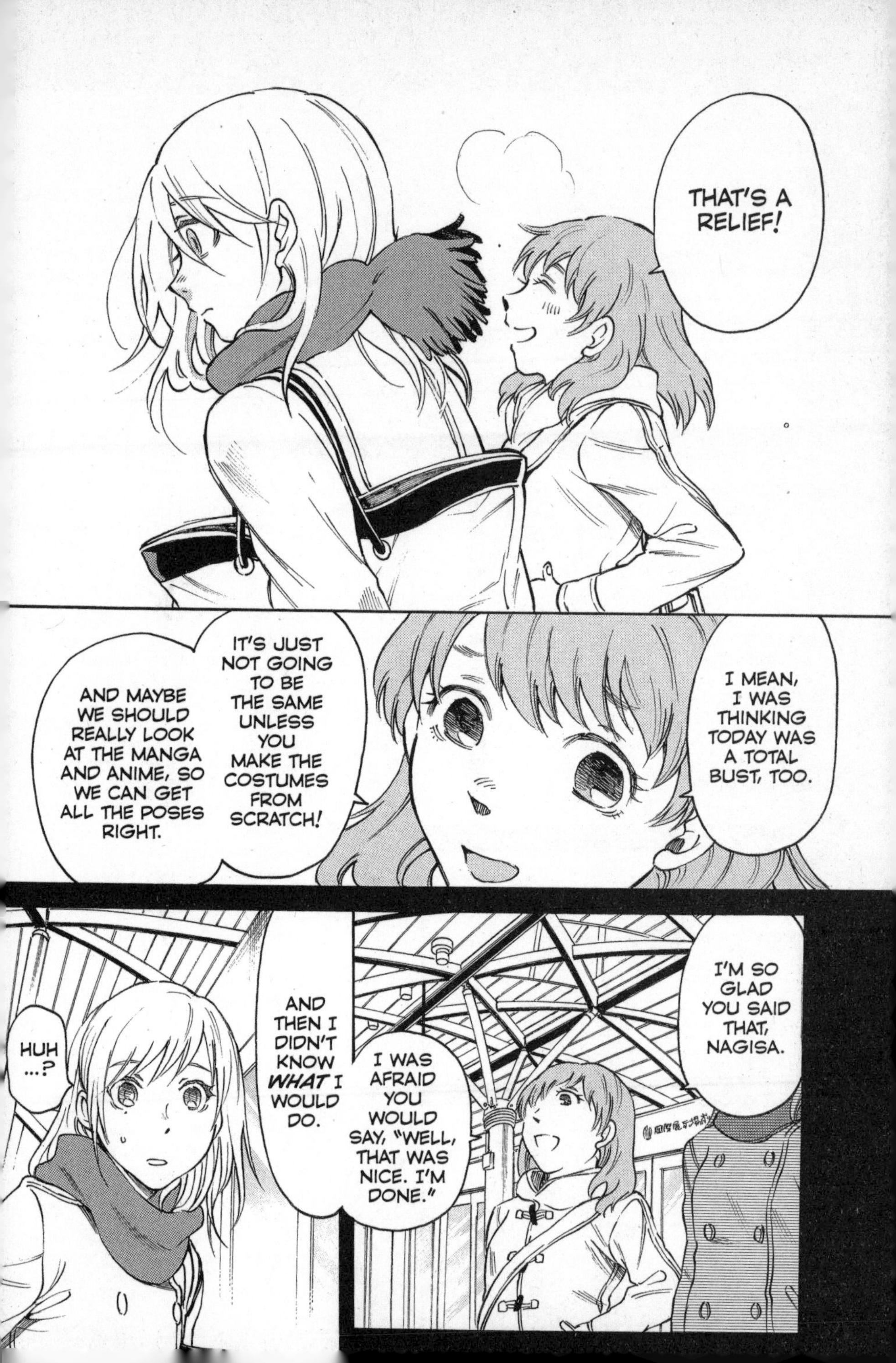
THAT'S A RELIEF!
I MEAN, I WAS THINKING TODAY WAS A TOTAL BUST, TOO.
IT'S JUST NOT GOING TO BE THE SAME UNLESS YOU MAKE THE COSTUMES FROM SCRATCH!
AND MAYBE WE SHOULD REALLY LOOK AT THE MANGA AND ANIME, SO WE CAN GET ALL THE POSES RIGHT.
I'M SO GLAD YOU SAID THAT, NAGISA.
I WAS AFRAID YOU WOULD SAY, "WELL, THAT WAS NICE. I'M DONE."
AND THEN I DIDN'T KNOW *WHAT* I WOULD DO.
HUH ...?

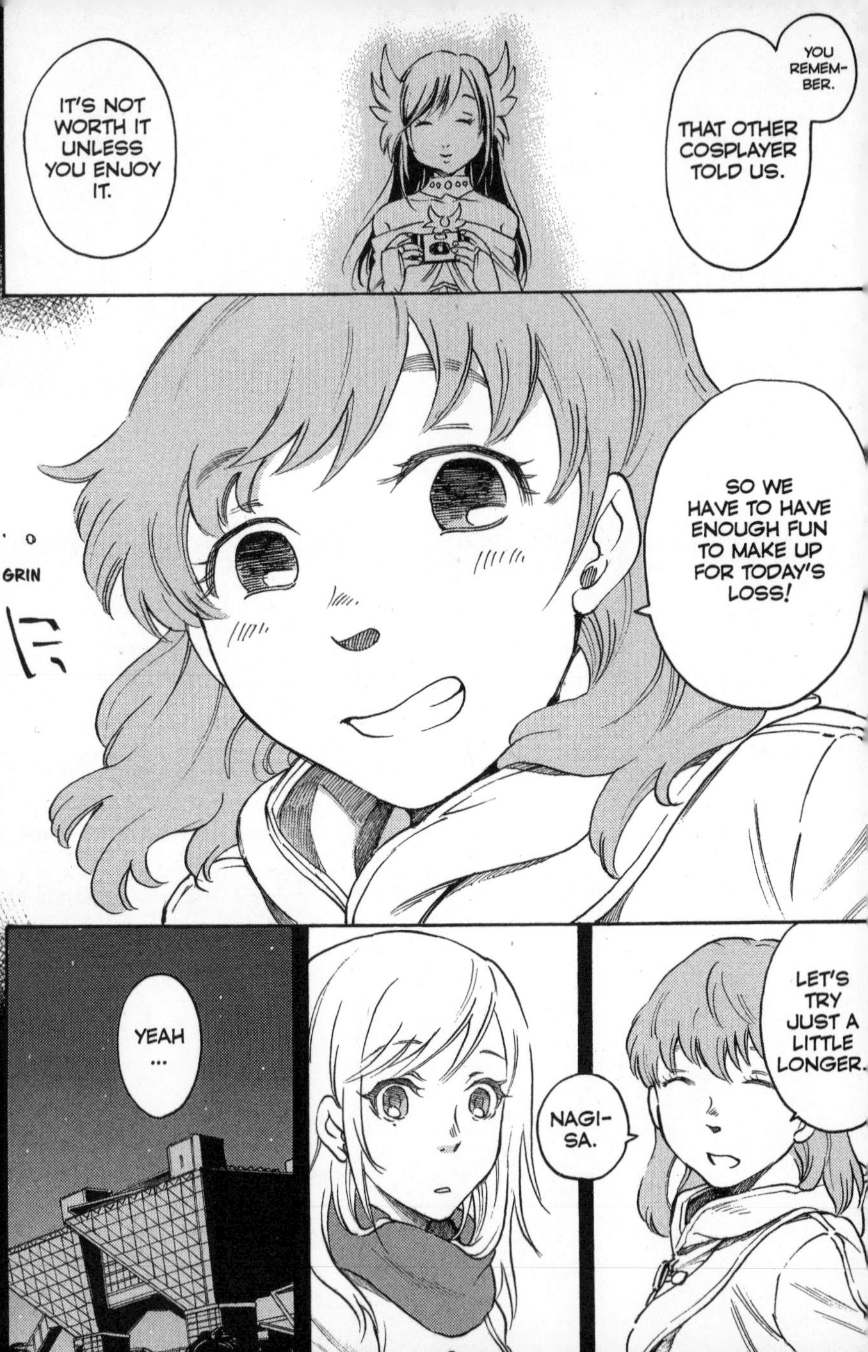
YOU REMEM-BER.
THAT OTHER COSPLAYER TOLD US.
IT'S NOT WORTH IT UNLESS YOU ENJOY IT.
SO WE HAVE TO HAVE ENOUGH FUN TO MAKE UP FOR TODAY'S LOSS!
GRIN
LET'S TRY JUST A LITTLE LONGER.
NAGI-SA.
YEAH ...

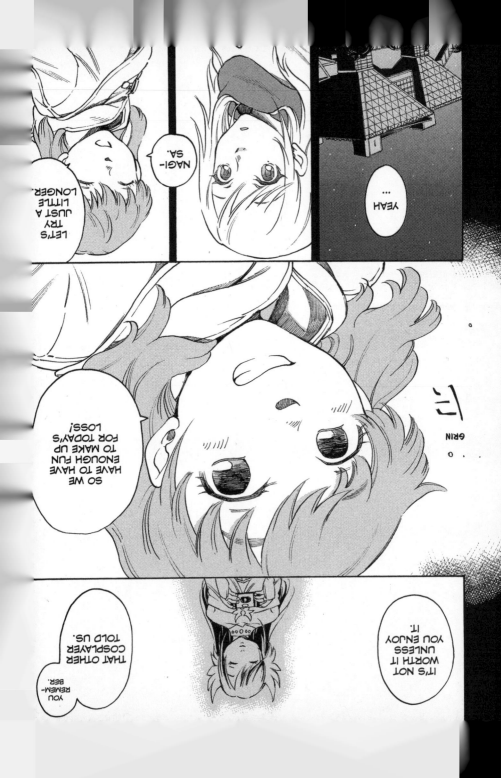

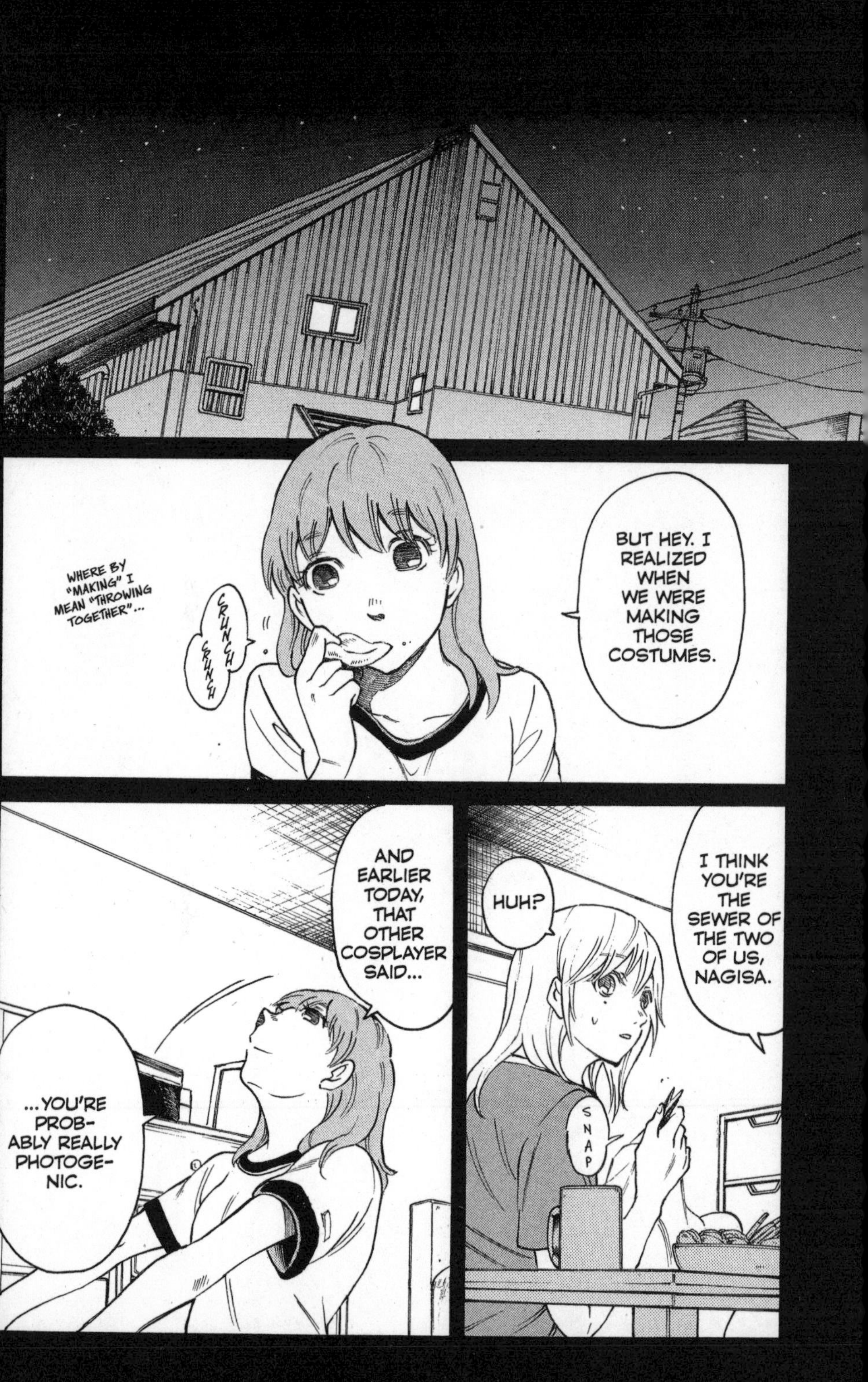
BUT HEY. I REALIZED WHEN WE WERE MAKING THOSE COSTUMES.
CRUNCH CRUNCH
WHERE BY "MAKING" I MEAN "THROWING TOGETHER"...
I THINK YOU'RE THE SEWER OF THE TWO OF US, NAGISA.
HUH?
SNAP
AND EARLIER TODAY, THAT OTHER COSPLAYER SAID...
...YOU'RE PROB-ABLY REALLY PHOTOGE-NIC.

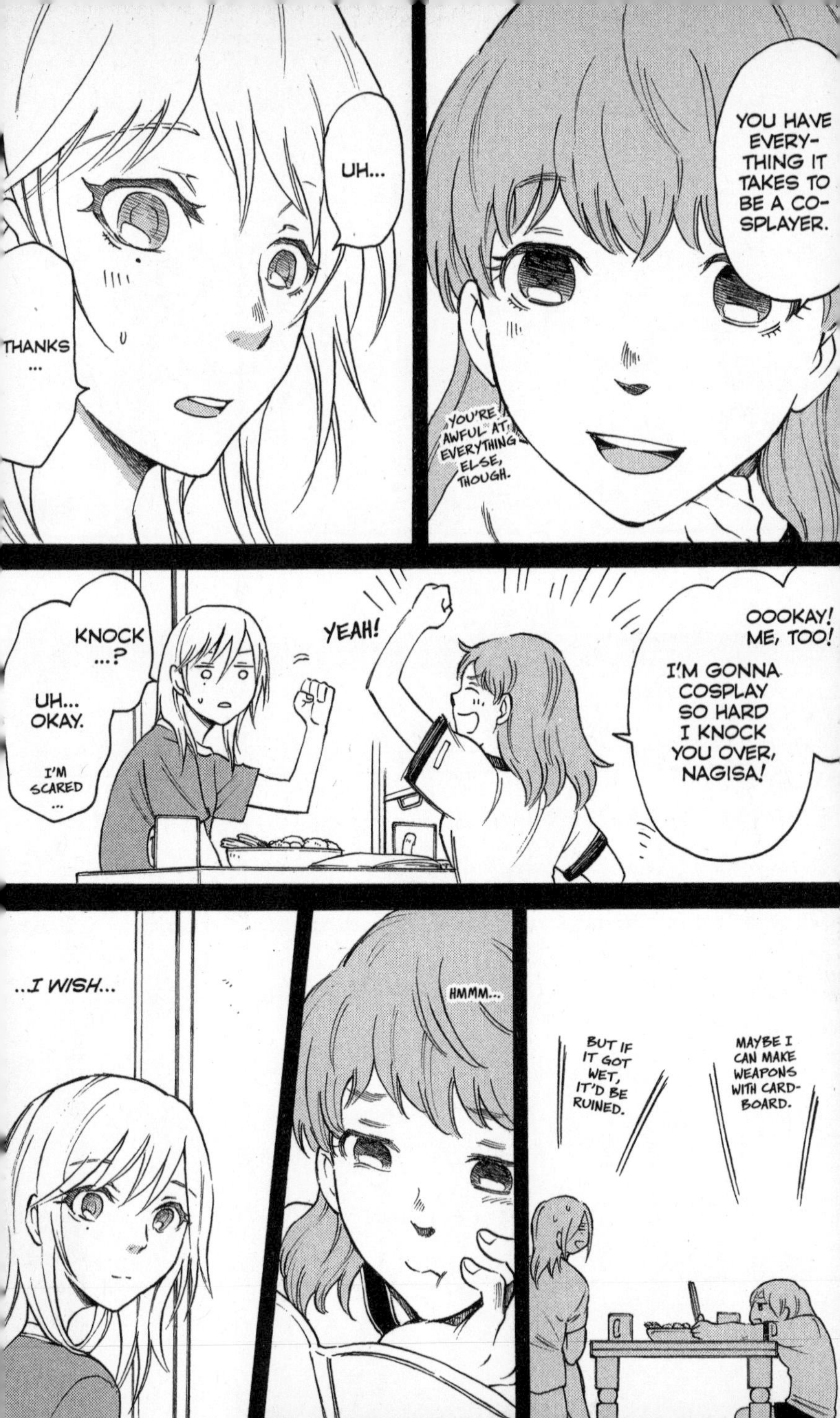
YOU HAVE EVERYTHING IT TAKES TO BE A COSPLAYER.
YOU'RE AWFUL AT EVERYTHING ELSE, THOUGH.
UH...
THANKS...
OOOKAY! ME, TOO!
I'M GONNA COSPLAY SO HARD I KNOCK YOU OVER, NAGISA!
YEAH!
KNOCK...?
UH... OKAY.
I'M SCARED...
MAYBE I CAN MAKE WEAPONS WITH CARDBOARD.
BUT IF IT GOT WET, IT'D BE RUINED.
HMMM...
...I WISH...

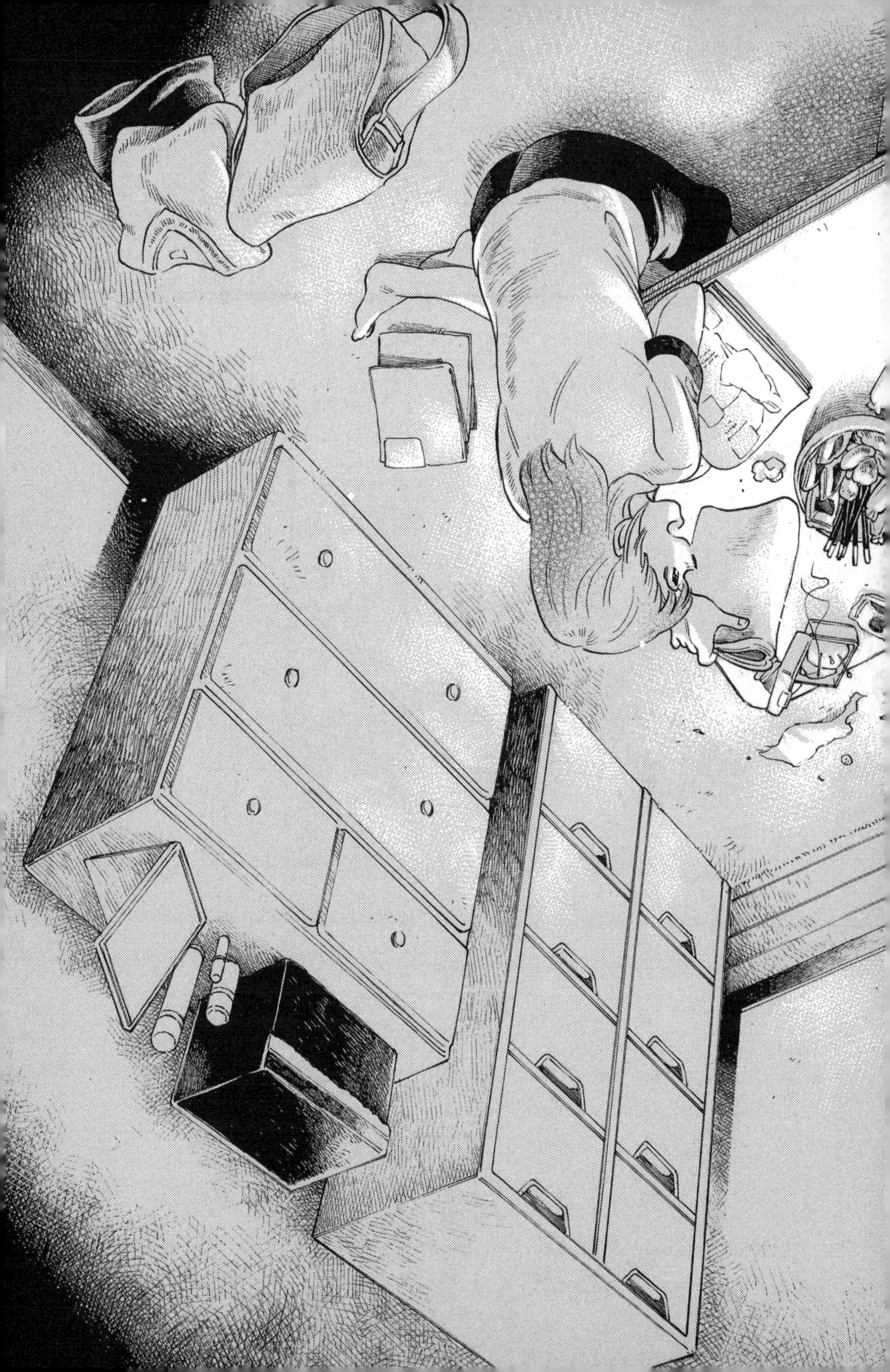

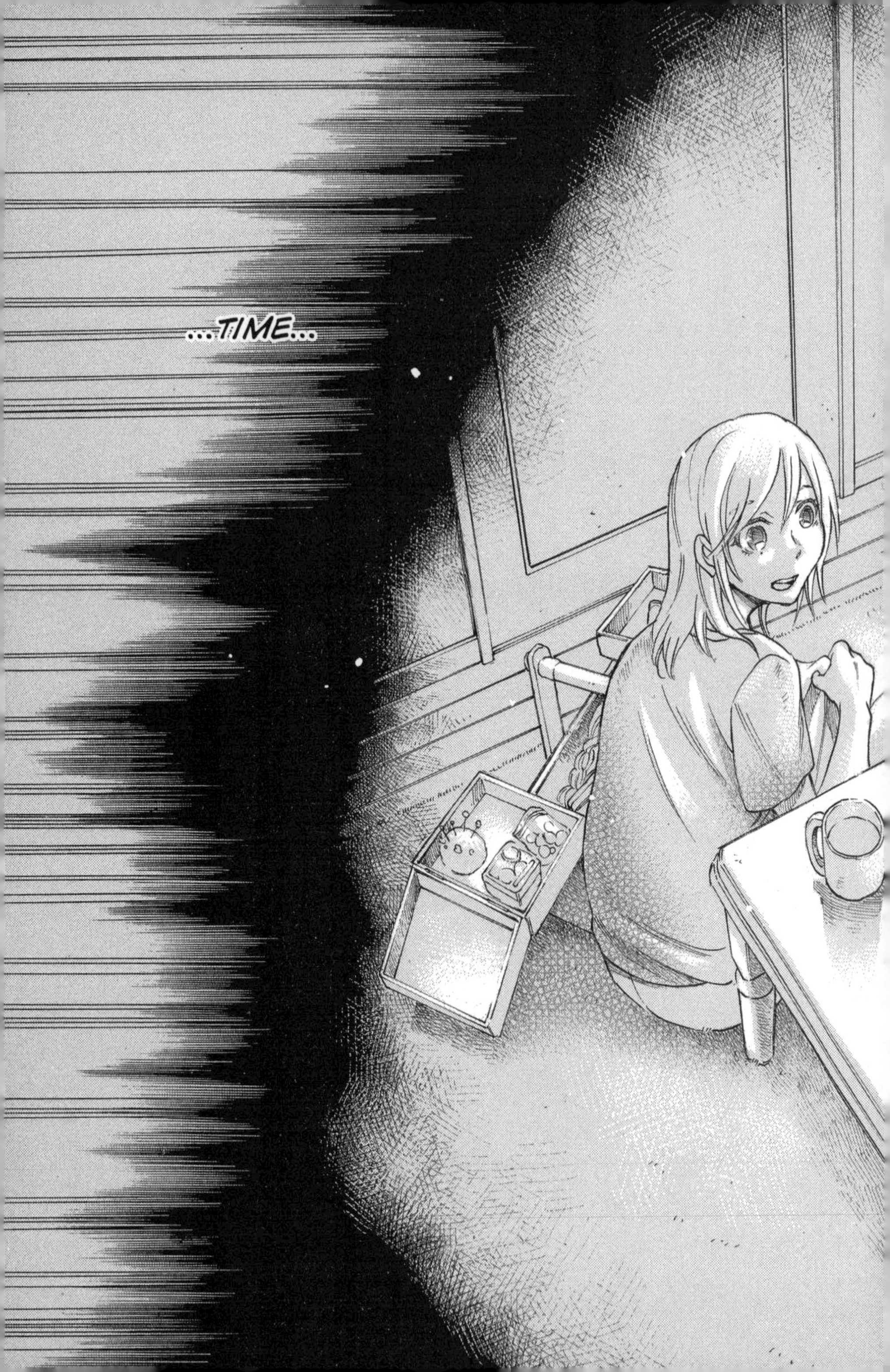
...TIME...

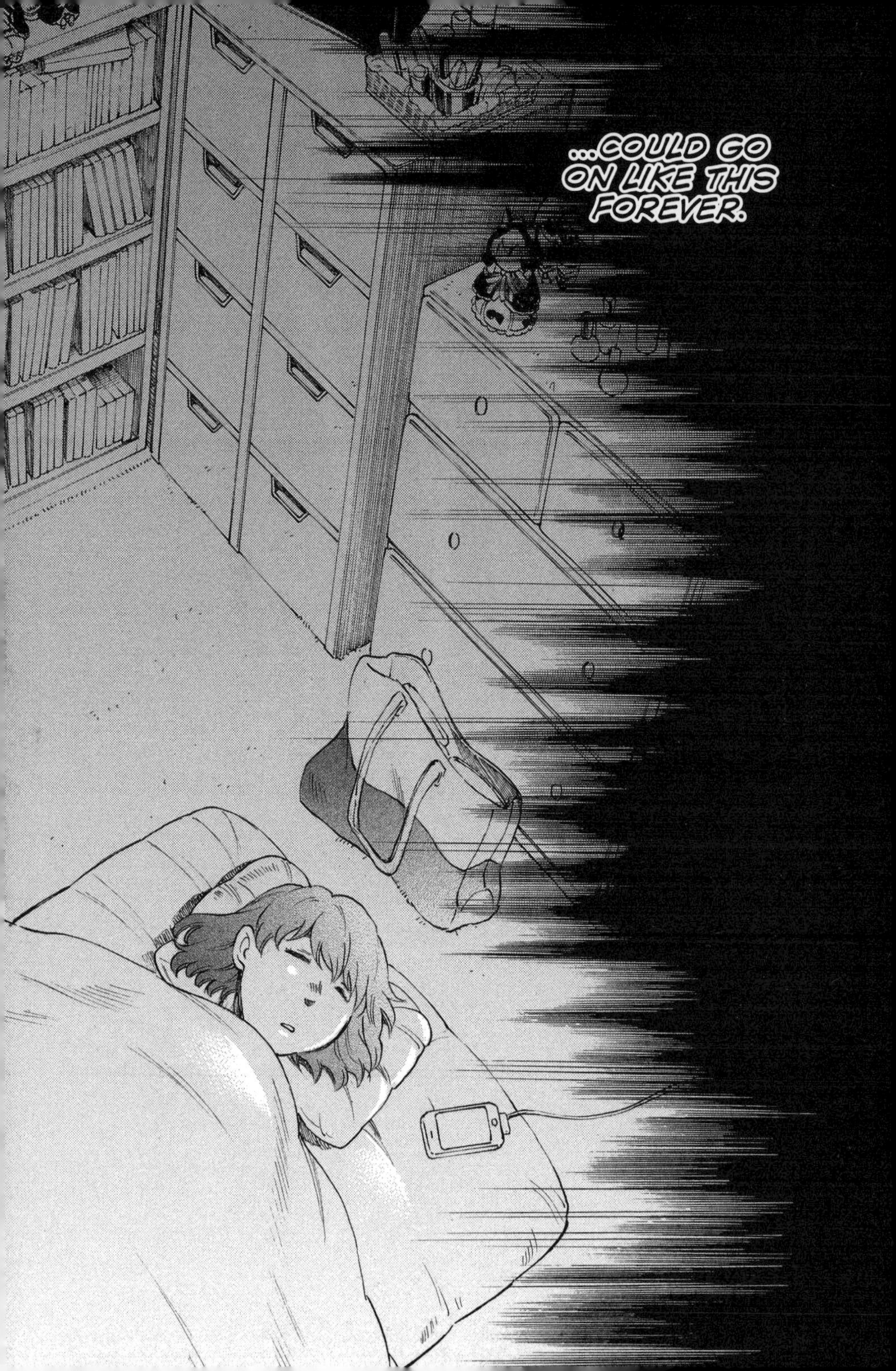
...COULD GO ON LIKE THIS FOREVER.

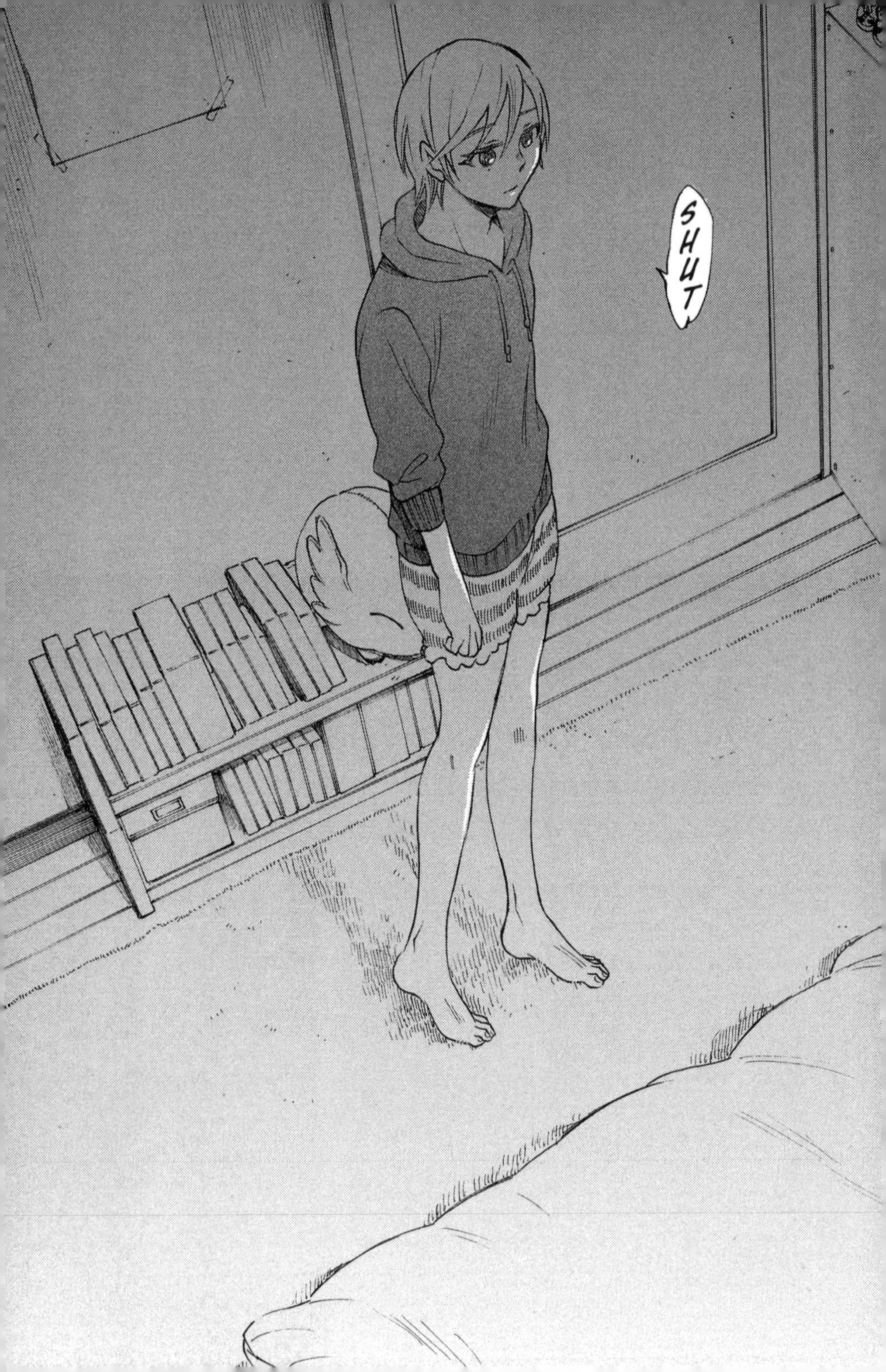
SHUT

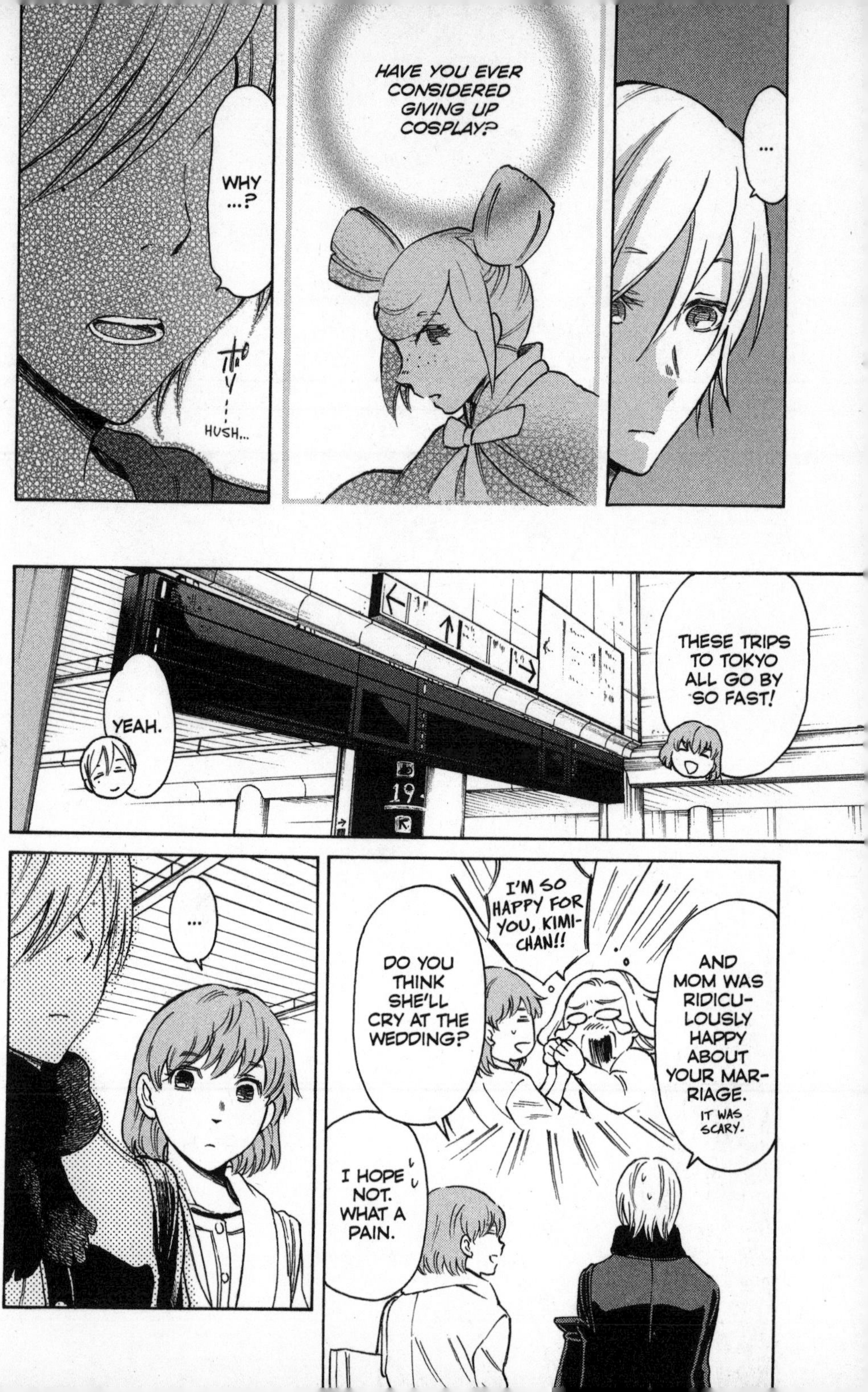
...
HAVE YOU EVER CONSIDERED GIVING UP COSPLAY?
WHY ...?
HUSH...
THESE TRIPS TO TOKYO ALL GO BY SO FAST!
YEAH.
AND MOM WAS RIDICULOUSLY HAPPY ABOUT YOUR MARRIAGE.
IT WAS SCARY.
I'M SO HAPPY FOR YOU, KIMI-CHAN!!
DO YOU THINK SHE'LL CRY AT THE WEDDING?
I HOPE NOT. WHAT A PAIN.
...

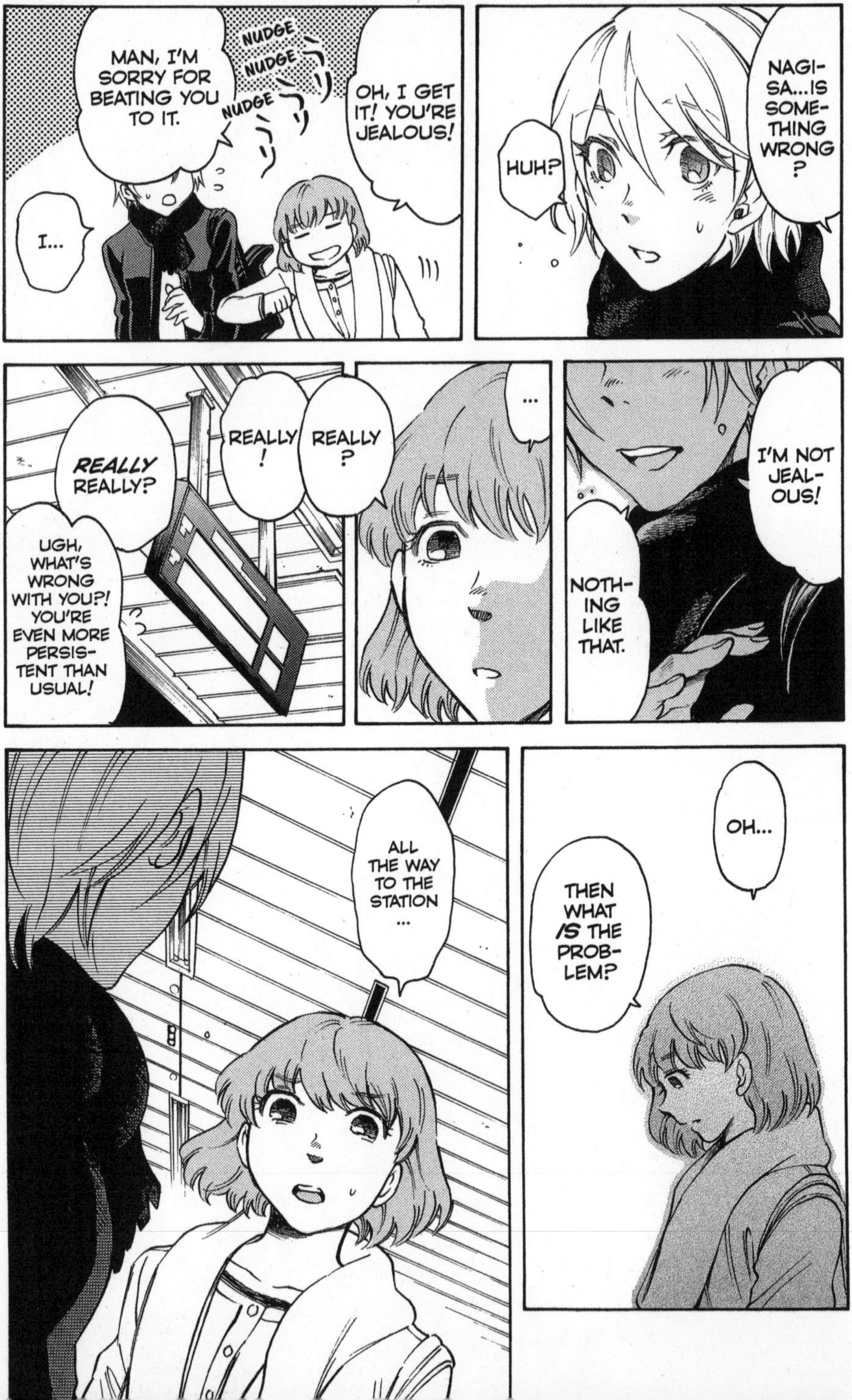
NAGI-SA...IS SOME-THING WRONG?
HUH?
OH, I GET IT! YOU'RE JEALOUS!
NUDGE
NUDGE
NUDGE
MAN, I'M SORRY FOR BEATING YOU TO IT.
I...
I'M NOT JEAL-OUS!
NOTH-ING LIKE THAT.
...
REALLY?
REALLY!
REALLY REALLY?
UGH, WHAT'S WRONG WITH YOU?! YOU'RE EVEN MORE PERSIS-TENT THAN USUAL!
OH...
THEN WHAT IS THE PROB-LEM?
ALL THE WAY TO THE STATION ...

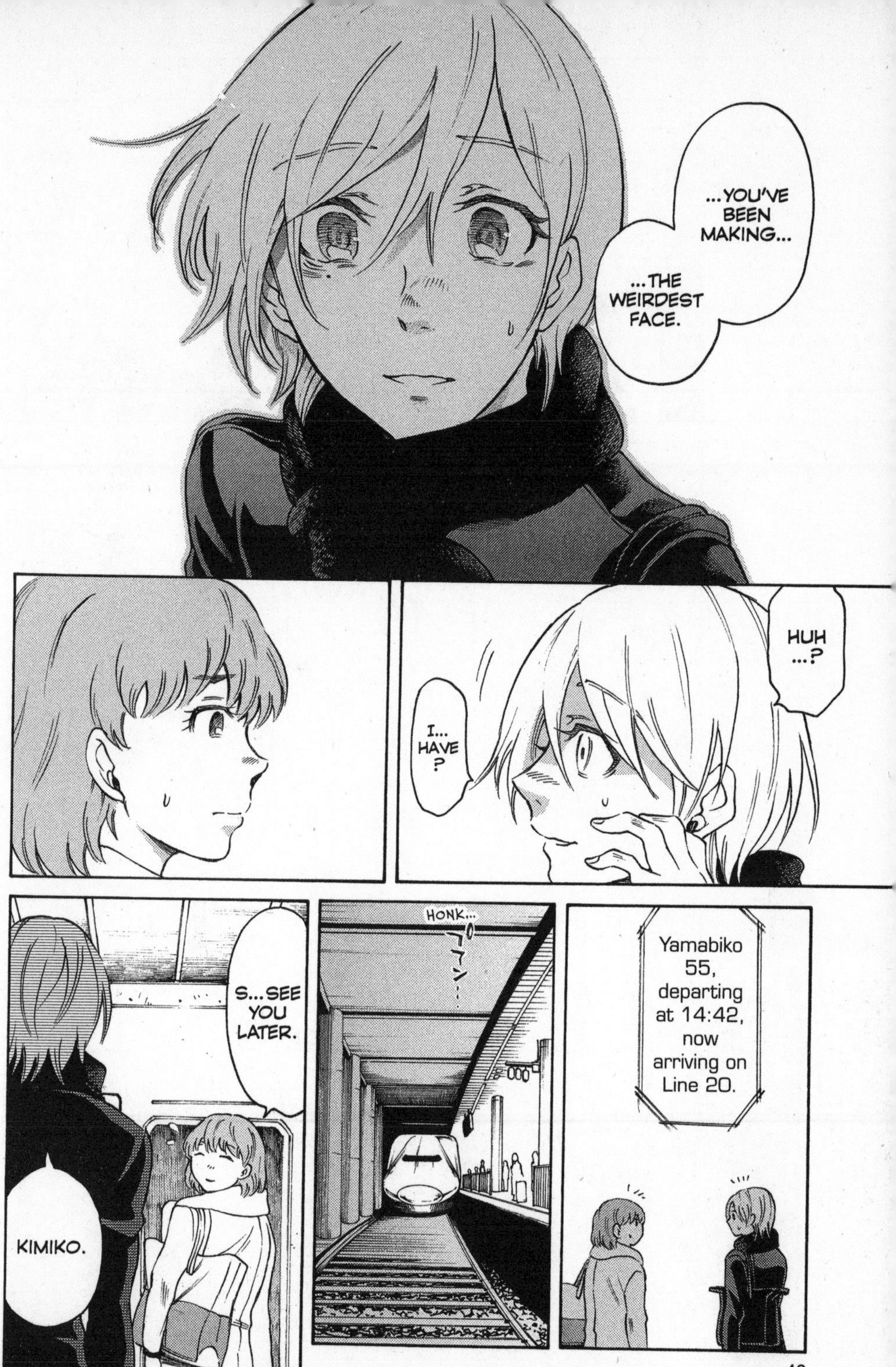
...YOU'VE BEEN MAKING...
...THE WEIRDEST FACE.
HUH ...?
I... HAVE ?
Yamabiko 55, departing at 14:42, now arriving on Line 20.
HONK...
S...SEE YOU LATER.
KIMIKO.

WHEN... CAN I SEE YOU AGAIN?
HUH...? UMM, NEXT TIME...
I DUNNO. I'M LOW ON FUNDS.
I'LL CALL YOU LATER.
FSHHH...
SHUT...

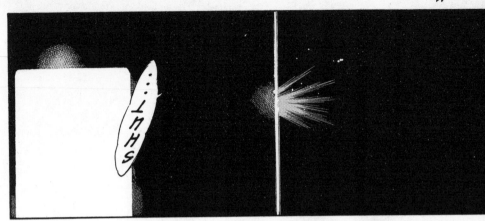

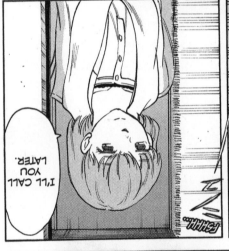

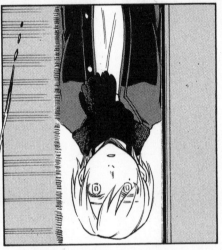

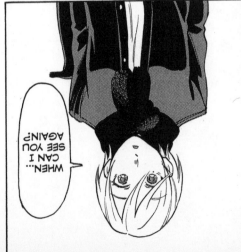

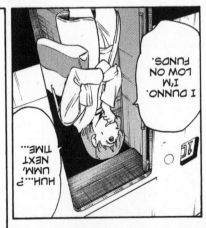

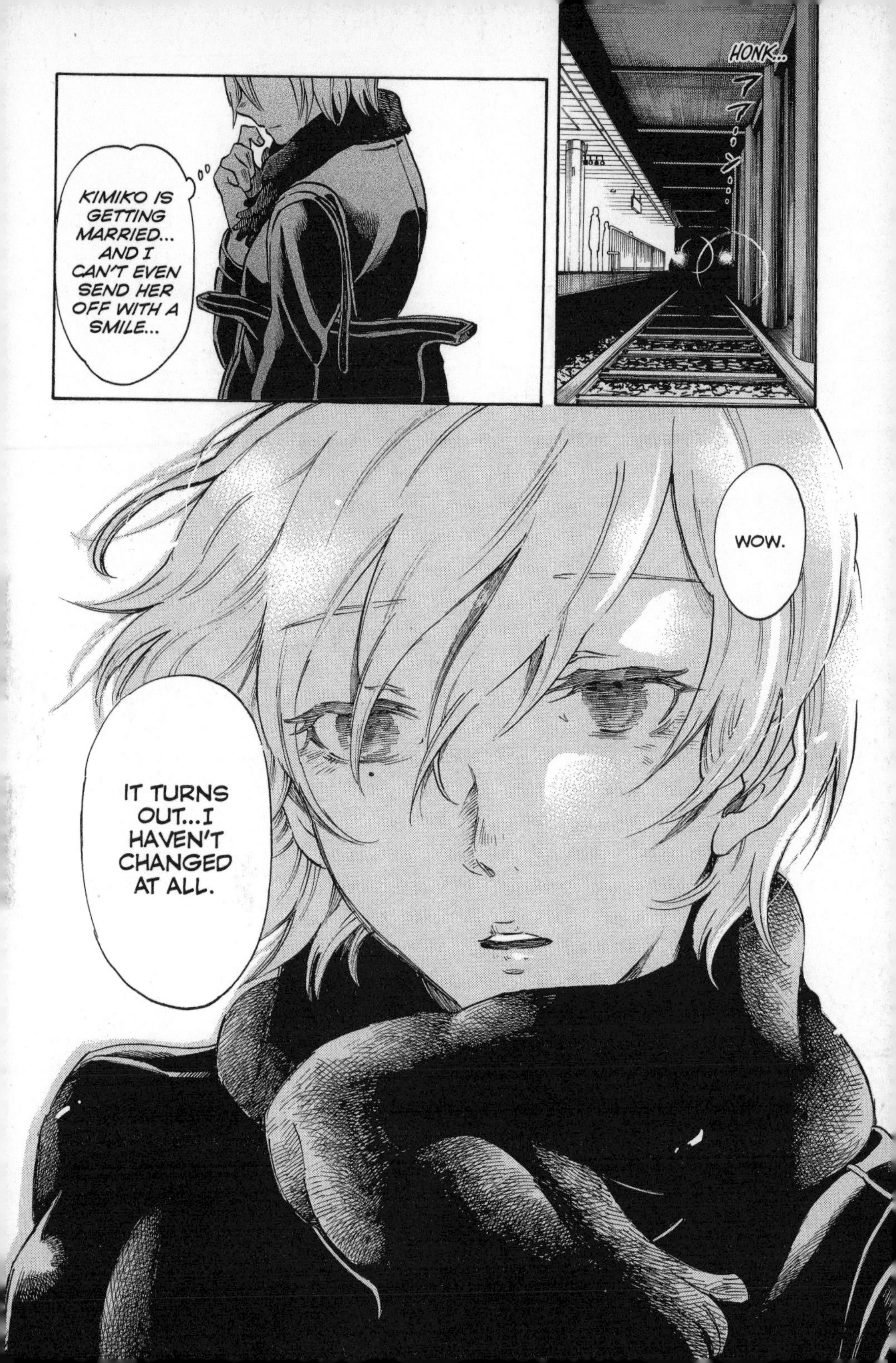
HONK...
KIMIKO IS GETTING MARRIED... AND I CAN'T EVEN SEND HER OFF WITH A SMILE...
WOW.
IT TURNS OUT...I HAVEN'T CHANGED AT ALL.

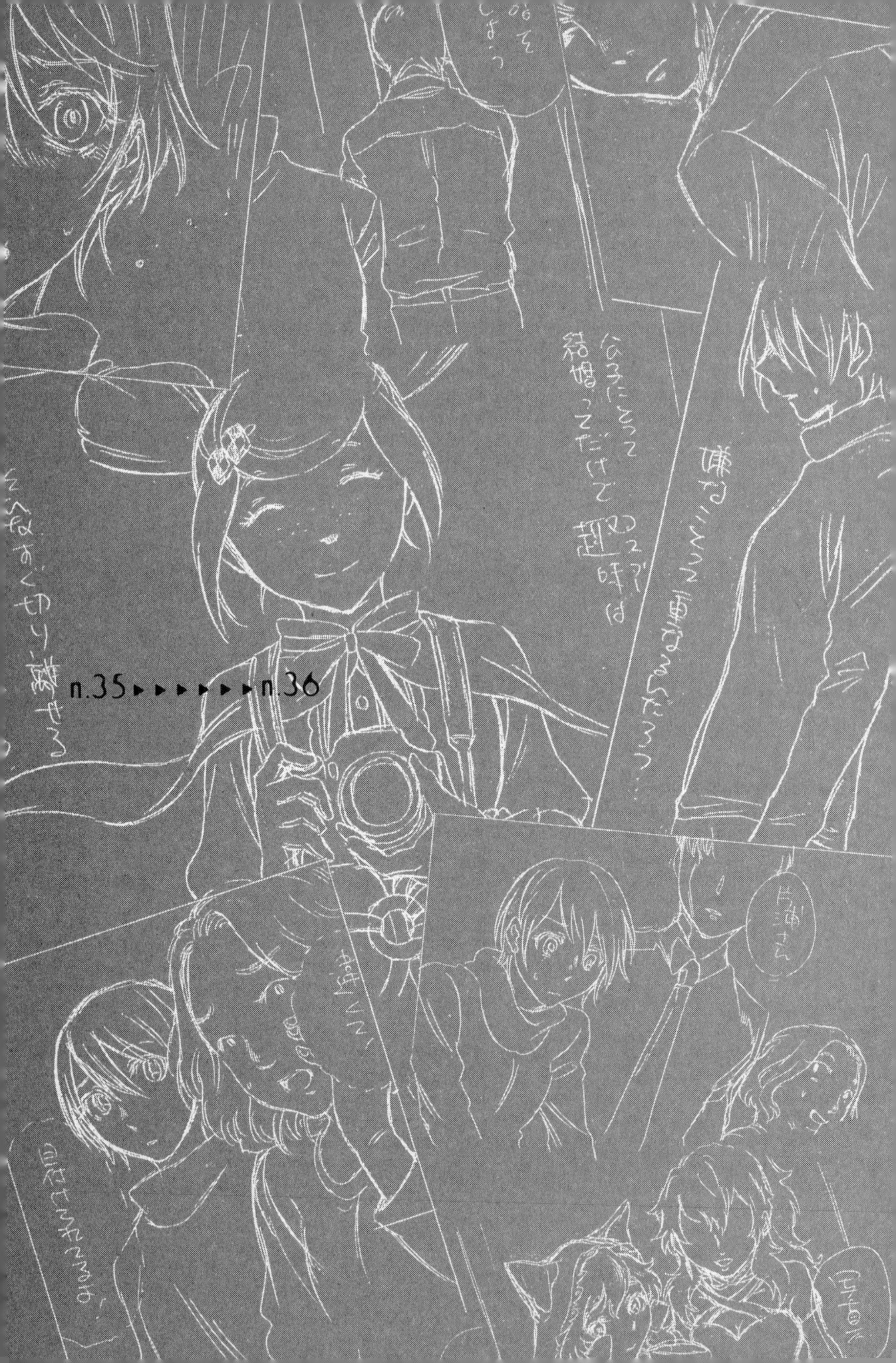

僕らはこうして重なるんだろう…
今はすぐやり直せる
n.35▸▸▸▸▸▸▸n.36
見せてもらえるよ

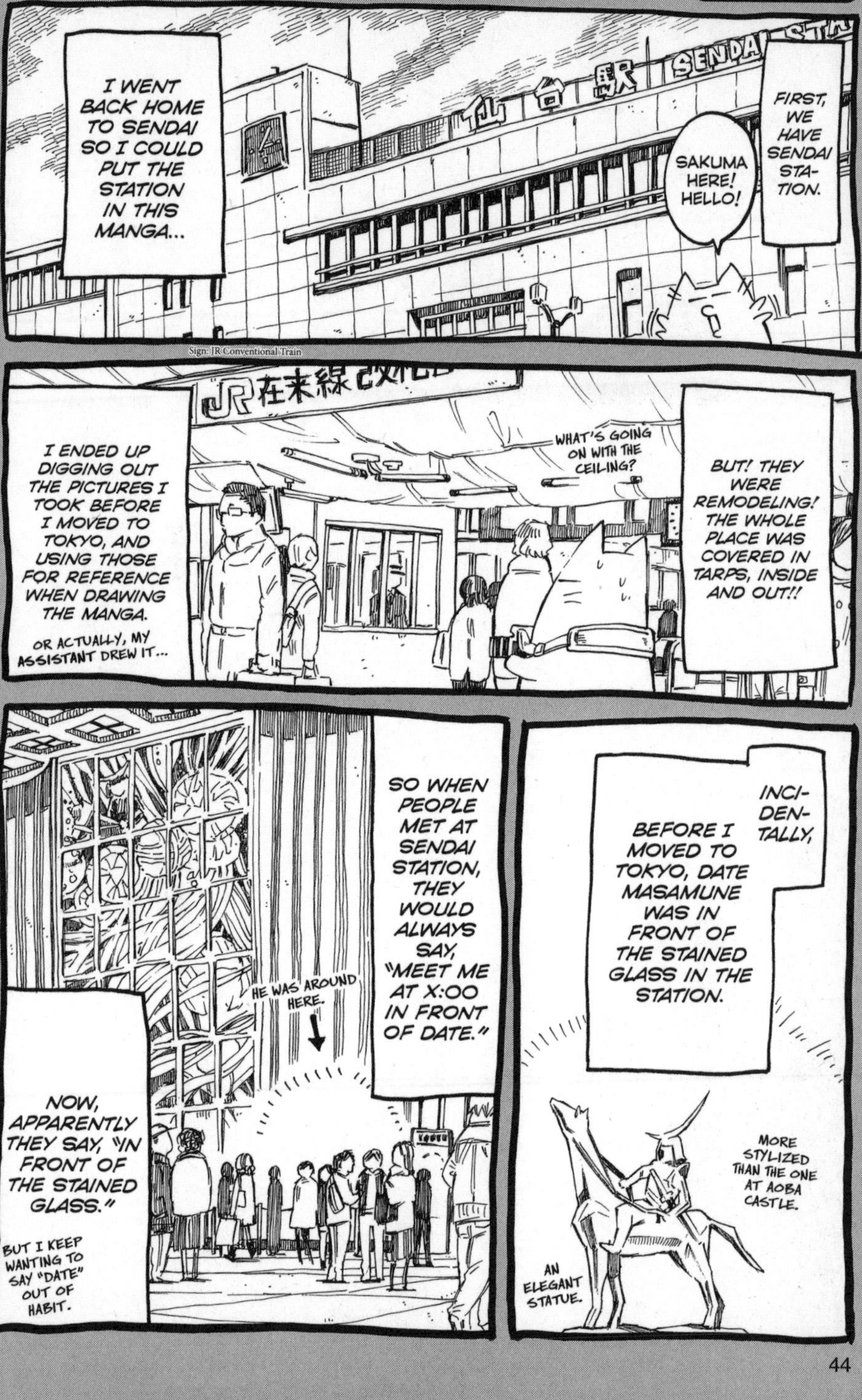
仙台駅 SENDAI
FIRST, WE HAVE SENDAI STA-TION.
SAKUMA HERE! HELLO!
I WENT BACK HOME TO SENDAI SO I COULD PUT THE STATION IN THIS MANGA...
JR 在来線
BUT! THEY WERE REMODELING! THE WHOLE PLACE WAS COVERED IN TARPS, INSIDE AND OUT!!
WHAT'S GOING ON WITH THE CEILING?
I ENDED UP DIGGING OUT THE PICTURES I TOOK BEFORE I MOVED TO TOKYO, AND USING THOSE FOR REFERENCE WHEN DRAWING THE MANGA.
OR ACTUALLY, MY ASSISTANT DREW IT...
INCI-DEN-TALLY,
BEFORE I MOVED TO TOKYO, DATE MASAMUNE WAS IN FRONT OF THE STAINED GLASS IN THE STATION.
MORE STYLIZED THAN THE ONE AT AOBA CASTLE.
AN ELEGANT STATUE.
SO WHEN PEOPLE MET AT SENDAI STATION, THEY WOULD ALWAYS SAY, "MEET ME AT X:00 IN FRONT OF DATE."
HE WAS AROUND HERE.
NOW, APPARENTLY THEY SAY, "IN FRONT OF THE STAINED GLASS."
BUT I KEEP WANTING TO SAY "DATE" OUT OF HABIT.

Sign: JR Conventional Train

HONK...
...
BACK TO MY JOB TOMORROW.
AND SO, EVERYTHING MOVES ON.
n.36
Complex age
I'M SCARED.

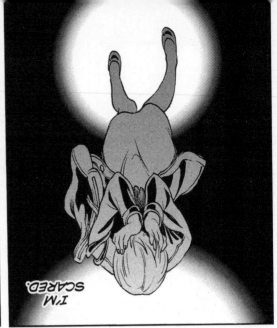

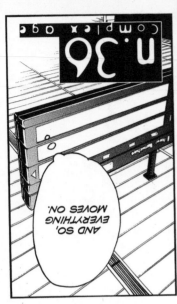

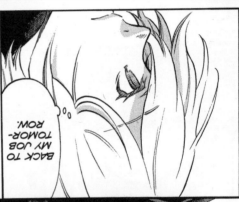

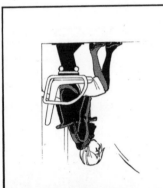

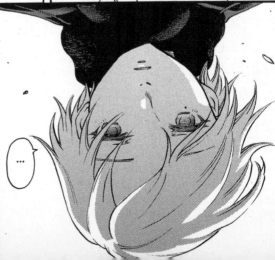

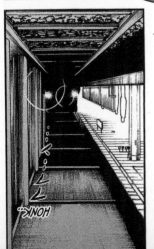

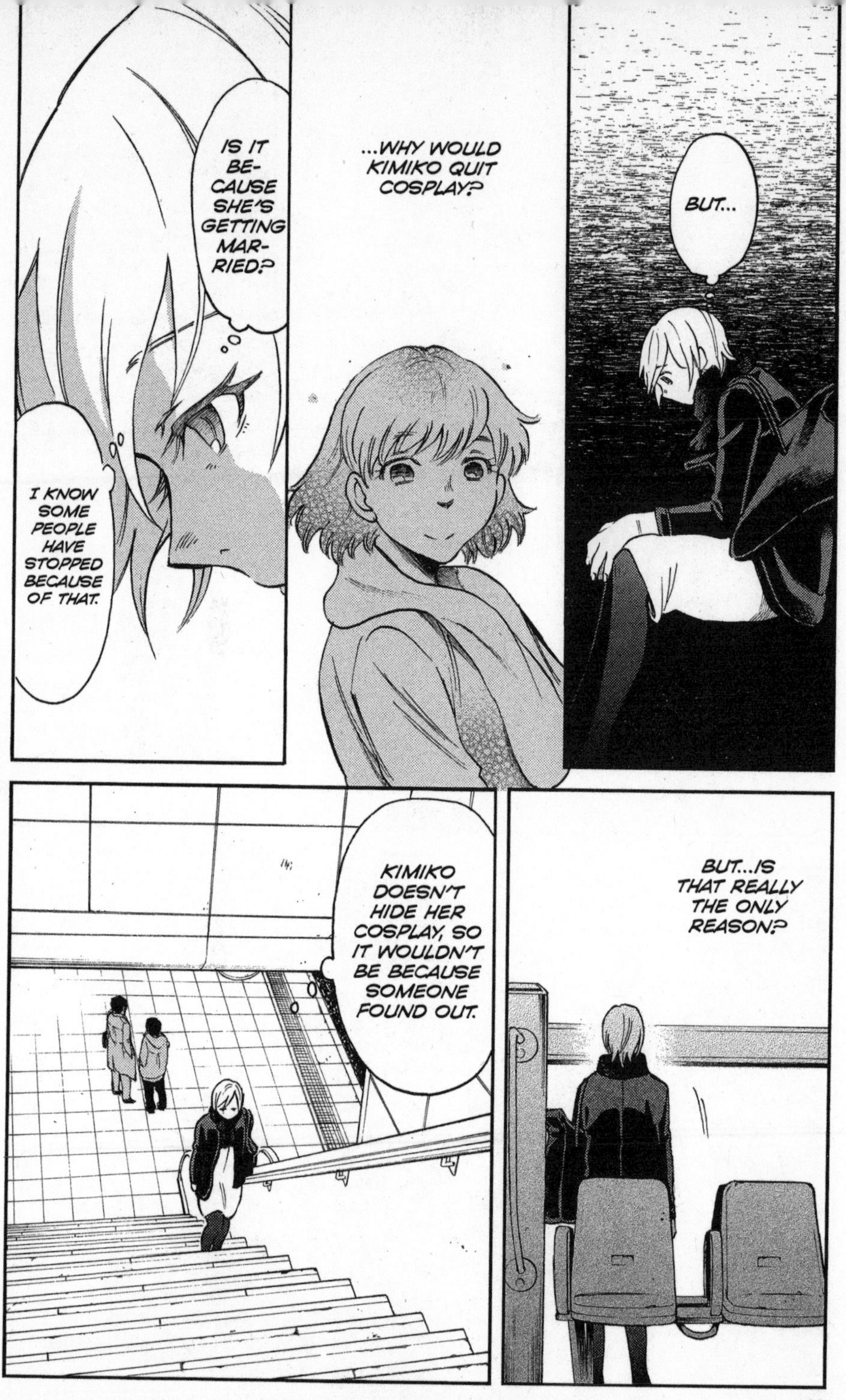
BUT...
...WHY WOULD KIMIKO QUIT COSPLAY?
IS IT BE-CAUSE SHE'S GETTING MAR-RIED?
I KNOW SOME PEOPLE HAVE STOPPED BECAUSE OF THAT.
BUT...IS THAT REALLY THE ONLY REASON?
KIMIKO DOESN'T HIDE HER COSPLAY, SO IT WOULDN'T BE BECAUSE SOMEONE FOUND OUT.

AND SHE SAID SHE'S GOING TO STOP, BUT THAT CAN MEAN ALL KINDS OF THINGS.
THERE HAS TO BE A GOOD REASON FOR IT.
AND THEN, SOME PEOPLE QUIT FOR A WHILE AND THEN TAKE IT UP AGAIN.
I JUST DON'T KNOW...
IT'S NOT LIKE YOU CAN DO IT FOREVER, ANYWAY.
I DON'T KNOW.
GNN...
BUT I'M NOT SURE KIMIKO IS THE TYPE OF PERSON...
...WHO COULD GIVE IT ALL UP JUST BECAUSE SHE'S GETTING MARRIED.

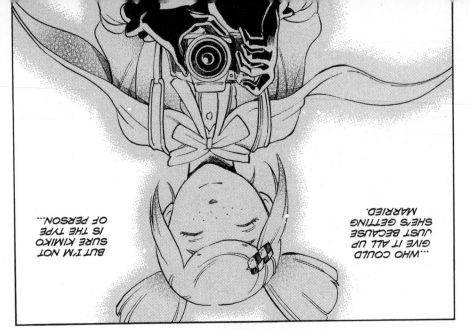

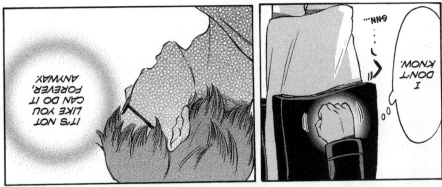

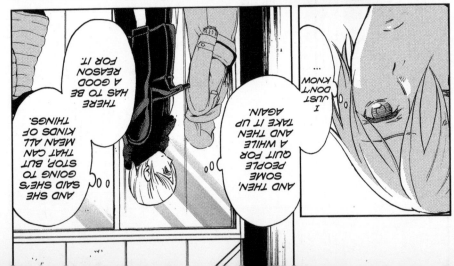

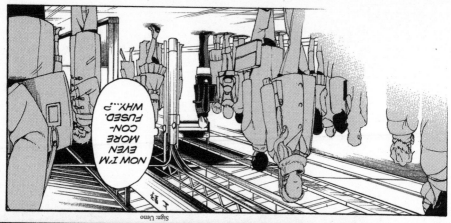

WHAT ... WHAT IF...
SHE WAS ONLY STILL DOING IT...
...BECAUSE IT WAS HER IDEA TO BEGIN WITH?
NO, THAT CAN'T POSSIBLY BE IT. THERE'S NO WAY.
SHE WOULDN'T DO SOMETHING IF SHE WASN'T ENJOYING IT.
Sign: Ueno
NOW I'M EVEN MORE CON-FUSED. WHY...?

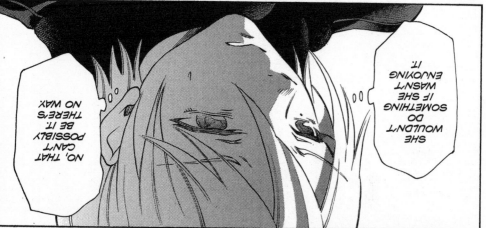

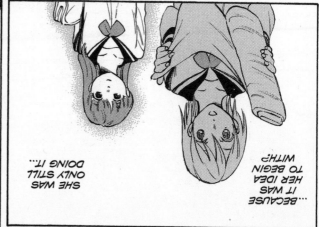

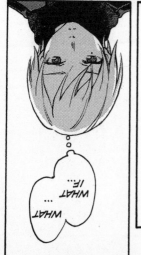

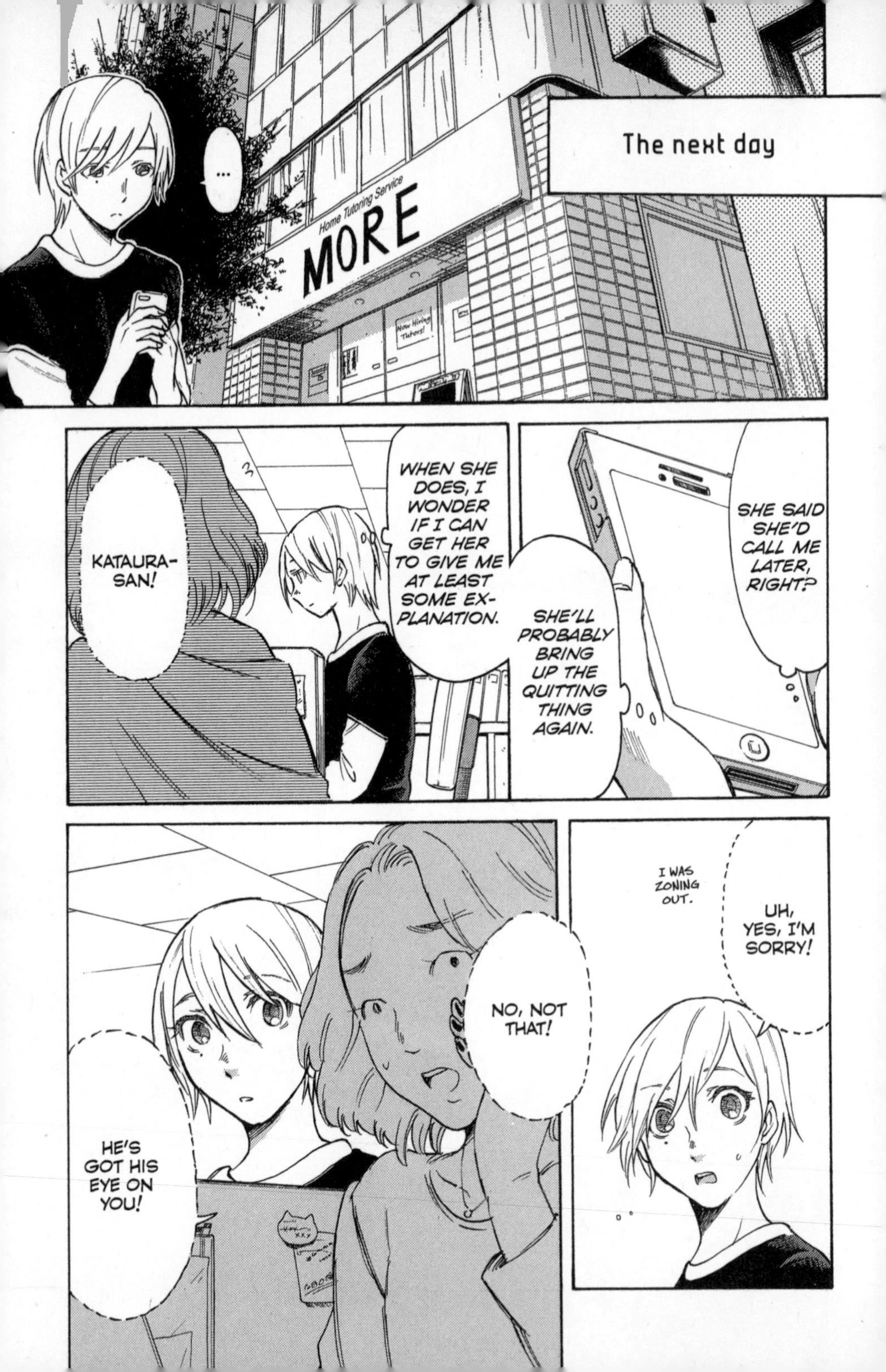
The next day
Home Tutoring Service
MORE
Now Hiring Tutors!
...
SHE SAID SHE'D CALL ME LATER, RIGHT?
SHE'LL PROBABLY BRING UP THE QUITTING THING AGAIN.
WHEN SHE DOES, I WONDER IF I CAN GET HER TO GIVE ME AT LEAST SOME EX-PLANATION.
KATAURA-SAN!
UH, YES, I'M SORRY!
I WAS ZONING OUT.
NO, NOT THAT!
HE'S GOT HIS EYE ON YOU!

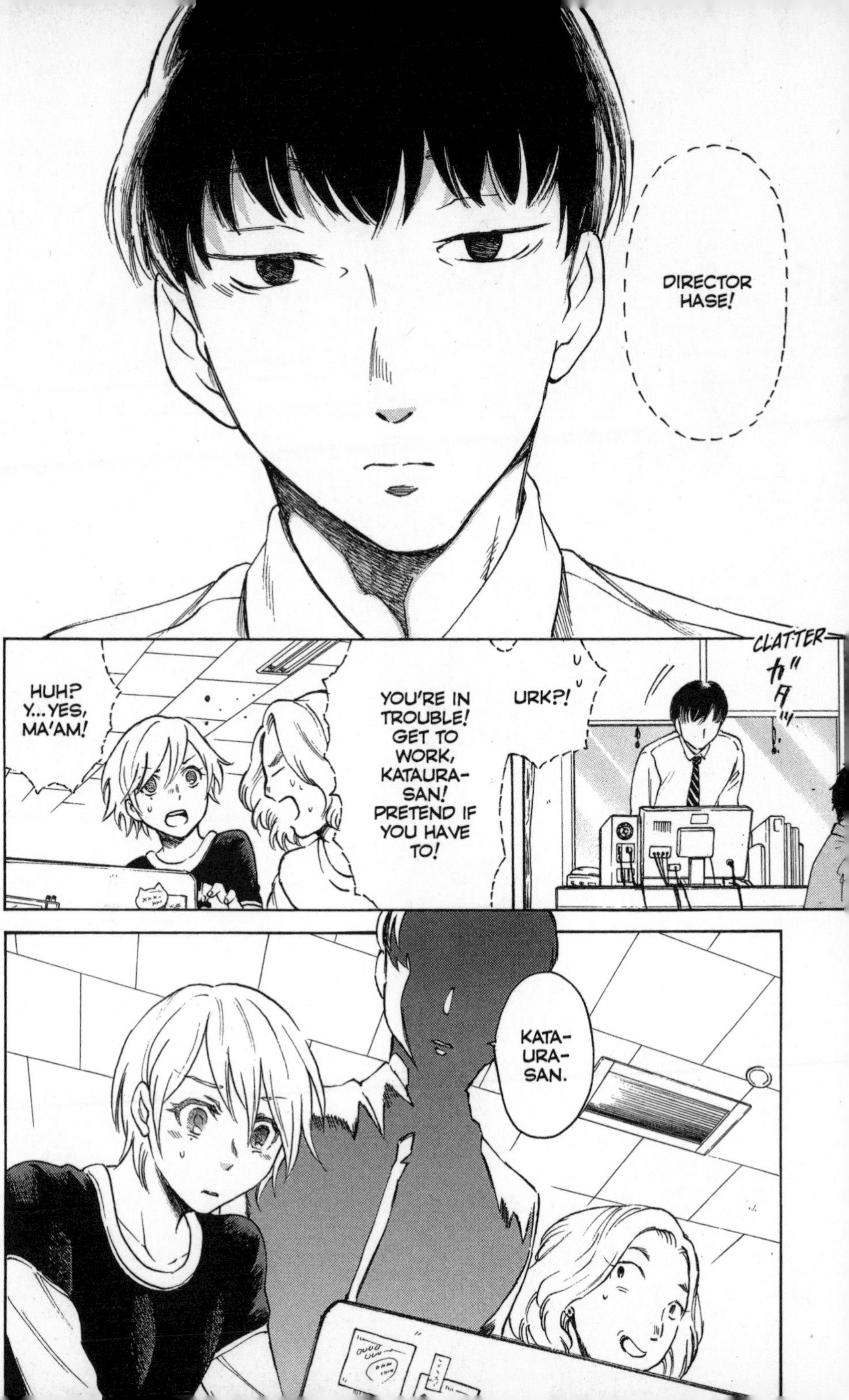
DIRECTOR HASE!
CLATTER
ガタ
URK?!
YOU'RE IN TROUBLE! GET TO WORK, KATAURA-SAN! PRETEND IF YOU HAVE TO!
HUH? Y...YES, MA'AM!
KATA-URA-SAN.

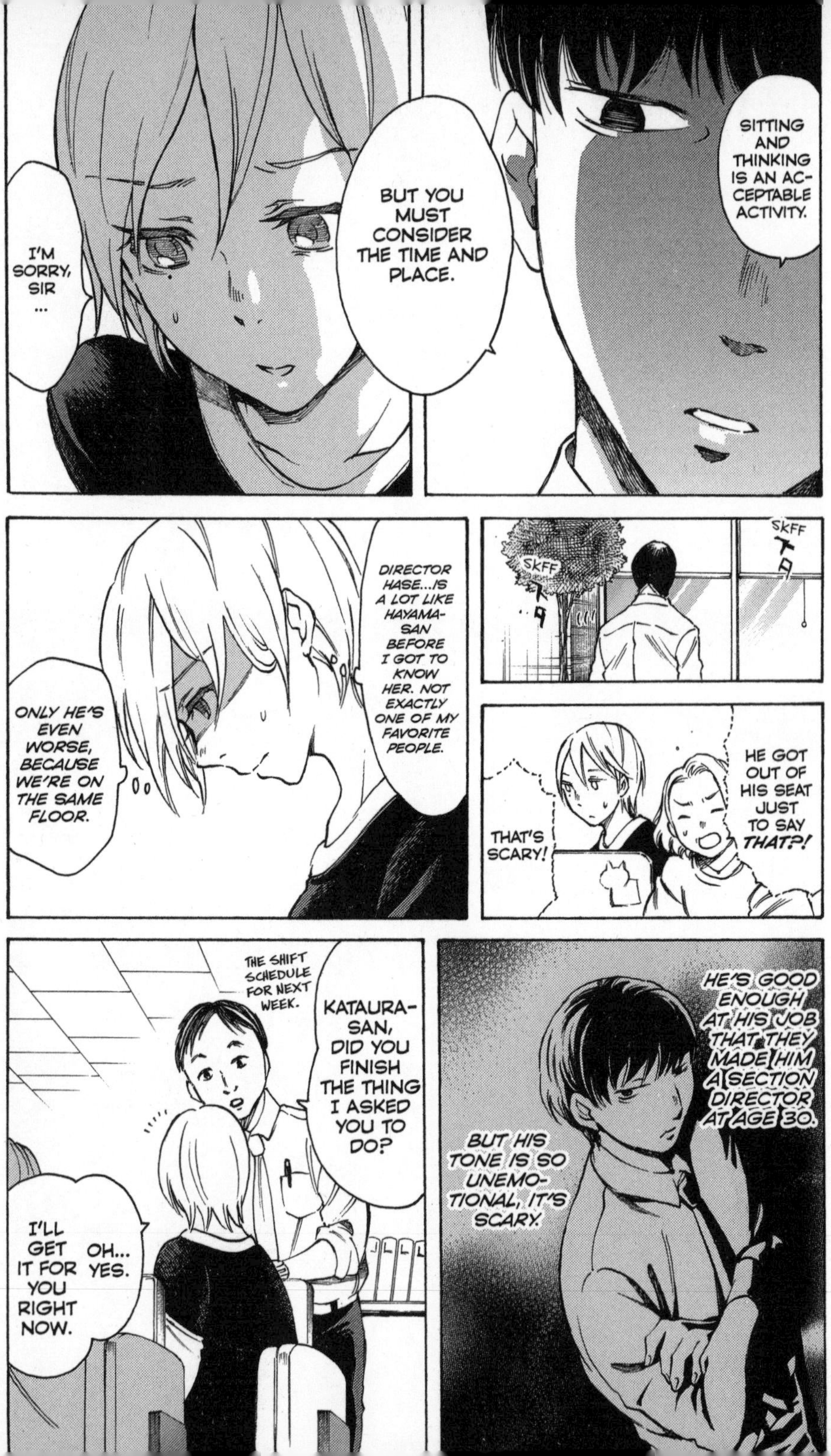
SITTING AND THINKING IS AN ACCEPTABLE ACTIVITY.
BUT YOU MUST CONSIDER THE TIME AND PLACE.
I'M SORRY, SIR ...
SKFF
SKFF
HE GOT OUT OF HIS SEAT JUST TO SAY THAT?!
THAT'S SCARY!
DIRECTOR HASE...IS A LOT LIKE HAYAMA-SAN BEFORE I GOT TO KNOW HER. NOT EXACTLY ONE OF MY FAVORITE PEOPLE.
ONLY HE'S EVEN WORSE, BECAUSE WE'RE ON THE SAME FLOOR.
HE'S GOOD ENOUGH AT HIS JOB THAT THEY MADE HIM A SECTION DIRECTOR AT AGE 30.
BUT HIS TONE IS SO UNEMOTIONAL, IT'S SCARY.
KATAURA-SAN, DID YOU FINISH THE THING I ASKED YOU TO DO?
THE SHIFT SCHEDULE FOR NEXT WEEK.
OH... YES.
I'LL GET IT FOR YOU RIGHT NOW.

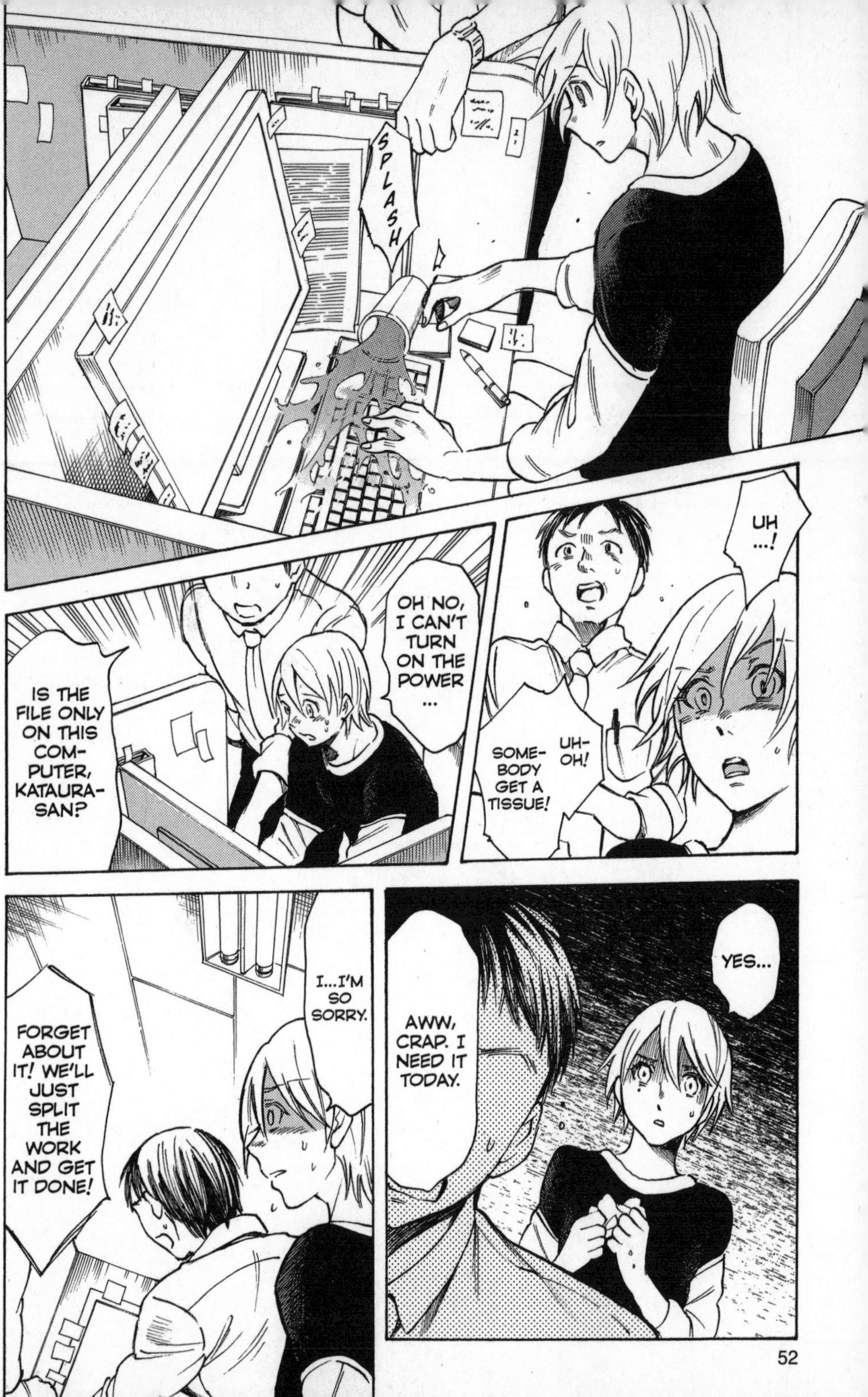
SPLASH
UH...!
UH-OH!
SOMEBODY GET A TISSUE!
OH NO, I CAN'T TURN ON THE POWER...
IS THE FILE ONLY ON THIS COMPUTER, KATAURA-SAN?
YES...
AWW, CRAP. I NEED IT TODAY.
I...I'M SO SORRY.
FORGET ABOUT IT! WE'LL JUST SPLIT THE WORK AND GET IT DONE!

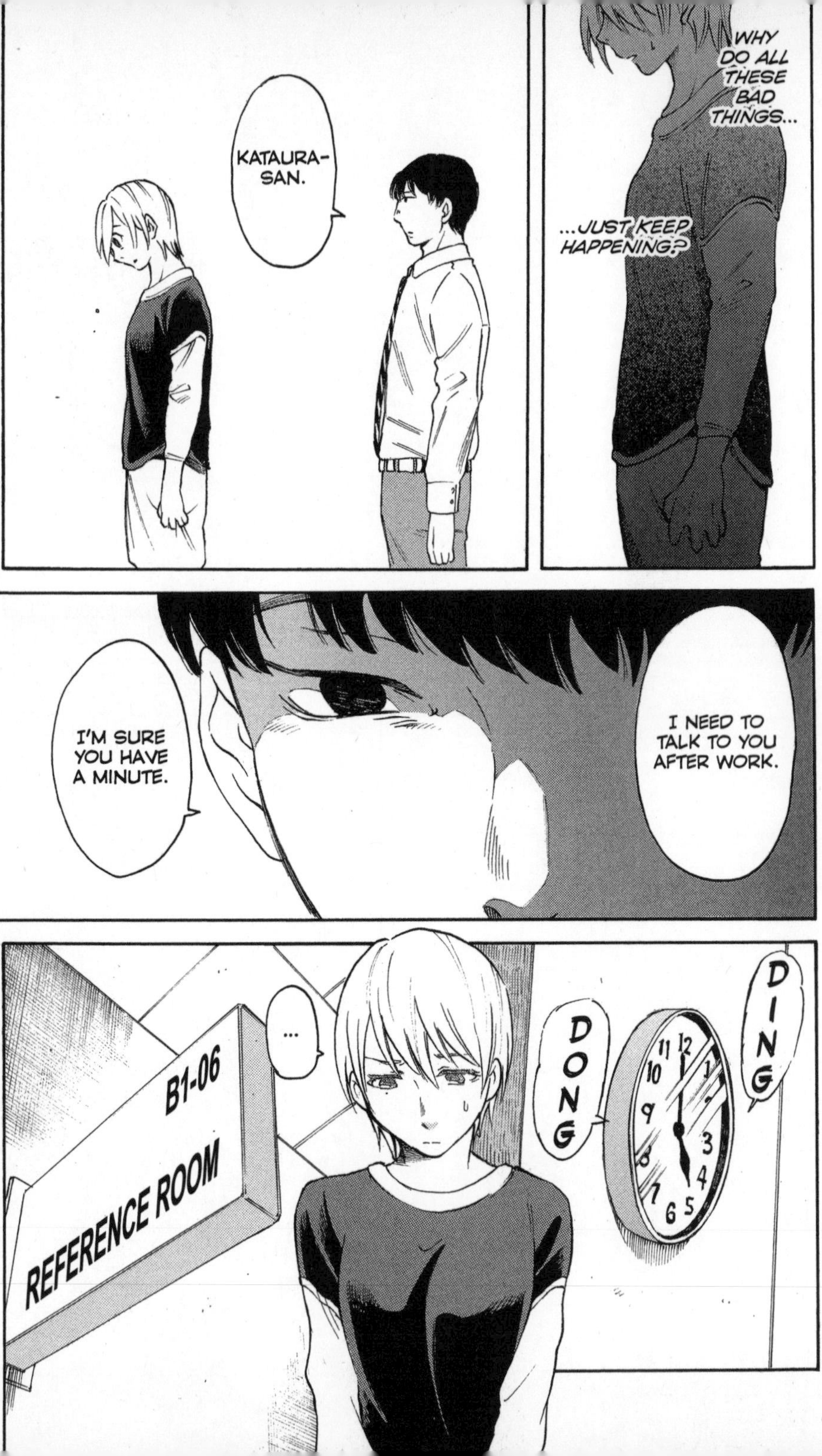
WHY DO ALL THESE BAD THINGS...
...JUST KEEP HAPPENING?
KATAURA-SAN.
I NEED TO TALK TO YOU AFTER WORK.
I'M SURE YOU HAVE A MINUTE.
DING
DONG
...
B1-06
REFERENCE ROOM

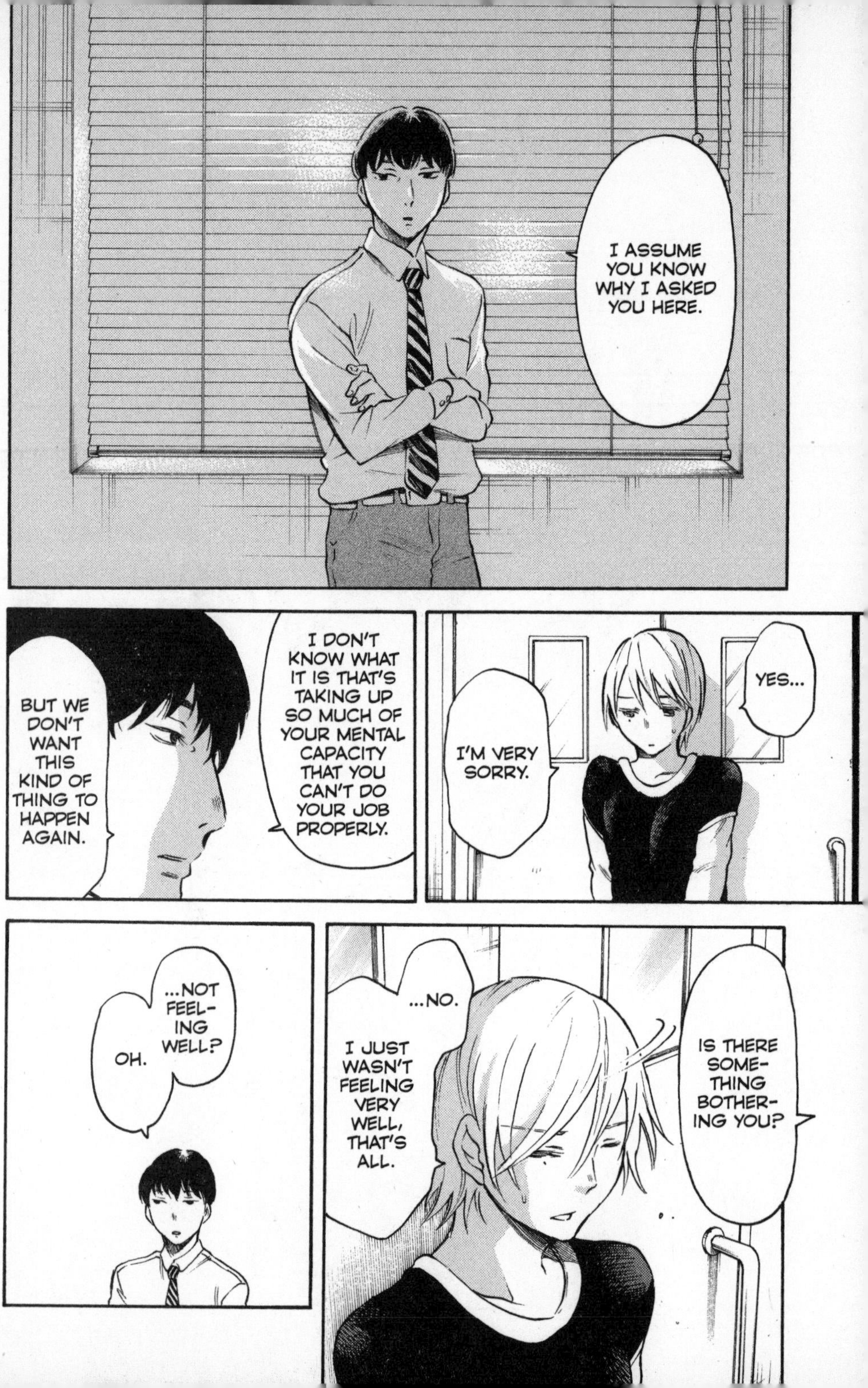
I ASSUME YOU KNOW WHY I ASKED YOU HERE.
YES...
I'M VERY SORRY.
I DON'T KNOW WHAT IT IS THAT'S TAKING UP SO MUCH OF YOUR MENTAL CAPACITY THAT YOU CAN'T DO YOUR JOB PROPERLY.
BUT WE DON'T WANT THIS KIND OF THING TO HAPPEN AGAIN.
IS THERE SOME-THING BOTHER-ING YOU?
...NO.
I JUST WASN'T FEELING VERY WELL, THAT'S ALL.
...NOT FEEL-ING WELL?
OH.

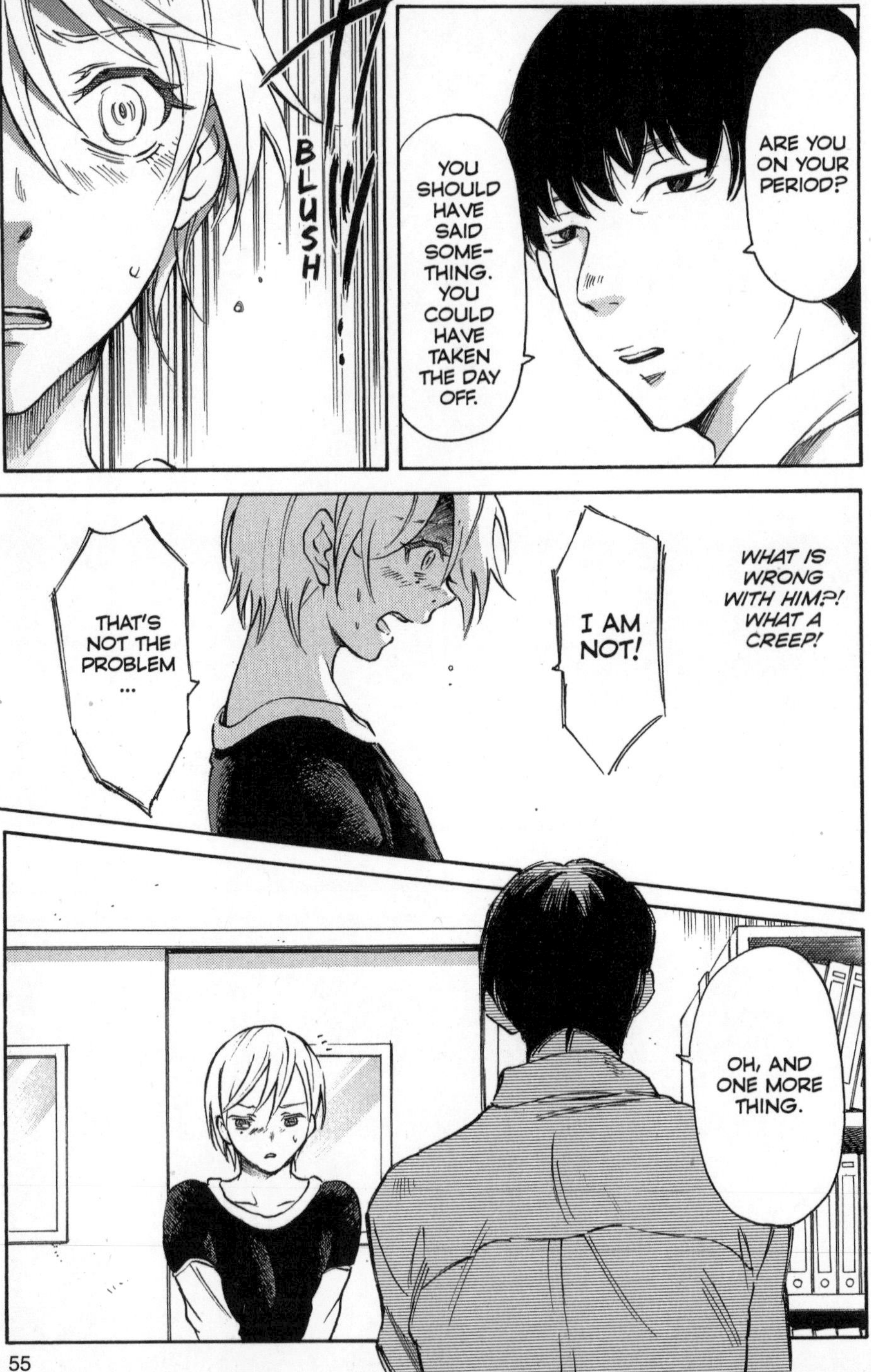
ARE YOU ON YOUR PERIOD?
YOU SHOULD HAVE SAID SOME-THING. YOU COULD HAVE TAKEN THE DAY OFF.
BLUSH
WHAT IS WRONG WITH HIM?! WHAT A CREEP!
I AM NOT!
THAT'S NOT THE PROBLEM ...
OH, AND ONE MORE THING.

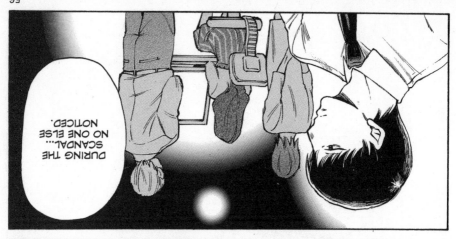

HOW IS HAYAMA-SAN DOING?
HUH...?
HE...
YOU DIDN'T TALK THAT MUCH AT WORK, BUT YOU TWO WERE FRIENDS, RIGHT?
HOW ...?
DURING THE SCANDAL... NO ONE ELSE NOTICED.

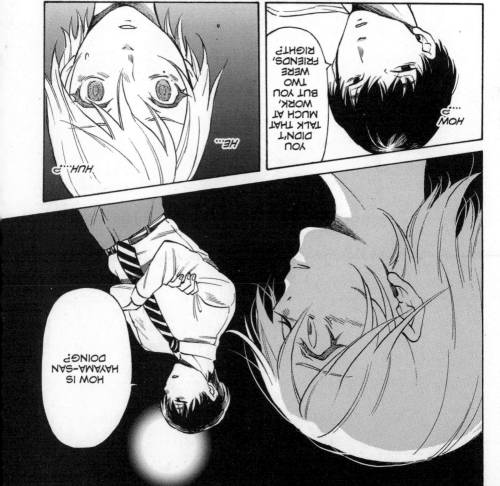

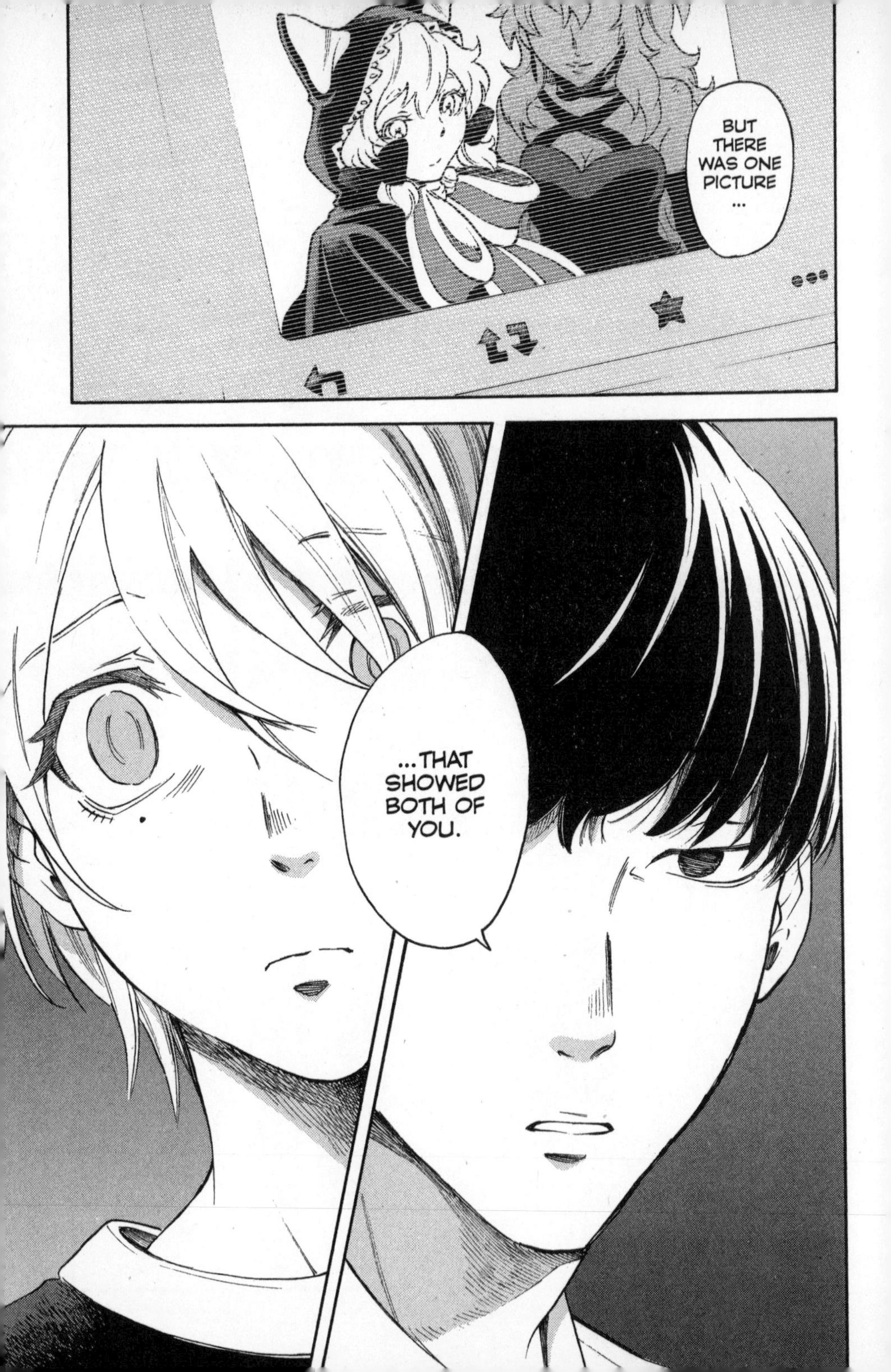
BUT THERE WAS ONE PICTURE ...
...THAT SHOWED BOTH OF YOU.

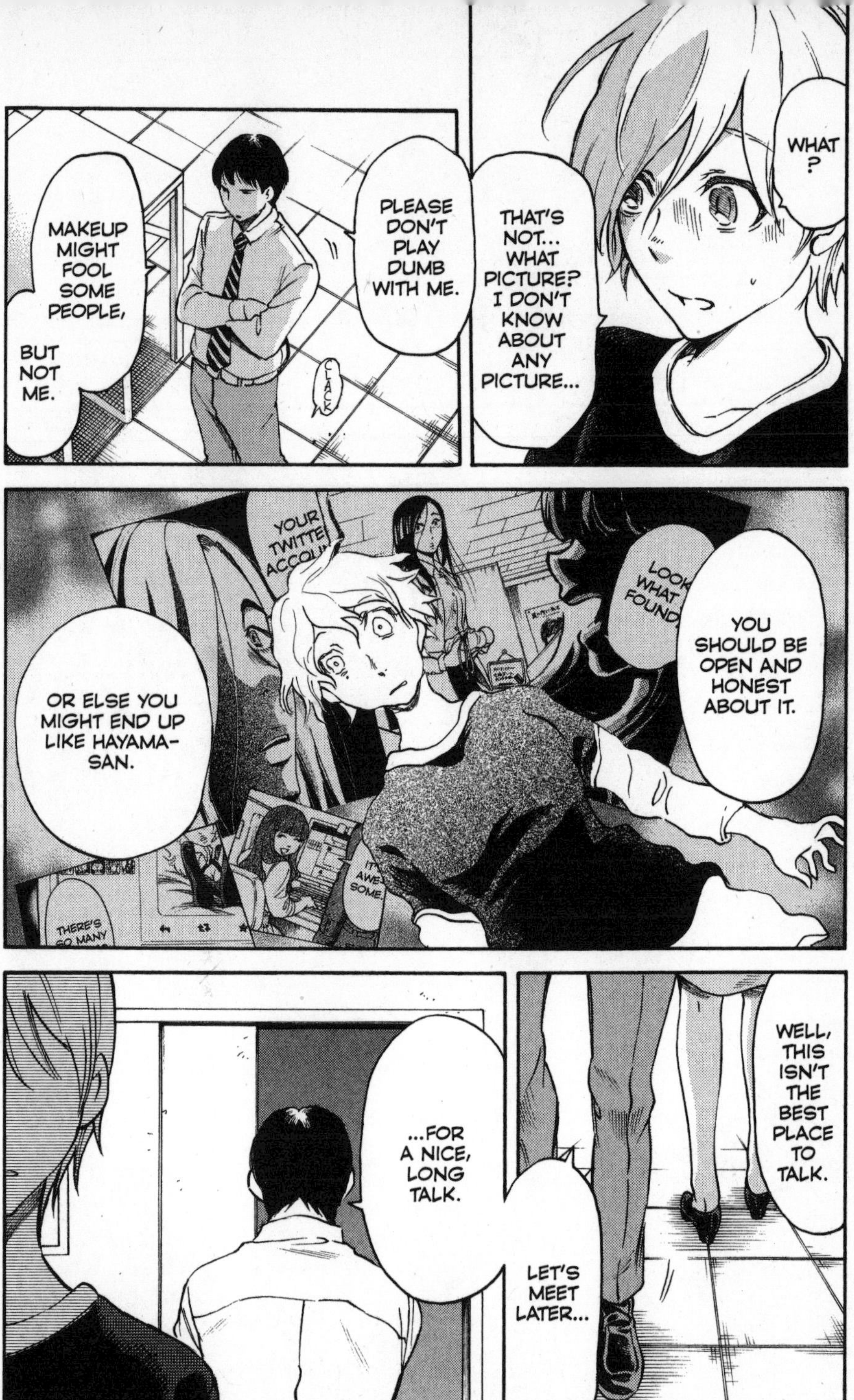
WHAT?
THAT'S NOT... WHAT PICTURE? I DON'T KNOW ABOUT ANY PICTURE...
PLEASE DON'T PLAY DUMB WITH ME.
CLACK
MAKEUP MIGHT FOOL SOME PEOPLE,
BUT NOT ME.
YOU SHOULD BE OPEN AND HONEST ABOUT IT.
OR ELSE YOU MIGHT END UP LIKE HAYAMA-SAN.
WELL, THIS ISN'T THE BEST PLACE TO TALK.
LET'S MEET LATER...
...FOR A NICE, LONG TALK.

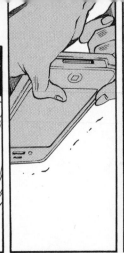

OR CAN I?

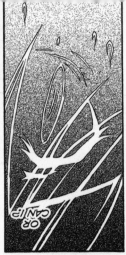

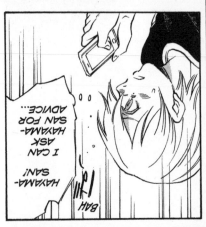

HAYAMA-SAN! I CAN ASK HAYAMA-SAN FOR ADVICE...

BAH!!

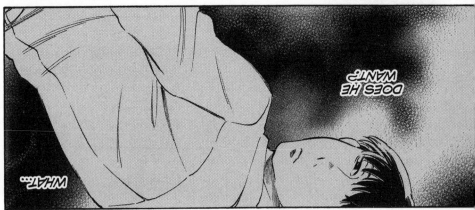

WHAT...

DOES HE WANT?

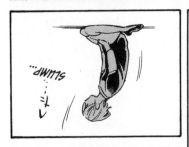

SLUMP...

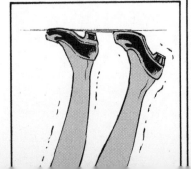

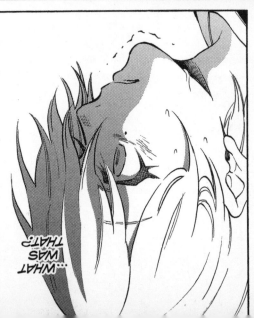

...WHAT WAS THAT?

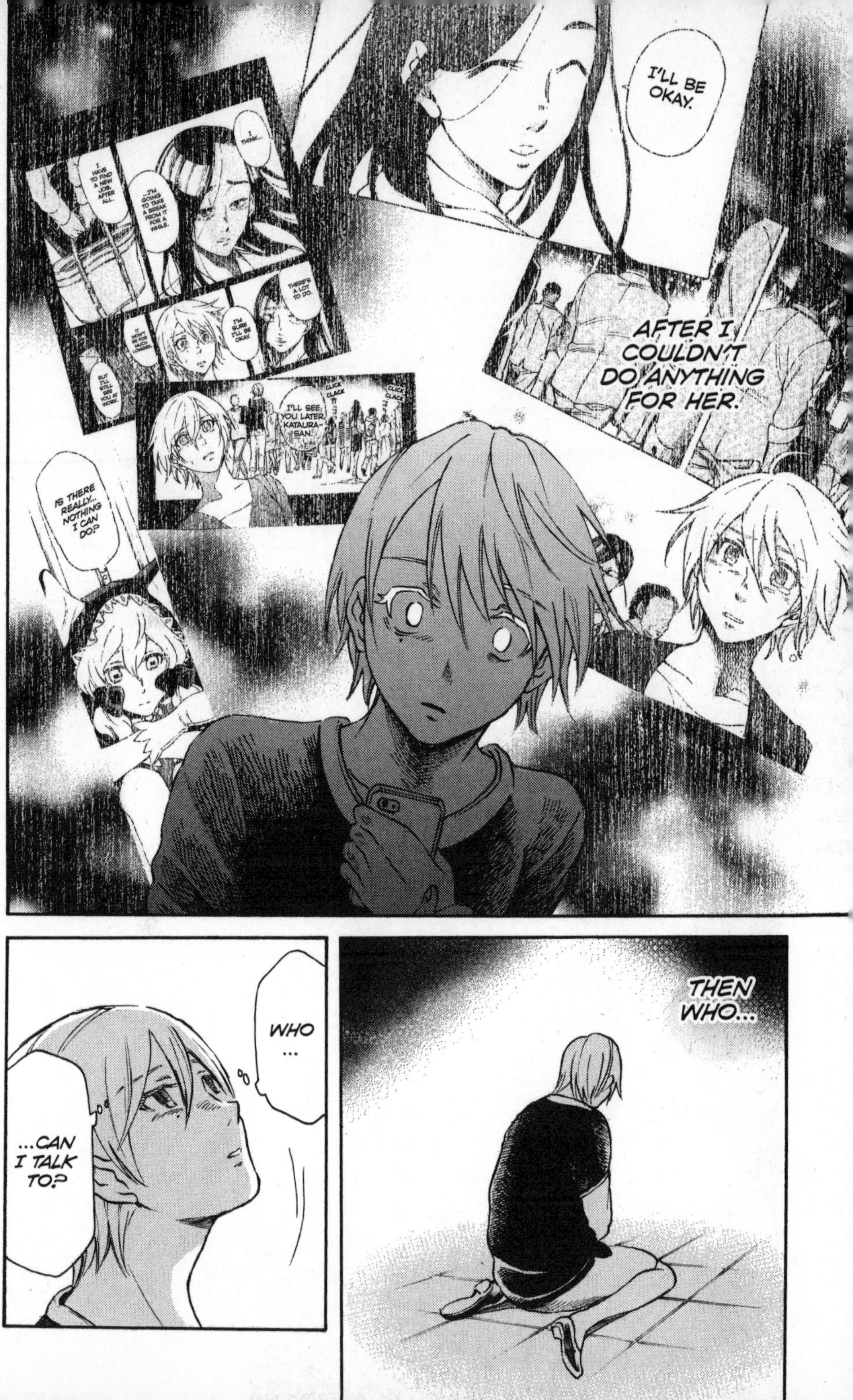
I'LL BE OKAY.
AFTER I COULDN'T DO ANYTHING FOR HER.
I THINK...
I HAVE TO FIND A NEW JOB AFTER ALL.
...I'M GOING TO TAKE A BREAK FROM IT FOR A WHILE.
THERE'S A LOT TO DO.
I'M SURE I'LL BE OKAY.
IT WON'T BE FOR MUCH LONGER.
BUT I'LL STILL SEE YOU AT WORK.
CLICK CLACK
CLICK CLACK
I'LL SEE YOU LATER, KATAURA-SAN.
IS THERE REALLY... NOTHING I CAN DO?
THEN WHO...
WHO ...
...CAN I TALK TO?

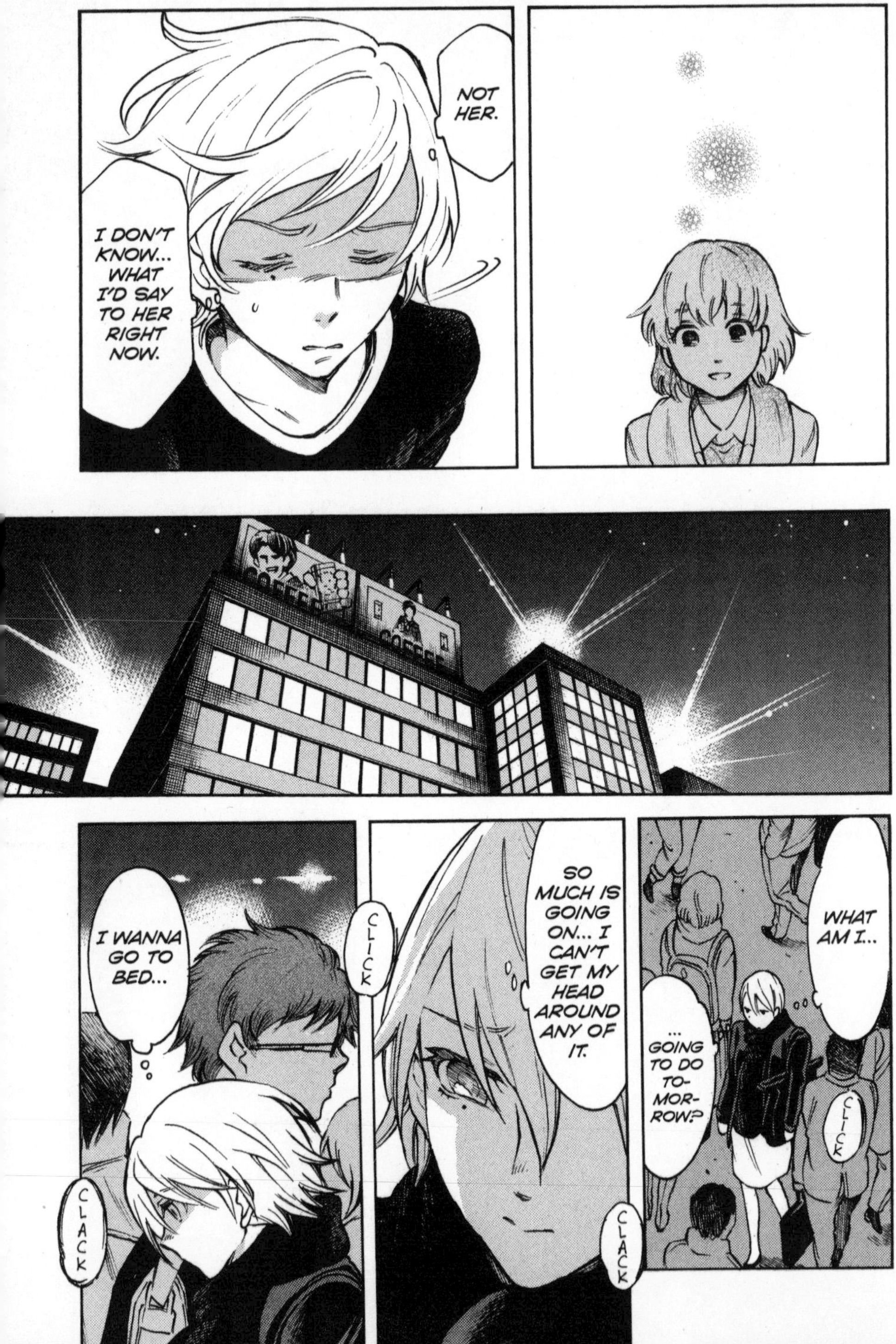
NOT HER.
I DON'T KNOW... WHAT I'D SAY TO HER RIGHT NOW.
WHAT AM I...
... GOING TO DO TO-MOR-ROW?
CLICK
SO MUCH IS GOING ON... I CAN'T GET MY HEAD AROUND ANY OF IT.
CLACK
CLICK
I WANNA GO TO BED...
CLACK

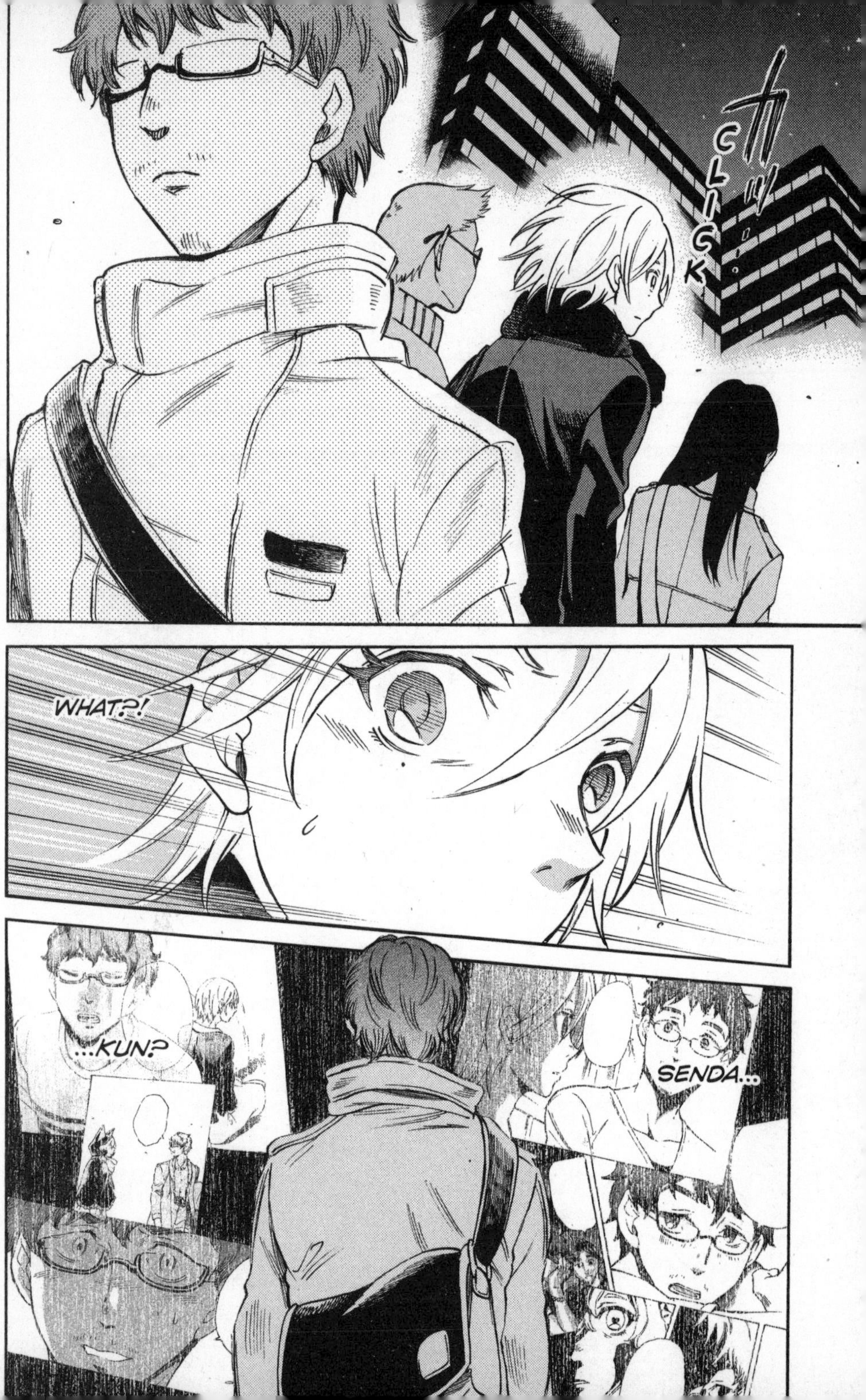
CLICK
WHAT?!
SENDA...
...KUN?

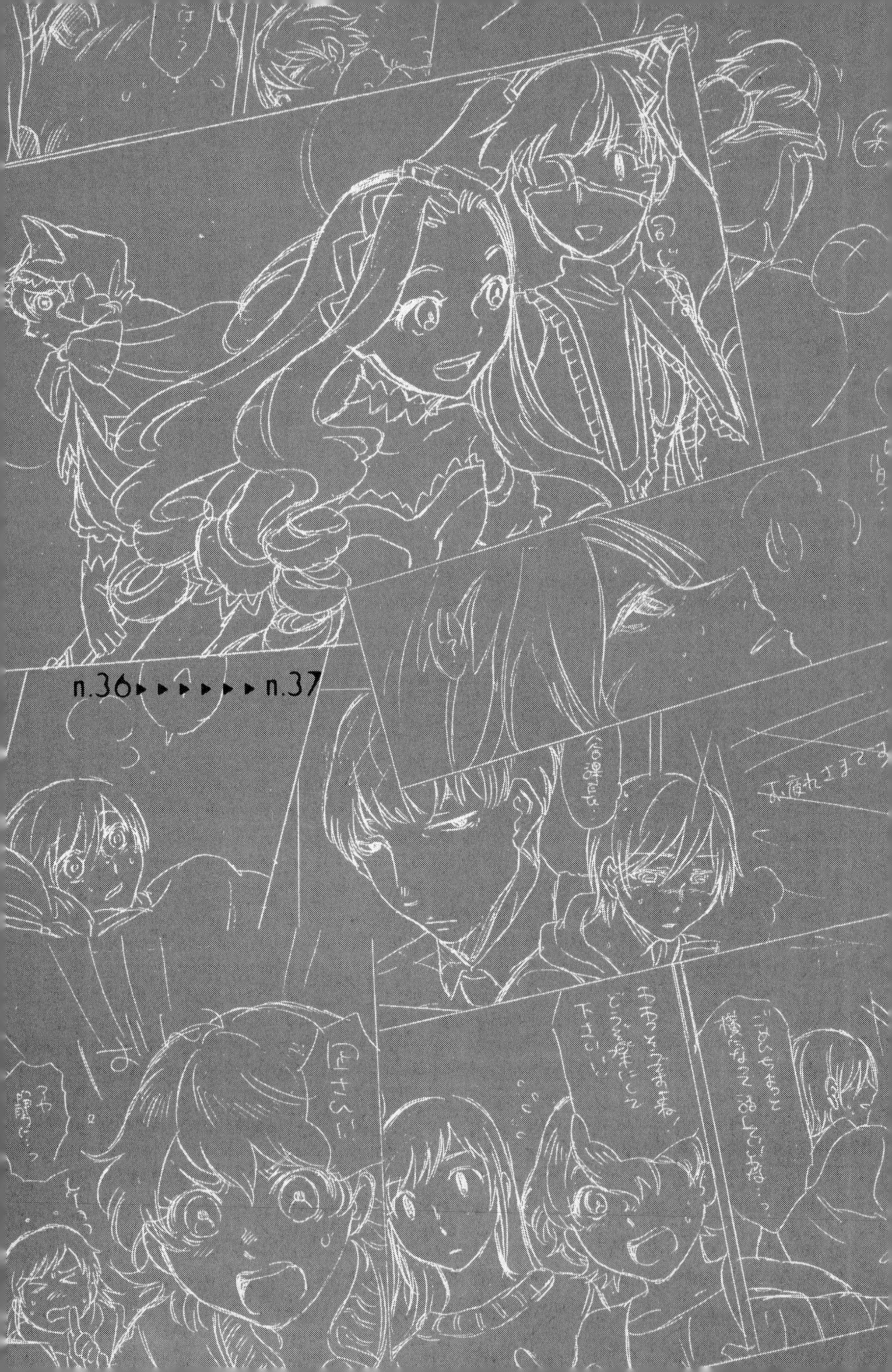
n.36▸▸▸▸▸▸▸▸n.37

SENDAI HIGH SCHOOL.
DANG DONG DING
NAGISA AND KIMIKO WENT TO NIAN HIGH SCHOOL.
IT'S IN TOKYO IN THE MANGA, BUT I DREW IT BASED ON MY ALMA MATER, SENDAI HIGH SCHOOL.
THERE I GO AGAIN!! TO BE ACCURATE, MY ASSISTANT DREW IT! THANK YOU!
THE SCHOOL MOTTO WAS "INDEPENDENCE AND SELF-RELIANCE,"
SO THE STUDENTS DIDN'T WEAR UNIFORMS TO SCHOOL.
OF COURSE, IN MY CASE, I ONLY HAD ABOUT THREE VARIATIONS OF PERSONAL FASHION. (DARK HISTORY)
NOT THAT ANYBODY CARES, BUT MY FATHER WENT TO THIS SCHOOL, TOO.
FOR CLUBS, I WAS IN BOTH THE ART CLUB AND THE ASTRONOMY AND EARTH SCIENCE CLUB.
STUDENTS WERE PROHIBITED FROM GOING ON THE ROOF, BUT THE EARTH SCIENCE CLUB MEMBERS HAD SPECIAL PERMISSION.
WE DID A LOT OF UNEXCITING THINGS LIKE LOOKING AT THE STARS AND GOING TO COLLECT ROCKS, BUT IT WAS RIDICULOUSLY FUN!
YOOHOO!
WE HAD AN ASTRONOMICAL OBSERVATORY ON THE ROOF.

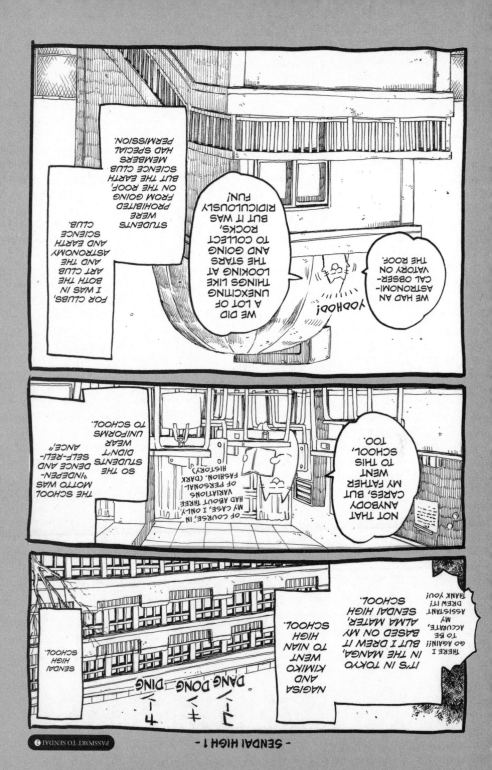

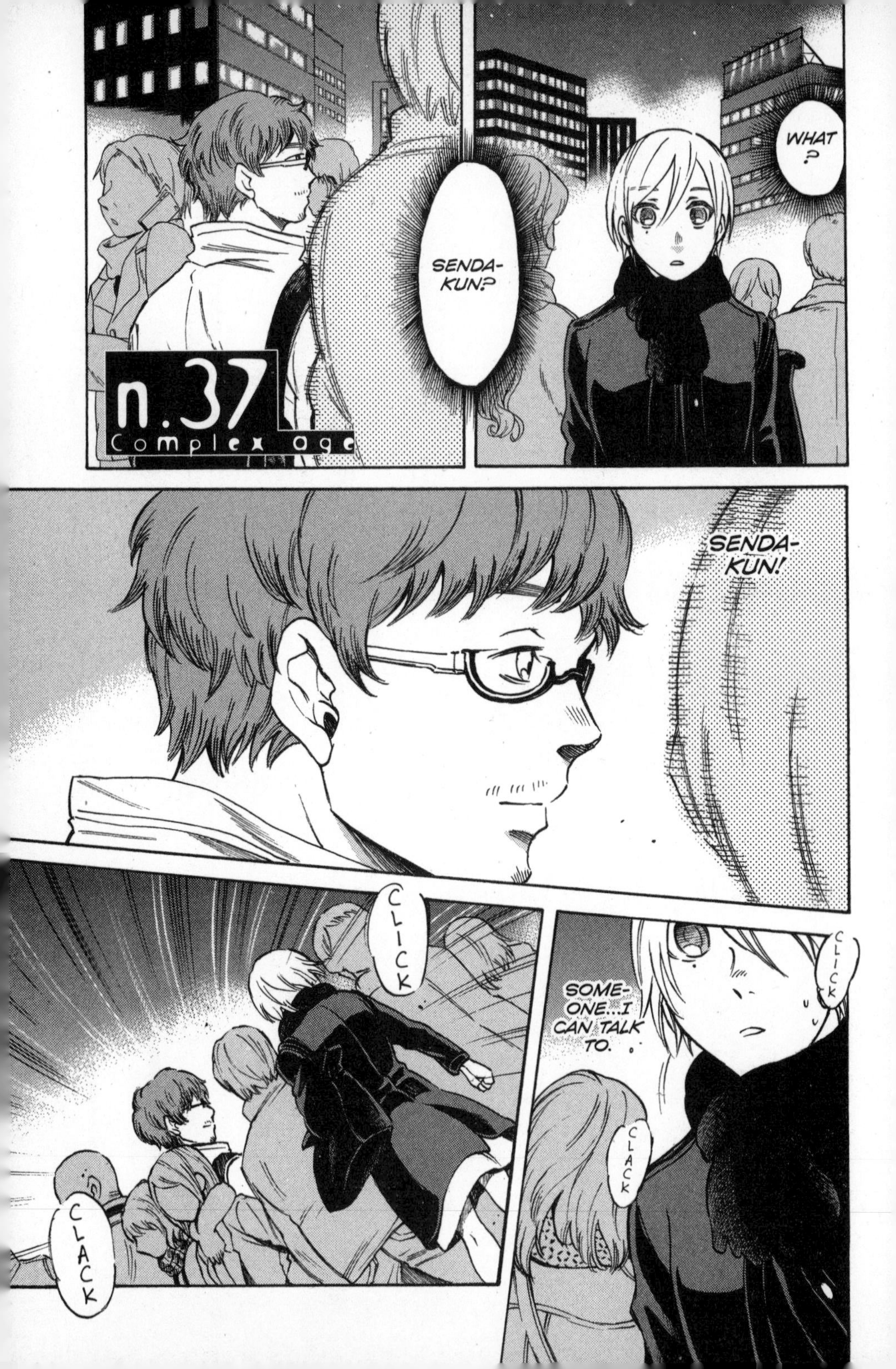
WHAT?
SENDA-KUN?
n.37
Complex age
SENDA-KUN!
CLICK
SOME-ONE...I CAN TALK TO.
CLACK
CLICK
CLACK

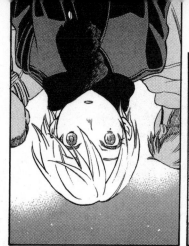
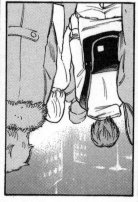
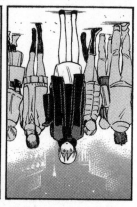
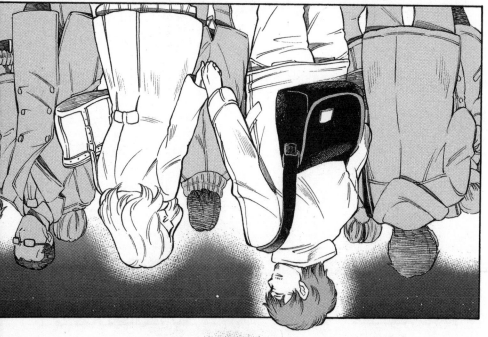
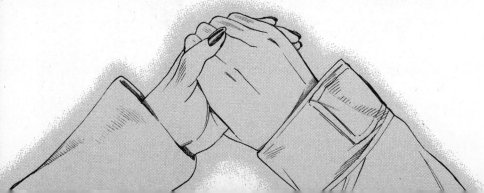

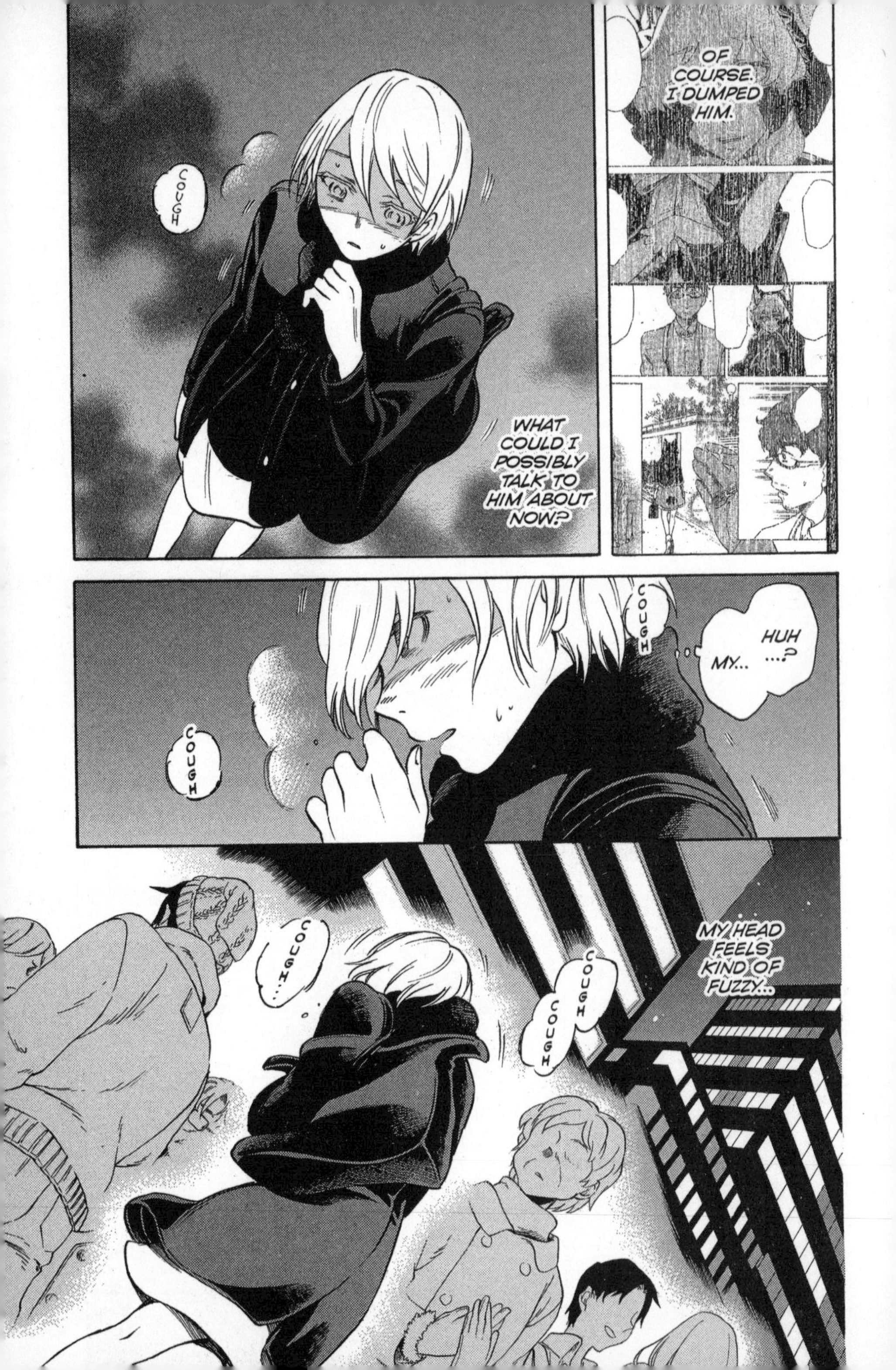
OF COURSE. I DUMPED HIM.
WHAT COULD I POSSIBLY TALK TO HIM ABOUT NOW?
COUGH
HUH ...?
MY...
COUGH
COUGH
MY HEAD FEELS KIND OF FUZZY...
COUGH
COUGH
COUGH...

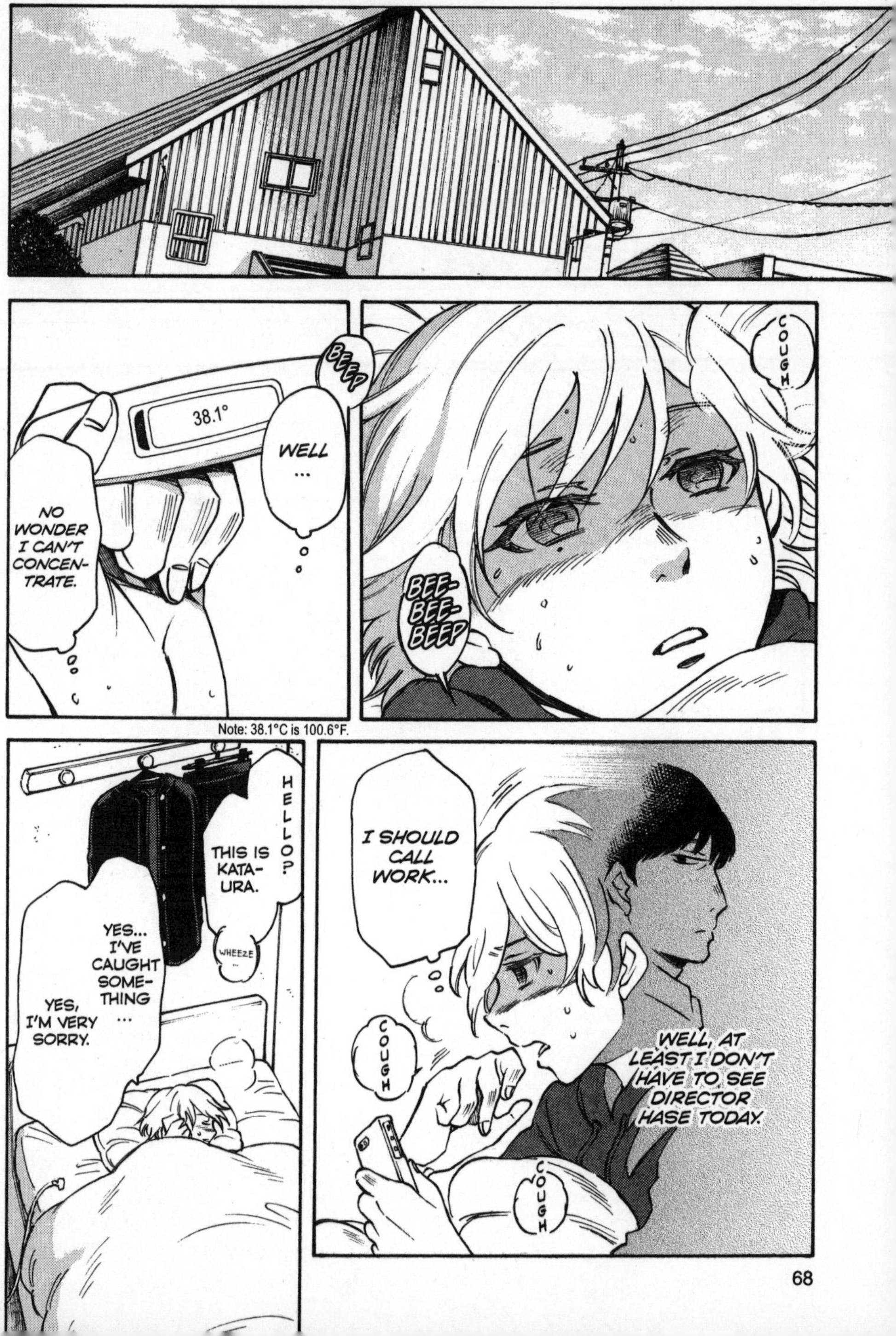
COUGH
BEE-BEE-BEEP
BEEP
WELL ...
NO WONDER I CAN'T CONCENTRATE.
I SHOULD CALL WORK...
COUGH
WELL, AT LEAST I DON'T HAVE TO SEE DIRECTOR HASE TODAY.
COUGH
HELLO?
THIS IS KATAURA.
WHEEZE ...
YES... I'VE CAUGHT SOMETHING ...
YES, I'M VERY SORRY.

Note: 38.1°C is 100.6°F.

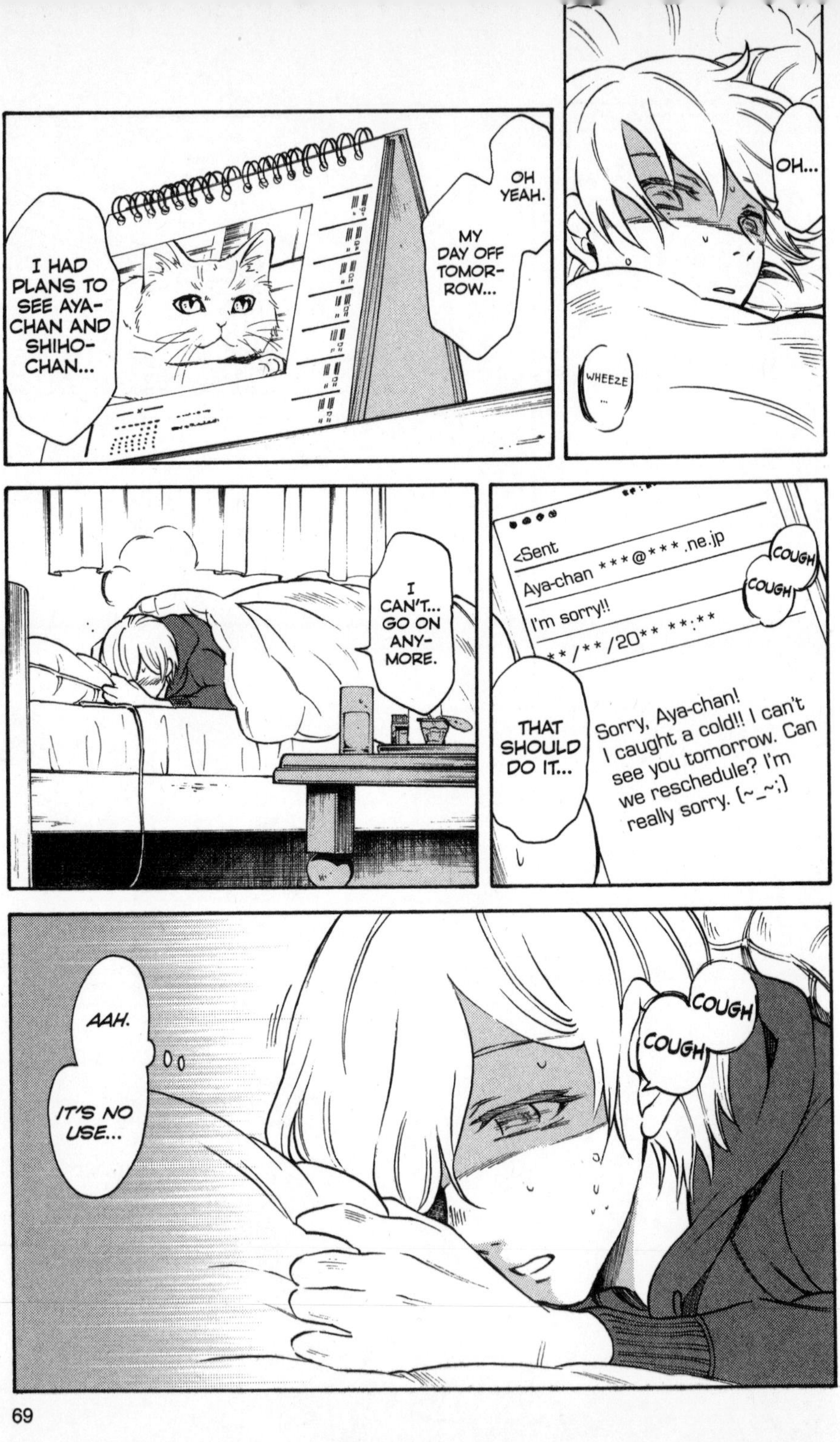

OH...
WHEEZE...
OH YEAH.
MY DAY OFF TOMORROW...
I HAD PLANS TO SEE AYA-CHAN AND SHIHO-CHAN...
<Sent
Aya-chan ***@***.ne.jp
I'm sorry!!
//20** **:**
COUGH
COUGH
Sorry, Aya-chan! I caught a cold!! I can't see you tomorrow. Can we reschedule? I'm really sorry. (~_~;)
THAT SHOULD DO IT...
I CAN'T... GO ON ANYMORE.
AAH.
IT'S NO USE...
COUGH
COUGH

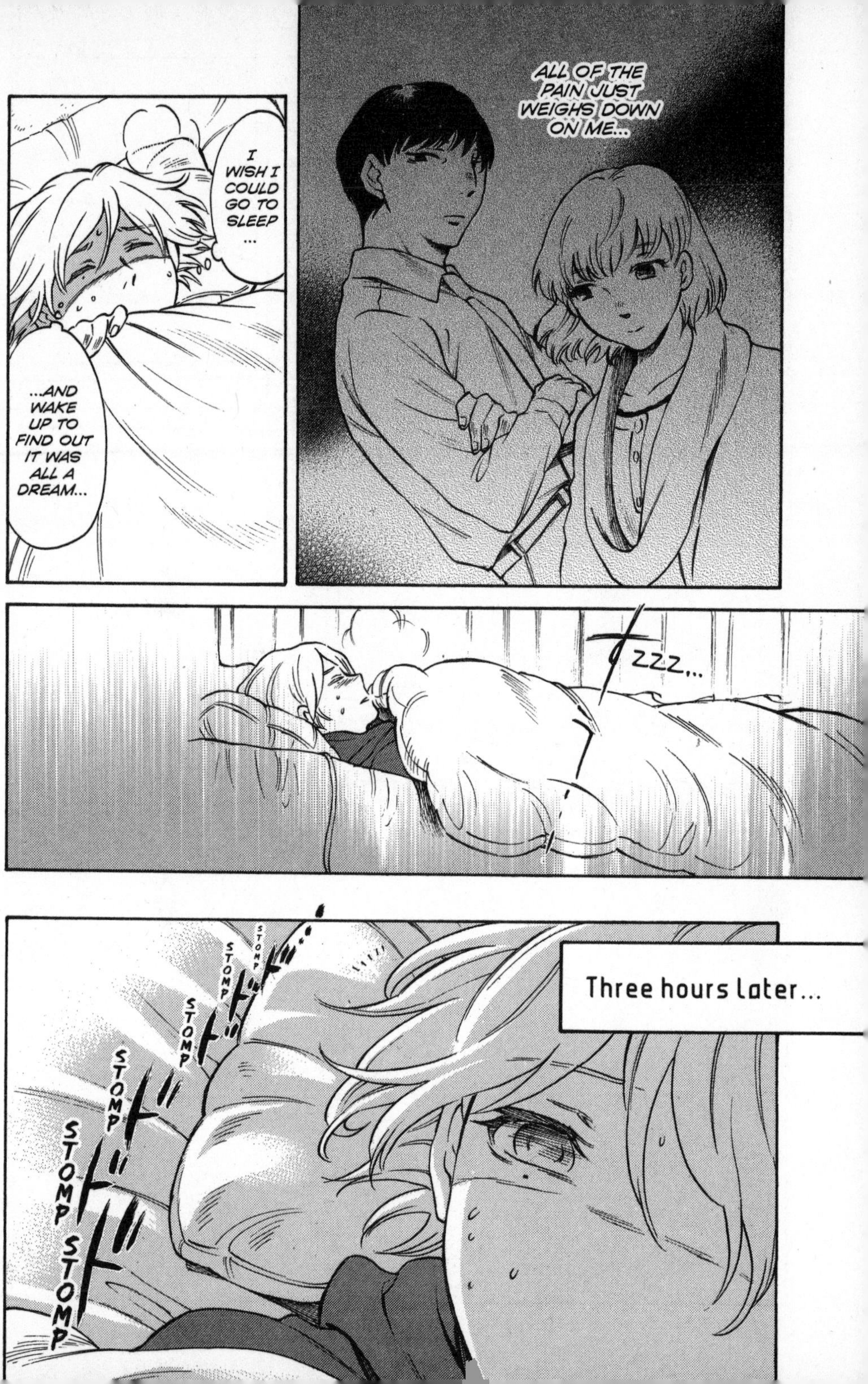
ALL OF THE PAIN JUST WEIGHS DOWN ON ME...
I WISH I COULD GO TO SLEEP...
...AND WAKE UP TO FIND OUT IT WAS ALL A DREAM...
ZZZ...
Three hours later...
STOMP
STOMP
STOMP
STOMP
STOMP STOMP
STOMP

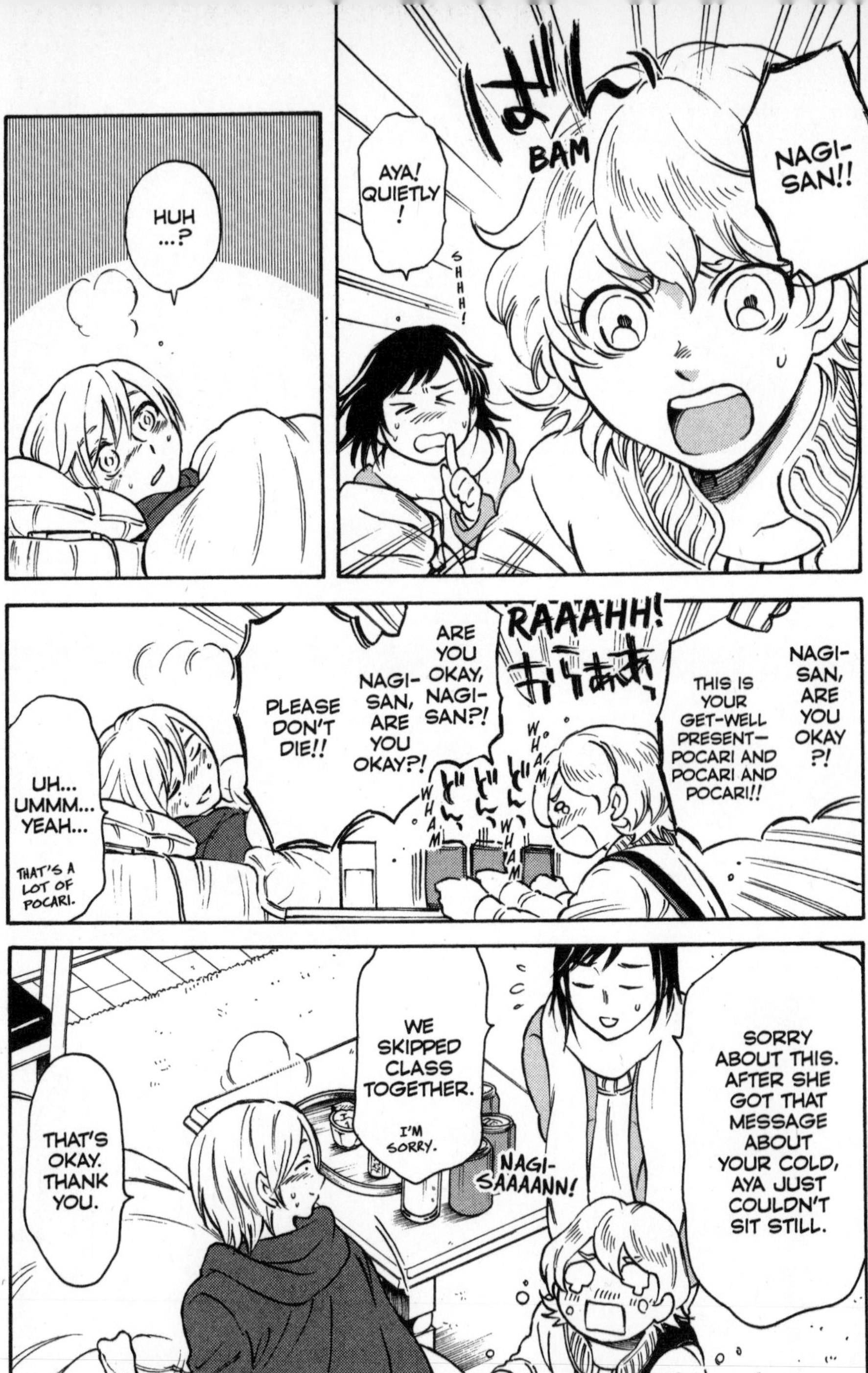
NAGI-SAN!!
BAM
AYA! QUIETLY!
SHHHH!
HUH...?
NAGI-SAN, ARE YOU OKAY?!
THIS IS YOUR GET-WELL PRESENT— POCARI AND POCARI AND POCARI!!
RAAAHH!
WHAM WHAM WHAM
ARE YOU OKAY, NAGI-SAN?!
NAGI-SAN, ARE YOU OKAY?!
PLEASE DON'T DIE!!
UH... UMMM... YEAH...
THAT'S A LOT OF POCARI.
SORRY ABOUT THIS. AFTER SHE GOT THAT MESSAGE ABOUT YOUR COLD, AYA JUST COULDN'T SIT STILL.
NAGI-SAAAANN!
WE SKIPPED CLASS TOGETHER.
I'M SORRY.
THAT'S OKAY. THANK YOU.

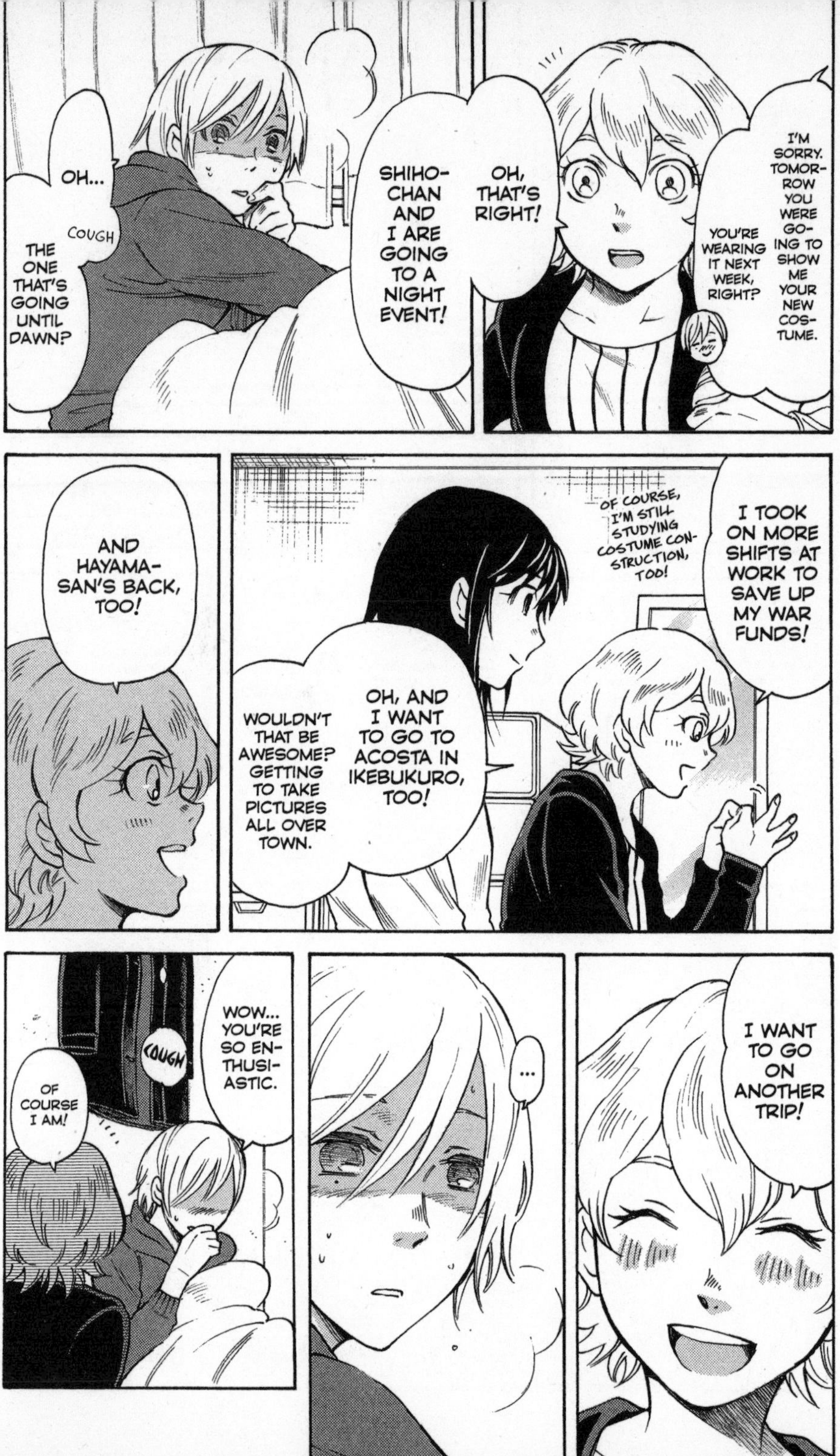
I'M SORRY. TOMORROW YOU WERE GOING TO SHOW ME YOUR NEW COSTUME.
YOU'RE WEARING IT NEXT WEEK, RIGHT?
OH, THAT'S RIGHT!
SHIHO-CHAN AND I ARE GOING TO A NIGHT EVENT!
OH...
COUGH
THE ONE THAT'S GOING UNTIL DAWN?
I TOOK ON MORE SHIFTS AT WORK TO SAVE UP MY WAR FUNDS!
OF COURSE, I'M STILL STUDYING COSTUME CONSTRUCTION, TOO!
OH, AND I WANT TO GO TO ACOSTA IN IKEBUKURO, TOO!
WOULDN'T THAT BE AWESOME? GETTING TO TAKE PICTURES ALL OVER TOWN.
AND HAYAMA-SAN'S BACK, TOO!
I WANT TO GO ON ANOTHER TRIP!
...
WOW... YOU'RE SO ENTHUSIASTIC.
COUGH
OF COURSE I AM!

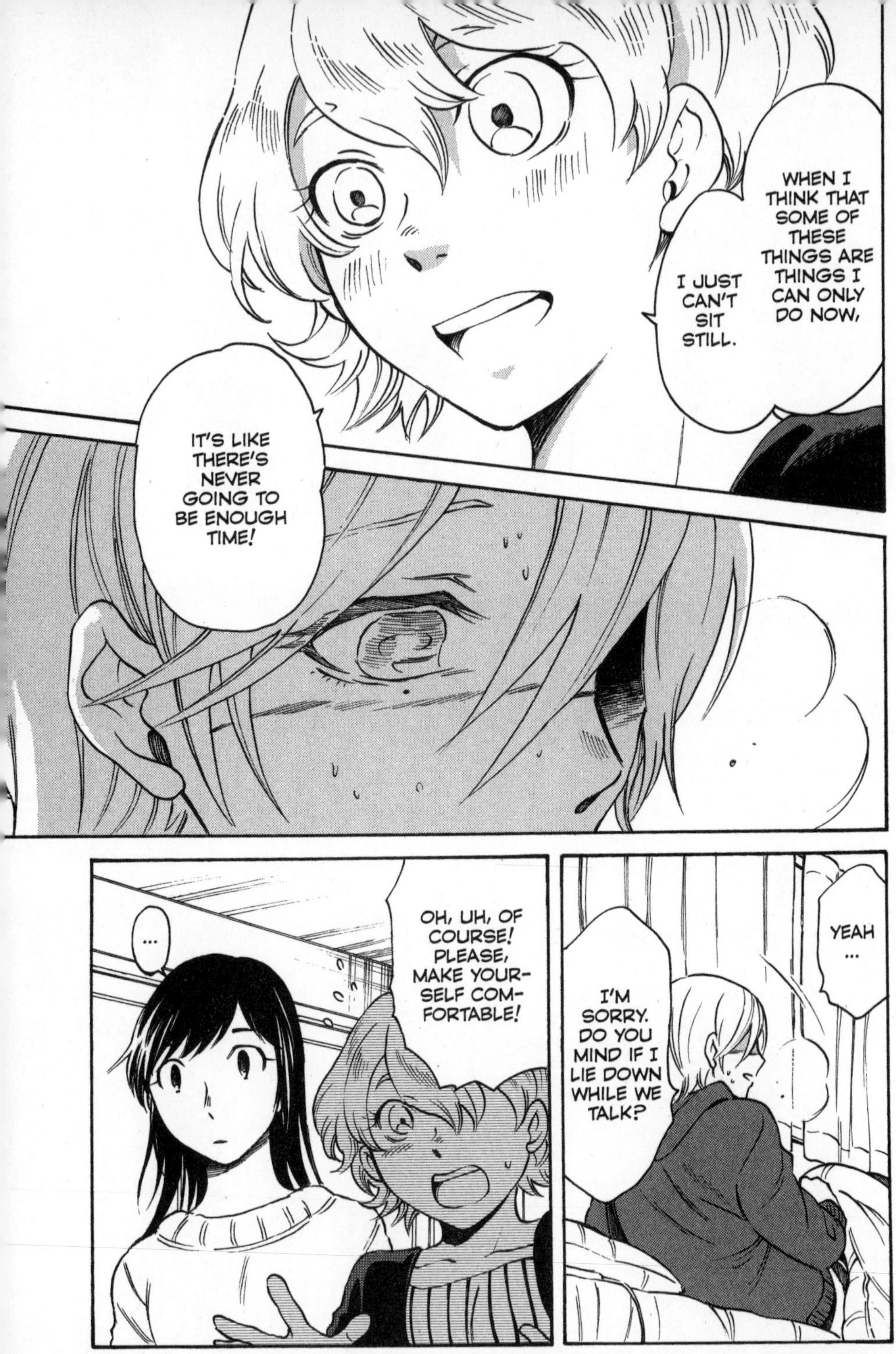
WHEN I THINK THAT SOME OF THESE THINGS ARE THINGS I CAN ONLY DO NOW,
I JUST CAN'T SIT STILL.
IT'S LIKE THERE'S NEVER GOING TO BE ENOUGH TIME!
YEAH ...
I'M SORRY. DO YOU MIND IF I LIE DOWN WHILE WE TALK?
OH, UH, OF COURSE! PLEASE, MAKE YOURSELF COMFORTABLE!
...

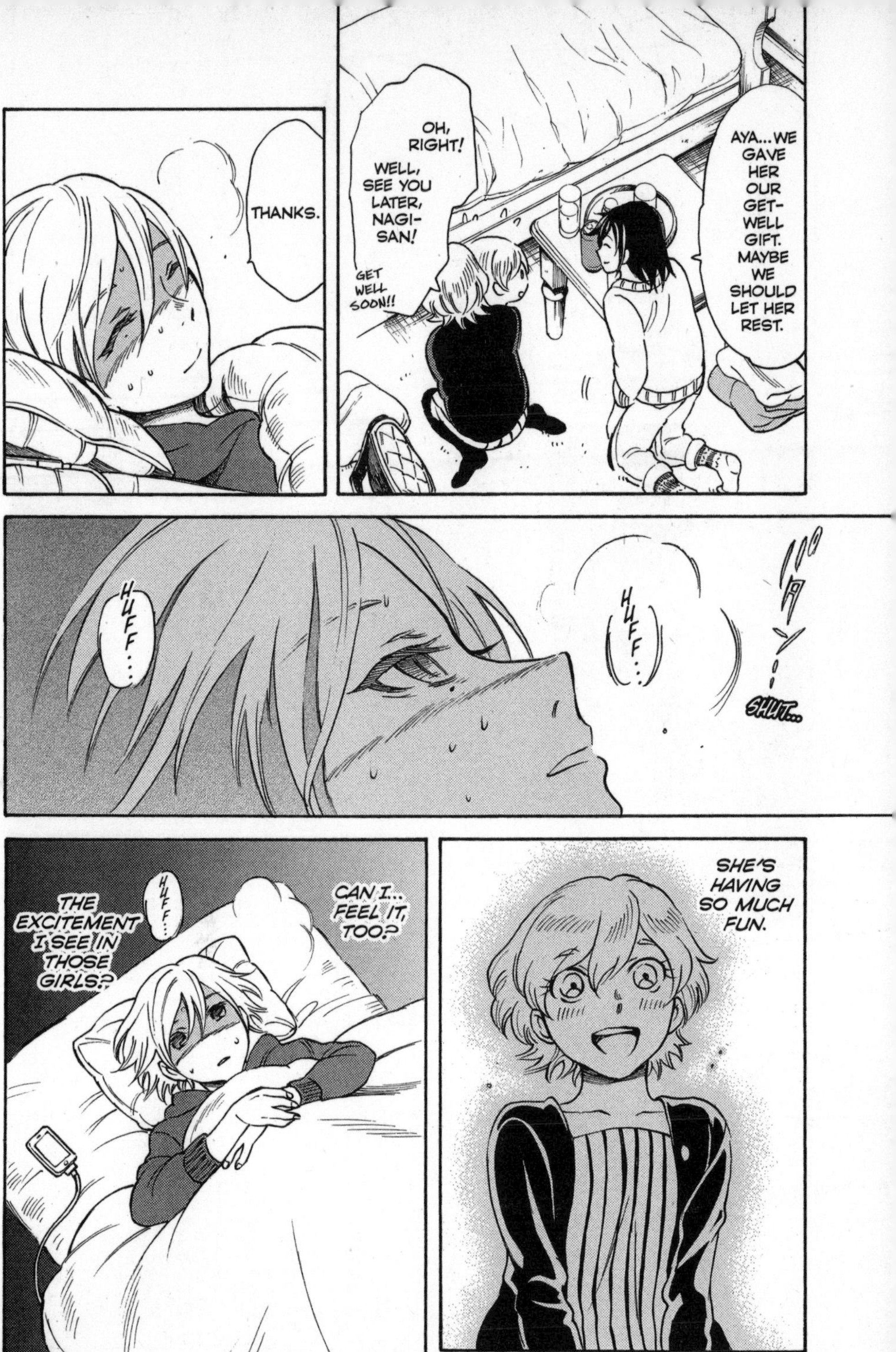
AYA...WE GAVE HER OUR GET-WELL GIFT. MAYBE WE SHOULD LET HER REST.
OH, RIGHT!
WELL, SEE YOU LATER, NAGI-SAN!
GET WELL SOON!!
THANKS.
HUFF...
HUFF...
SHUT...
SHE'S HAVING SO MUCH FUN.
CAN I... FEEL IT, TOO?
HUFF...
THE EXCITEMENT I SEE IN THOSE GIRLS?

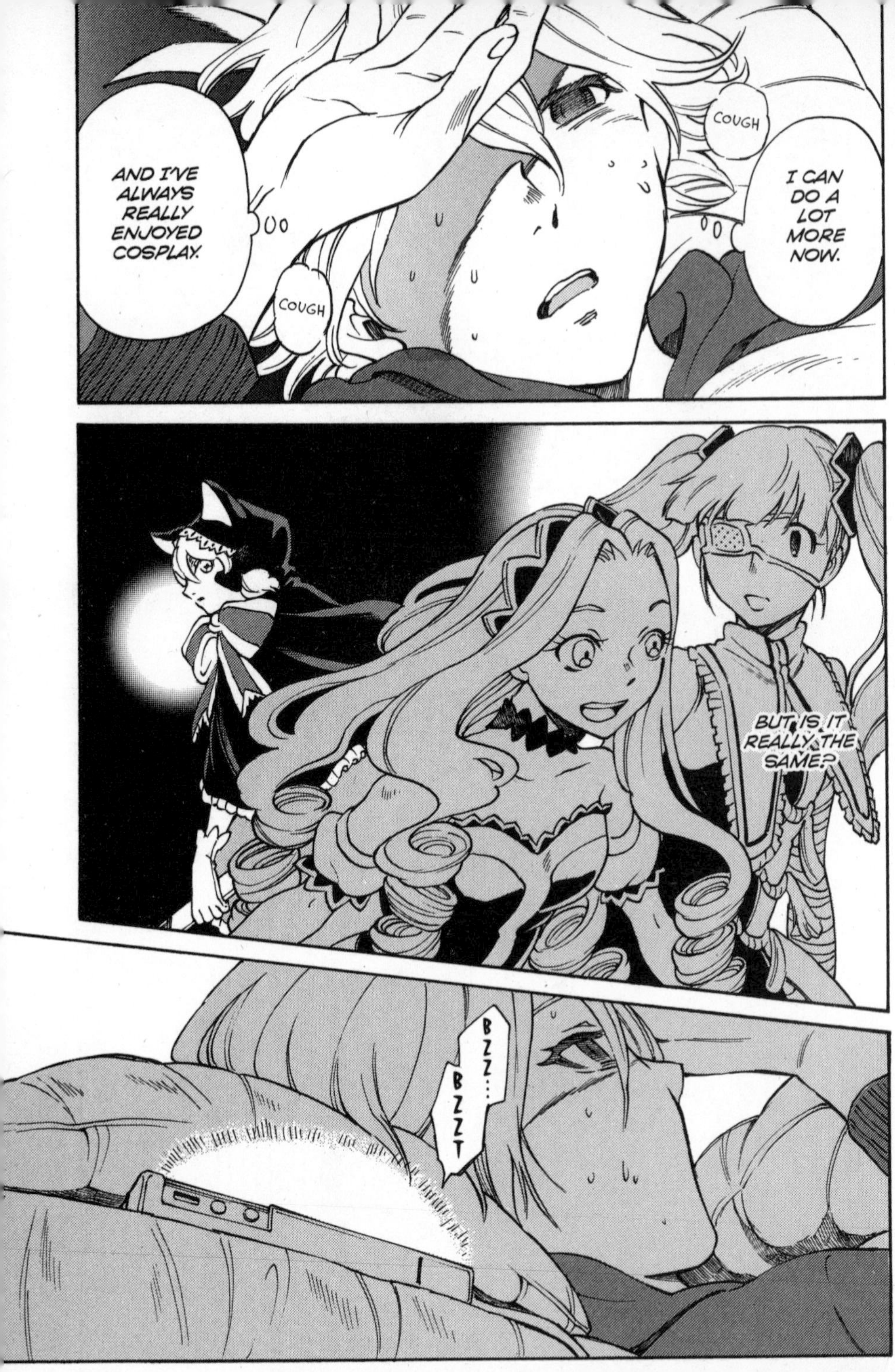
COUGH
I CAN DO A LOT MORE NOW.
AND I'VE ALWAYS REALLY ENJOYED COSPLAY.
COUGH
BUT IS IT REALLY THE SAME?
BZZ... BZZT

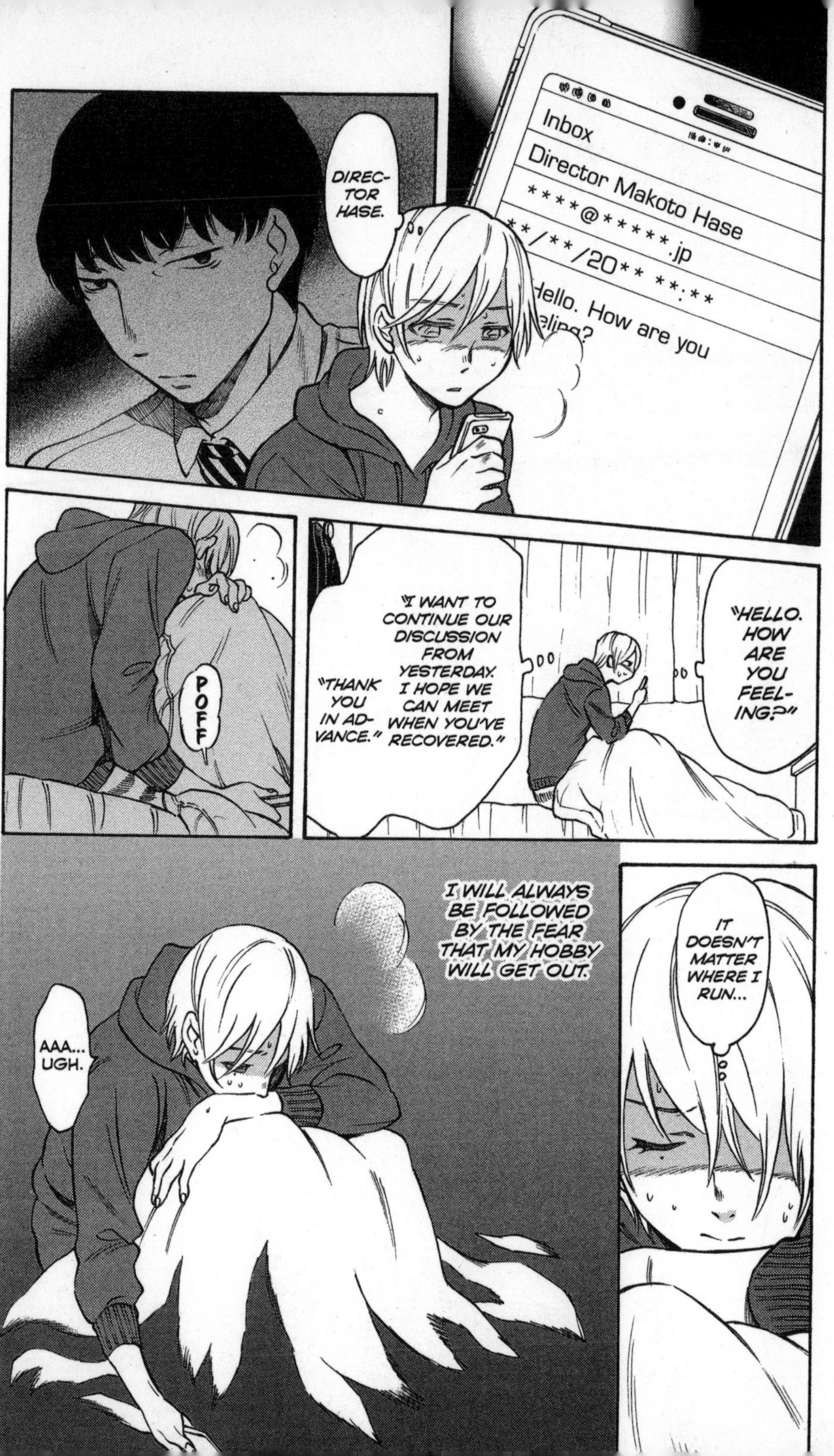
Inbox
Director Makoto Hase
****@*****.jp
//20** **:**
Hello. How are you feeling?
DIRECTOR HASE.
"HELLO. HOW ARE YOU FEELING?"
"I WANT TO CONTINUE OUR DISCUSSION FROM YESTERDAY. I HOPE WE CAN MEET WHEN YOU'VE RECOVERED."
"THANK YOU IN ADVANCE."
POFF
IT DOESN'T MATTER WHERE I RUN...
I WILL ALWAYS BE FOLLOWED BY THE FEAR THAT MY HOBBY WILL GET OUT.
AAA... UGH.

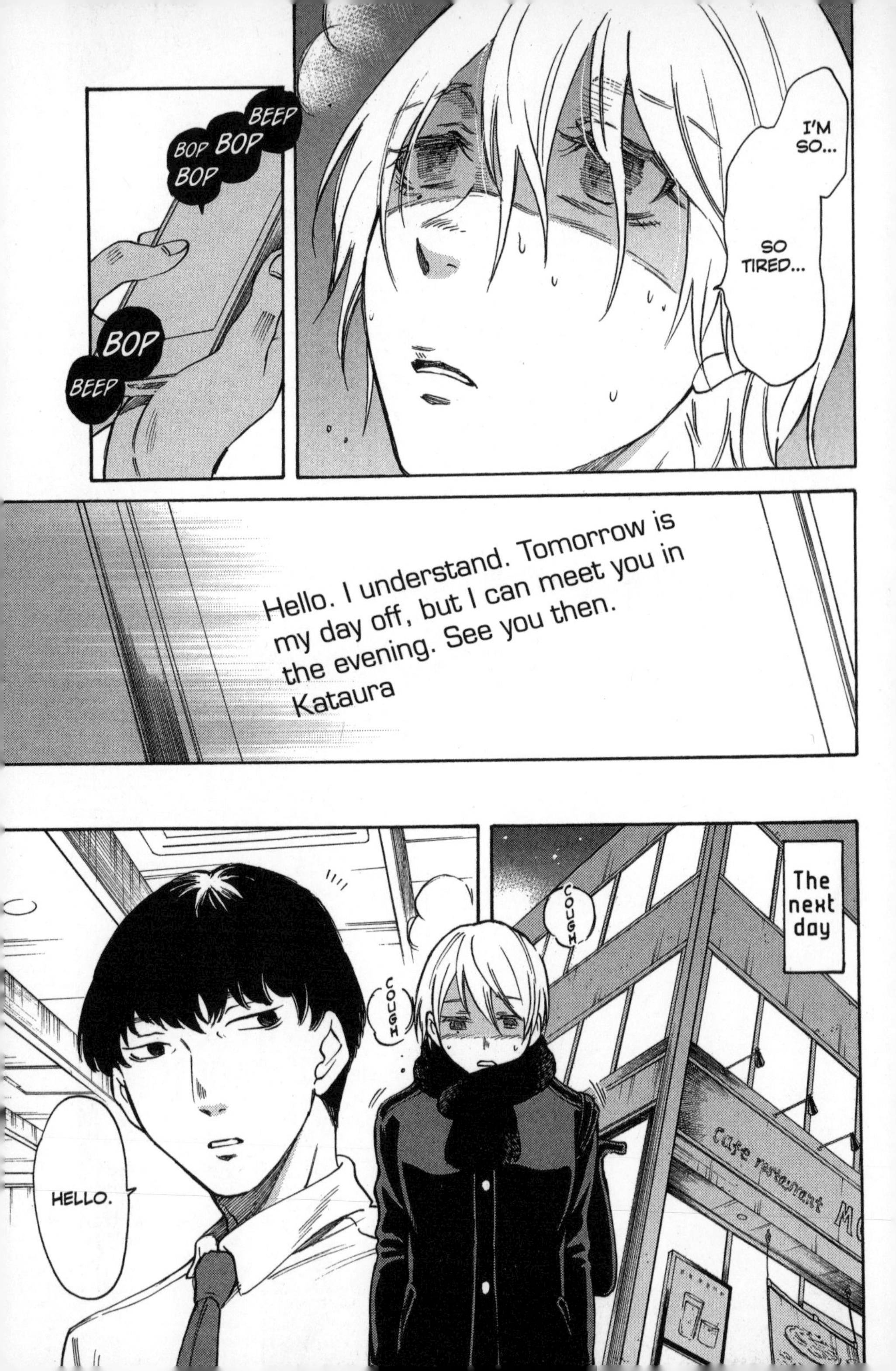
I'M SO...
SO TIRED...
BEEP BOP BOP BOP
BOP BEEP
Hello. I understand. Tomorrow is my day off, but I can meet you in the evening. See you then.
Kataura
The next day
COUGH
COUGH
Cafe restaurant M
HELLO.

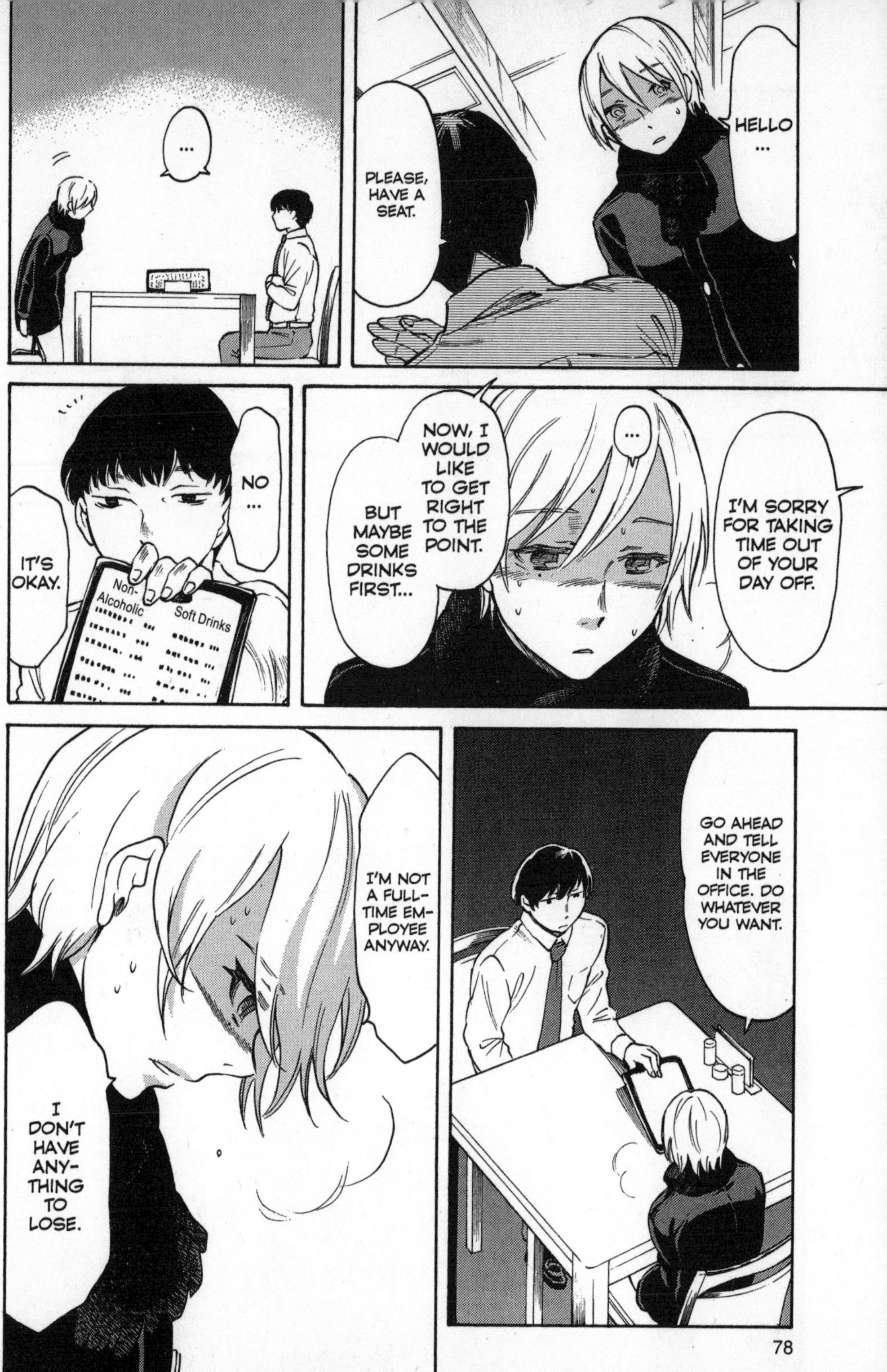
HELLO ...
PLEASE, HAVE A SEAT.
...
I'M SORRY FOR TAKING TIME OUT OF YOUR DAY OFF.
...
NOW, I WOULD LIKE TO GET RIGHT TO THE POINT.
BUT MAYBE SOME DRINKS FIRST...
NO ...
IT'S OKAY.
Non-Alcoholic
Soft Drinks
GO AHEAD AND TELL EVERYONE IN THE OFFICE. DO WHATEVER YOU WANT.
I'M NOT A FULL-TIME EMPLOYEE ANYWAY.
I DON'T HAVE ANYTHING TO LOSE.

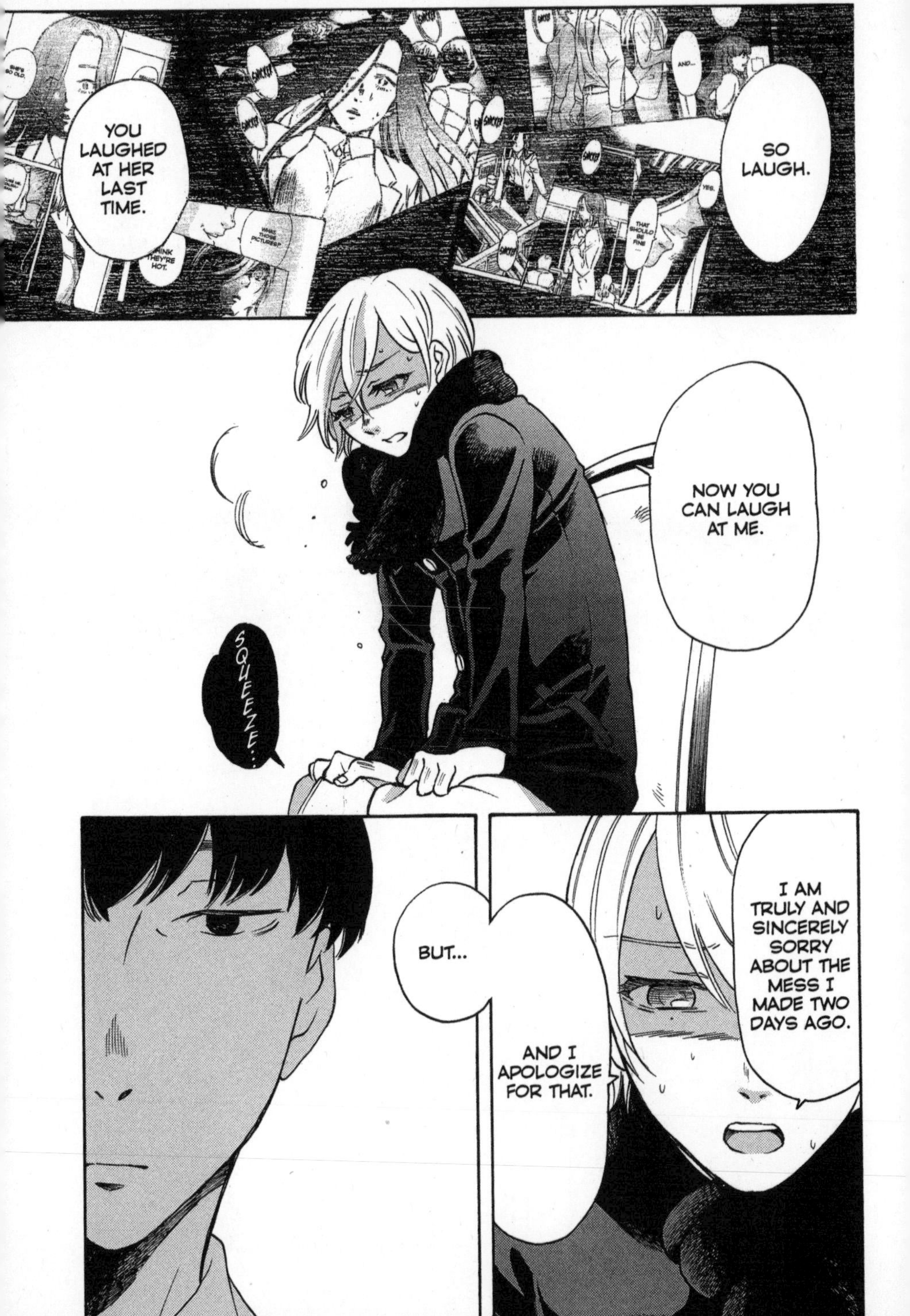
YOU LAUGHED AT HER LAST TIME.
SO LAUGH.
AND...
YES.
THAT SHOULD BE FINE.
SHE'S SO OLD.
WHAT ARE THOSE PICTURES?
NOW YOU CAN LAUGH AT ME.
SQUEEZE...
I AM TRULY AND SINCERELY SORRY ABOUT THE MESS I MADE TWO DAYS AGO.
AND I APOLOGIZE FOR THAT.
BUT...

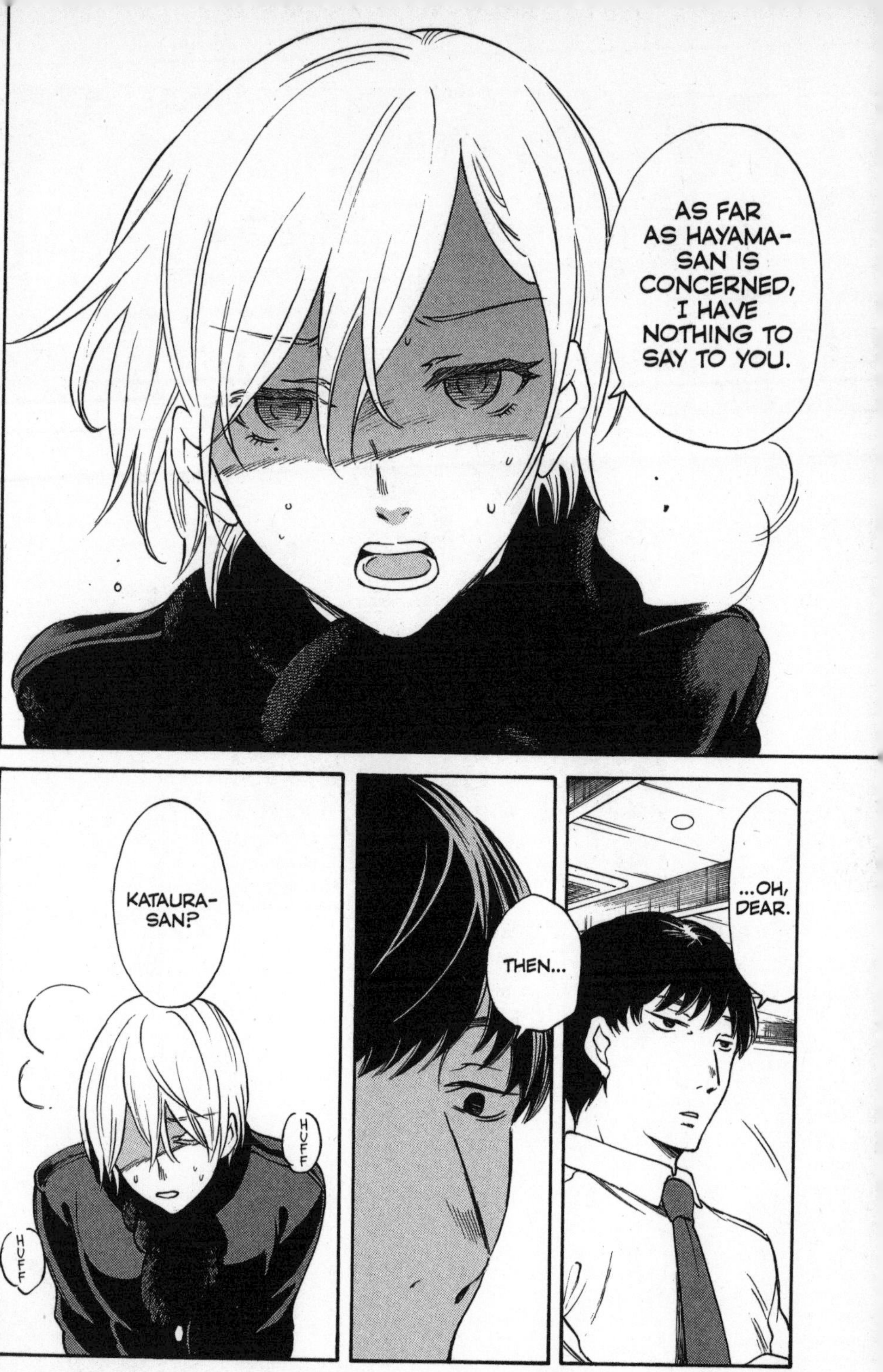
AS FAR AS HAYAMA-SAN IS CONCERNED, I HAVE NOTHING TO SAY TO YOU.
...OH, DEAR.
THEN...
KATAURA-SAN?
HUFF
HUFF

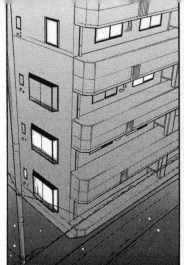

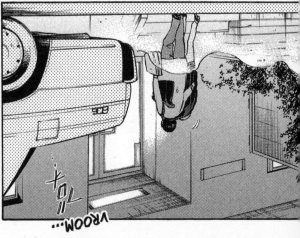

VROOM...

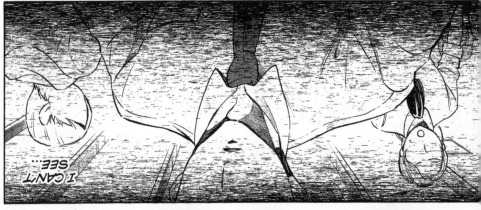

I CAN'T SEE...

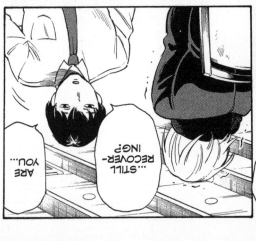

...ARE YOU...

...STILL RECOVER-ING?

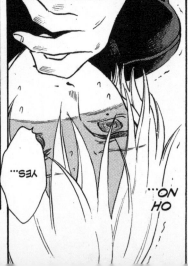

...YES...

OH NO...

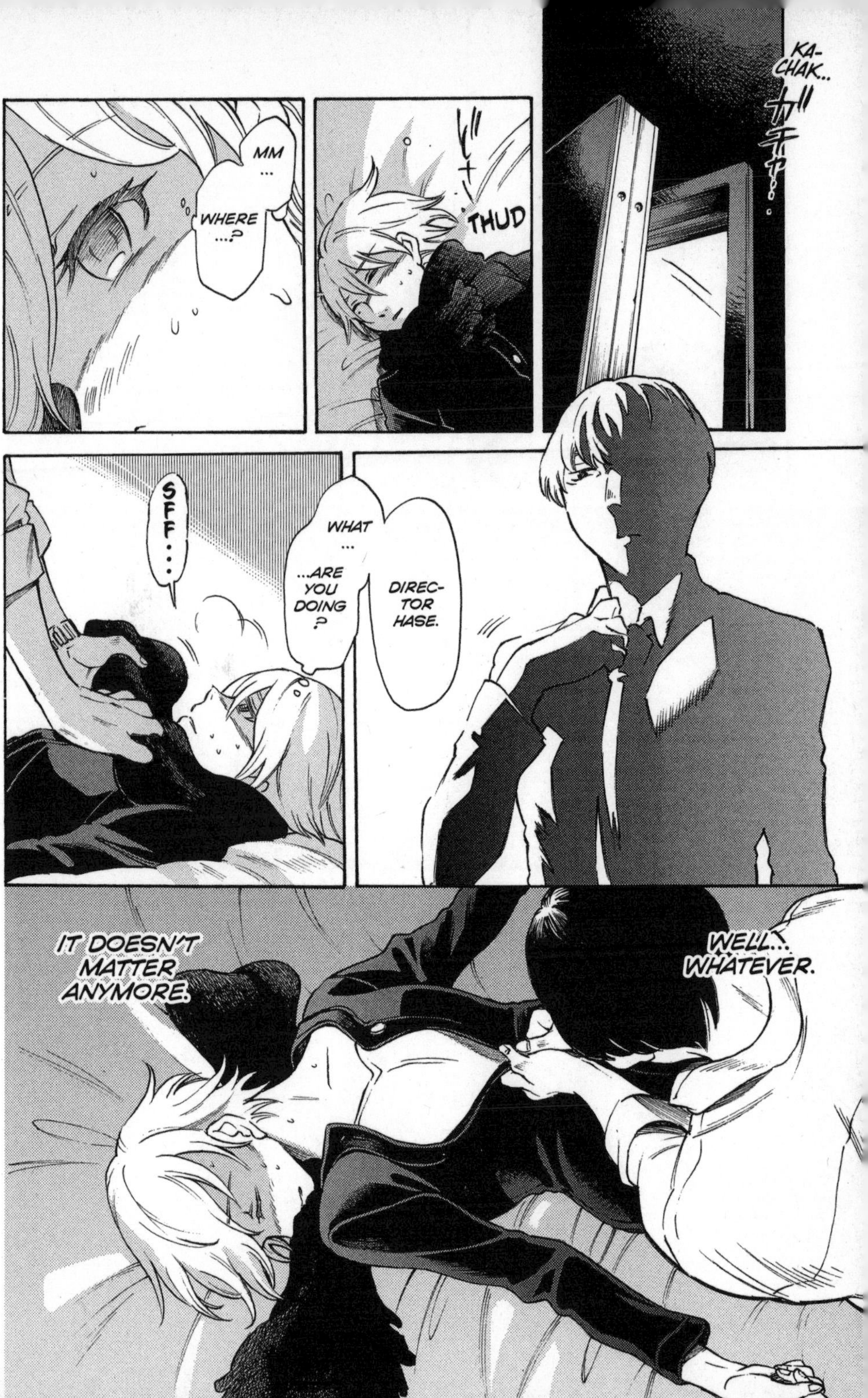
KA-CHAK...
THUD
MM ...
WHERE ...?
WHAT ...
...ARE YOU DOING?
DIREC-TOR HASE.
SFF...
WELL... WHATEVER.
IT DOESN'T MATTER ANYMORE.

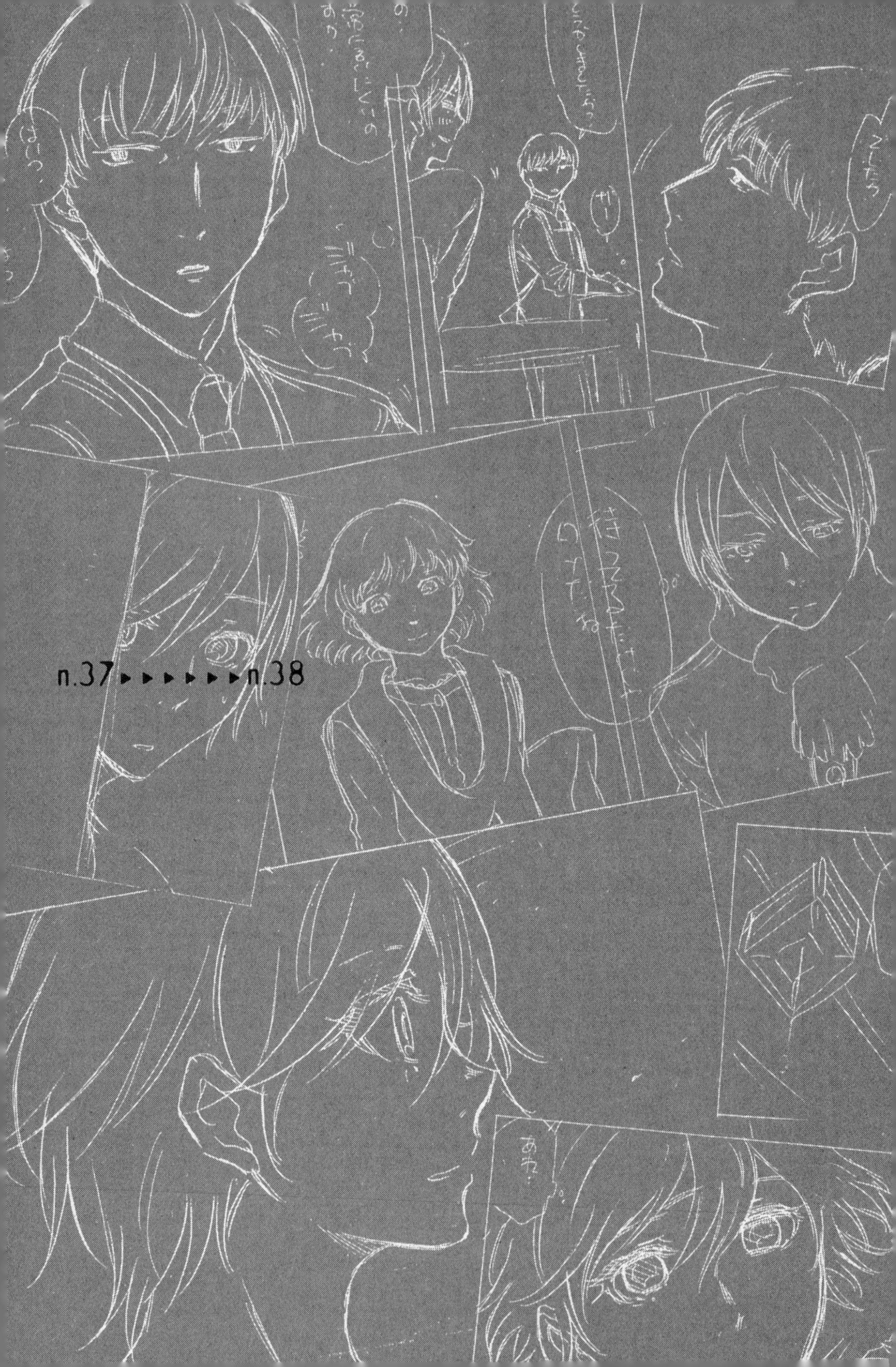
n.37▸▸▸▸▸▸▸n.38

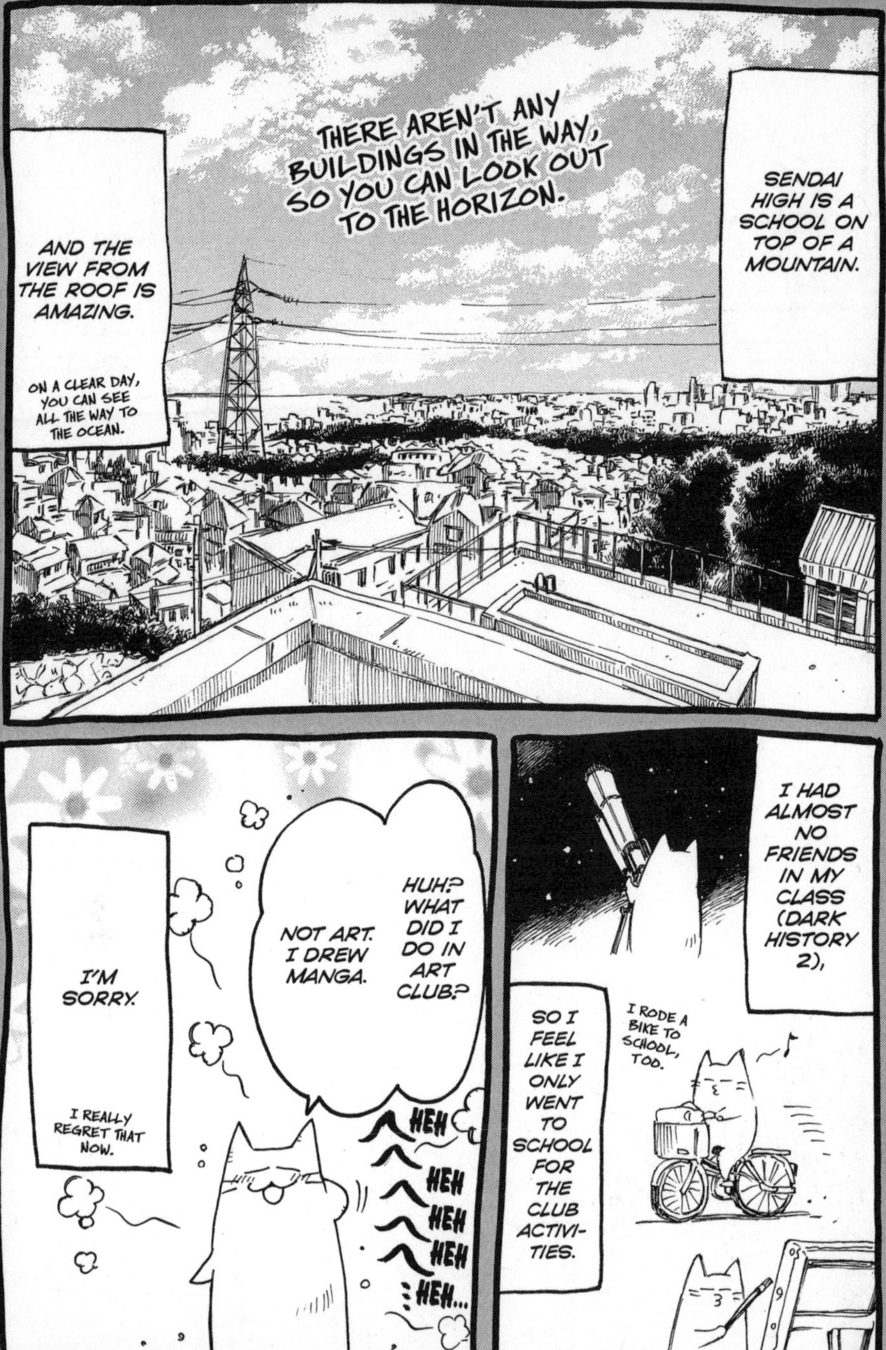
SENDAI HIGH IS A SCHOOL ON TOP OF A MOUNTAIN.
THERE AREN'T ANY BUILDINGS IN THE WAY, SO YOU CAN LOOK OUT TO THE HORIZON.
AND THE VIEW FROM THE ROOF IS AMAZING.
ON A CLEAR DAY, YOU CAN SEE ALL THE WAY TO THE OCEAN.
I HAD ALMOST NO FRIENDS IN MY CLASS (DARK HISTORY 2),
I RODE A BIKE TO SCHOOL, TOO.
SO I FEEL LIKE I ONLY WENT TO SCHOOL FOR THE CLUB ACTIVITIES.
HUH? WHAT DID I DO IN ART CLUB?
NOT ART. I DREW MANGA.
HEH HEH HEH HEH HEH...
I'M SORRY.
I REALLY REGRET THAT NOW.

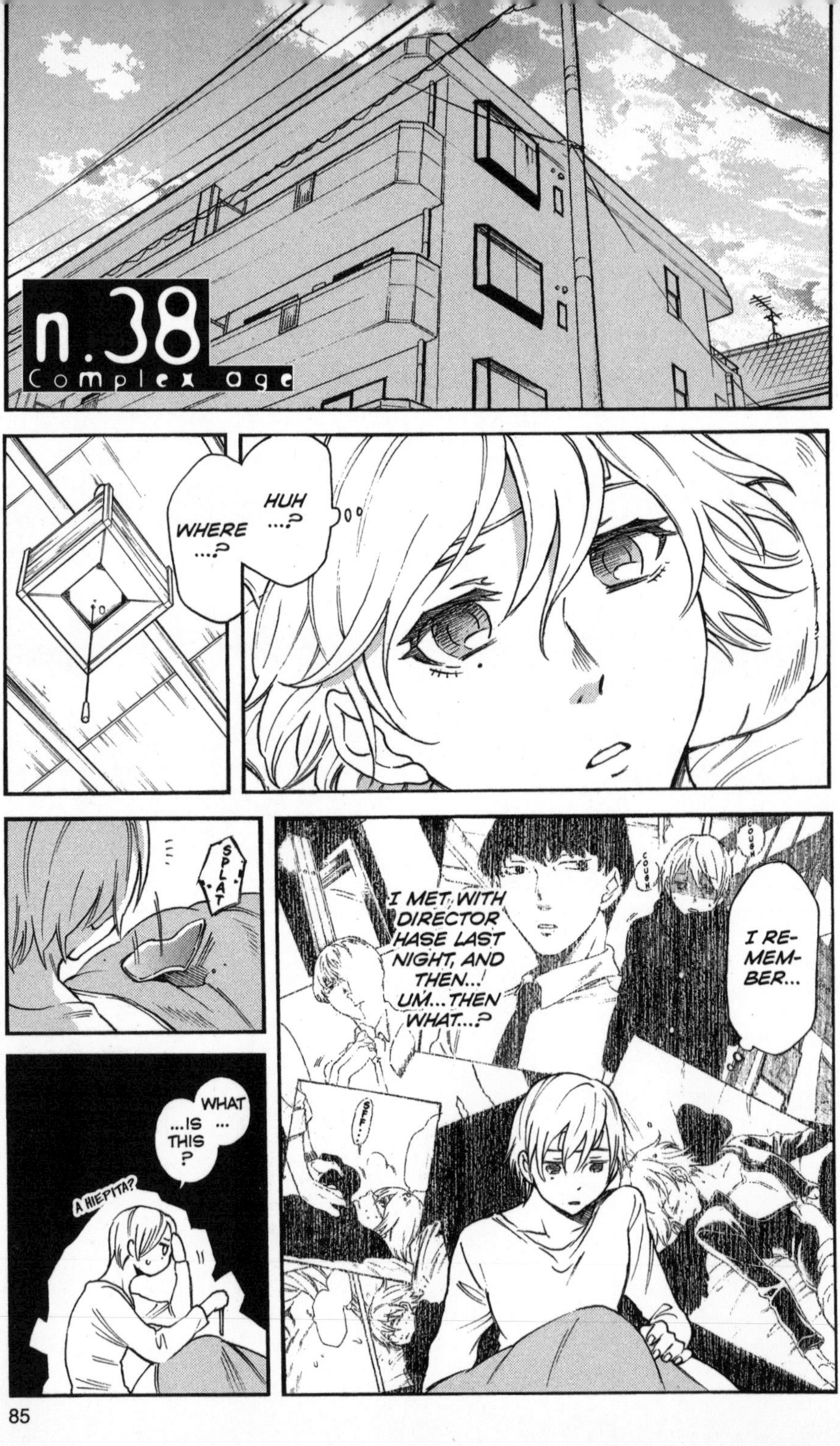
n.38
Complex age
HUH ...?
WHERE ...?
COUGH
COUGH
I RE-MEMBER...
I MET WITH DIRECTOR HASE LAST NIGHT, AND THEN... UM...THEN WHAT...?
SFF...
SPLAT
WHAT ...
...IS THIS ?
A HIEPITA?

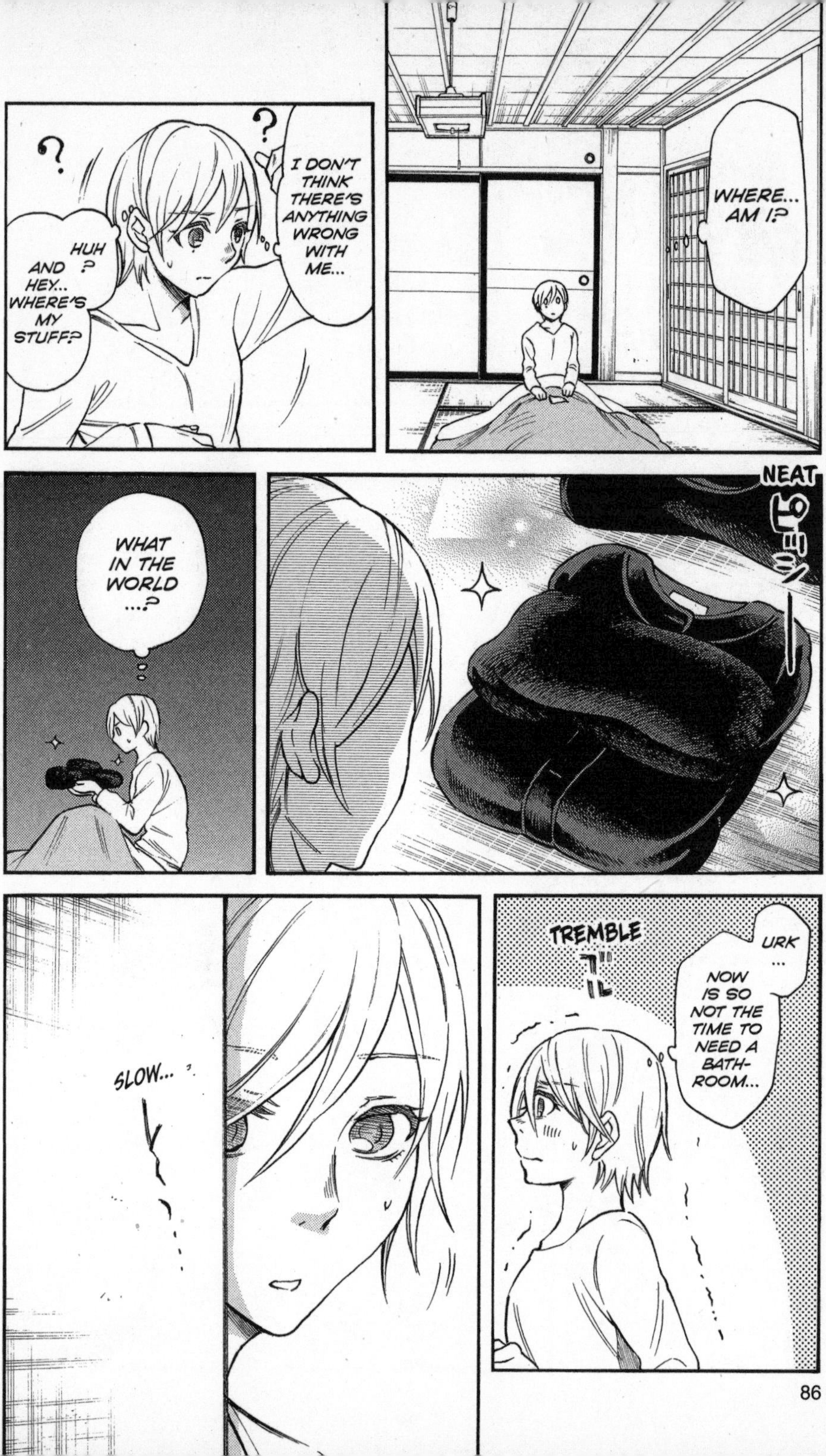
WHERE... AM I?
I DON'T THINK THERE'S ANYTHING WRONG WITH ME...
HUH? AND HEY... WHERE'S MY STUFF?
NEAT
WHAT IN THE WORLD ...?
TREMBLE
URK ... NOW IS SO NOT THE TIME TO NEED A BATH-ROOM...
SLOW...

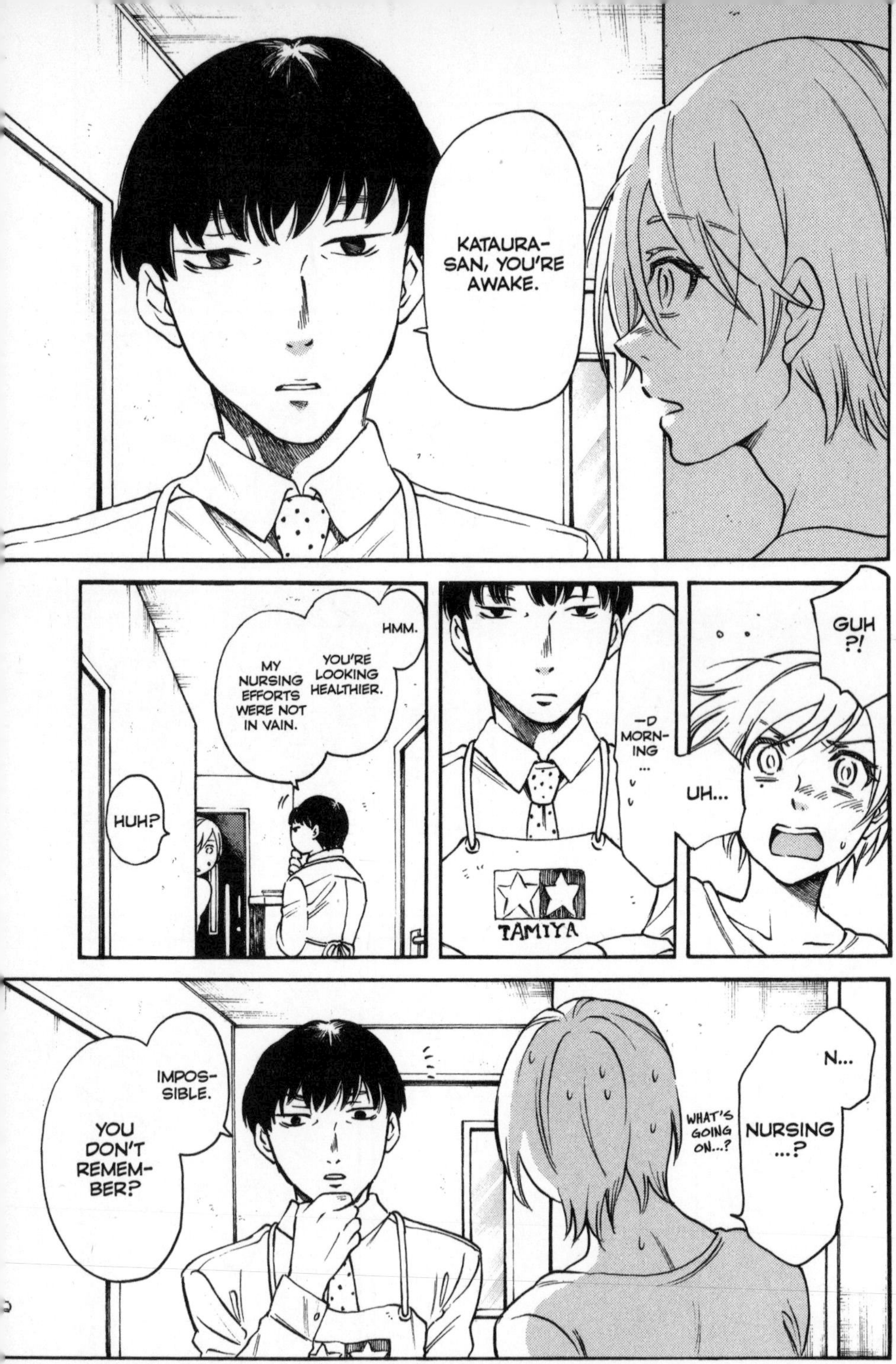
KATAURA-SAN, YOU'RE AWAKE.
GUH ?!
UH...
—D MORNING ...
HMM.
YOU'RE LOOKING HEALTHIER.
MY NURSING EFFORTS WERE NOT IN VAIN.
HUH?
N...
NURSING ...?
WHAT'S GOING ON...?
IMPOSSIBLE.
YOU DON'T REMEMBER?

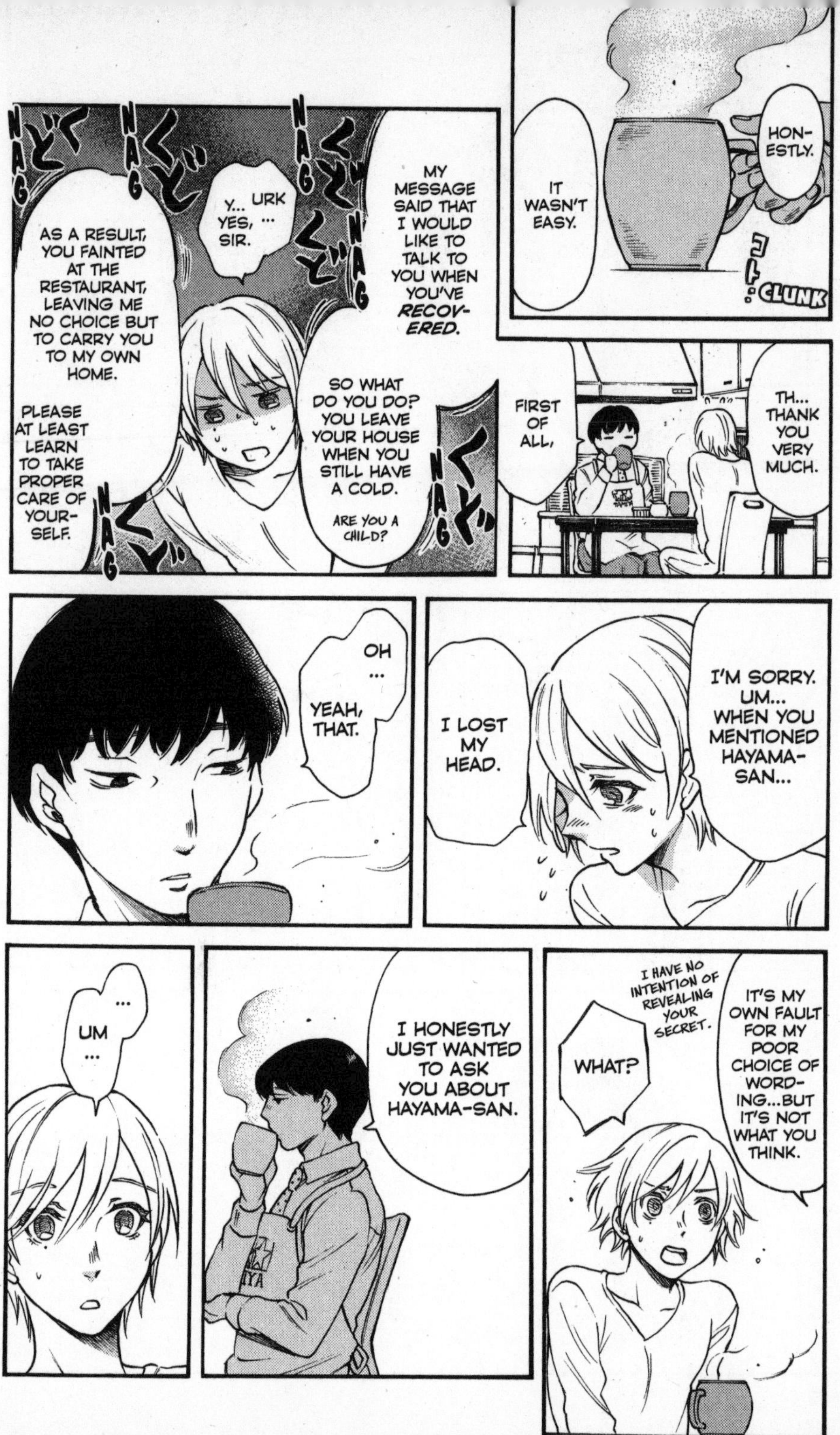
HON-ESTLY.
IT WASN'T EASY.
CLUNK
TH... THANK YOU VERY MUCH.
FIRST OF ALL,
MY MESSAGE SAID THAT I WOULD LIKE TO TALK TO YOU WHEN YOU'VE RECOVERED.
Y... URK YES, ... SIR.
SO WHAT DO YOU DO? YOU LEAVE YOUR HOUSE WHEN YOU STILL HAVE A COLD.
ARE YOU A CHILD?
AS A RESULT, YOU FAINTED AT THE RESTAURANT, LEAVING ME NO CHOICE BUT TO CARRY YOU TO MY OWN HOME.
PLEASE AT LEAST LEARN TO TAKE PROPER CARE OF YOUR-SELF.
NAG NAG NAG NAG NAG NAG
I'M SORRY. UM... WHEN YOU MENTIONED HAYAMA-SAN...
I LOST MY HEAD.
OH ... YEAH, THAT.
IT'S MY OWN FAULT FOR MY POOR CHOICE OF WORD-ING...BUT IT'S NOT WHAT YOU THINK.
I HAVE NO INTENTION OF REVEALING YOUR SECRET.
WHAT?
I HONESTLY JUST WANTED TO ASK YOU ABOUT HAYAMA-SAN.
... UM ...

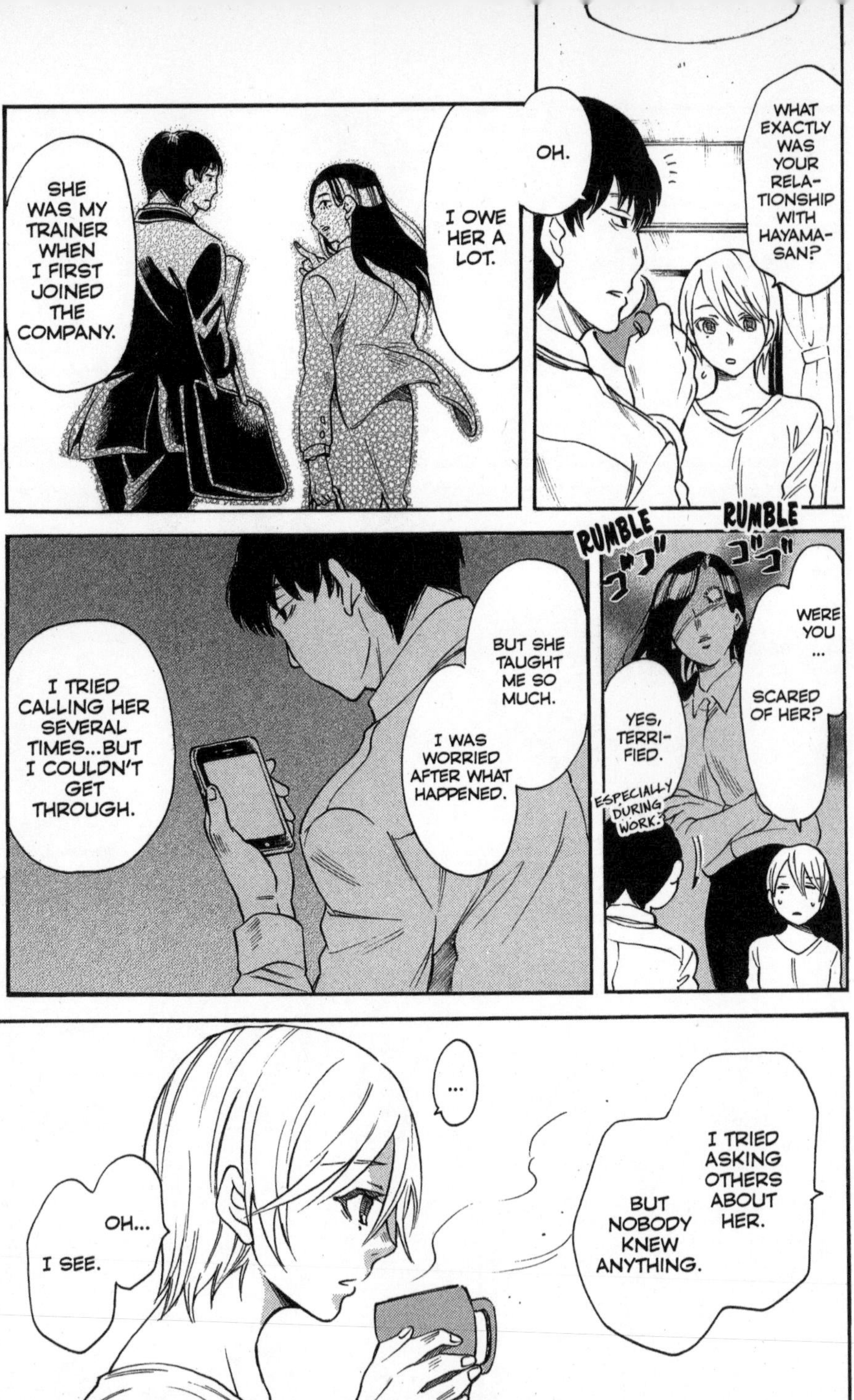
WHAT EXACTLY WAS YOUR RELATIONSHIP WITH HAYAMA-SAN?
OH.
I OWE HER A LOT.
SHE WAS MY TRAINER WHEN I FIRST JOINED THE COMPANY.
RUMBLE
RUMBLE
WERE YOU ... SCARED OF HER?
YES, TERRIFIED.
ESPECIALLY DURING WORK.
BUT SHE TAUGHT ME SO MUCH.
I WAS WORRIED AFTER WHAT HAPPENED.
I TRIED CALLING HER SEVERAL TIMES...BUT I COULDN'T GET THROUGH.
I TRIED ASKING OTHERS ABOUT HER.
BUT NOBODY KNEW ANYTHING.
...
OH... I SEE.

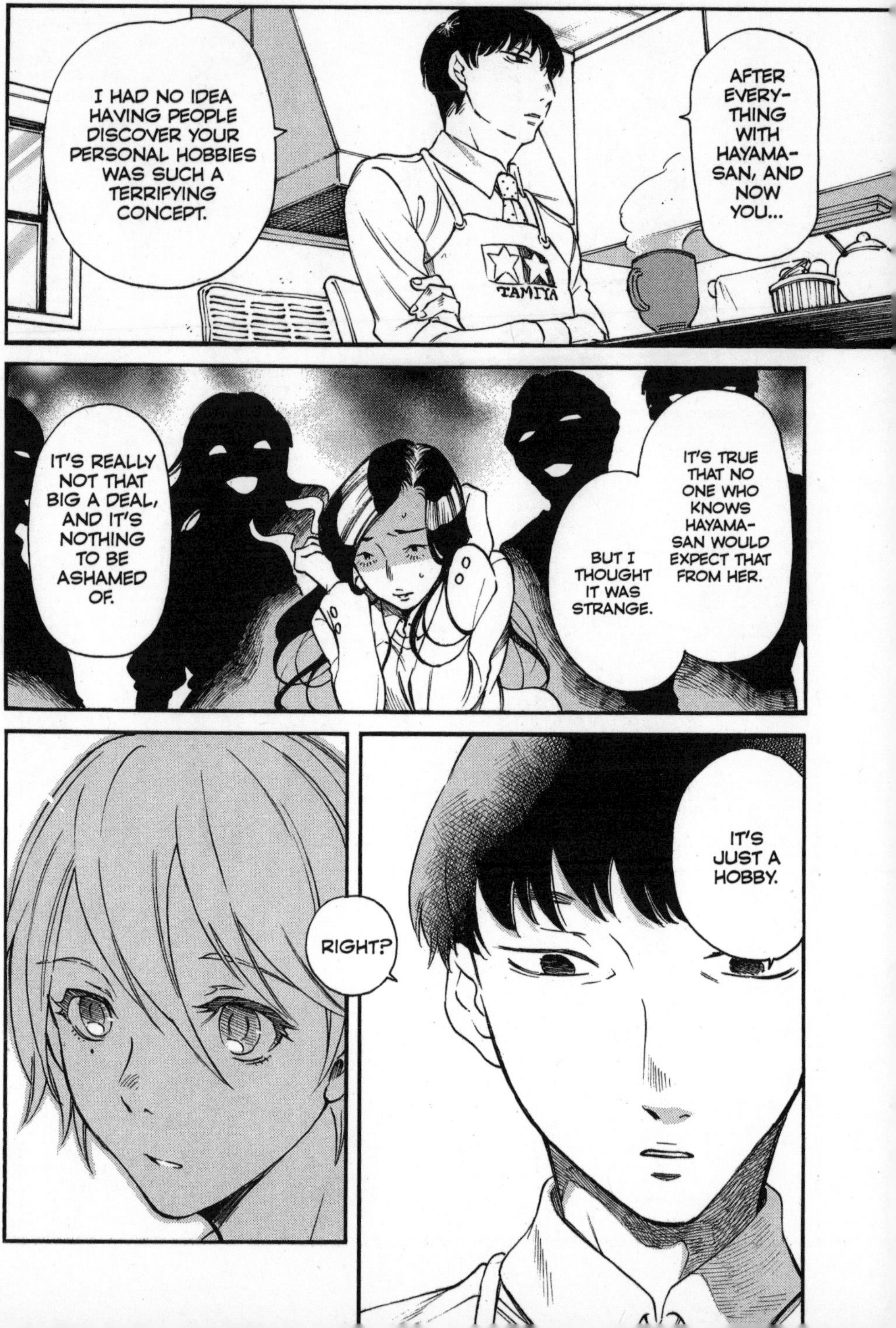
AFTER EVERYTHING WITH HAYAMA-SAN, AND NOW YOU...
I HAD NO IDEA HAVING PEOPLE DISCOVER YOUR PERSONAL HOBBIES WAS SUCH A TERRIFYING CONCEPT.
IT'S TRUE THAT NO ONE WHO KNOWS HAYAMA-SAN WOULD EXPECT THAT FROM HER.
BUT I THOUGHT IT WAS STRANGE.
IT'S REALLY NOT THAT BIG A DEAL, AND IT'S NOTHING TO BE ASHAMED OF.
IT'S JUST A HOBBY.
RIGHT?
TAMIYA

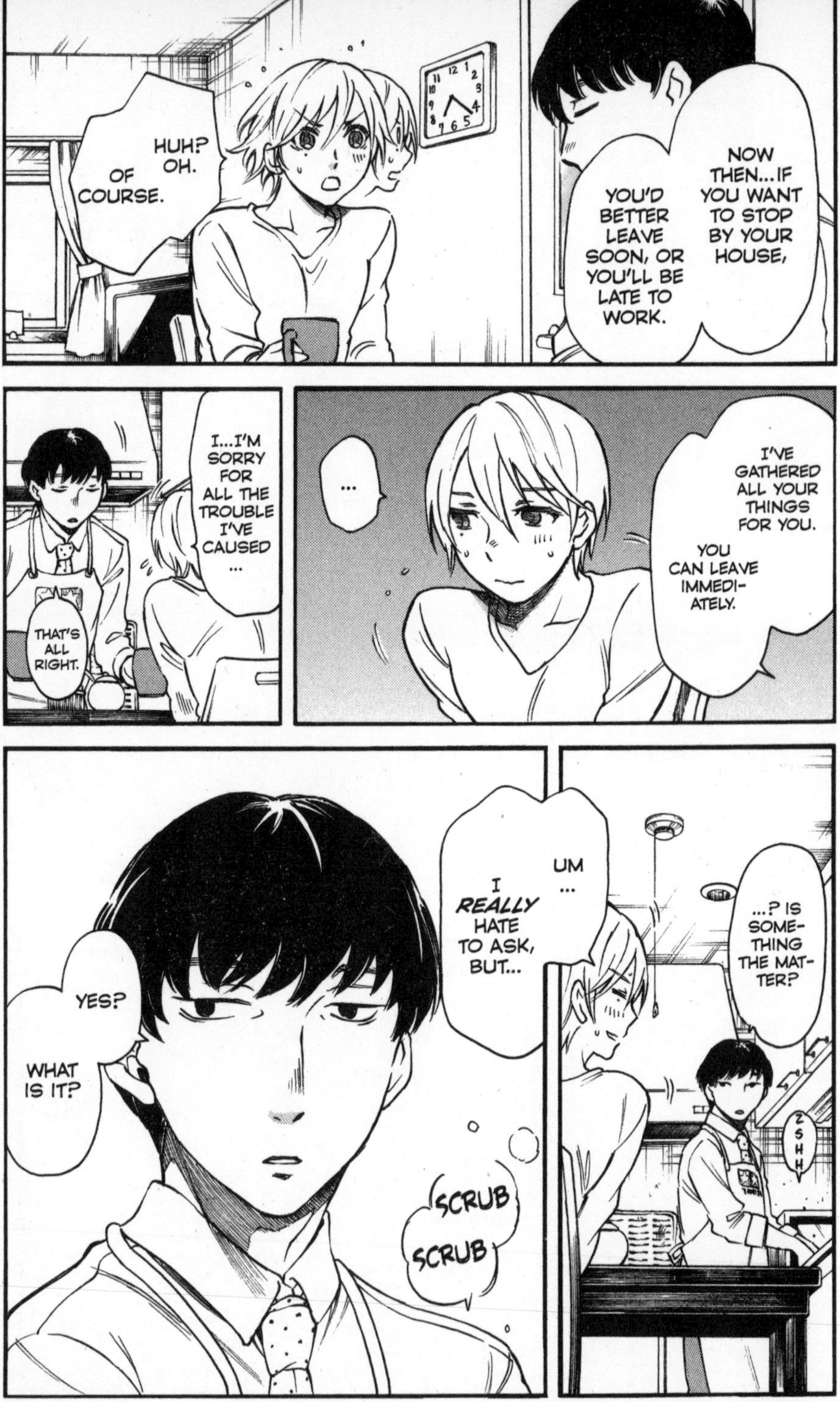
NOW THEN...IF YOU WANT TO STOP BY YOUR HOUSE,
YOU'D BETTER LEAVE SOON, OR YOU'LL BE LATE TO WORK.
HUH? OH.
OF COURSE.
I'VE GATHERED ALL YOUR THINGS FOR YOU.
YOU CAN LEAVE IMMEDI-ATELY.
...
I...I'M SORRY FOR ALL THE TROUBLE I'VE CAUSED ...
THAT'S ALL RIGHT.
...? IS SOME-THING THE MAT-TER?
ZSHH
UM ...
I REALLY HATE TO ASK, BUT...
SCRUB
SCRUB
YES?
WHAT IS IT?

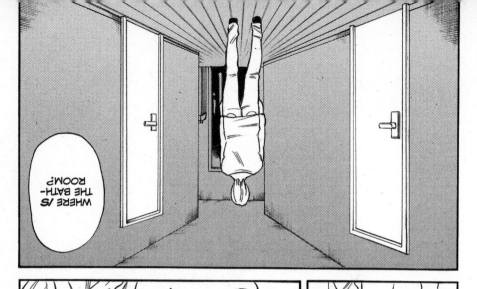

MAY I... USE YOUR REST-ROOM?
...
GO AHEAD.
...CHAK
WHEW ...
THAT WAS SCARY ...
BUT I'M GLAD IT WAS NOTHING. ...FOR SO MANY REASONS.
WAIT.
WHERE IS THE BATH-ROOM?

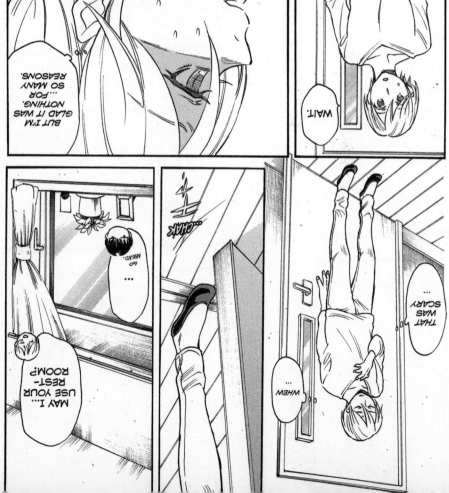

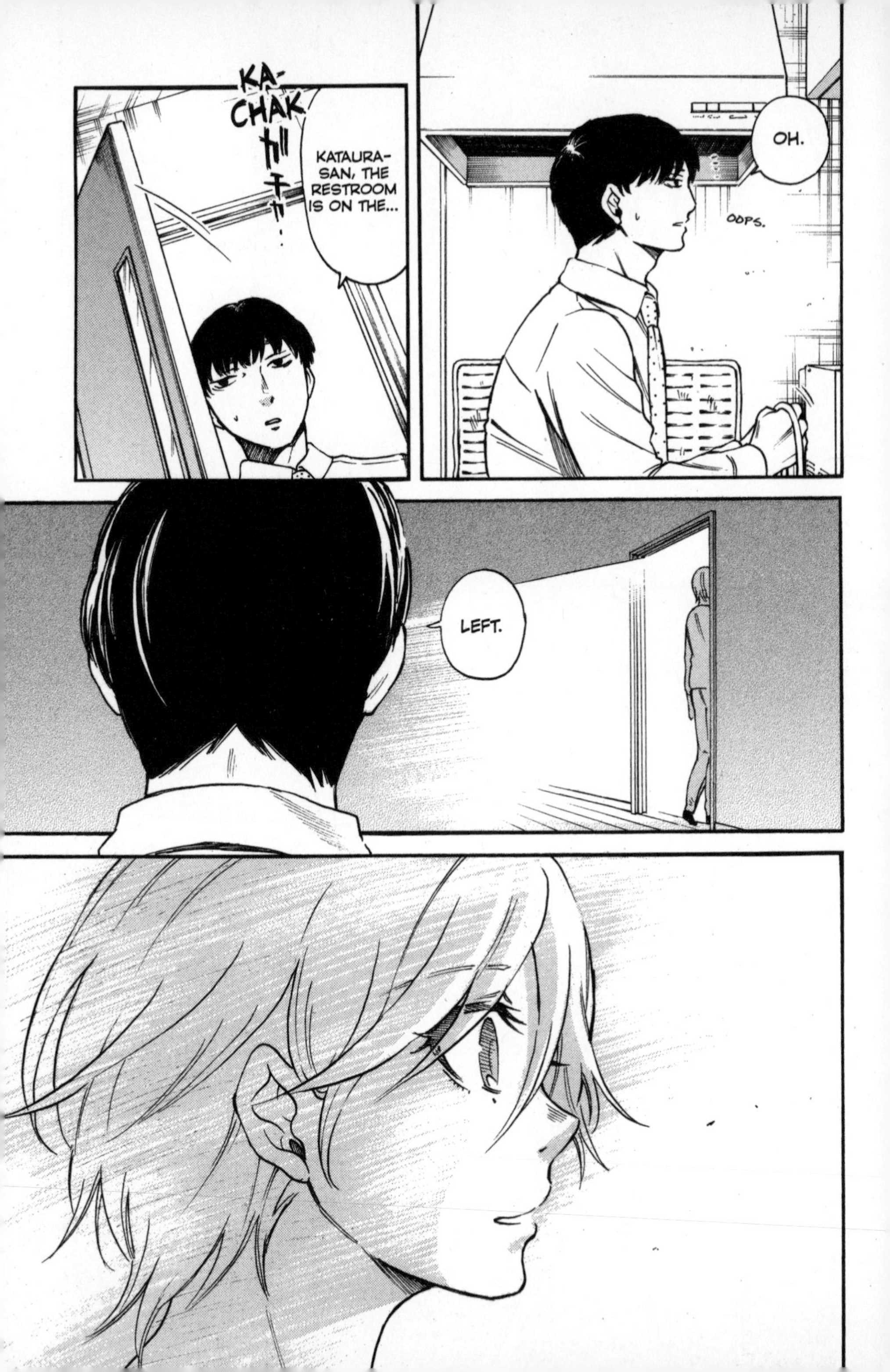
OH.
OOPS.
KA-CHAK
カチャ…
KATAURA-SAN, THE RESTROOM IS ON THE...
LEFT.

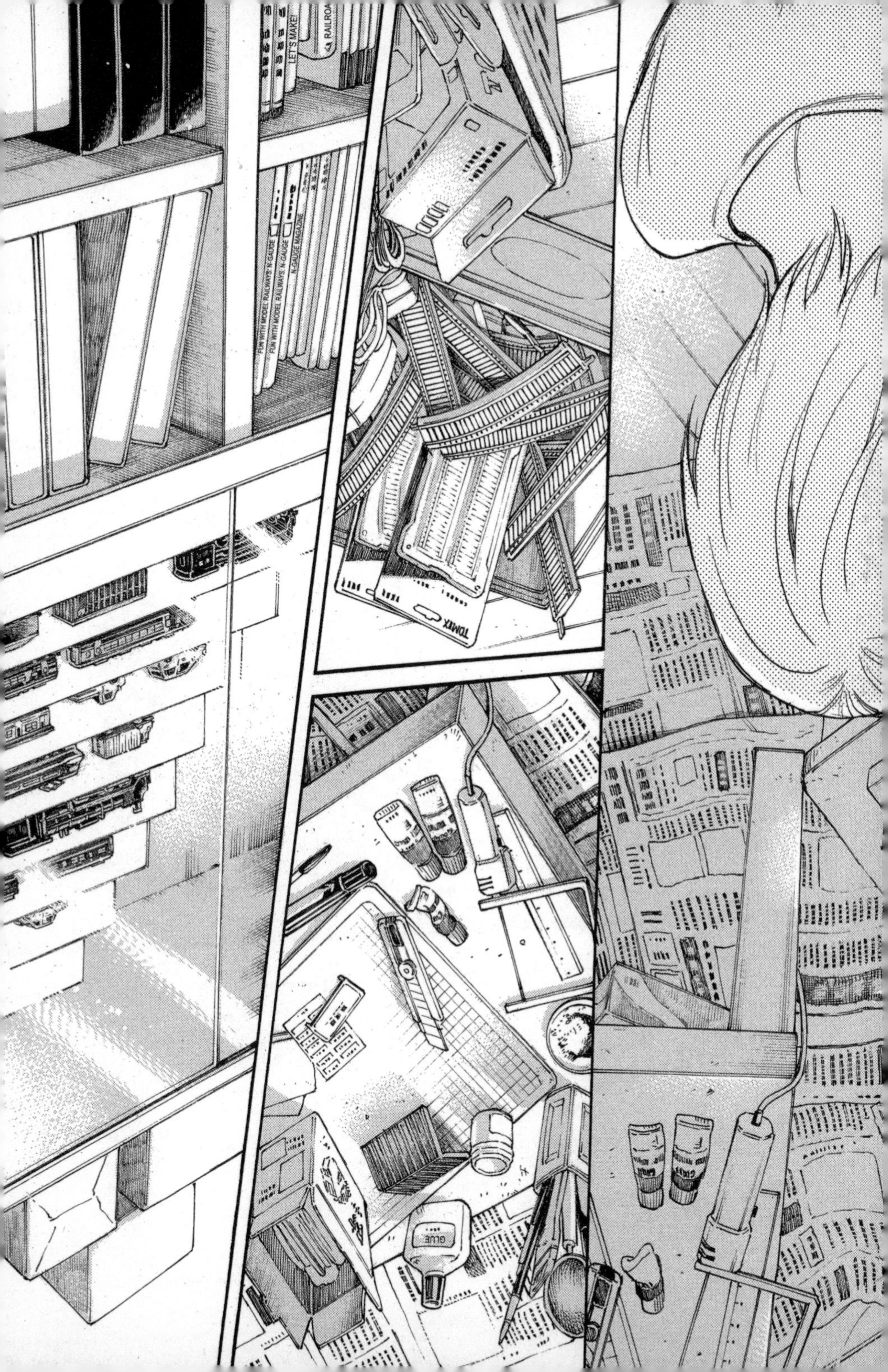
LET'S MAKE!
RAILROAD
FUN WITH MODEL RAILWAYS N-GAUGE
FUN WITH MODEL RAILWAYS N-GAUGE
N-GAUGE MAGAZINE
TOMIX
GLUE

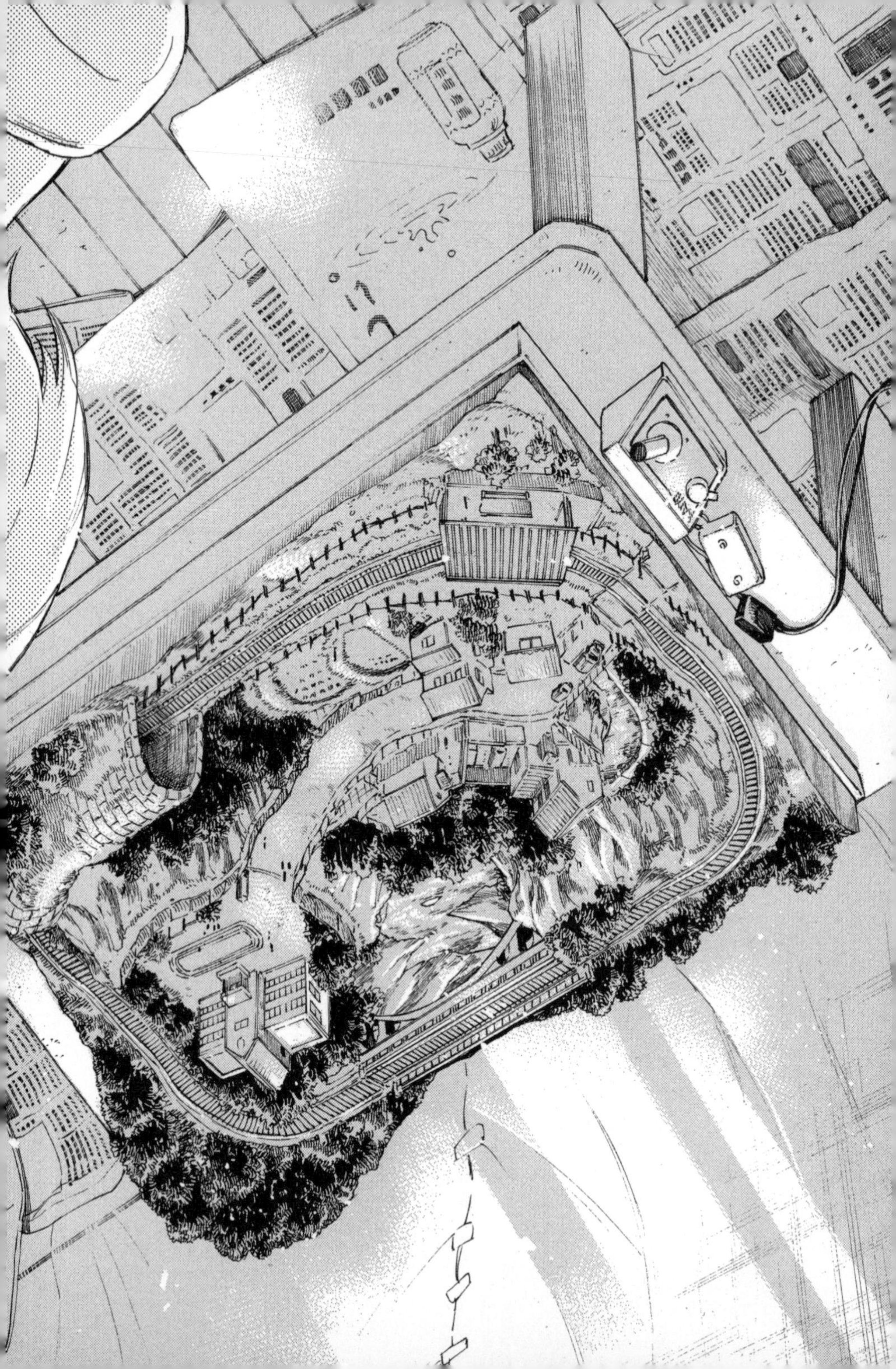

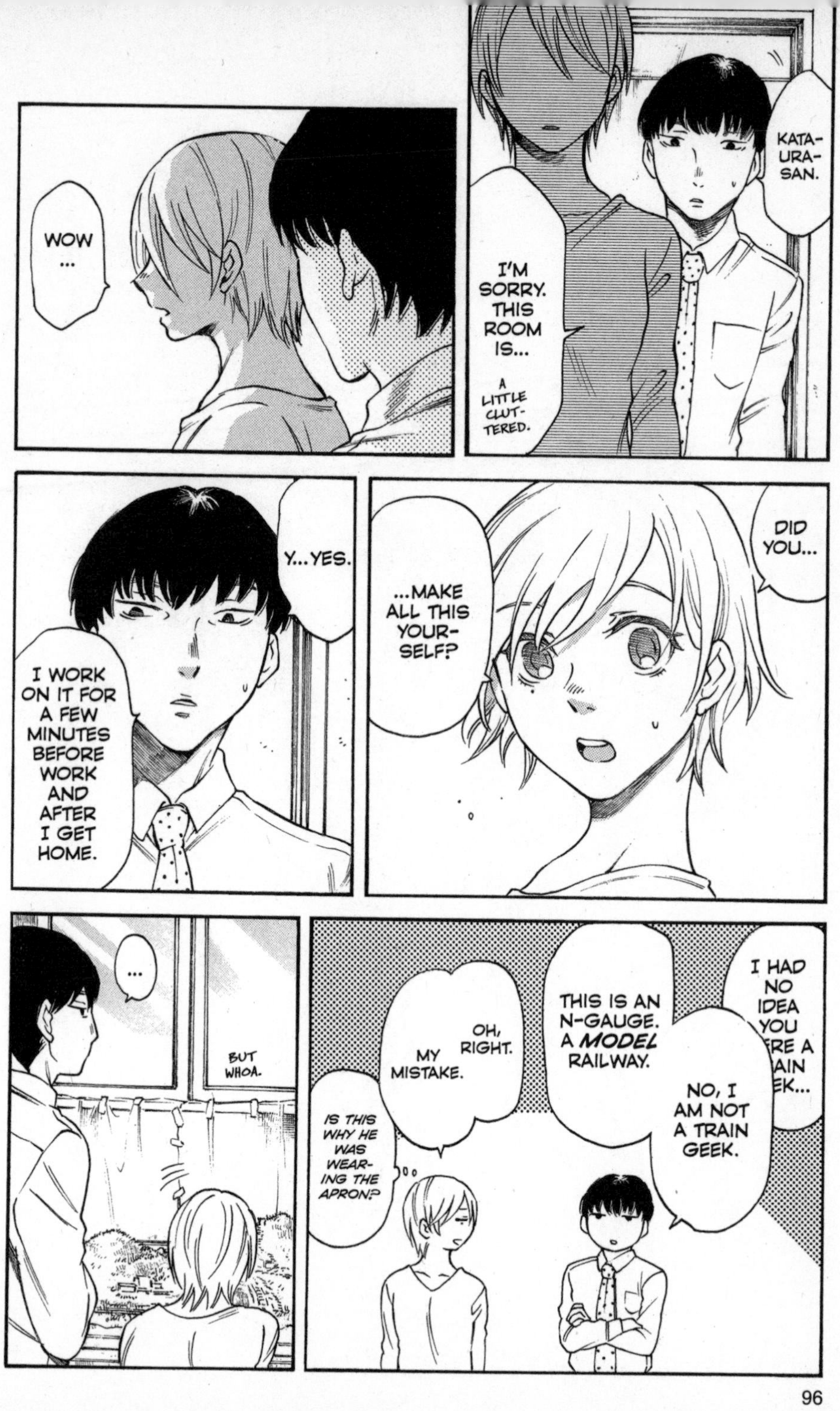
KATA-URA-SAN.
I'M SORRY. THIS ROOM IS...
A LITTLE CLUTTERED.
WOW...
DID YOU...
...MAKE ALL THIS YOURSELF?
Y...YES.
I WORK ON IT FOR A FEW MINUTES BEFORE WORK AND AFTER I GET HOME.
I HAD NO IDEA YOU
THIS IS AN N-GAUGE. A ***MODEL*** RAILWAY.
NO, I AM NOT A TRAIN GEEK.
OH, RIGHT. MY MISTAKE.
IS THIS WHY HE WAS WEARING THE APRON?
BUT WHOA.
...

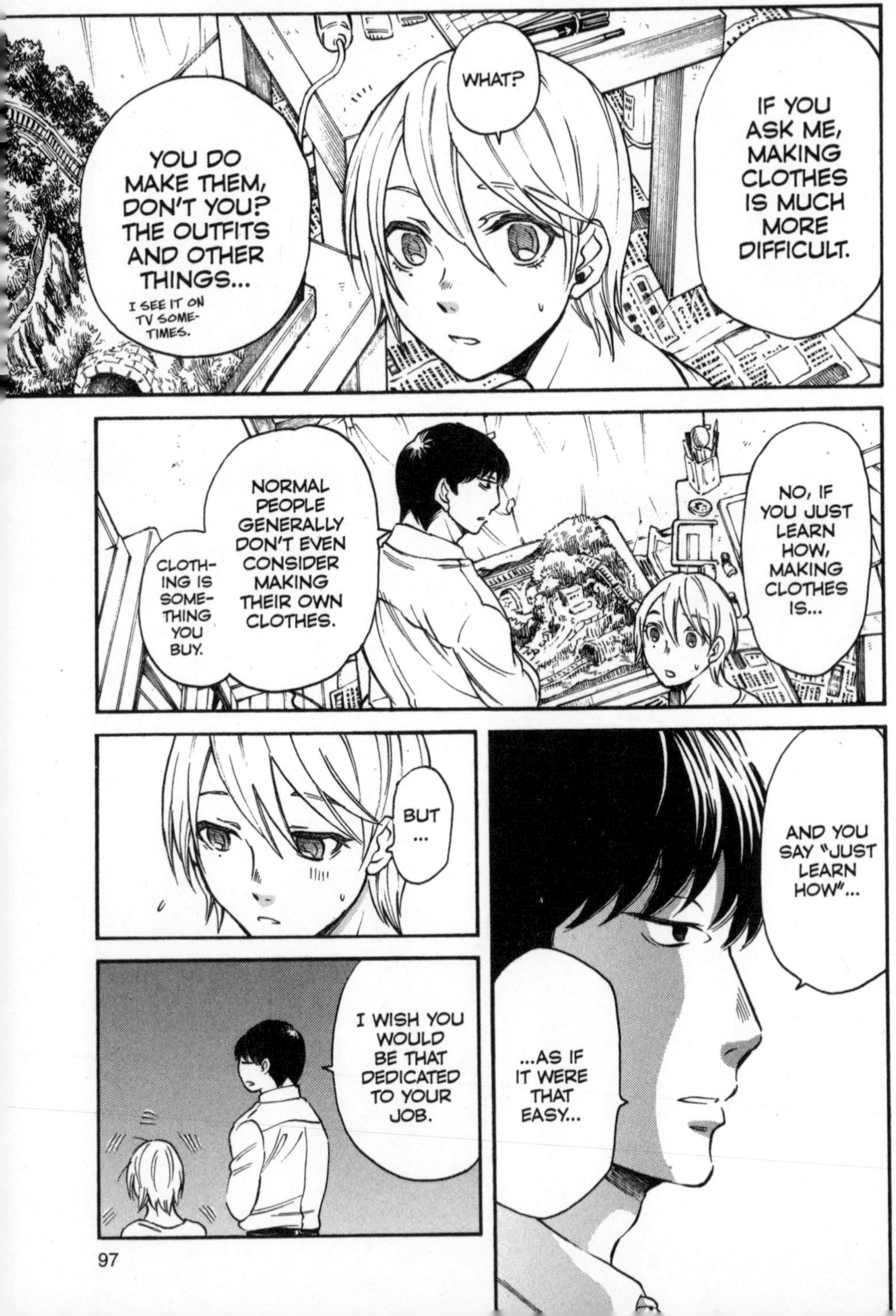
IF YOU ASK ME, MAKING CLOTHES IS MUCH MORE DIFFICULT.
WHAT?
YOU DO MAKE THEM, DON'T YOU? THE OUTFITS AND OTHER THINGS...
I SEE IT ON TV SOME-TIMES.
NO, IF YOU JUST LEARN HOW, MAKING CLOTHES IS...
NORMAL PEOPLE GENERALLY DON'T EVEN CONSIDER MAKING THEIR OWN CLOTHES.
CLOTH-ING IS SOME-THING YOU BUY.
AND YOU SAY "JUST LEARN HOW"...
...AS IF IT WERE THAT EASY...
BUT ...
I WISH YOU WOULD BE THAT DEDICATED TO YOUR JOB.

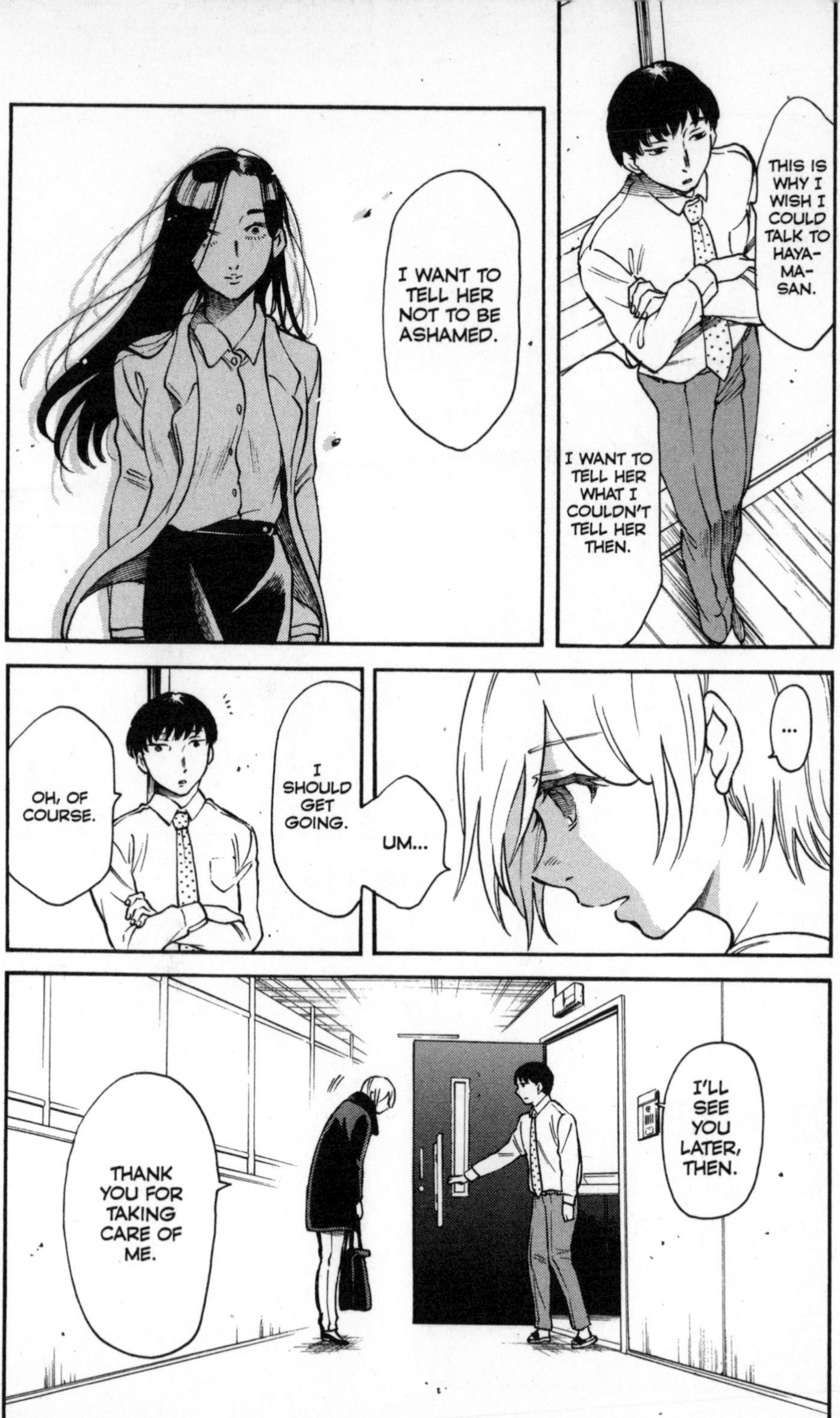
THIS IS WHY I WISH I COULD TALK TO HAYA-MA-SAN.
I WANT TO TELL HER WHAT I COULDN'T TELL HER THEN.
I WANT TO TELL HER NOT TO BE ASHAMED.
...
UM...
I SHOULD GET GOING.
OH, OF COURSE.
I'LL SEE YOU LATER, THEN.
THANK YOU FOR TAKING CARE OF ME.

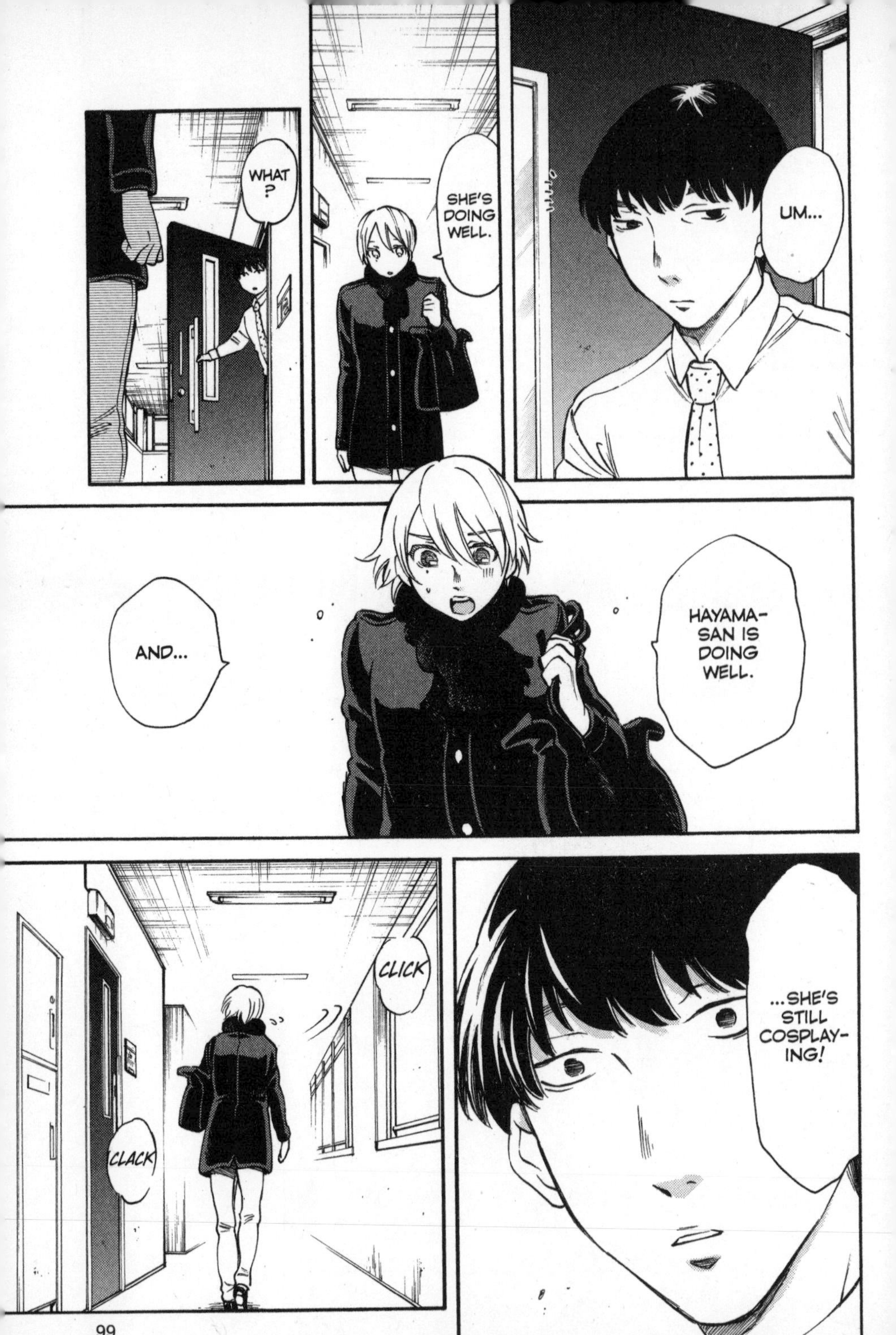
UM...
SHE'S DOING WELL.
WHAT ?
HAYAMA-SAN IS DOING WELL.
AND...
...SHE'S STILL COSPLAYING!
CLICK
CLACK

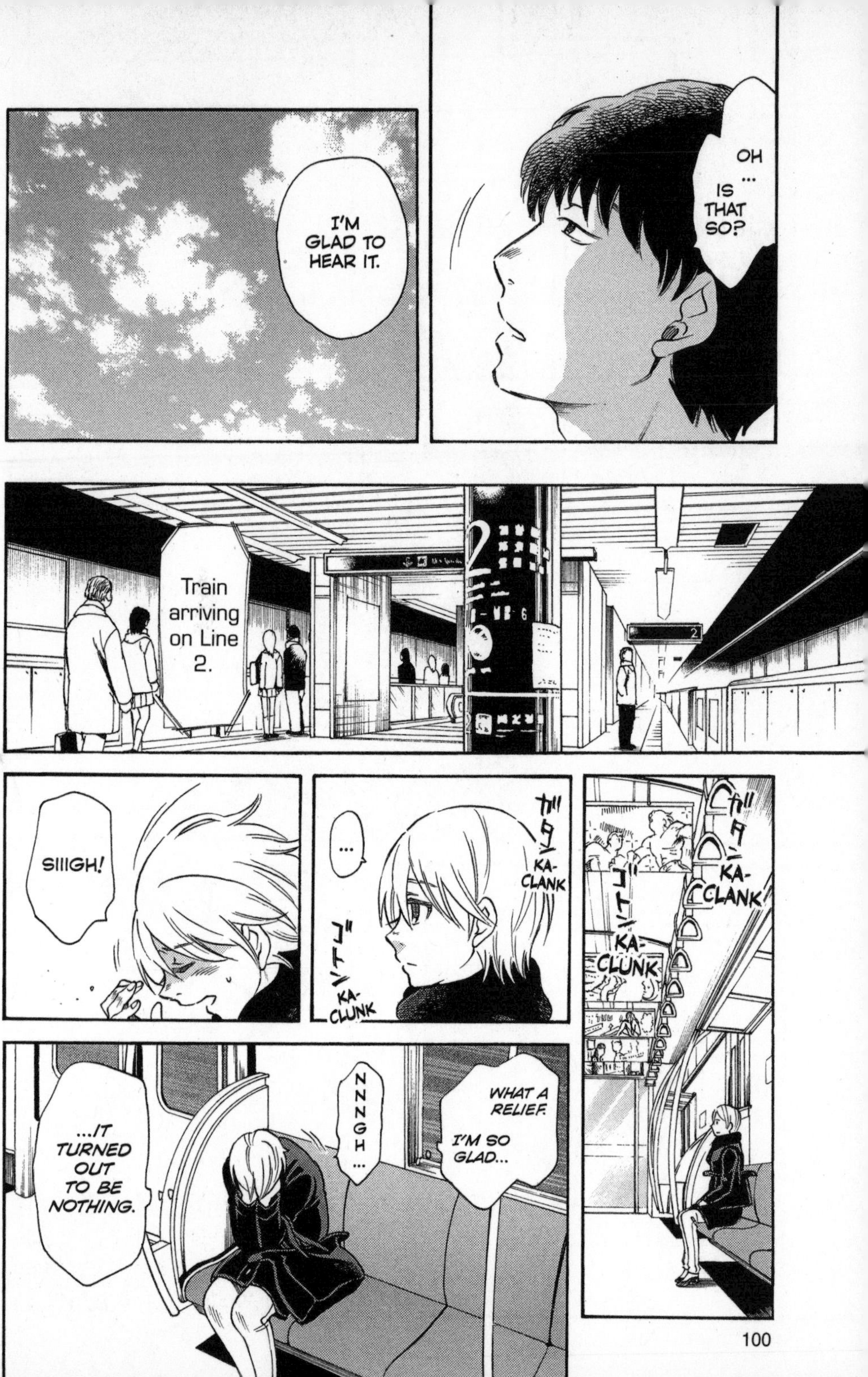
OH ... IS THAT SO?
I'M GLAD TO HEAR IT.
Train arriving on Line 2.
KA-CLANK
KA-CLUNK
...
KA-CLANK
KA-CLUNK
SIIIGH!
WHAT A RELIEF.
I'M SO GLAD...
NNNGH ...
...IT TURNED OUT TO BE NOTHING.

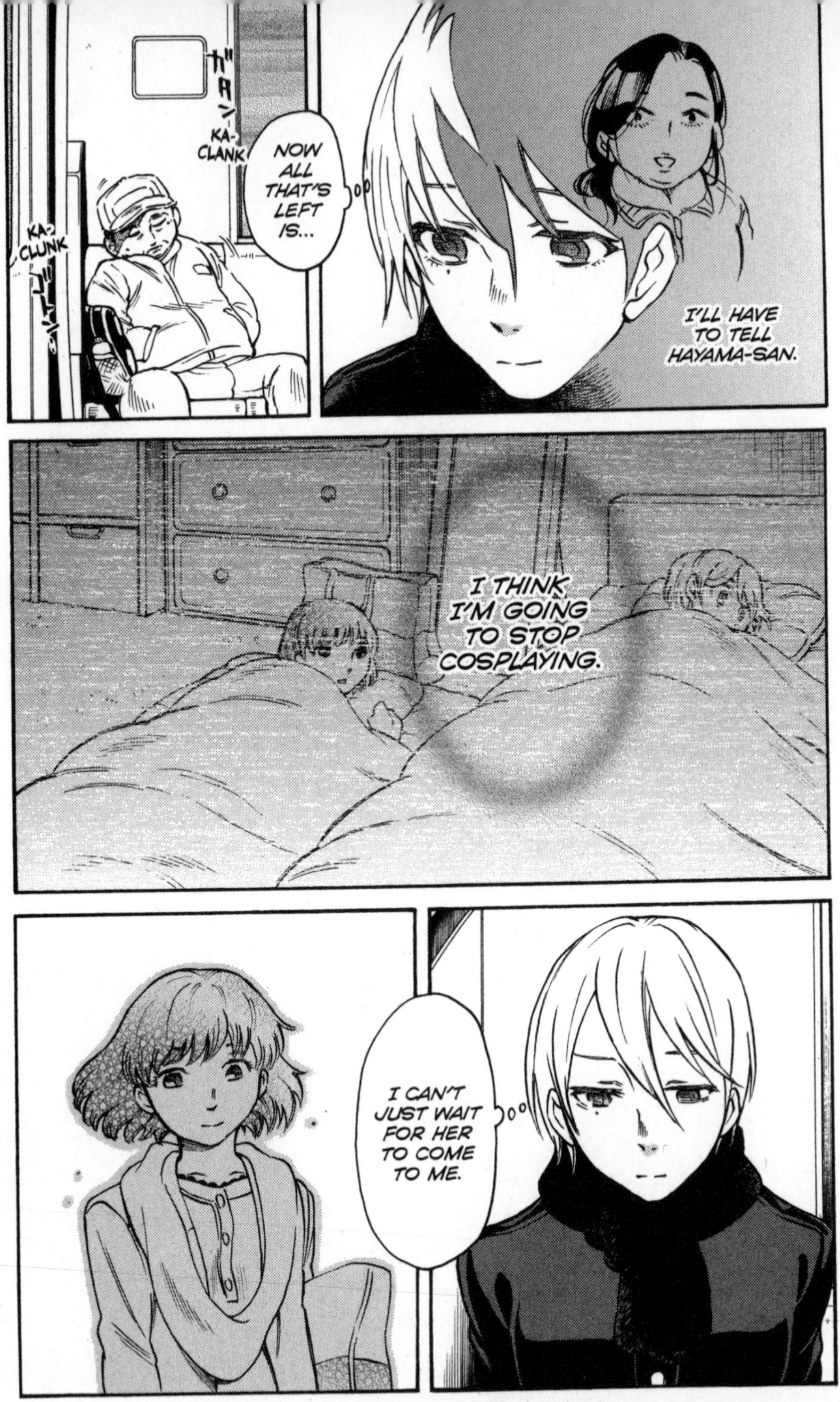
I'LL HAVE TO TELL HAYAMA-SAN.
NOW ALL THAT'S LEFT IS...
KA-CLANK
KA-CLUNK
I THINK I'M GOING TO STOP COSPLAYING.
I CAN'T JUST WAIT FOR HER TO COME TO ME.

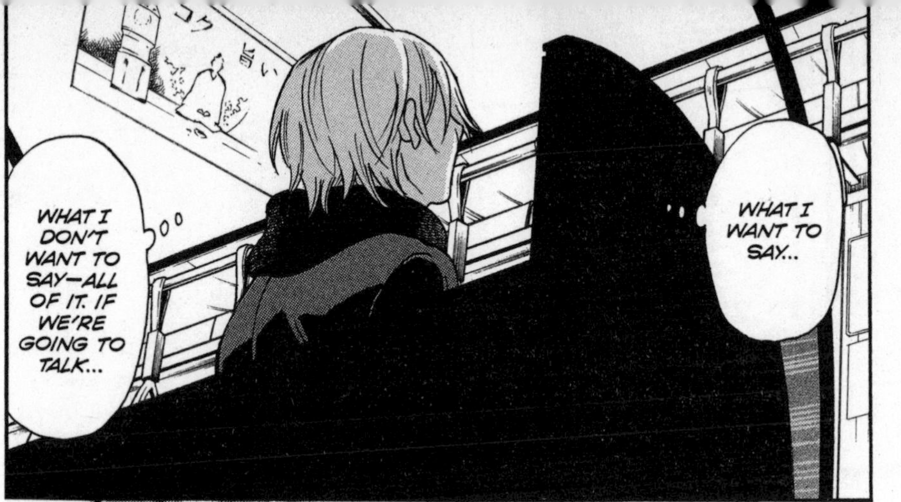
WHAT I WANT TO SAY...
WHAT I DON'T WANT TO SAY—ALL OF IT. IF WE'RE GOING TO TALK...
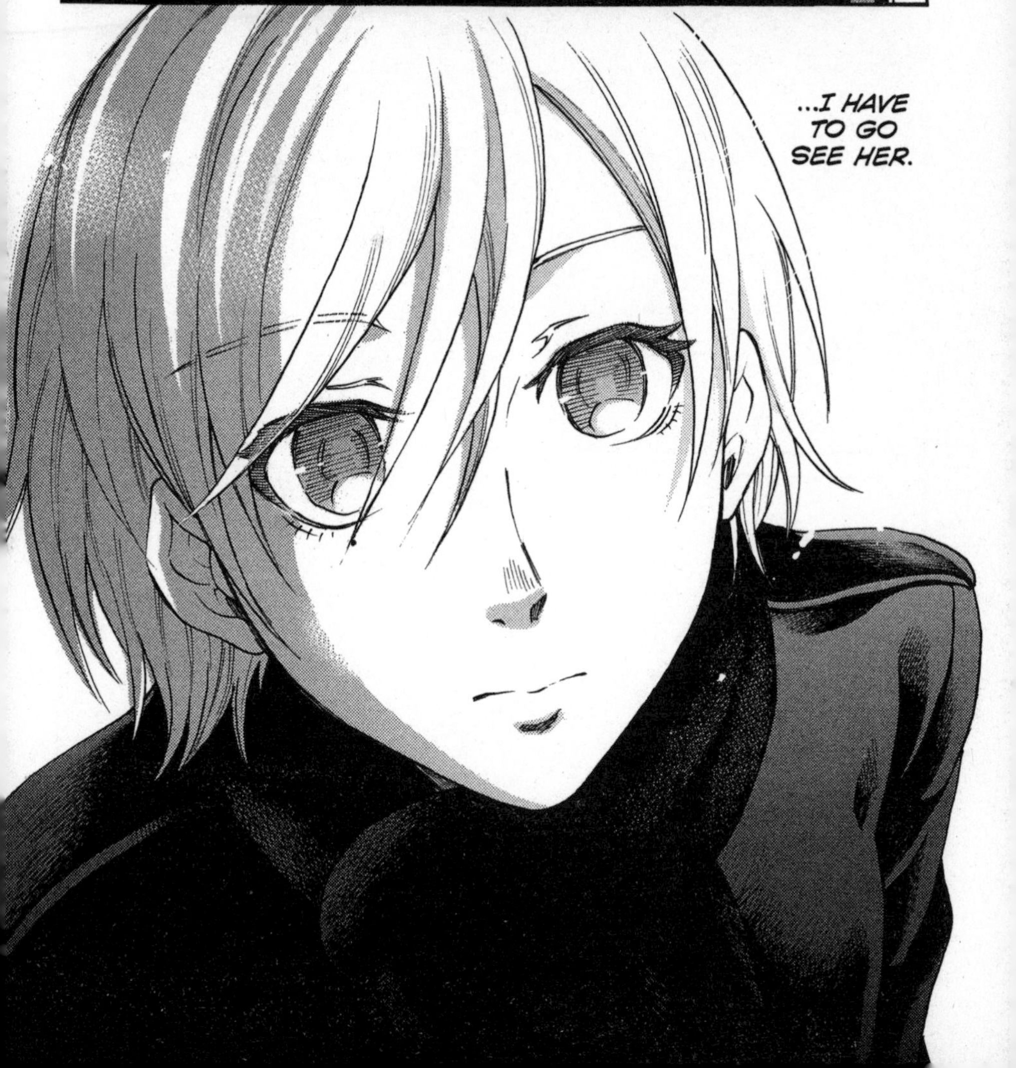
...I HAVE TO GO SEE HER.

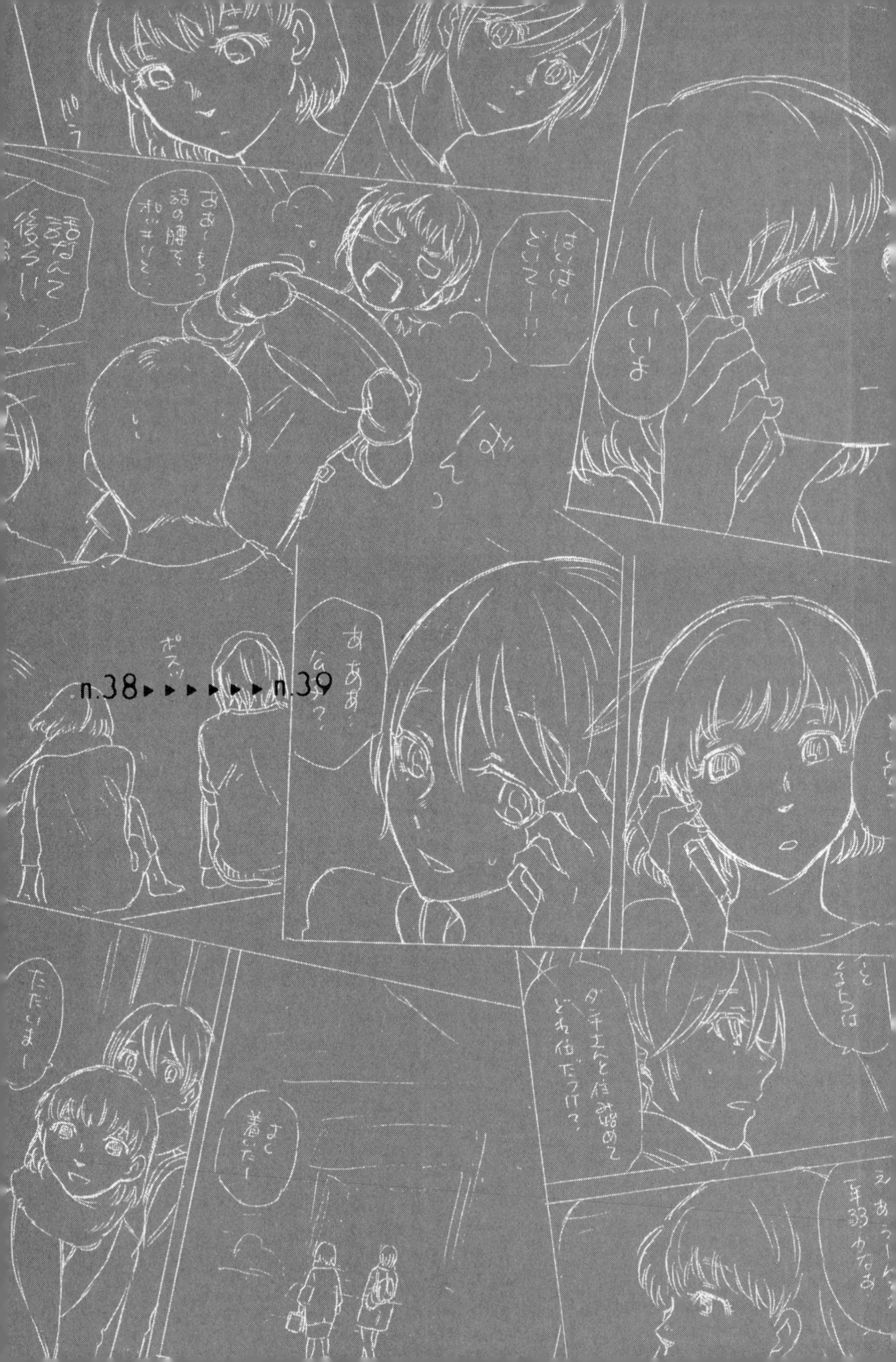

いいよ
n.38▶▶▶▶▶▶▶n.39
ただいまー

- MIYAGI MIYA-GIFTS -

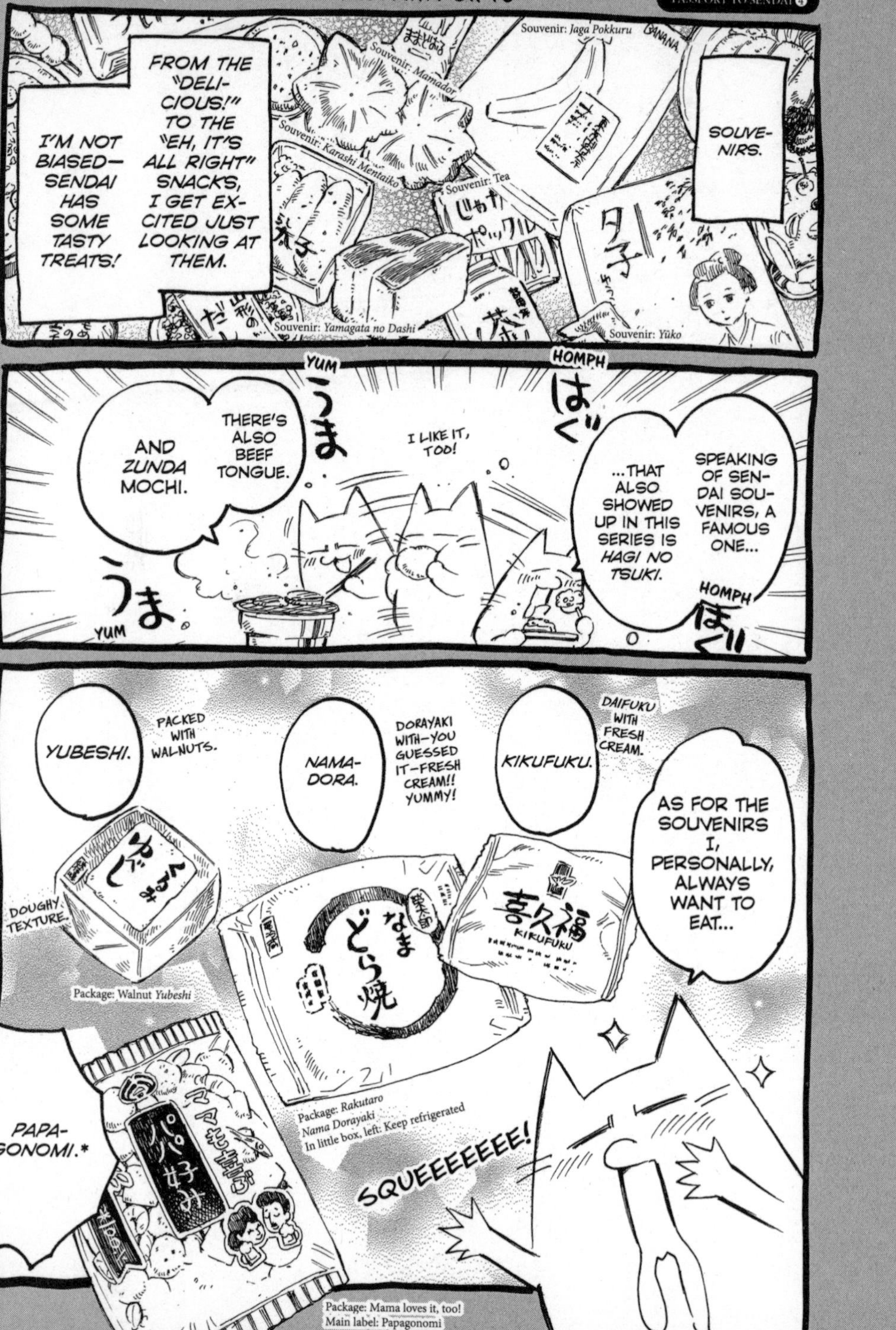
SOUVENIRS.
FROM THE "DELICIOUS!" TO THE "EH, IT'S ALL RIGHT" SNACKS, I GET EXCITED JUST LOOKING AT THEM.
I'M NOT BIASED—SENDAI HAS SOME TASTY TREATS!
Souvenir: Jaga Pokkuru
Souvenir: Mamador
Souvenir: Karashi Mentaiko
Souvenir: Tea
Souvenir: Yamagata no Dashi
Souvenir: Yūko
SPEAKING OF SENDAI SOUVENIRS, A FAMOUS ONE...
...THAT ALSO SHOWED UP IN THIS SERIES IS HAGI NO TSUKI.
HOMPH
HOMPH
I LIKE IT, TOO!
YUM
THERE'S ALSO BEEF TONGUE.
AND ZUNDA MOCHI.
YUM
AS FOR THE SOUVENIRS I, PERSONALLY, ALWAYS WANT TO EAT...
DAIFUKU WITH FRESH CREAM.
KIKUFUKU.
DORAYAKI WITH—YOU GUESSED IT—FRESH CREAM!! YUMMY!
NAMA-DORA.
PACKED WITH WALNUTS.
YUBESHI.
DOUGHY TEXTURE.
Package: Walnut Yubeshi
Package: Rakutaro
Nama Dorayaki
In little box, left: Keep refrigerated
SQUEEEEEEEE!
PAPA-GONOMI.*
Package: Mama loves it, too!
Main label: Papagonomi

*SEE THE NEXT ONE FOR AN EXPLANATION.

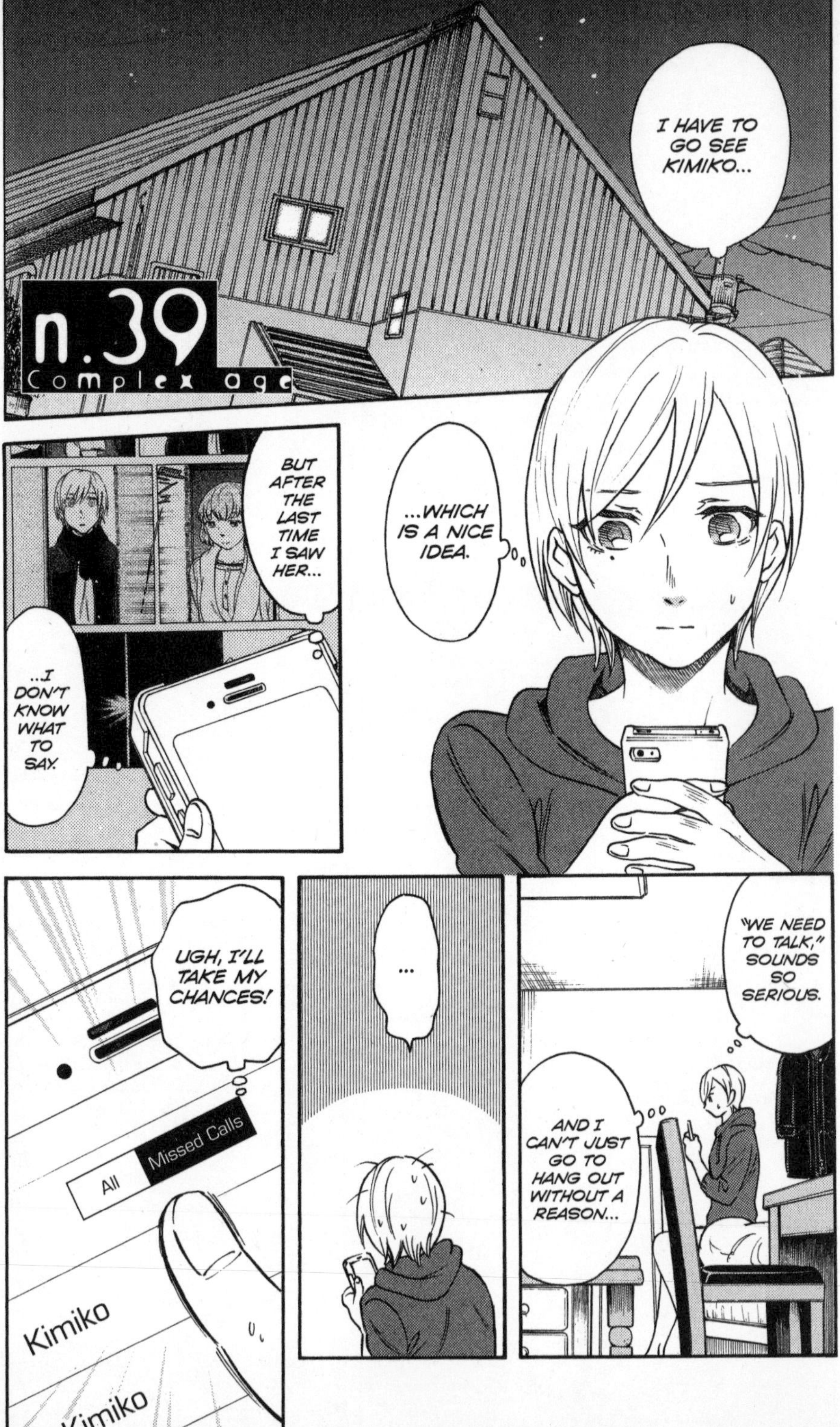
n.39
Complex age
I HAVE TO GO SEE KIMIKO...
...WHICH IS A NICE IDEA.
BUT AFTER THE LAST TIME I SAW HER...
...I DON'T KNOW WHAT TO SAY.
"WE NEED TO TALK," SOUNDS SO SERIOUS.
AND I CAN'T JUST GO TO HANG OUT WITHOUT A REASON...
...
UGH, I'LL TAKE MY CHANCES!
All
Missed Calls
Kimiko
Kimiko

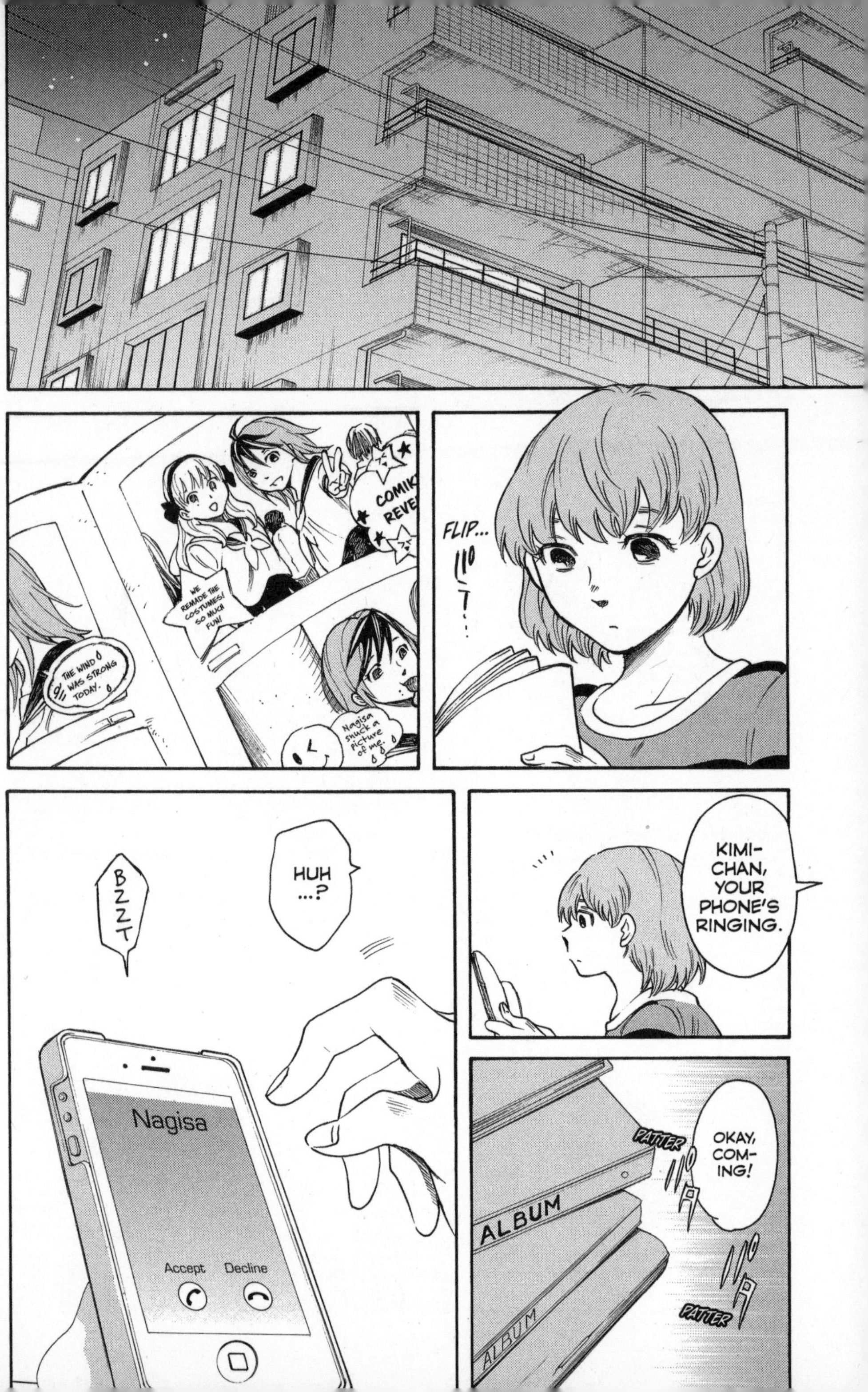
FLIP...
WE REMADE THE COSTUMES! SO MUCH FUN!
THE WIND WAS STRONG TODAY.
Nagisa snuck a picture of me.
KIMI-CHAN, YOUR PHONE'S RINGING.
OKAY, COM-ING!
PATTER
ALBUM
ALBUM
PATTER
BZZT
HUH ...?
Nagisa
Accept
Decline

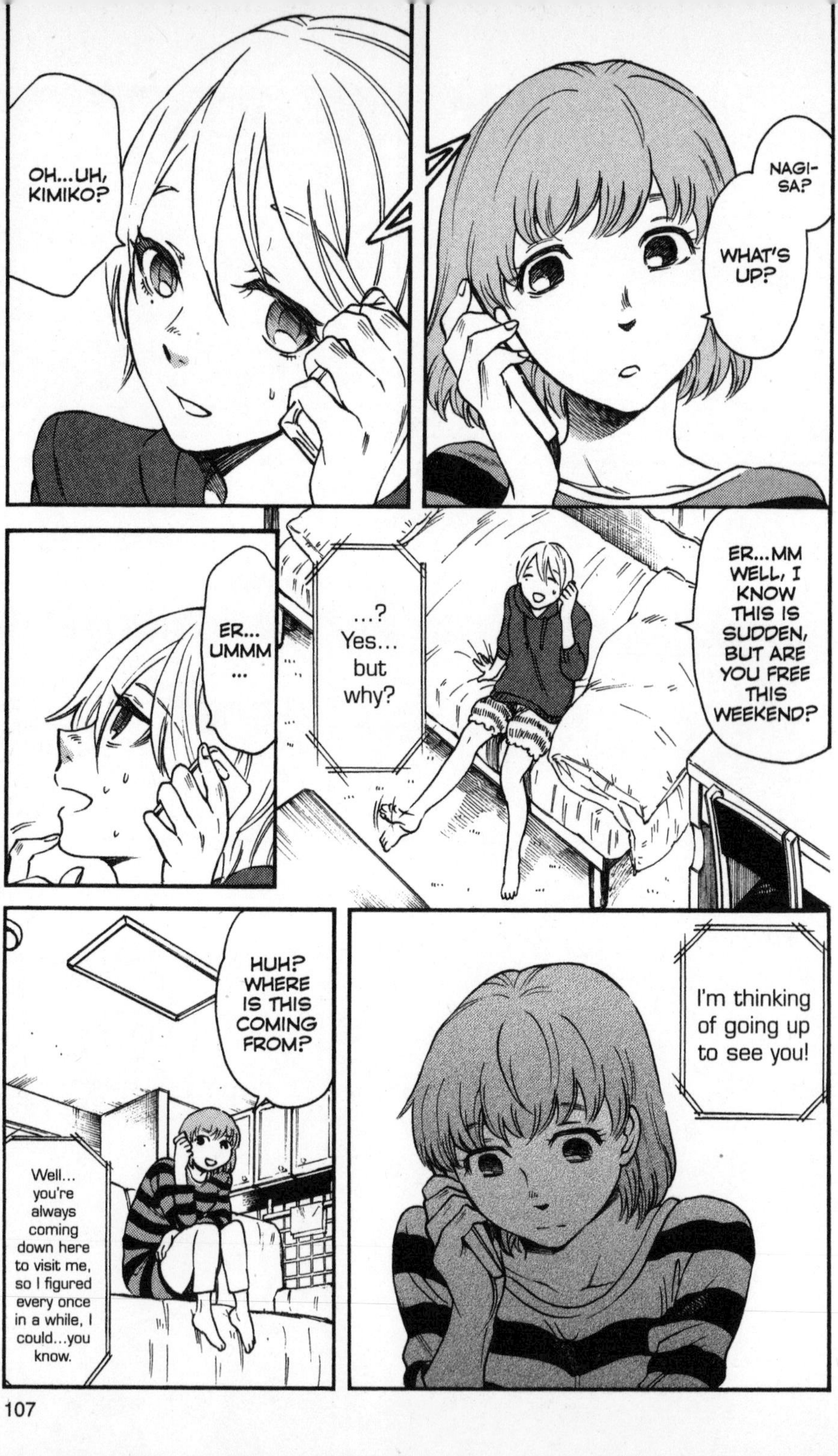
NAGI-SA?
WHAT'S UP?
OH...UH, KIMIKO?
ER...MM WELL, I KNOW THIS IS SUDDEN, BUT ARE YOU FREE THIS WEEKEND?
...? Yes... but why?
ER... UMMM ...
I'm thinking of going up to see you!
HUH? WHERE IS THIS COMING FROM?
Well... you're always coming down here to visit me, so I figured every once in a while, I could...you know.

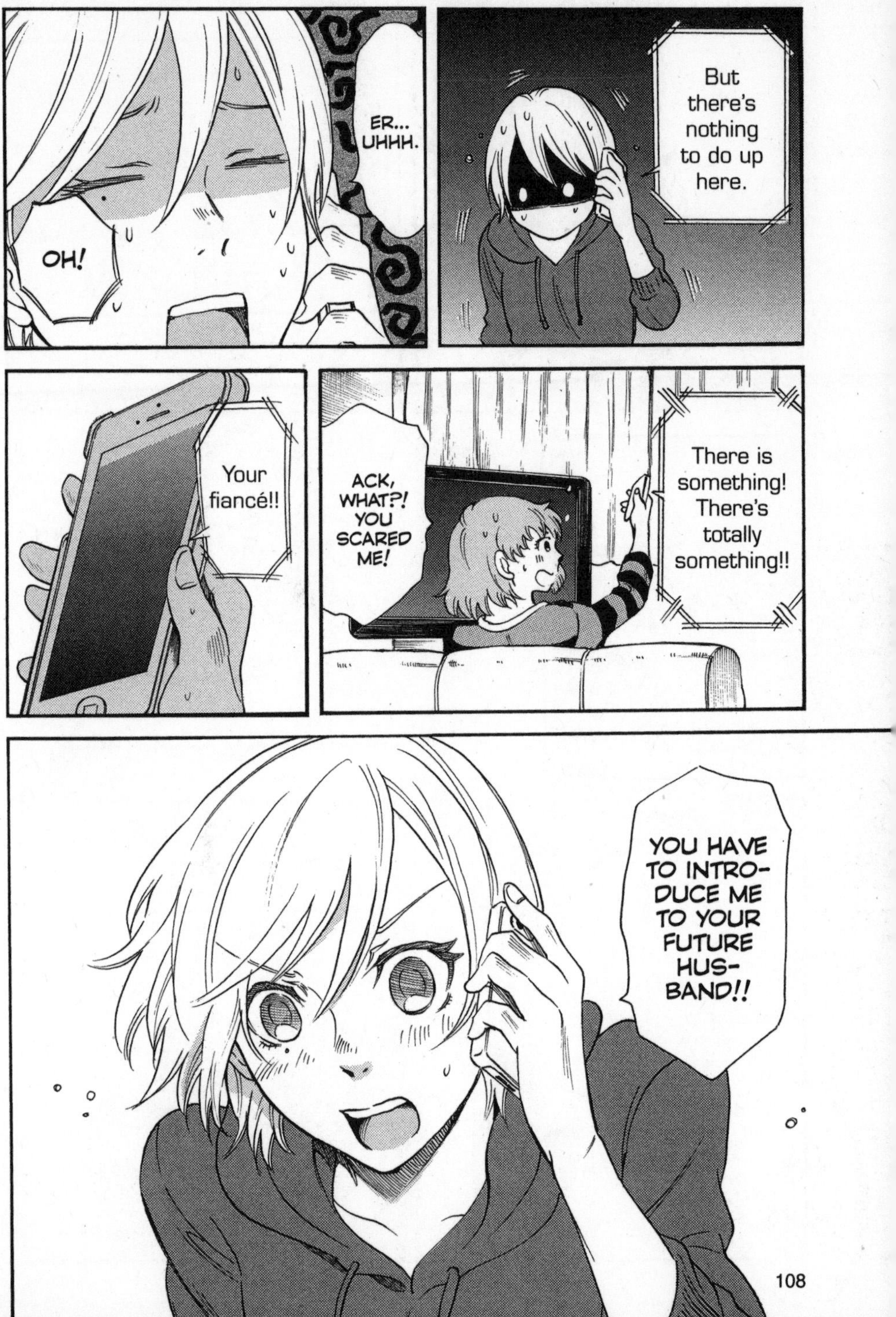
But there's nothing to do up here.
ER... UHHH.
OH!
There is something! There's totally something!!
ACK, WHAT?! YOU SCARED ME!
Your fiancé!!
YOU HAVE TO INTRO-DUCE ME TO YOUR FUTURE HUS-BAND!!

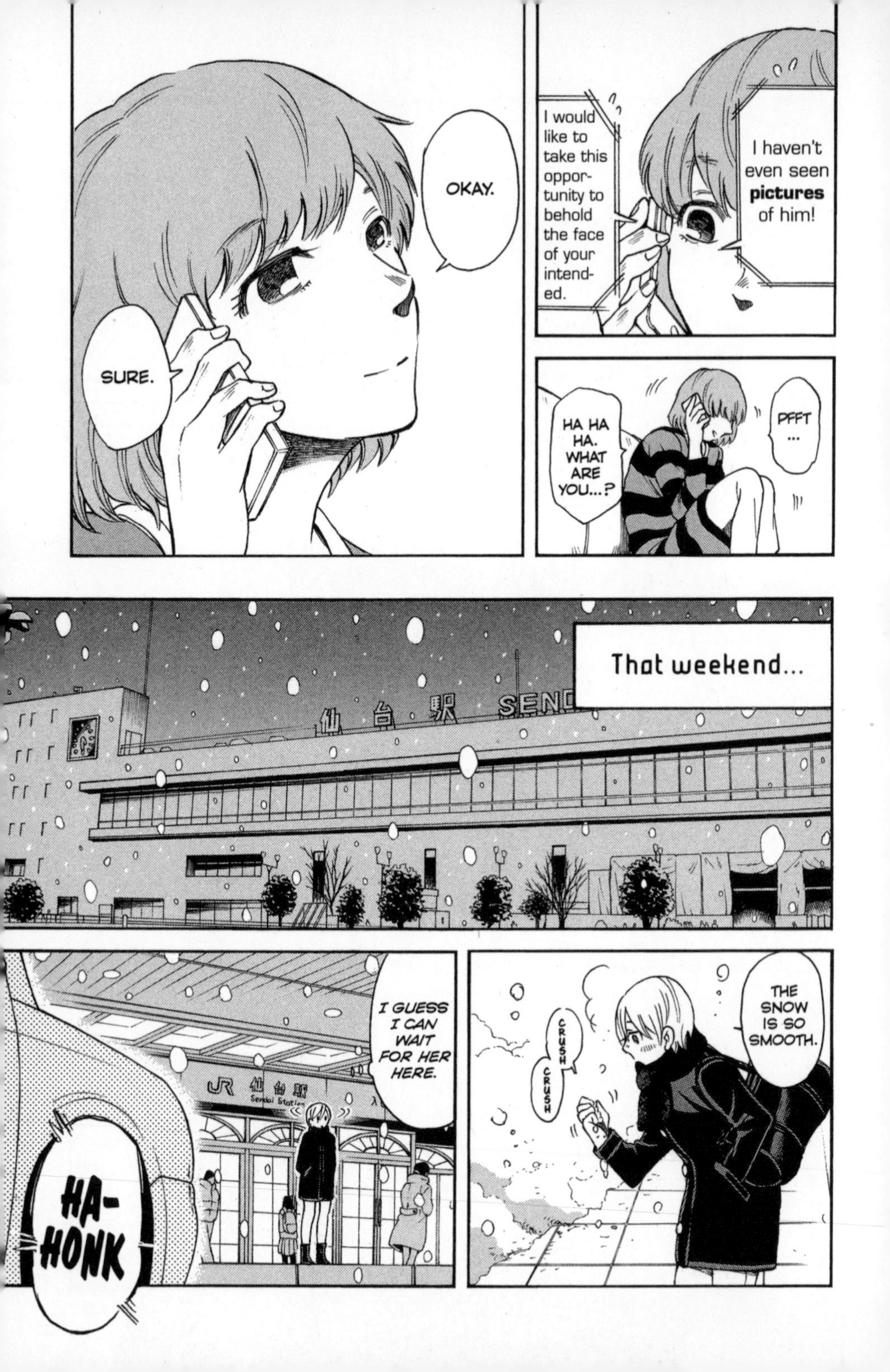
I haven't even seen **pictures** of him!
I would like to take this opportunity to behold the face of your intended.
PFFT ...
HA HA HA. WHAT ARE YOU...?
OKAY.
SURE.
That weekend...
仙台駅 SEND
THE SNOW IS SO SMOOTH.
CRUSH CRUSH
I GUESS I CAN WAIT FOR HER HERE.
JR 仙台駅
Sendai Station
HA-HONK

NAGISA!
LONG TRIP, HUH? GET ON IN!
BAM
THANKS FOR HAVING ME.
THANKS FOR COMING.
VVVN
...
SO... UM, THE PLACE YOU LIVE NOW...
YOU'RE SHARING IT WITH YOUR FIANCÉ? HOW LONG SINCE YOU MOVED IN TOGETHER?
HUH? HMM... JUST UNDER A YEAR, I GUESS.

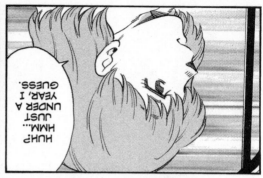

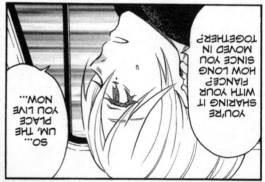

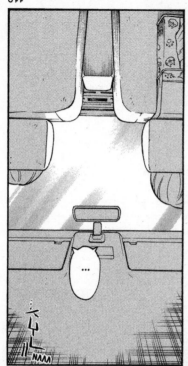

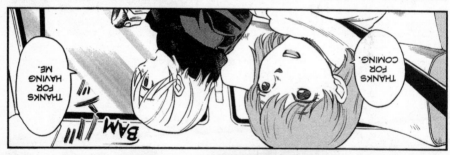

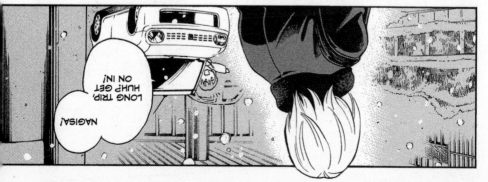

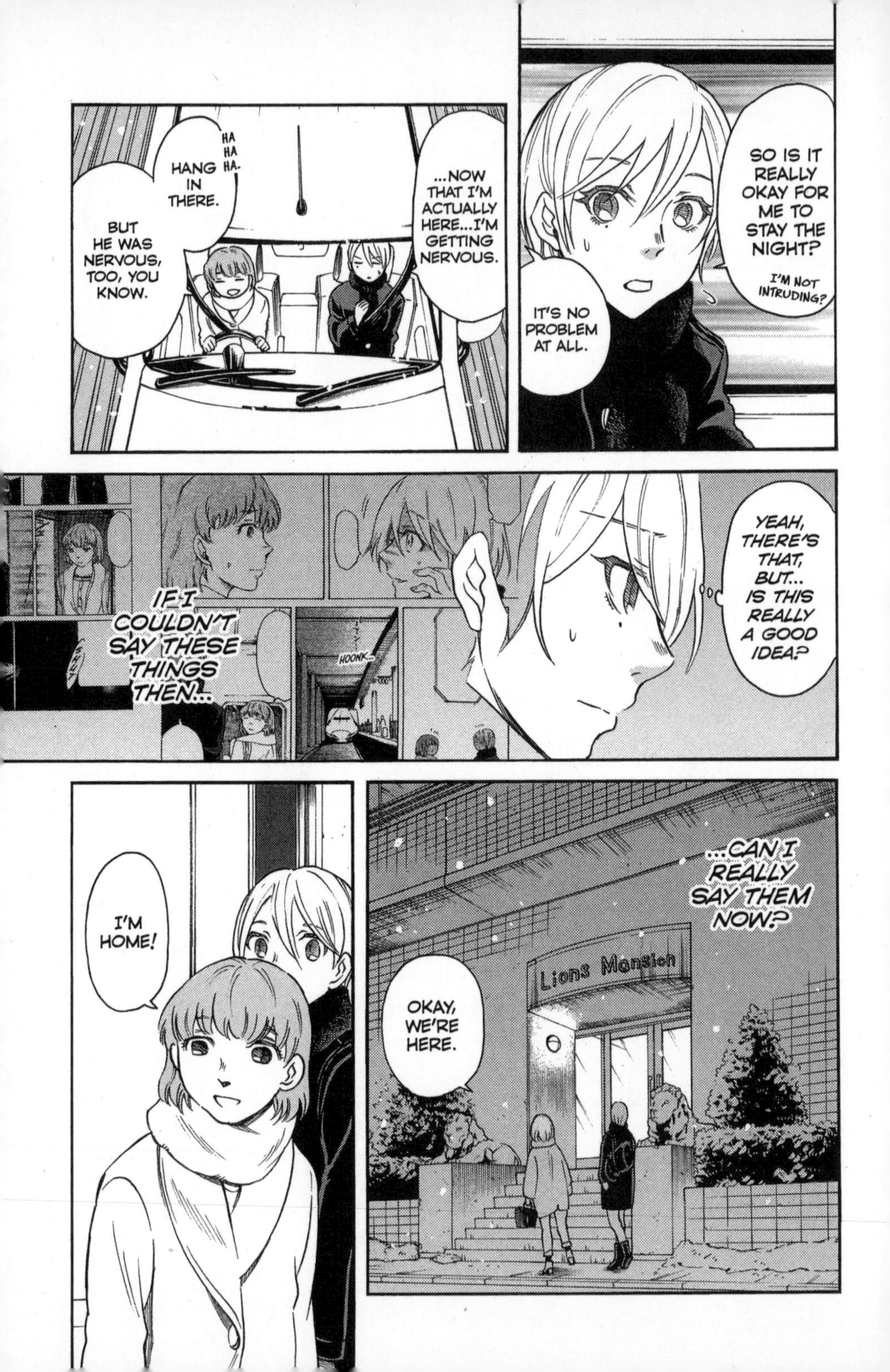
SO IS IT REALLY OKAY FOR ME TO STAY THE NIGHT?
I'M NOT INTRUDING?
IT'S NO PROBLEM AT ALL.
...NOW THAT I'M ACTUALLY HERE...I'M GETTING NERVOUS.
HA HA HA.
HANG IN THERE.
BUT HE WAS NERVOUS, TOO, YOU KNOW.
YEAH, THERE'S THAT, BUT... IS THIS REALLY A GOOD IDEA?
HOONK...
IF I COULDN'T SAY THESE THINGS THEN...
...CAN I REALLY SAY THEM NOW?
Lions Mansion
OKAY, WE'RE HERE.
I'M HOME!

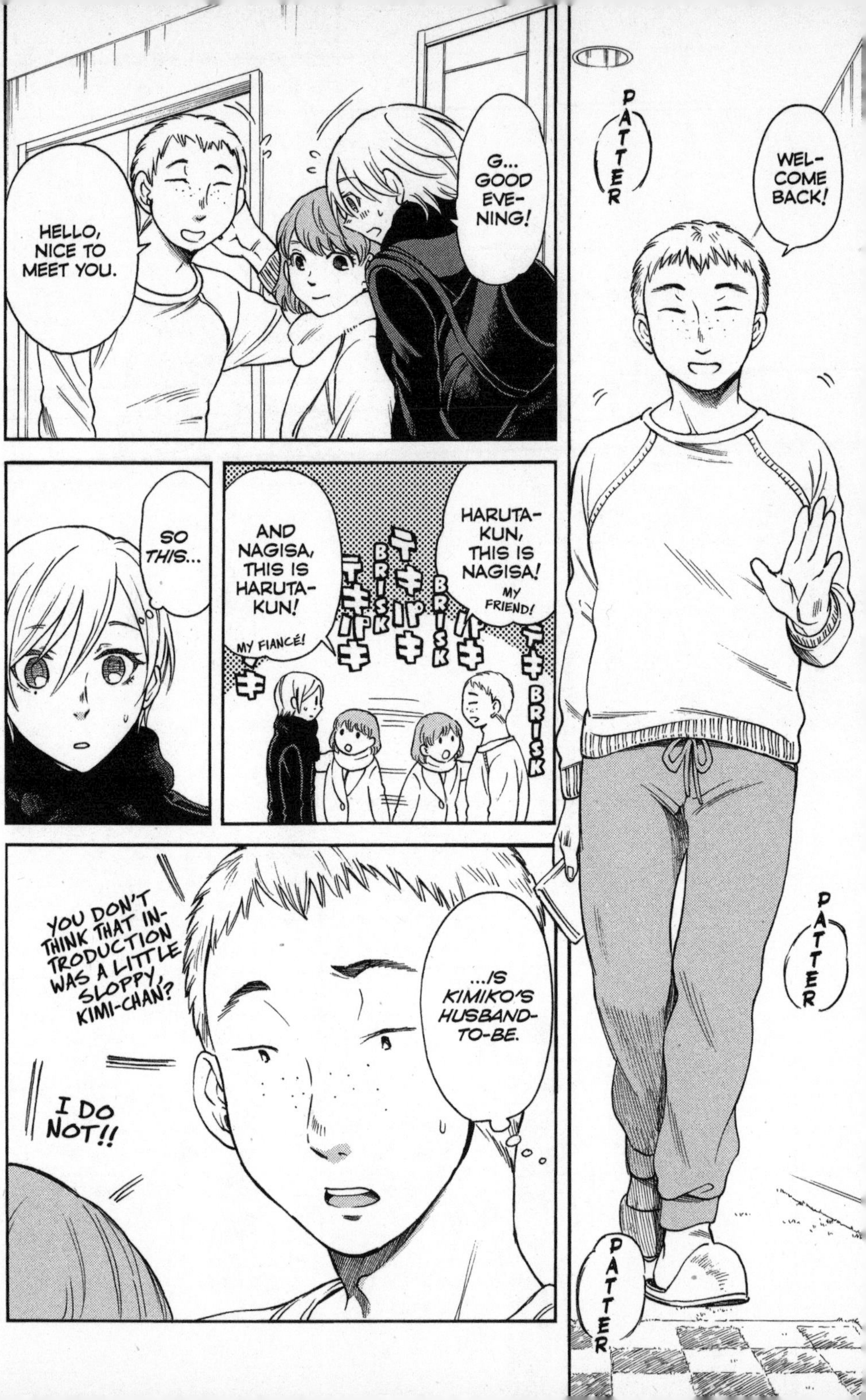

PATTER
WEL-COME BACK!
PATTER
PATTER
G... GOOD EVE-NING!
HELLO, NICE TO MEET YOU.
HARUTA-KUN, THIS IS NAGISA!
MY FRIEND!
AND NAGISA, THIS IS HARUTA-KUN!
MY FIANCÉ!
BRISK
BRISK
BRISK
SO THIS...
...IS KIMIKO'S HUSBAND-TO-BE.
YOU DON'T THINK THAT IN-TRODUCTION WAS A LITTLE SLOPPY, KIMI-CHAN?
I DO NOT!!

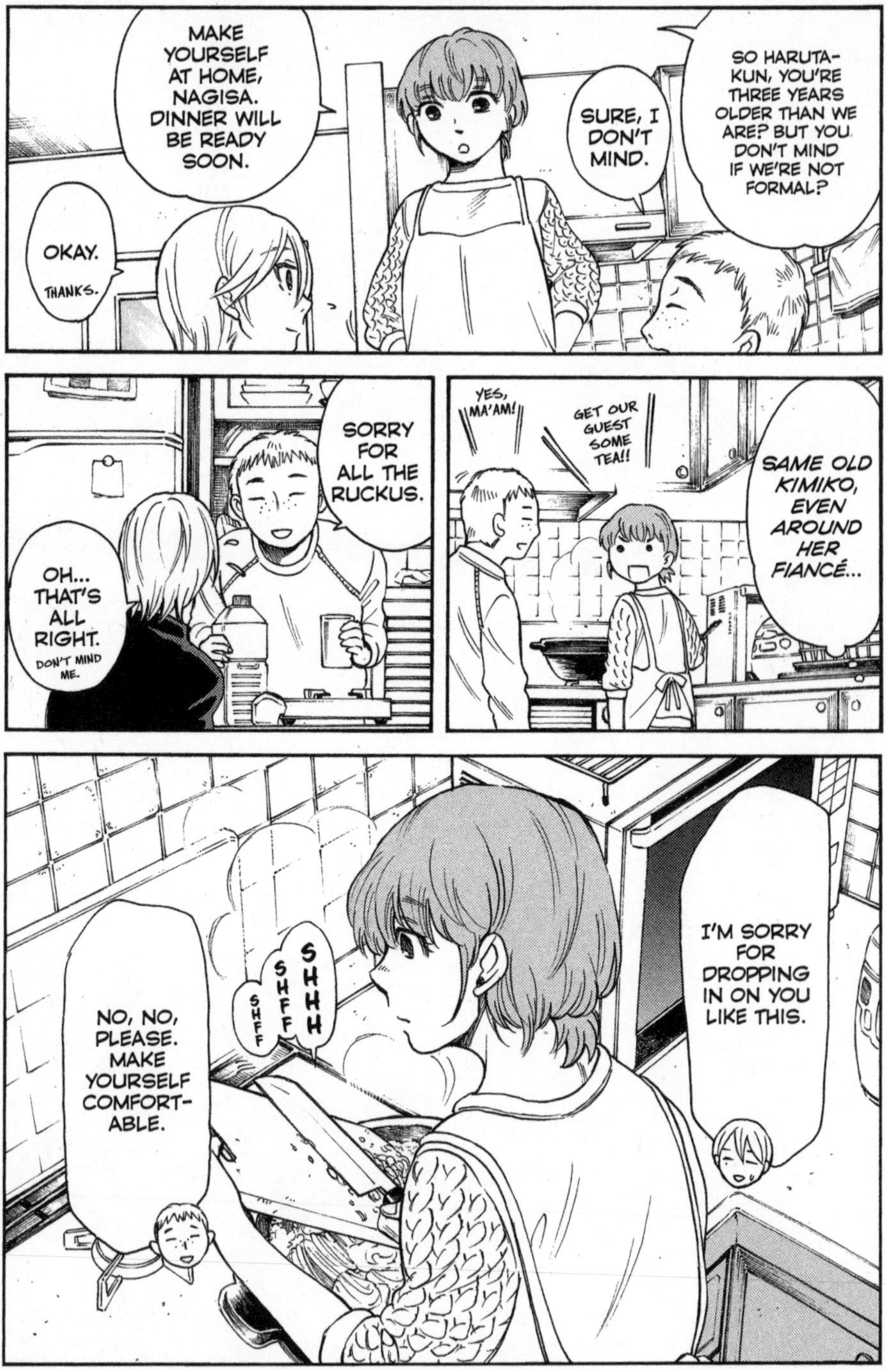
SO HARUTA-KUN, YOU'RE THREE YEARS OLDER THAN WE ARE? BUT YOU DON'T MIND IF WE'RE NOT FORMAL?
SURE, I DON'T MIND.
MAKE YOURSELF AT HOME, NAGISA. DINNER WILL BE READY SOON.
OKAY.
THANKS.
SAME OLD KIMIKO, EVEN AROUND HER FIANCÉ...
GET OUR GUEST SOME TEA!!
YES, MA'AM!
SORRY FOR ALL THE RUCKUS.
OH... THAT'S ALL RIGHT.
DON'T MIND ME.
I'M SORRY FOR DROPPING IN ON YOU LIKE THIS.
SHHH
SHFF
SHFF
NO, NO, PLEASE. MAKE YOURSELF COMFORT-ABLE.

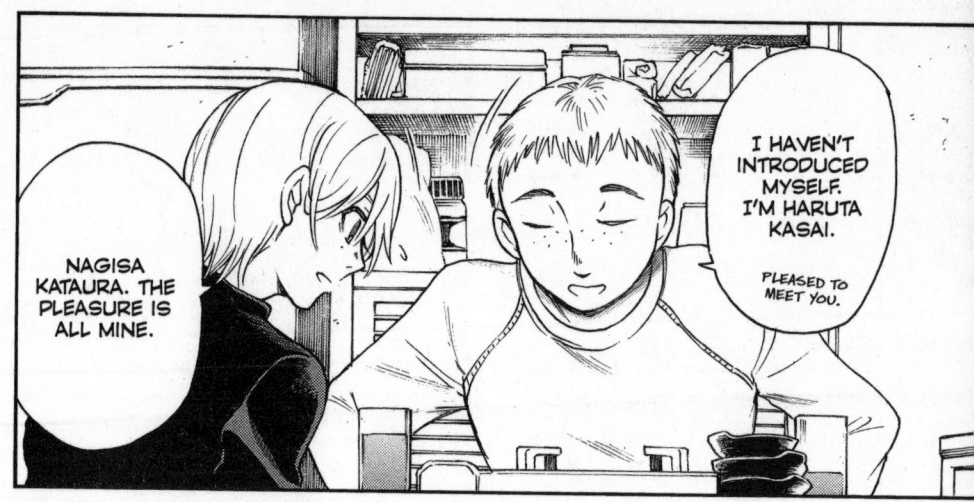

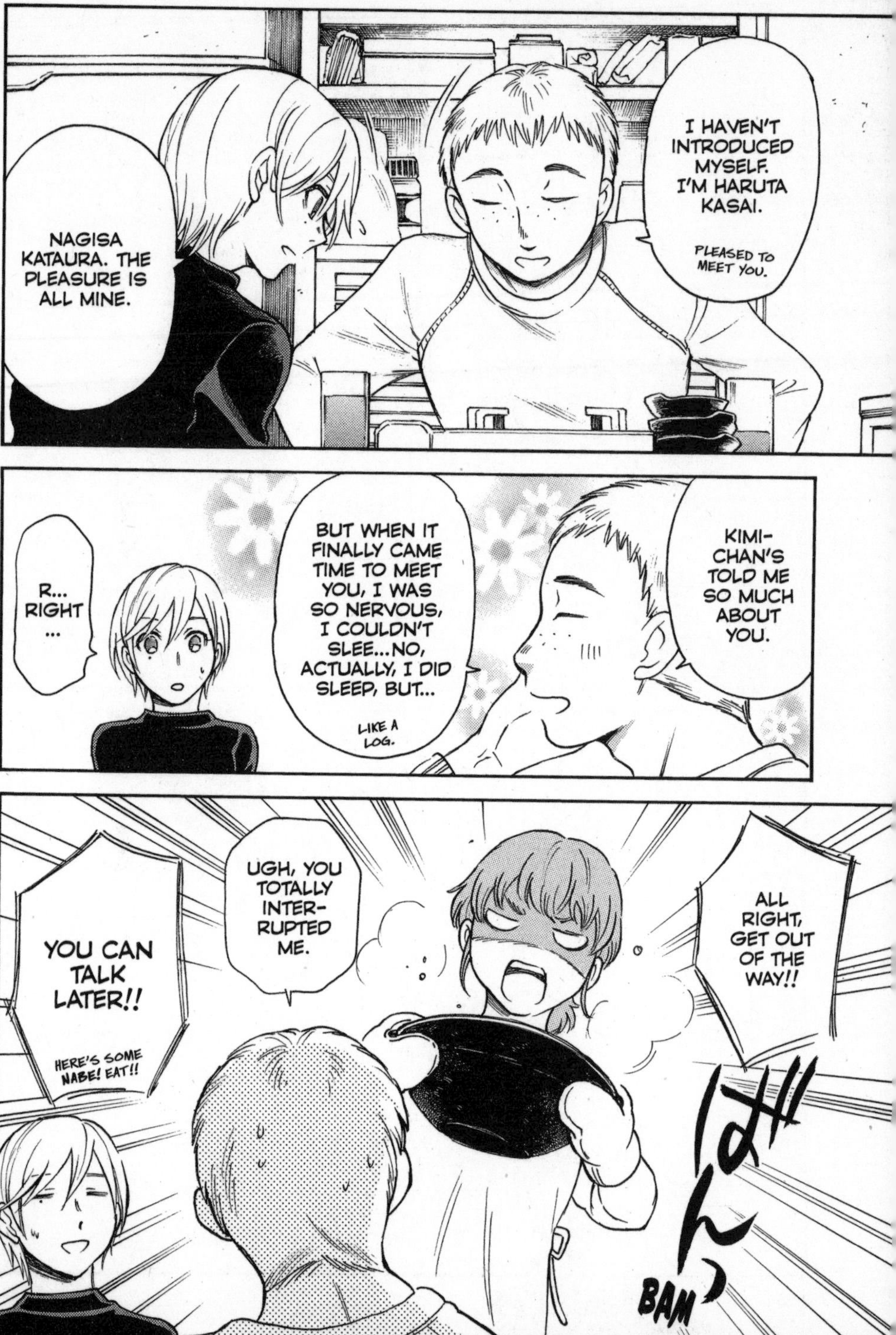

I HAVEN'T INTRODUCED MYSELF. I'M HARUTA KASAI.

PLEASED TO MEET YOU.

NAGISA KATAURA. THE PLEASURE IS ALL MINE.

KIMI-CHAN'S TOLD ME SO MUCH ABOUT YOU.

BUT WHEN IT FINALLY CAME TIME TO MEET YOU, I WAS SO NERVOUS, I COULDN'T SLEE...NO, ACTUALLY, I DID SLEEP, BUT...

LIKE A LOG.

R... RIGHT...

ALL RIGHT, GET OUT OF THE WAY!!

UGH, YOU TOTALLY INTER-RUPTED ME.

YOU CAN TALK LATER!!

HERE'S SOME NABE! EAT!!

BAM

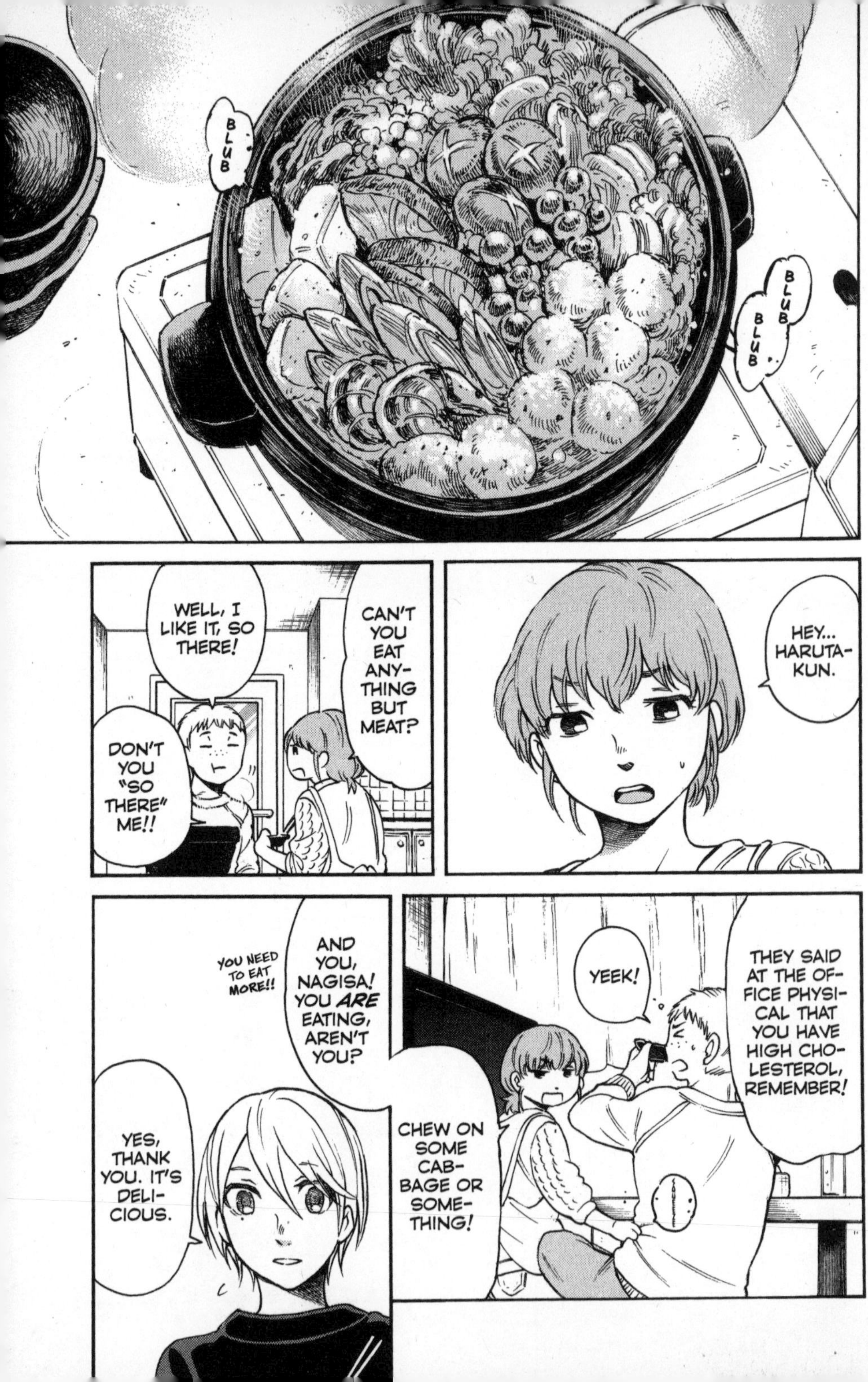
BLUB BLUB
BLUB
HEY... HARUTA-KUN.
CAN'T YOU EAT ANY-THING BUT MEAT?
WELL, I LIKE IT, SO THERE!
DON'T YOU "SO THERE" ME!!
THEY SAID AT THE OF-FICE PHYSI-CAL THAT YOU HAVE HIGH CHO-LESTEROL, REMEMBER!
YEEK!
CHEW ON SOME CAB-BAGE OR SOME-THING!
AND YOU, NAGISA! YOU *ARE* EATING, AREN'T YOU?
YOU NEED TO EAT MORE!!
YES, THANK YOU. IT'S DELI-CIOUS.

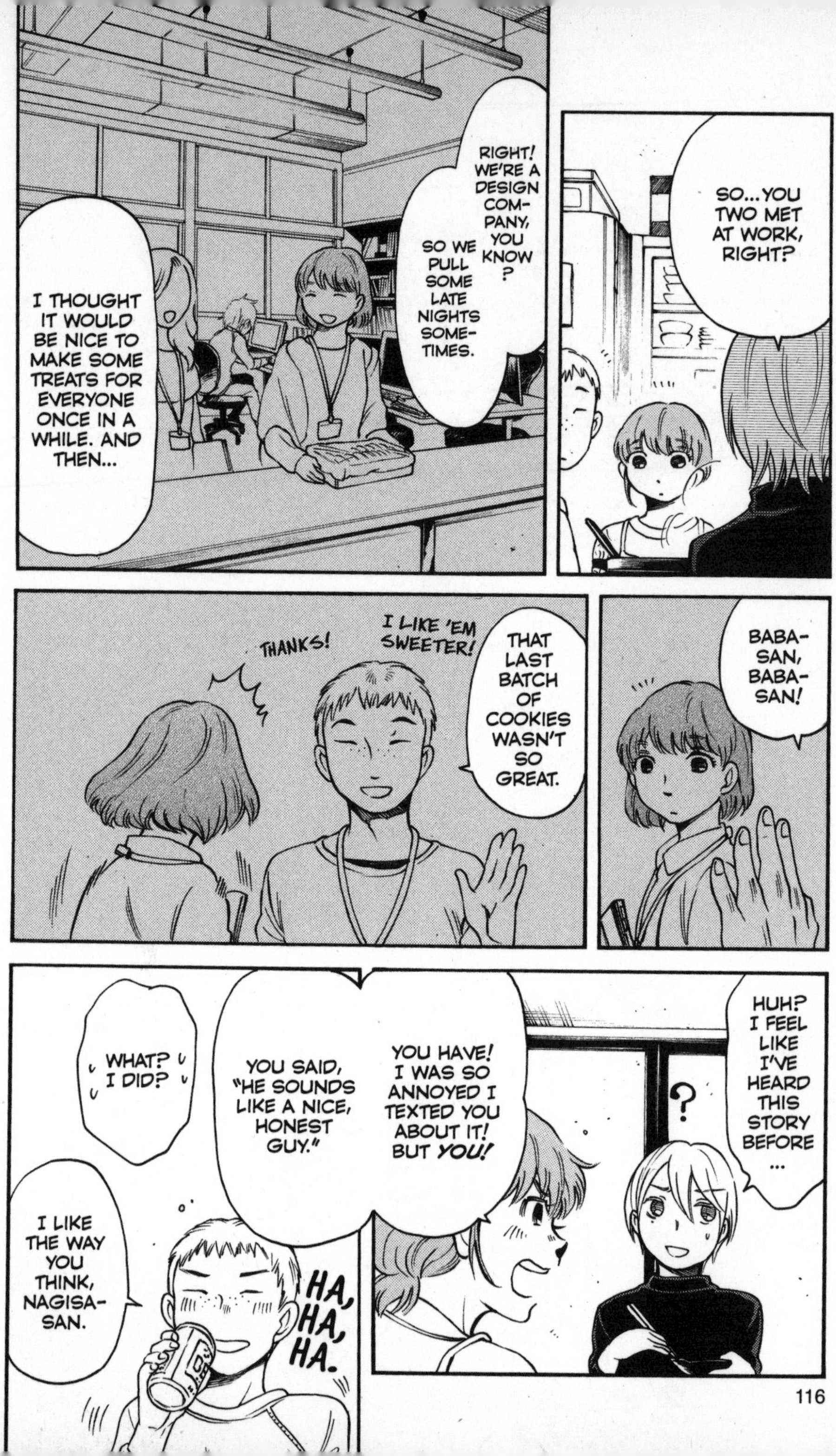
SO...YOU TWO MET AT WORK, RIGHT?
RIGHT! WE'RE A DESIGN COMPANY, YOU KNOW?
SO WE PULL SOME LATE NIGHTS SOMETIMES.
I THOUGHT IT WOULD BE NICE TO MAKE SOME TREATS FOR EVERYONE ONCE IN A WHILE. AND THEN...
BABA-SAN, BABA-SAN!
THAT LAST BATCH OF COOKIES WASN'T SO GREAT.
I LIKE 'EM SWEETER!
THANKS!
HUH? I FEEL LIKE I'VE HEARD THIS STORY BEFORE...
?
YOU HAVE! I WAS SO ANNOYED I TEXTED YOU ABOUT IT! BUT YOU!
YOU SAID, "HE SOUNDS LIKE A NICE, HONEST GUY."
WHAT? I DID?
I LIKE THE WAY YOU THINK, NAGISA-SAN.
HA, HA, HA.

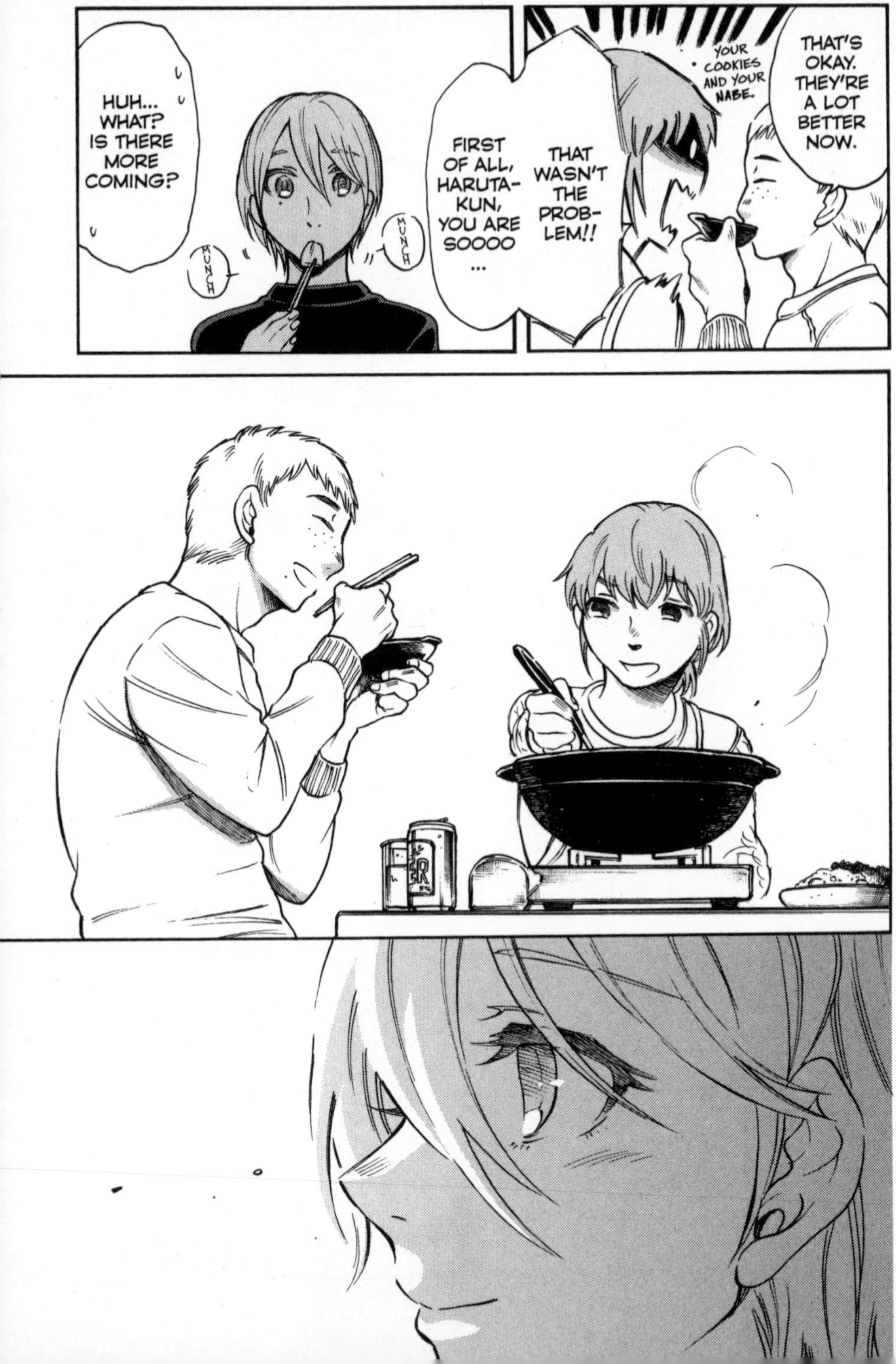
THAT'S OKAY. THEY'RE A LOT BETTER NOW.
YOUR COOKIES AND YOUR NABE.
THAT WASN'T THE PROB-LEM!!
FIRST OF ALL, HARUTA-KUN, YOU ARE SOOOO ...
MUNCH
MUNCH
HUH... WHAT? IS THERE MORE COMING?

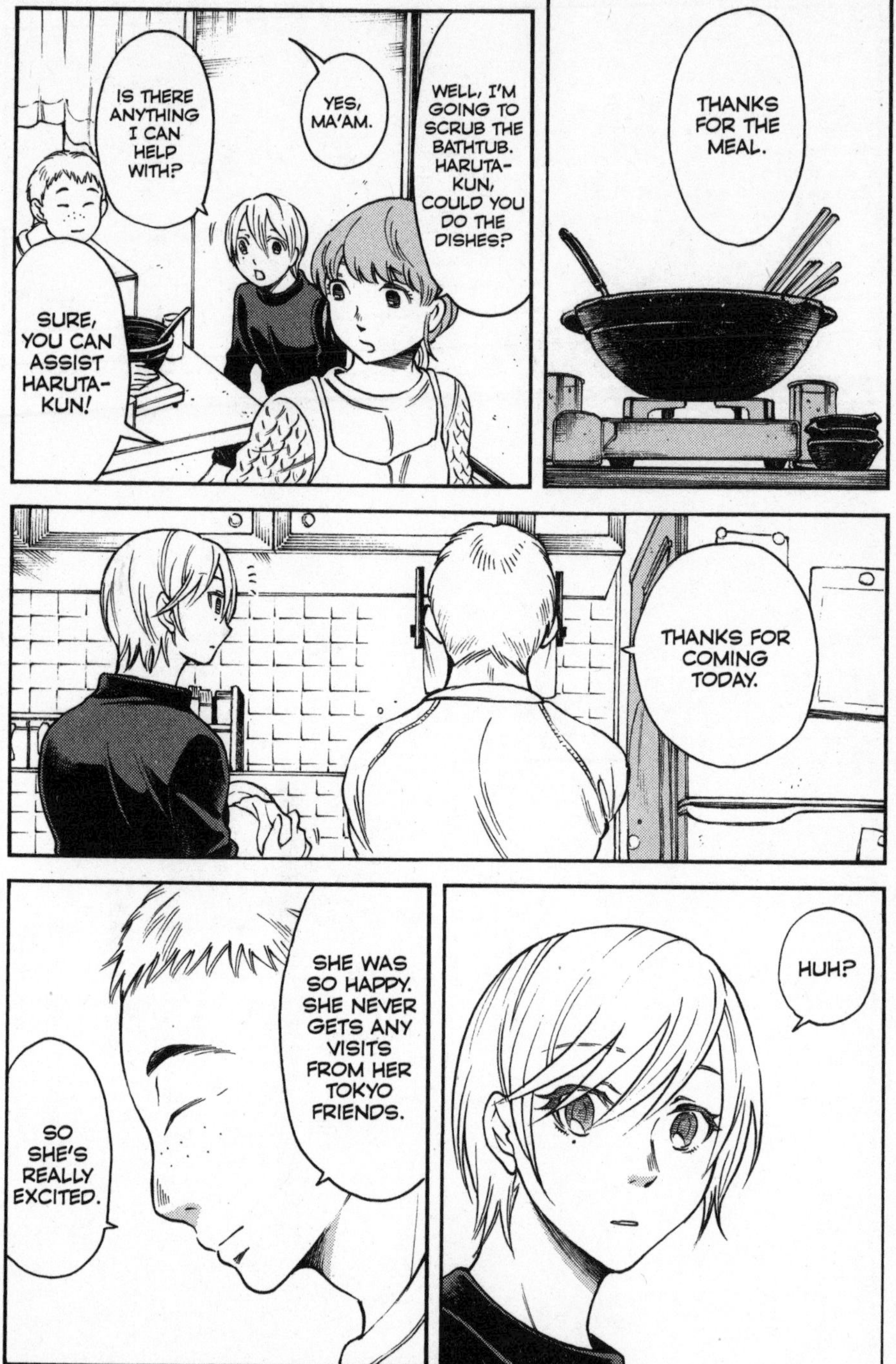
THANKS FOR THE MEAL.
WELL, I'M GOING TO SCRUB THE BATHTUB. HARUTA-KUN, COULD YOU DO THE DISHES?
YES, MA'AM.
IS THERE ANYTHING I CAN HELP WITH?
SURE, YOU CAN ASSIST HARUTA-KUN!
THANKS FOR COMING TODAY.
HUH?
SHE WAS SO HAPPY. SHE NEVER GETS ANY VISITS FROM HER TOKYO FRIENDS.
SO SHE'S REALLY EXCITED.

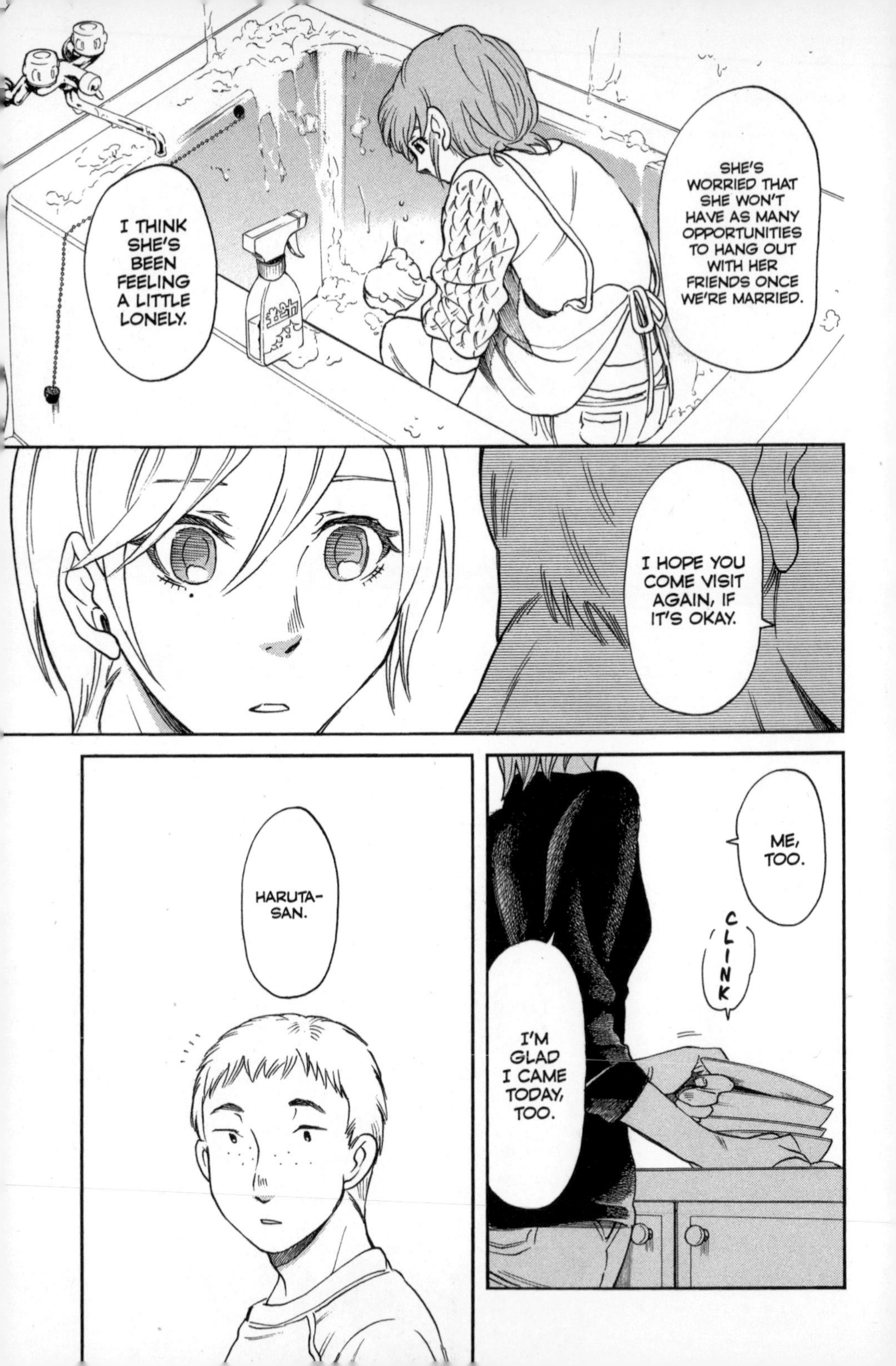
SHE'S WORRIED THAT SHE WON'T HAVE AS MANY OPPORTUNITIES TO HANG OUT WITH HER FRIENDS ONCE WE'RE MARRIED.
I THINK SHE'S BEEN FEELING A LITTLE LONELY.
I HOPE YOU COME VISIT AGAIN, IF IT'S OKAY.
ME, TOO.
CLINK
I'M GLAD I CAME TODAY, TOO.
HARUTA-SAN.

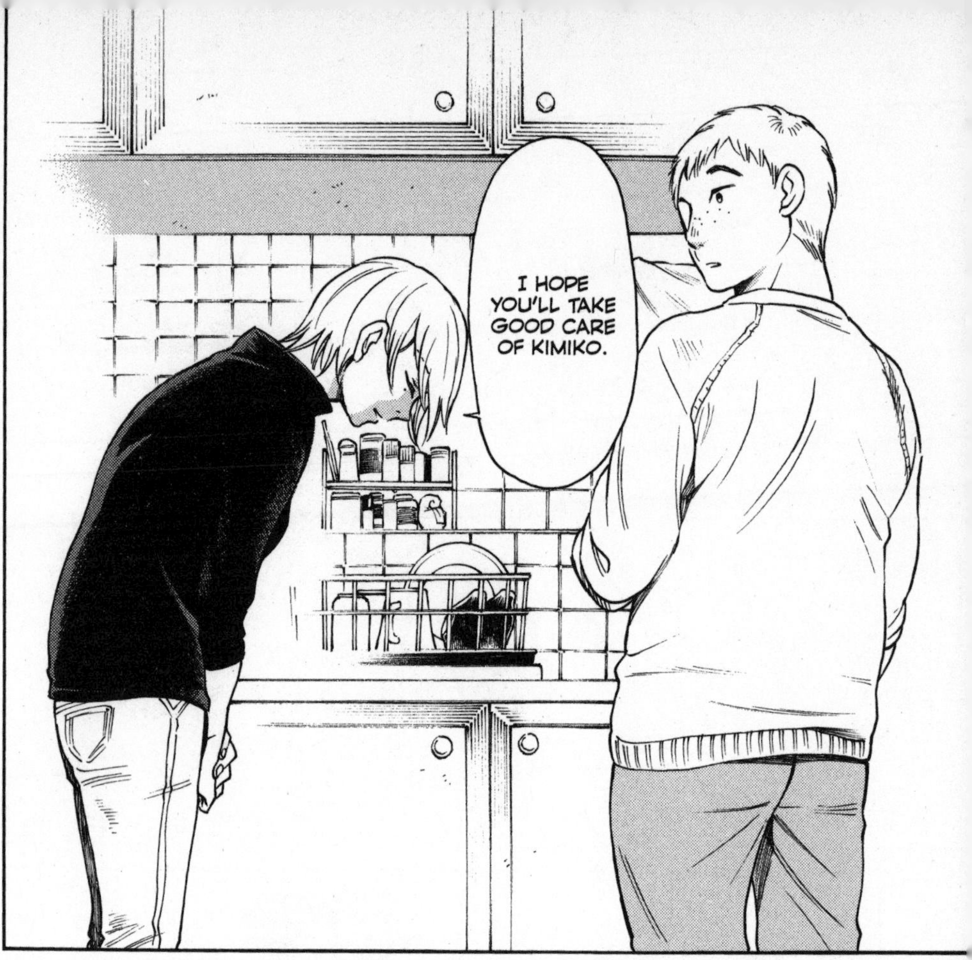
I HOPE YOU'LL TAKE GOOD CARE OF KIMIKO.
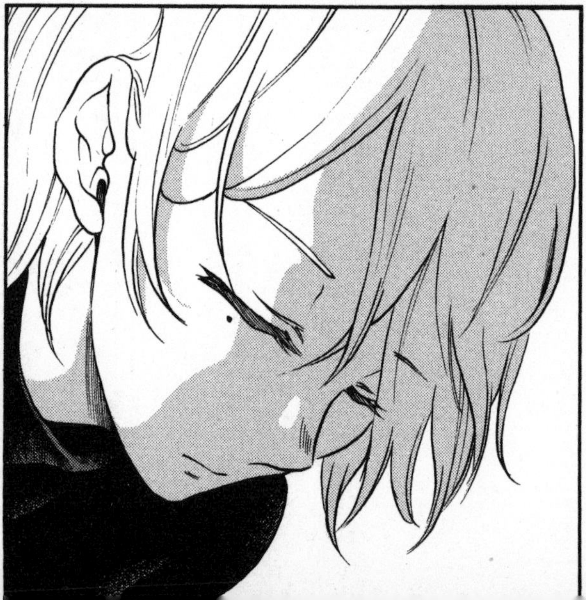
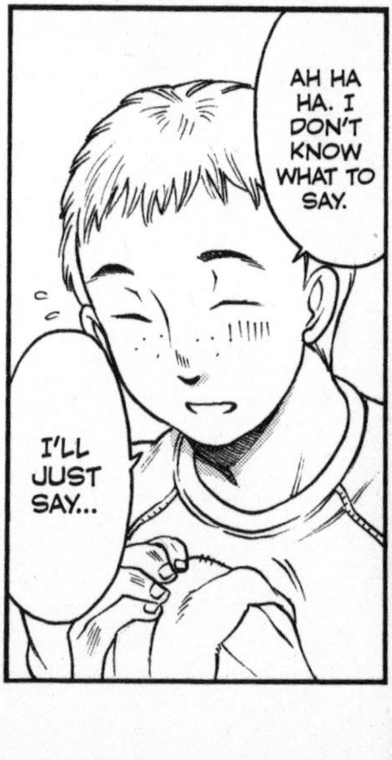
AH HA HA. I DON'T KNOW WHAT TO SAY.
I'LL JUST SAY...

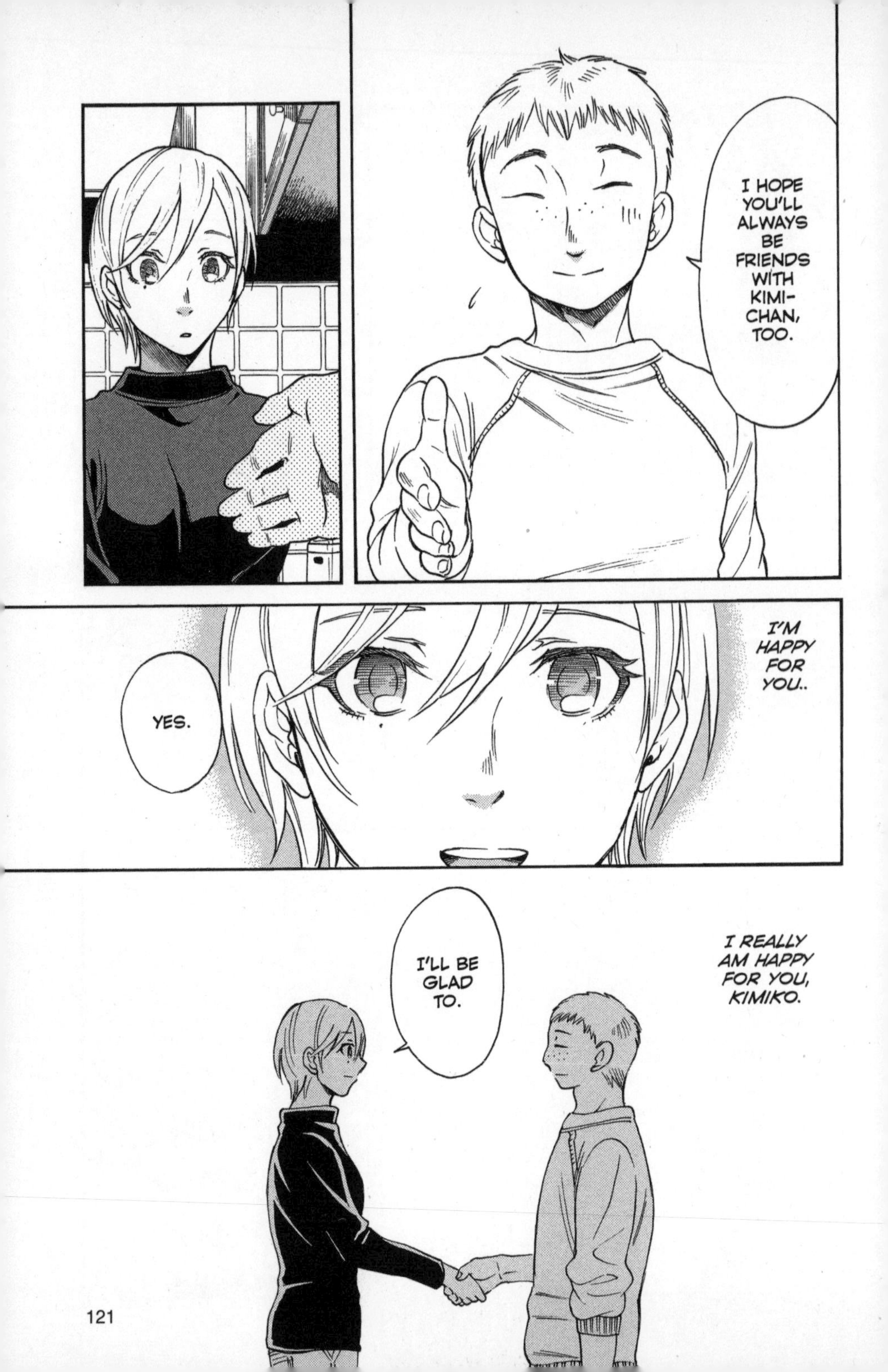
I HOPE YOU'LL ALWAYS BE FRIENDS WITH KIMI-CHAN, TOO.
I'M HAPPY FOR YOU..
YES.
I REALLY AM HAPPY FOR YOU, KIMIKO.
I'LL BE GLAD TO.

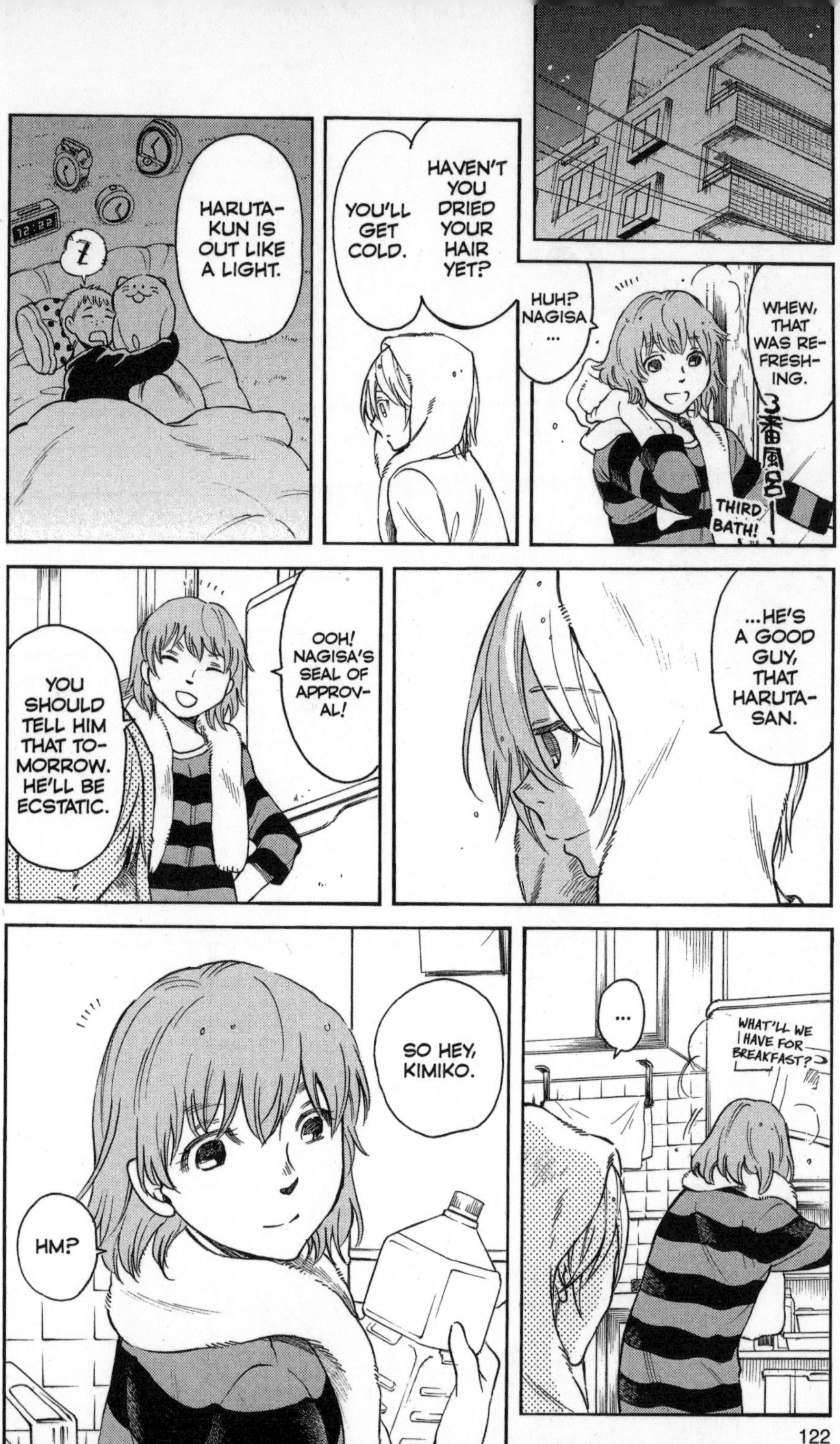
WHEW, THAT WAS RE-FRESH-ING.
3番風呂
THIRD BATH!
HUH? NAGISA ...
HAVEN'T YOU DRIED YOUR HAIR YET?
YOU'LL GET COLD.
HARUTA-KUN IS OUT LIKE A LIGHT.
Z
...HE'S A GOOD GUY, THAT HARUTA-SAN.
OOH! NAGISA'S SEAL OF APPROV-AL!
YOU SHOULD TELL HIM THAT TO-MORROW. HE'LL BE ECSTATIC.
WHAT'LL WE HAVE FOR BREAKFAST?
...
SO HEY, KIMIKO.
HM?

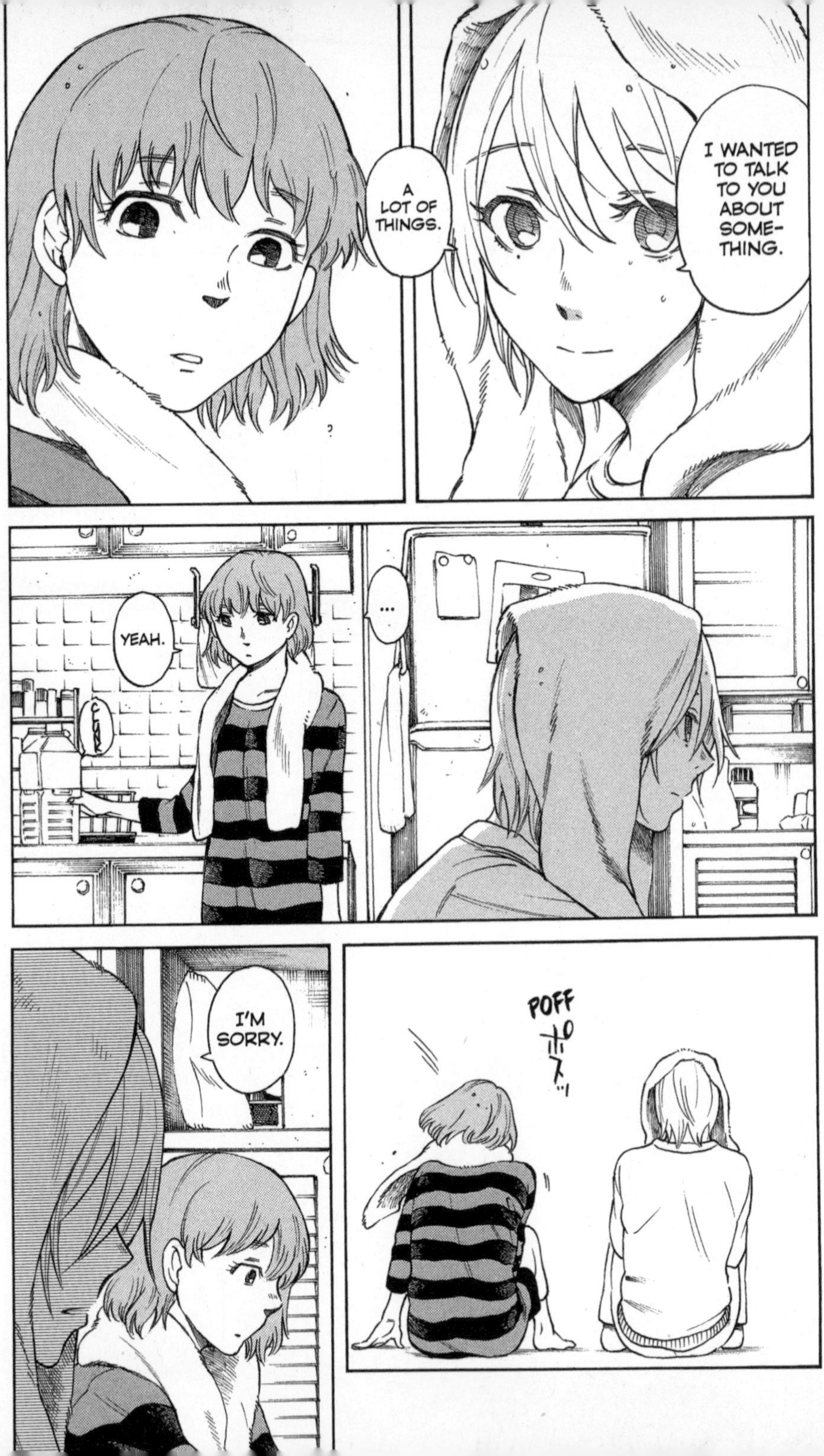
I WANTED TO TALK TO YOU ABOUT SOME-THING.
A LOT OF THINGS.
...
YEAH.
CLINK
POFF
I'M SORRY.

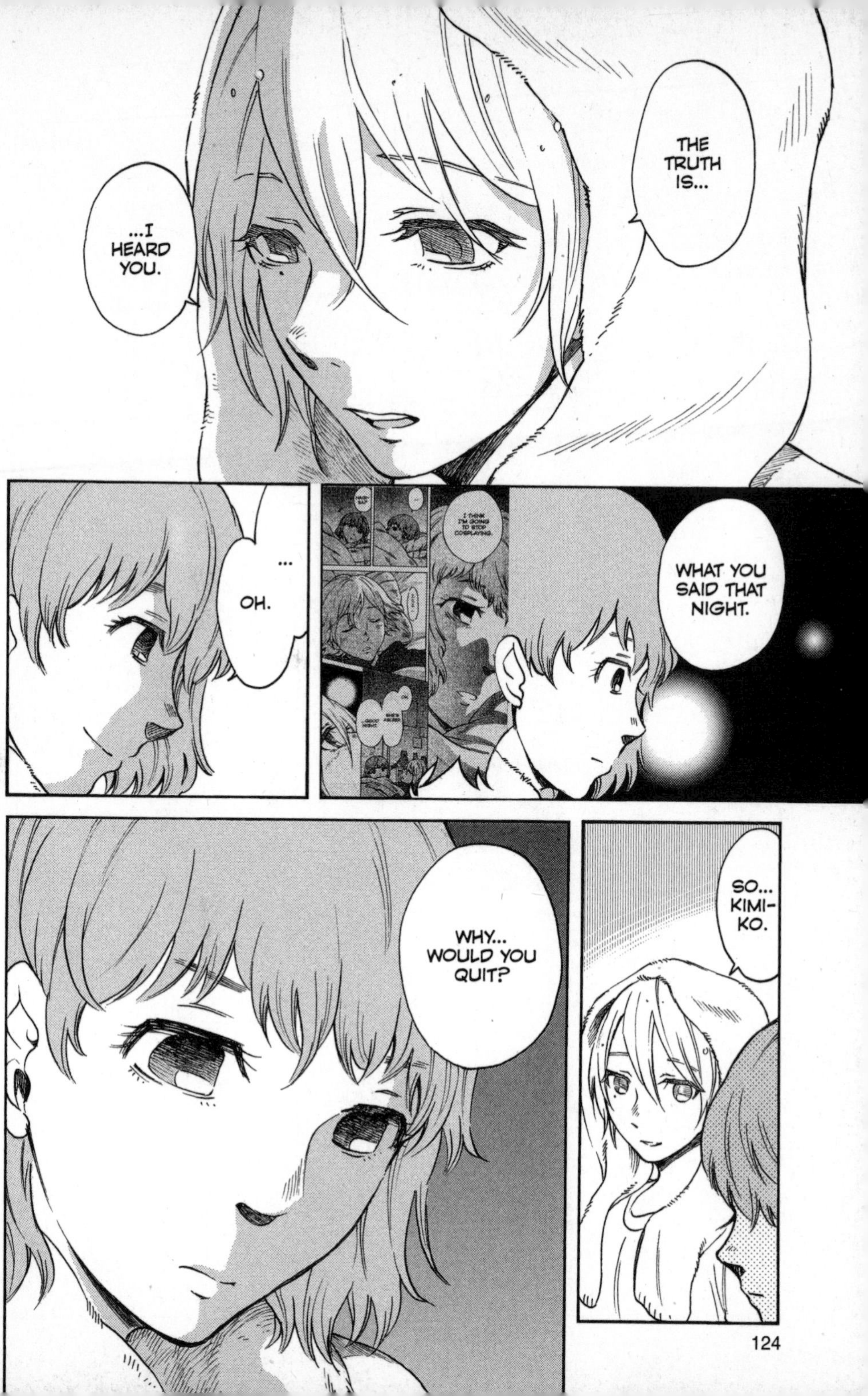
THE TRUTH IS...
...I HEARD YOU.
WHAT YOU SAID THAT NIGHT.
I THINK I'M GOING TO STOP COSPLAYING.
...
OH.
SO... KIMI-KO.
WHY... WOULD YOU QUIT?

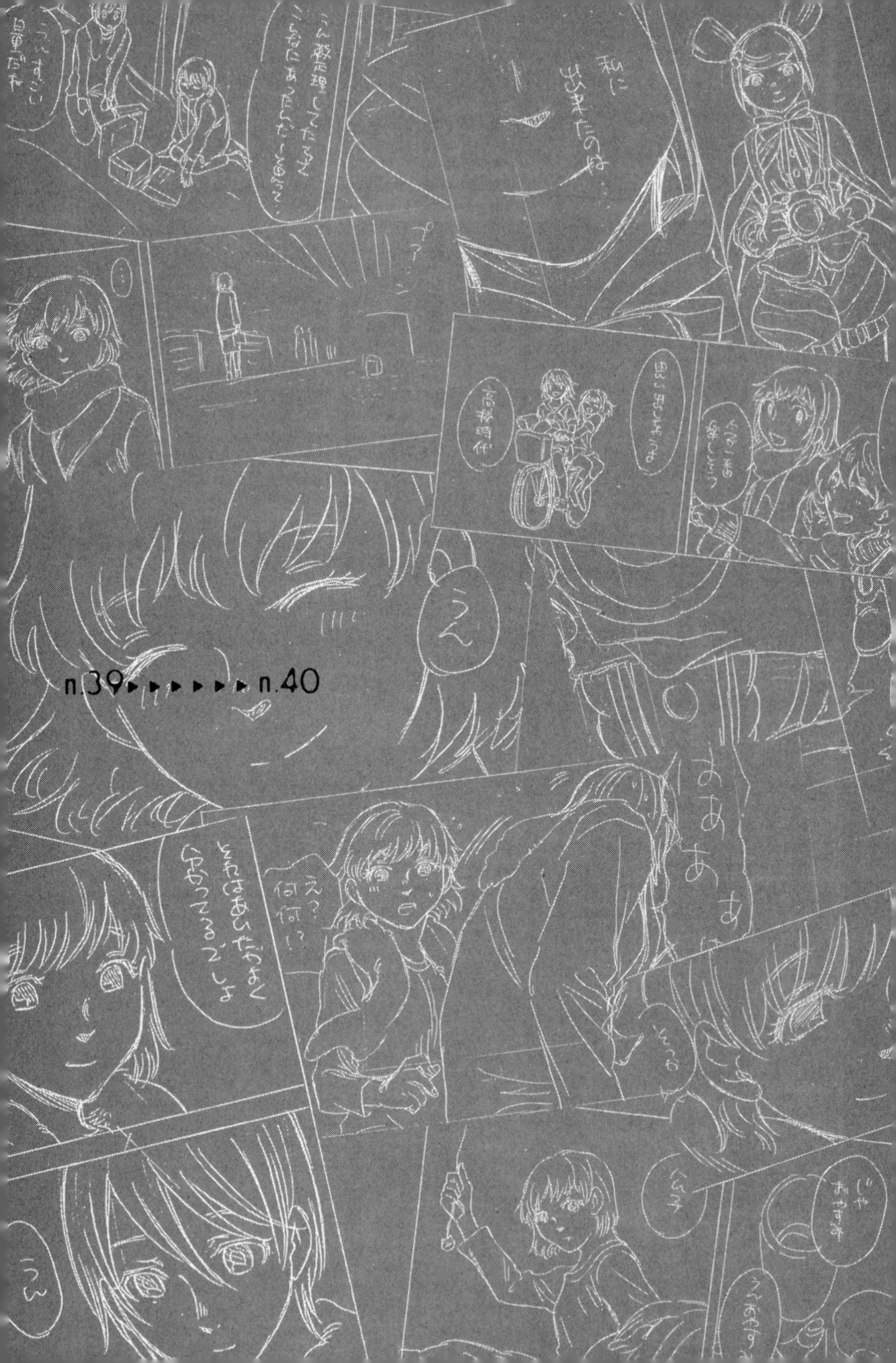
私に出来たのは…
うへすごい量だね
高校時代
え
え？何何っ
それはあんたがよく分かってるでしょ
じゃおやすみ
うんおやす
うん
n.39▸▸▸▸▸▸▸n.40

- MIYAGI MIYA-GIFTS 2 -

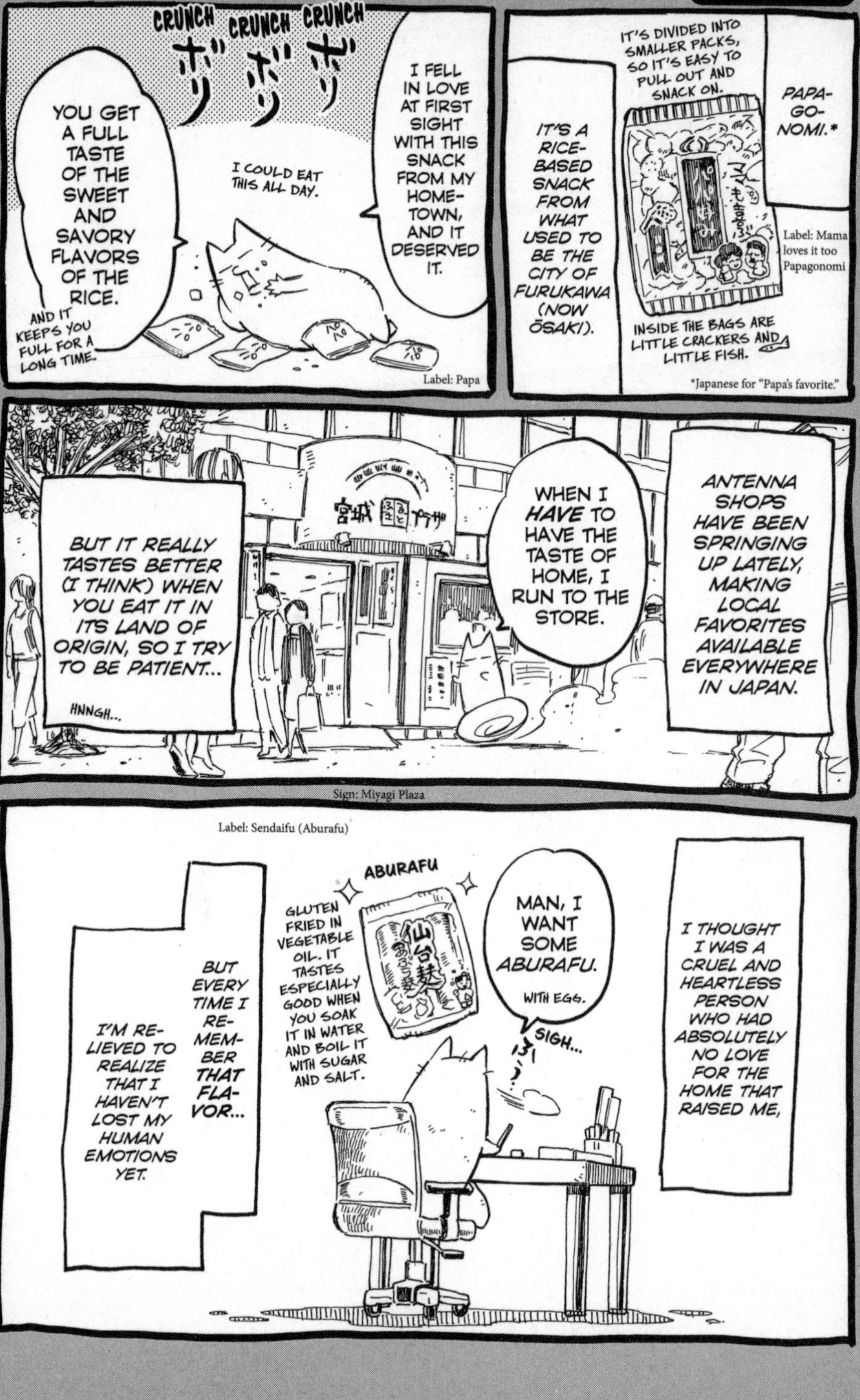
PAPA-GO-NOMI.*
IT'S DIVIDED INTO SMALLER PACKS, SO IT'S EASY TO PULL OUT AND SNACK ON.
IT'S A RICE-BASED SNACK FROM WHAT USED TO BE THE CITY OF FURUKAWA (NOW ŌSAKI).
Label: Mama loves it too Papagonomi
INSIDE THE BAGS ARE LITTLE CRACKERS AND LITTLE FISH.
*Japanese for "Papa's favorite."
CRUNCH CRUNCH CRUNCH
ボリ ボリ ボリ
I FELL IN LOVE AT FIRST SIGHT WITH THIS SNACK FROM MY HOMETOWN, AND IT DESERVED IT.
I COULD EAT THIS ALL DAY.
YOU GET A FULL TASTE OF THE SWEET AND SAVORY FLAVORS OF THE RICE.
AND IT KEEPS YOU FULL FOR A LONG TIME.
Label: Papa
ANTENNA SHOPS HAVE BEEN SPRINGING UP LATELY, MAKING LOCAL FAVORITES AVAILABLE EVERYWHERE IN JAPAN.
WHEN I HAVE TO HAVE THE TASTE OF HOME, I RUN TO THE STORE.
宮城 ふるさと プラザ
BUT IT REALLY TASTES BETTER (I THINK) WHEN YOU EAT IT IN ITS LAND OF ORIGIN, SO I TRY TO BE PATIENT...
HNNGH...
Sign: Miyagi Plaza
Label: Sendaifu (Aburafu)
I THOUGHT I WAS A CRUEL AND HEARTLESS PERSON WHO HAD ABSOLUTELY NO LOVE FOR THE HOME THAT RAISED ME,
MAN, I WANT SOME ABURAFU.
WITH EGG.
SIGH...
ABURAFU
GLUTEN FRIED IN VEGETABLE OIL. IT TASTES ESPECIALLY GOOD WHEN YOU SOAK IT IN WATER AND BOIL IT WITH SUGAR AND SALT.
BUT EVERY TIME I REMEMBER THAT FLAVOR...
I'M RELIEVED TO REALIZE THAT I HAVEN'T LOST MY HUMAN EMOTIONS YET.

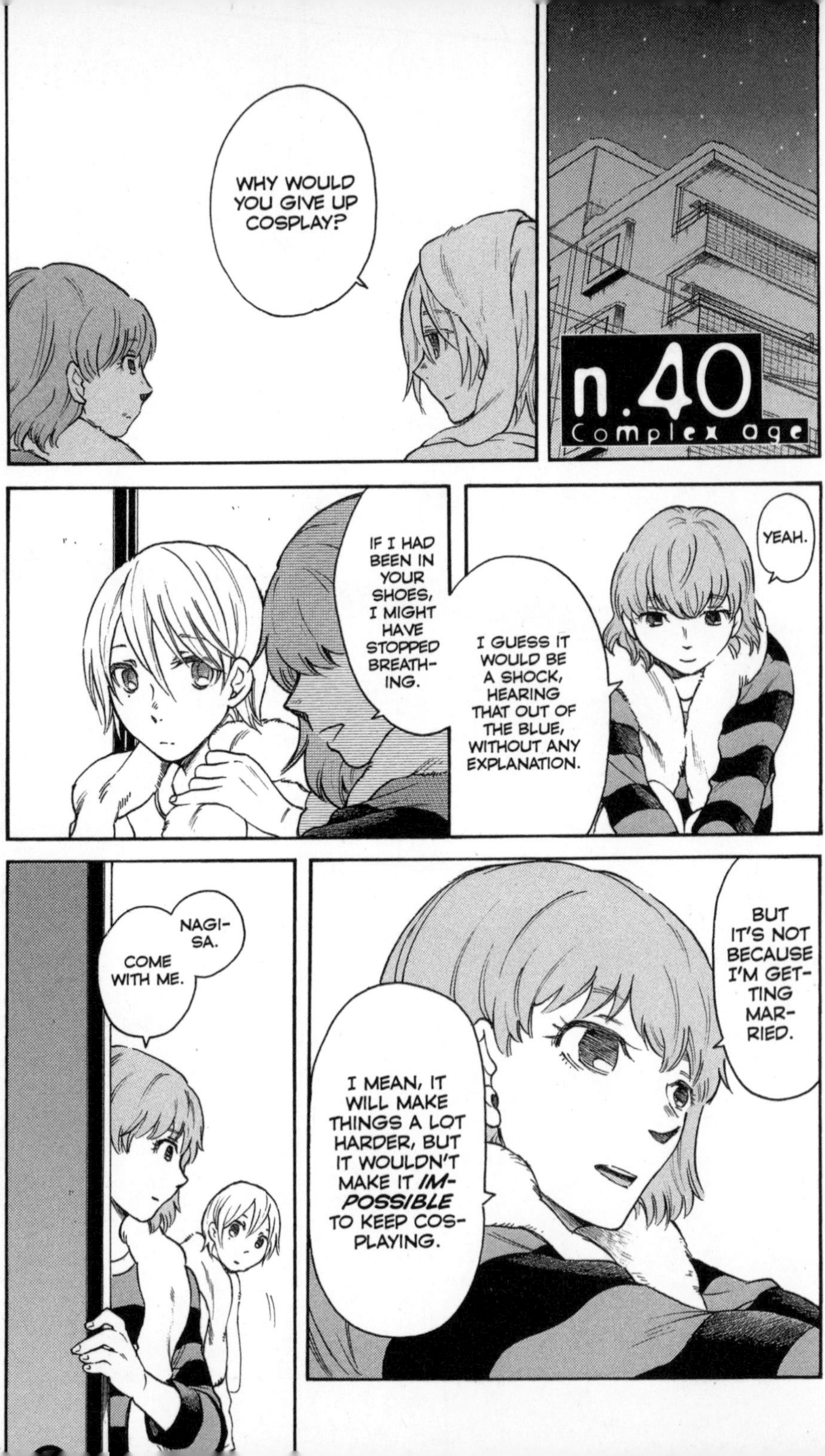
n.40
Complex age
WHY WOULD YOU GIVE UP COSPLAY?
YEAH.
I GUESS IT WOULD BE A SHOCK, HEARING THAT OUT OF THE BLUE, WITHOUT ANY EXPLANATION.
IF I HAD BEEN IN YOUR SHOES, I MIGHT HAVE STOPPED BREATH-ING.
BUT IT'S NOT BECAUSE I'M GET-TING MAR-RIED.
I MEAN, IT WILL MAKE THINGS A LOT HARDER, BUT IT WOULDN'T MAKE IT *IM-POSSIBLE* TO KEEP COS-PLAYING.
NAGI-SA.
COME WITH ME.

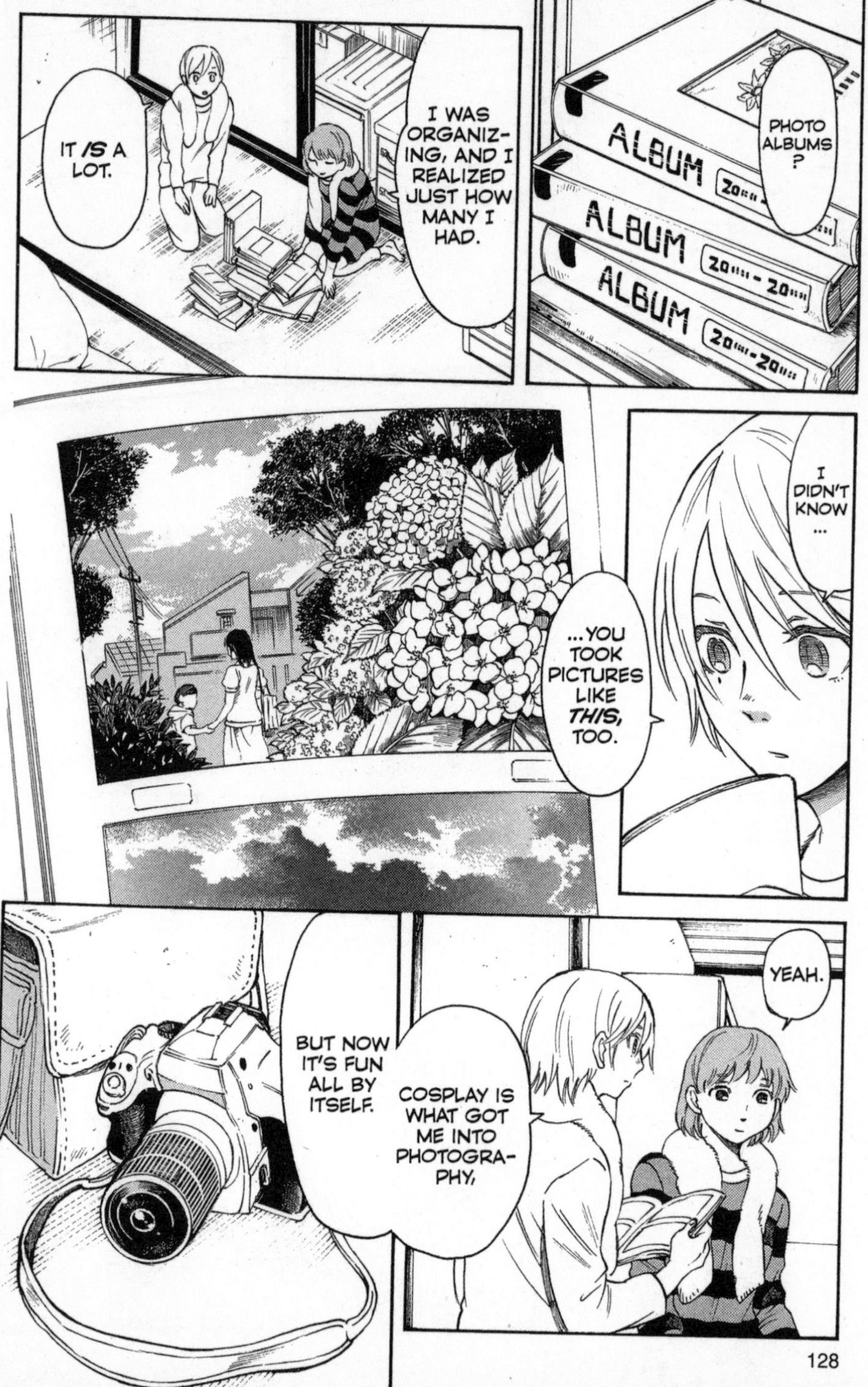
PHOTO ALBUMS ?
ALBUM
ALBUM
ALBUM
I WAS ORGANIZ-ING, AND I REALIZED JUST HOW MANY I HAD.
IT IS A LOT.
I DIDN'T KNOW ...
...YOU TOOK PICTURES LIKE *THIS,* TOO.
YEAH.
COSPLAY IS WHAT GOT ME INTO PHOTOGRA-PHY,
BUT NOW IT'S FUN ALL BY ITSELF.

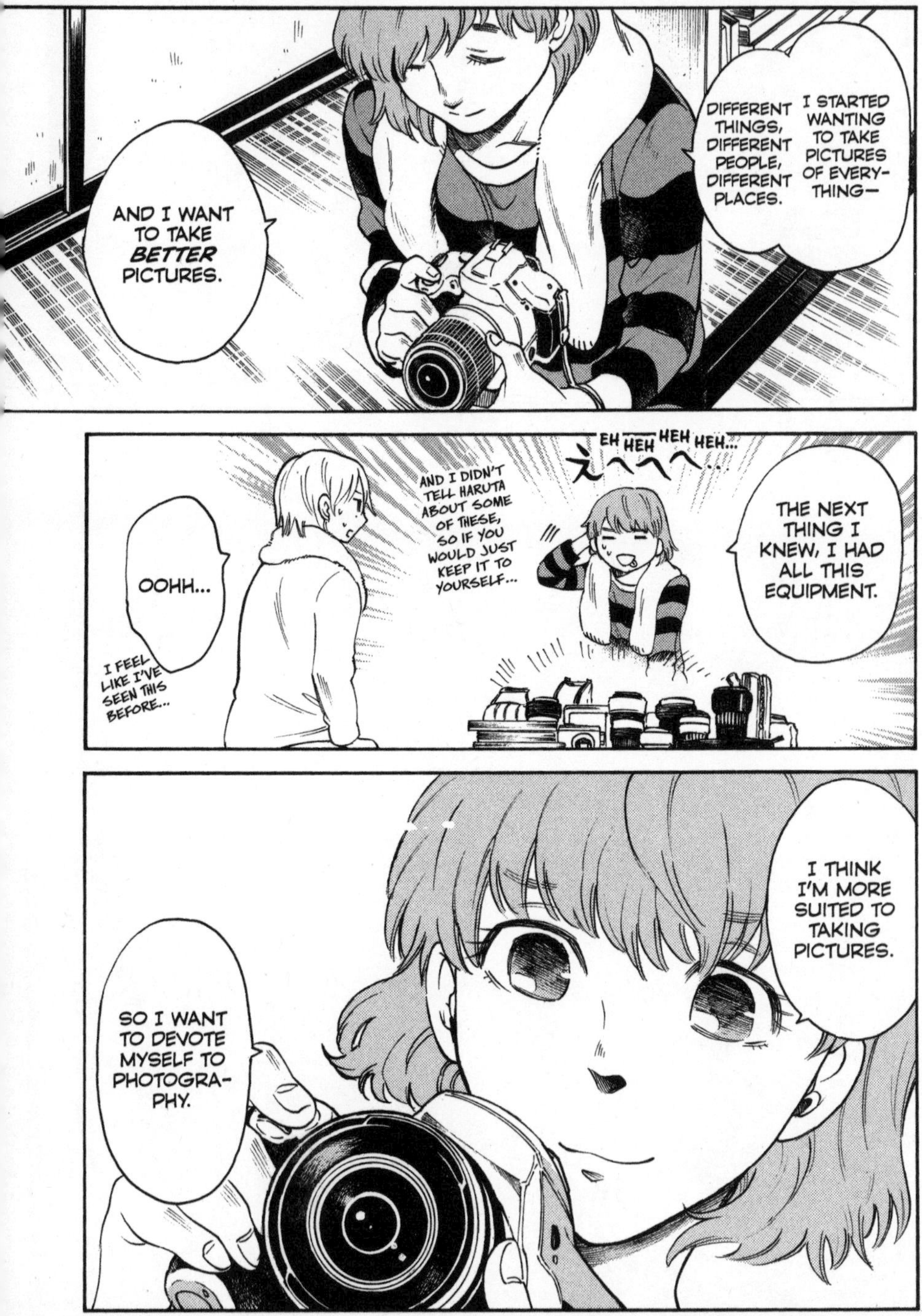
I STARTED WANTING TO TAKE PICTURES OF EVERY-THING—
DIFFERENT THINGS, DIFFERENT PEOPLE, DIFFERENT PLACES.
AND I WANT TO TAKE **BETTER** PICTURES.
EH HEH HEH HEH...
THE NEXT THING I KNEW, I HAD ALL THIS EQUIPMENT.
AND I DIDN'T TELL HARUTA ABOUT SOME OF THESE, SO IF YOU WOULD JUST KEEP IT TO YOURSELF...
OOHH...
I FEEL LIKE I'VE SEEN THIS BEFORE...
I THINK I'M MORE SUITED TO TAKING PICTURES.
SO I WANT TO DEVOTE MYSELF TO PHOTOGRA-PHY.

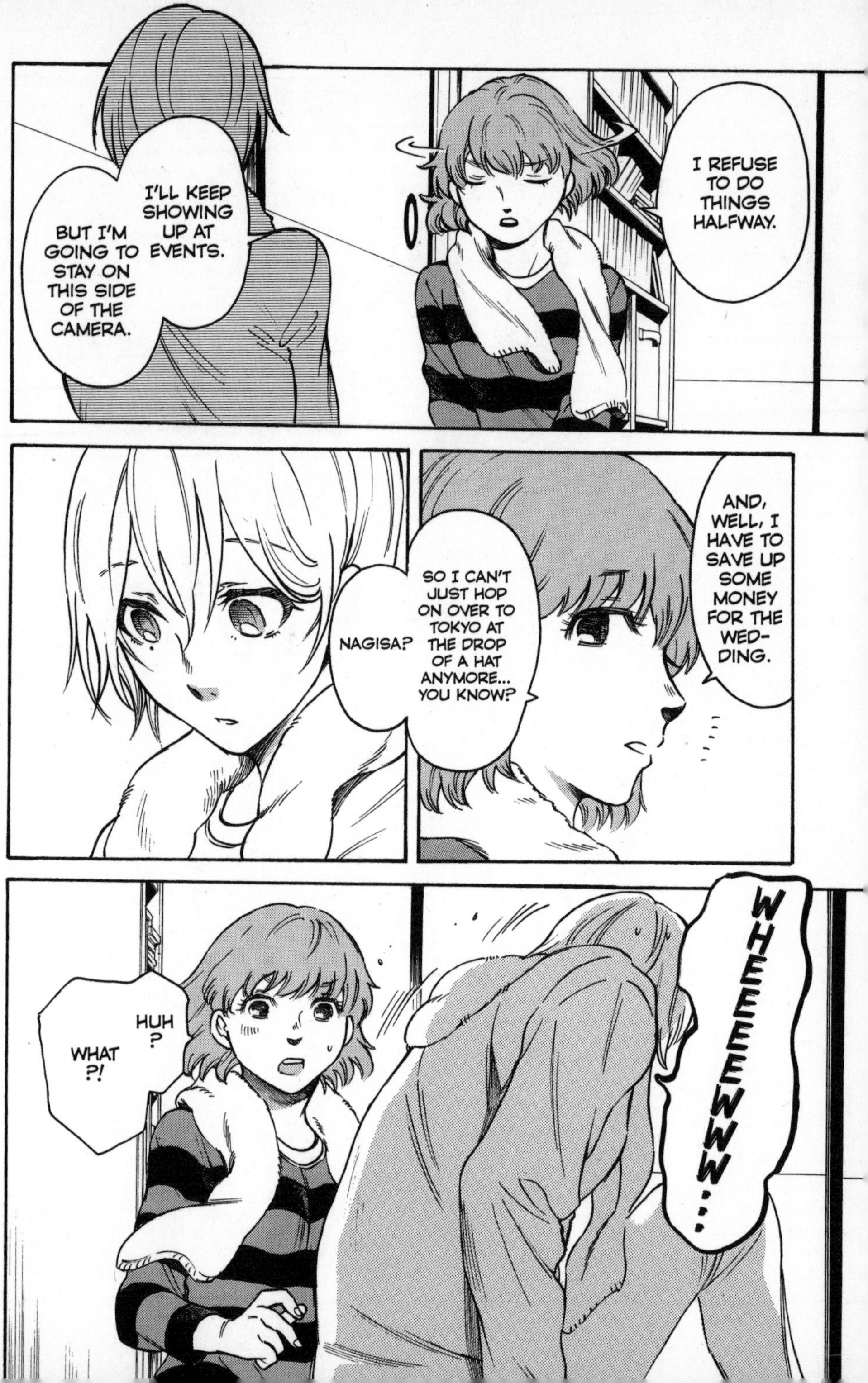
I REFUSE TO DO THINGS HALFWAY.
I'LL KEEP SHOWING UP AT EVENTS.
BUT I'M GOING TO STAY ON THIS SIDE OF THE CAMERA.
AND, WELL, I HAVE TO SAVE UP SOME MONEY FOR THE WED-DING.
SO I CAN'T JUST HOP ON OVER TO TOKYO AT THE DROP OF A HAT ANYMORE... YOU KNOW?
...
NAGISA?
WHEEEEEWWW...
HUH?
WHAT?!

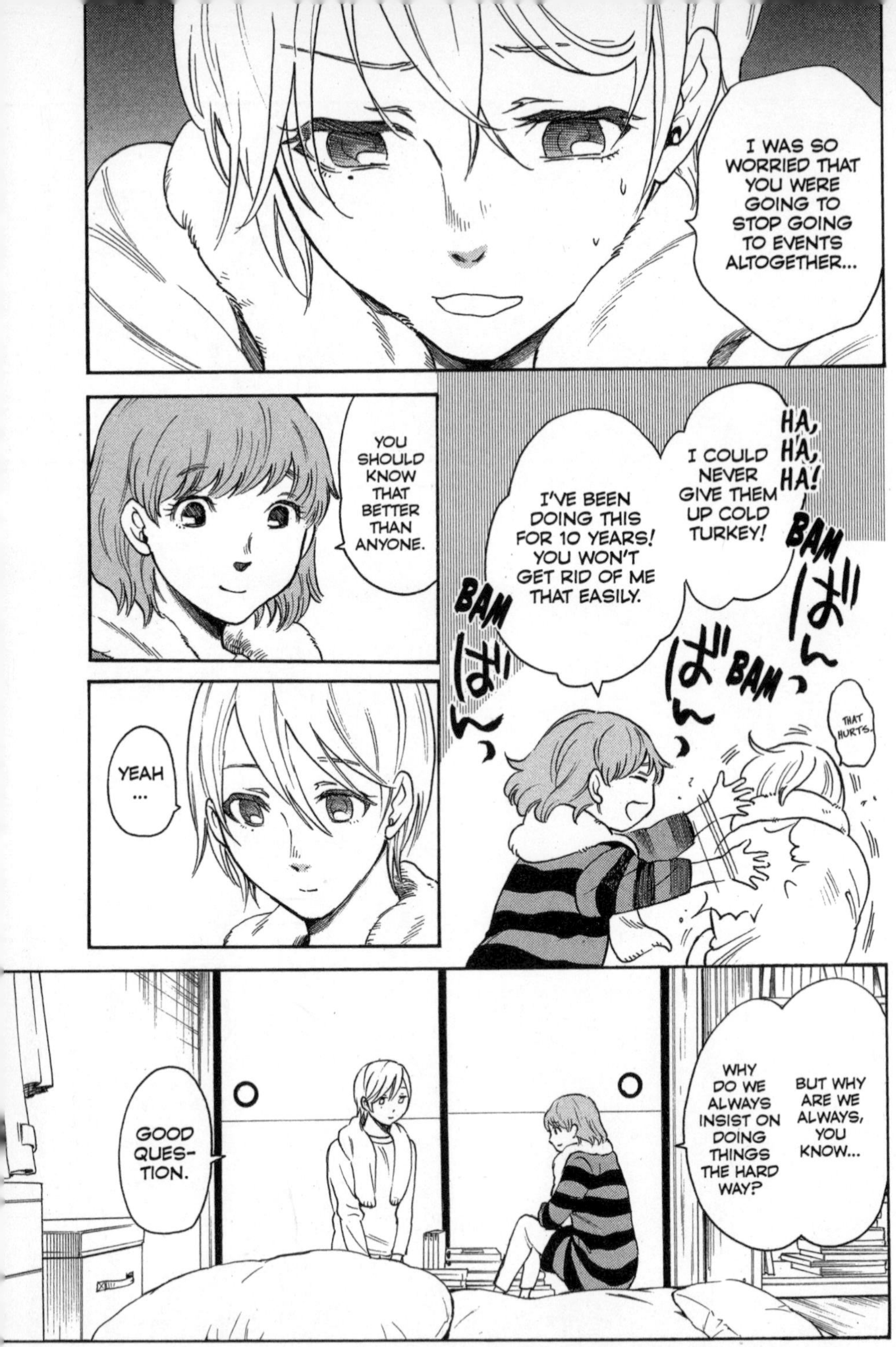
I WAS SO WORRIED THAT YOU WERE GOING TO STOP GOING TO EVENTS ALTOGETHER...
HA, HA, HA!
I COULD NEVER GIVE THEM UP COLD TURKEY!
I'VE BEEN DOING THIS FOR 10 YEARS! YOU WON'T GET RID OF ME THAT EASILY.
BAM ばん
BAM ばん
BAM ばん
THAT HURTS.
YOU SHOULD KNOW THAT BETTER THAN ANYONE.
YEAH ...
BUT WHY ARE WE ALWAYS, YOU KNOW...
WHY DO WE ALWAYS INSIST ON DOING THINGS THE HARD WAY?
GOOD QUES-TION.

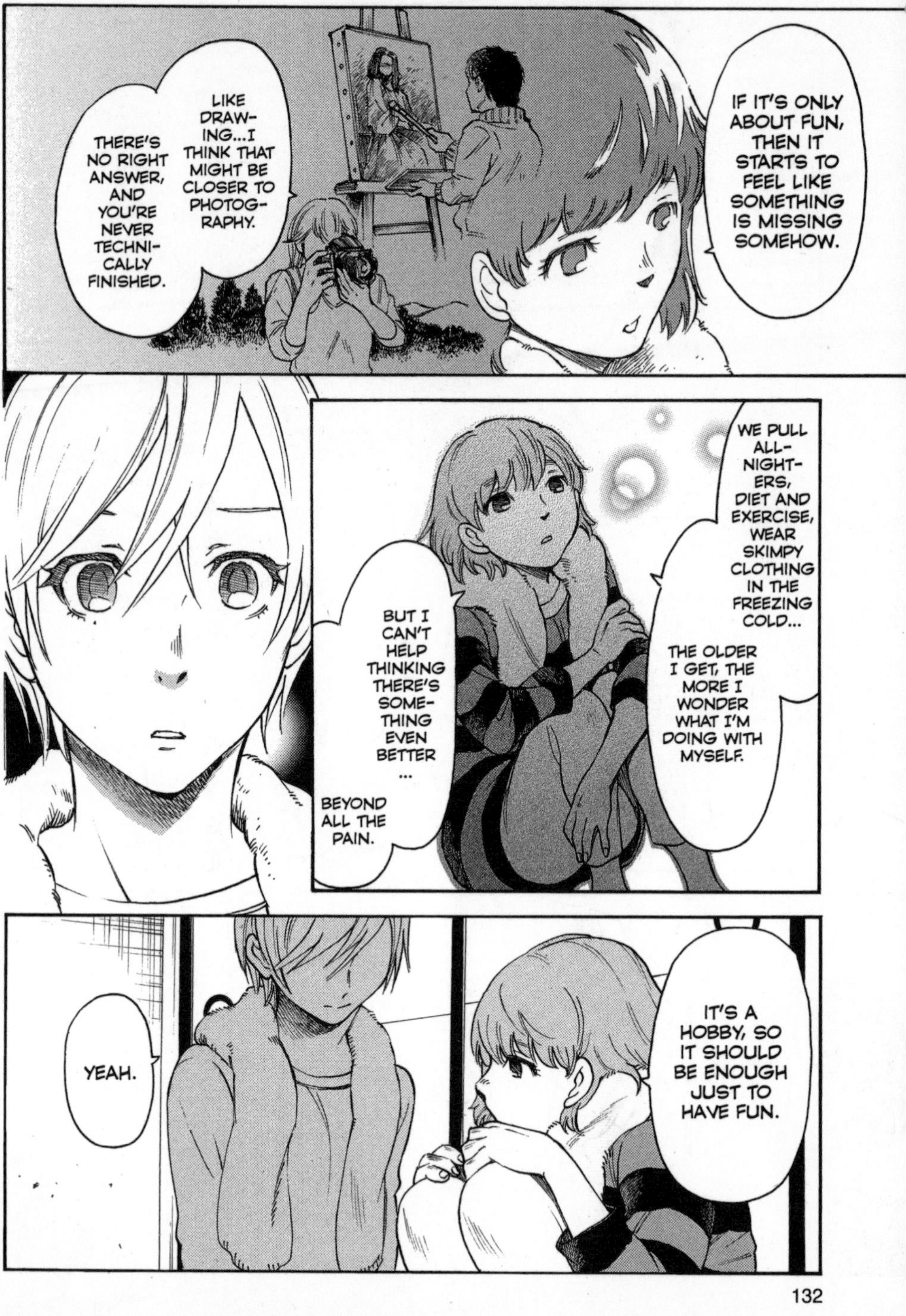
IF IT'S ONLY ABOUT FUN, THEN IT STARTS TO FEEL LIKE SOMETHING IS MISSING SOMEHOW.
LIKE DRAWING...I THINK THAT MIGHT BE CLOSER TO PHOTOGRAPHY.
THERE'S NO RIGHT ANSWER, AND YOU'RE NEVER TECHNICALLY FINISHED.
WE PULL ALL-NIGHTERS, DIET AND EXERCISE, WEAR SKIMPY CLOTHING IN THE FREEZING COLD...
THE OLDER I GET, THE MORE I WONDER WHAT I'M DOING WITH MYSELF.
BUT I CAN'T HELP THINKING THERE'S SOMETHING EVEN BETTER ...
BEYOND ALL THE PAIN.
IT'S A HOBBY, SO IT SHOULD BE ENOUGH JUST TO HAVE FUN.
YEAH.

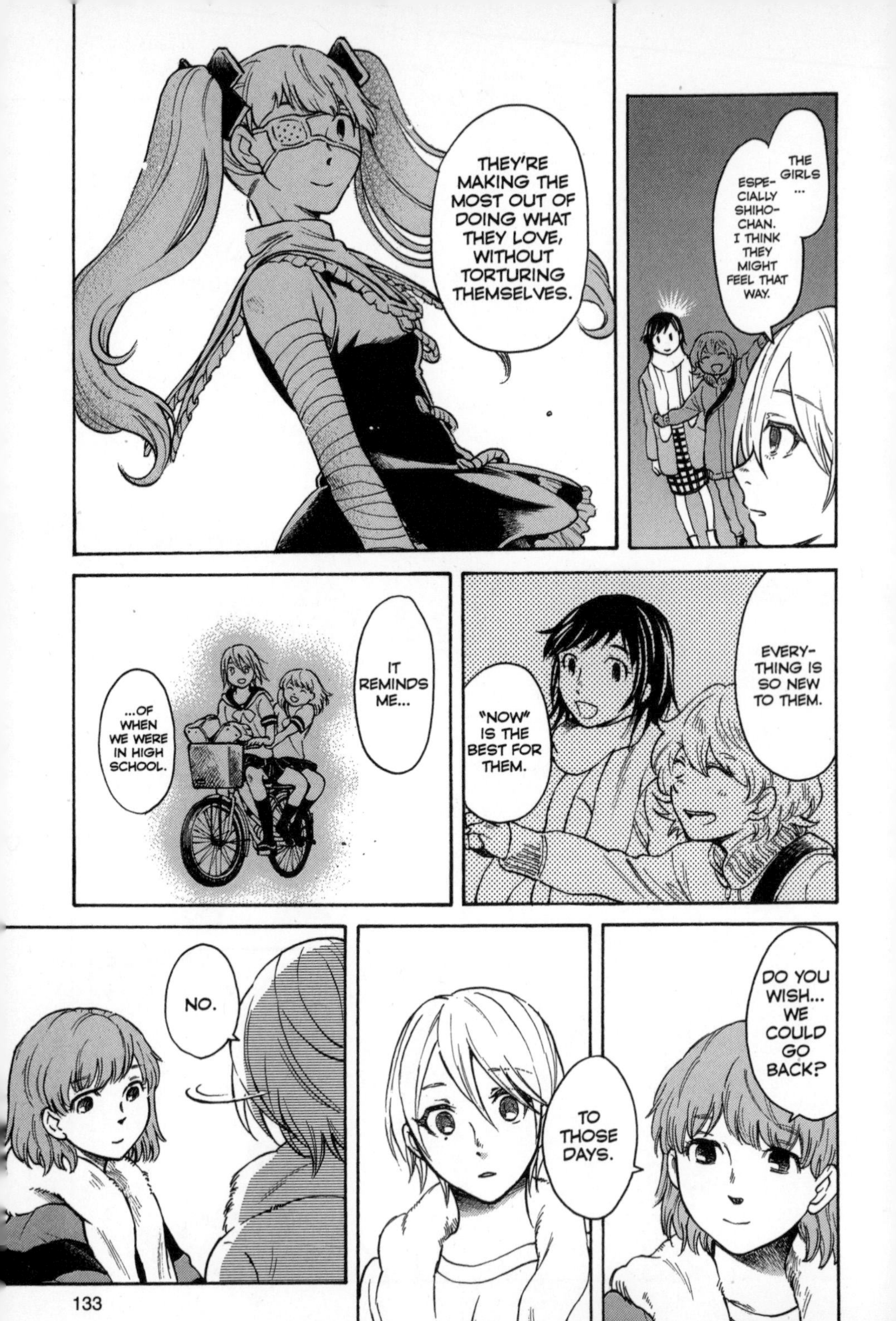
THE GIRLS ...
ESPECIALLY SHIHO-CHAN. I THINK THEY MIGHT FEEL THAT WAY.
THEY'RE MAKING THE MOST OUT OF DOING WHAT THEY LOVE, WITHOUT TORTURING THEMSELVES.
EVERYTHING IS SO NEW TO THEM.
"NOW" IS THE BEST FOR THEM.
IT REMINDS ME...
...OF WHEN WE WERE IN HIGH SCHOOL.
DO YOU WISH... WE COULD GO BACK?
TO THOSE DAYS.
NO.

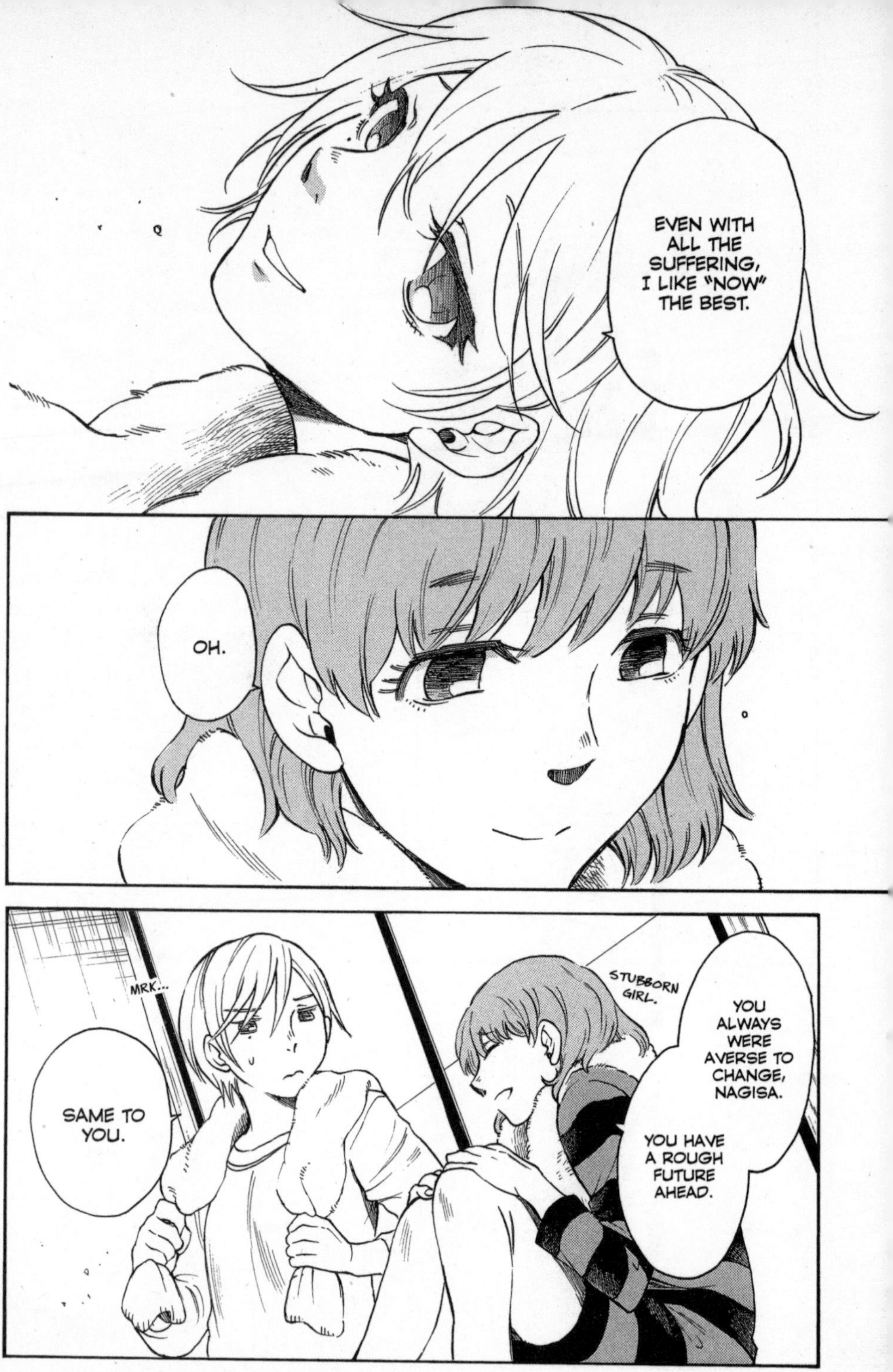
EVEN WITH ALL THE SUFFERING, I LIKE "NOW" THE BEST.
OH.
YOU ALWAYS WERE AVERSE TO CHANGE, NAGISA.
YOU HAVE A ROUGH FUTURE AHEAD.
STUBBORN GIRL.
MRK...
SAME TO YOU.

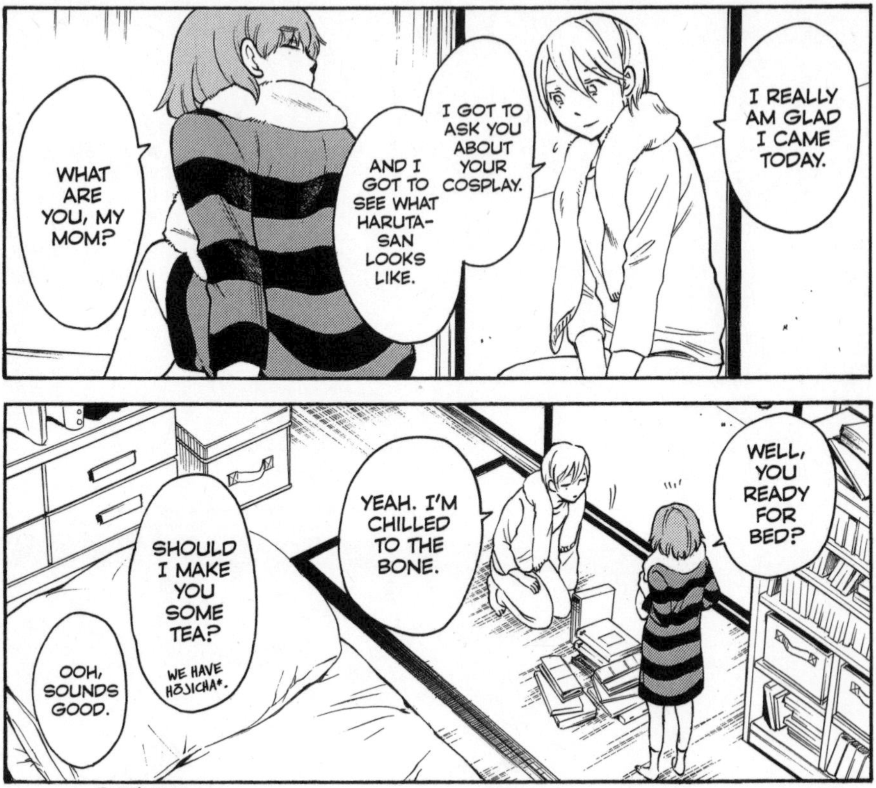
I REALLY AM GLAD I CAME TODAY.
I GOT TO ASK YOU ABOUT YOUR COSPLAY.
AND I GOT TO SEE WHAT HARUTA-SAN LOOKS LIKE.
WHAT ARE YOU, MY MOM?
WELL, YOU READY FOR BED?
YEAH. I'M CHILLED TO THE BONE.
SHOULD I MAKE YOU SOME TEA?
WE HAVE HŌJICHA*.
OOH, SOUNDS GOOD.

*Roasted green tea

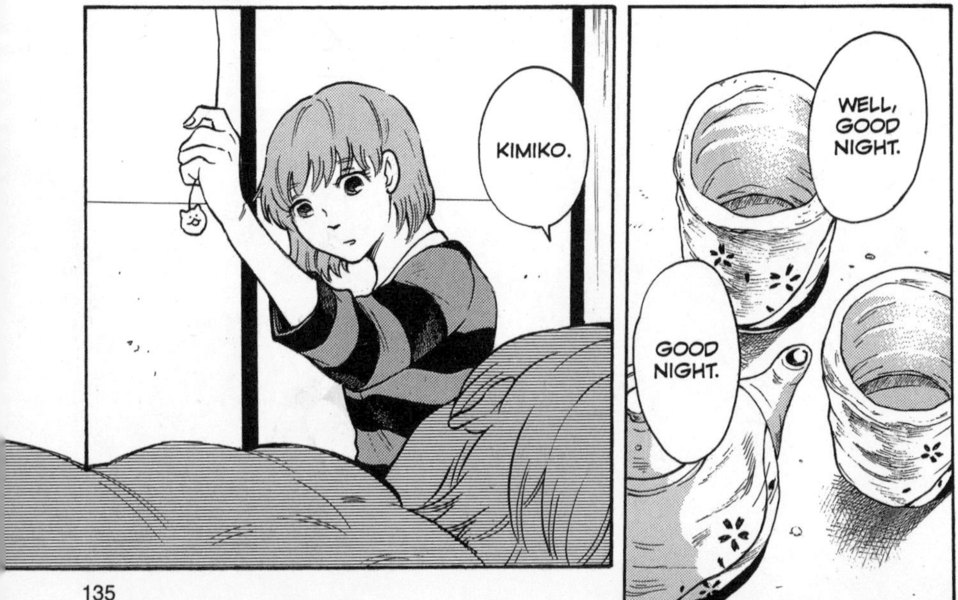
WELL, GOOD NIGHT.
GOOD NIGHT.
KIMIKO.

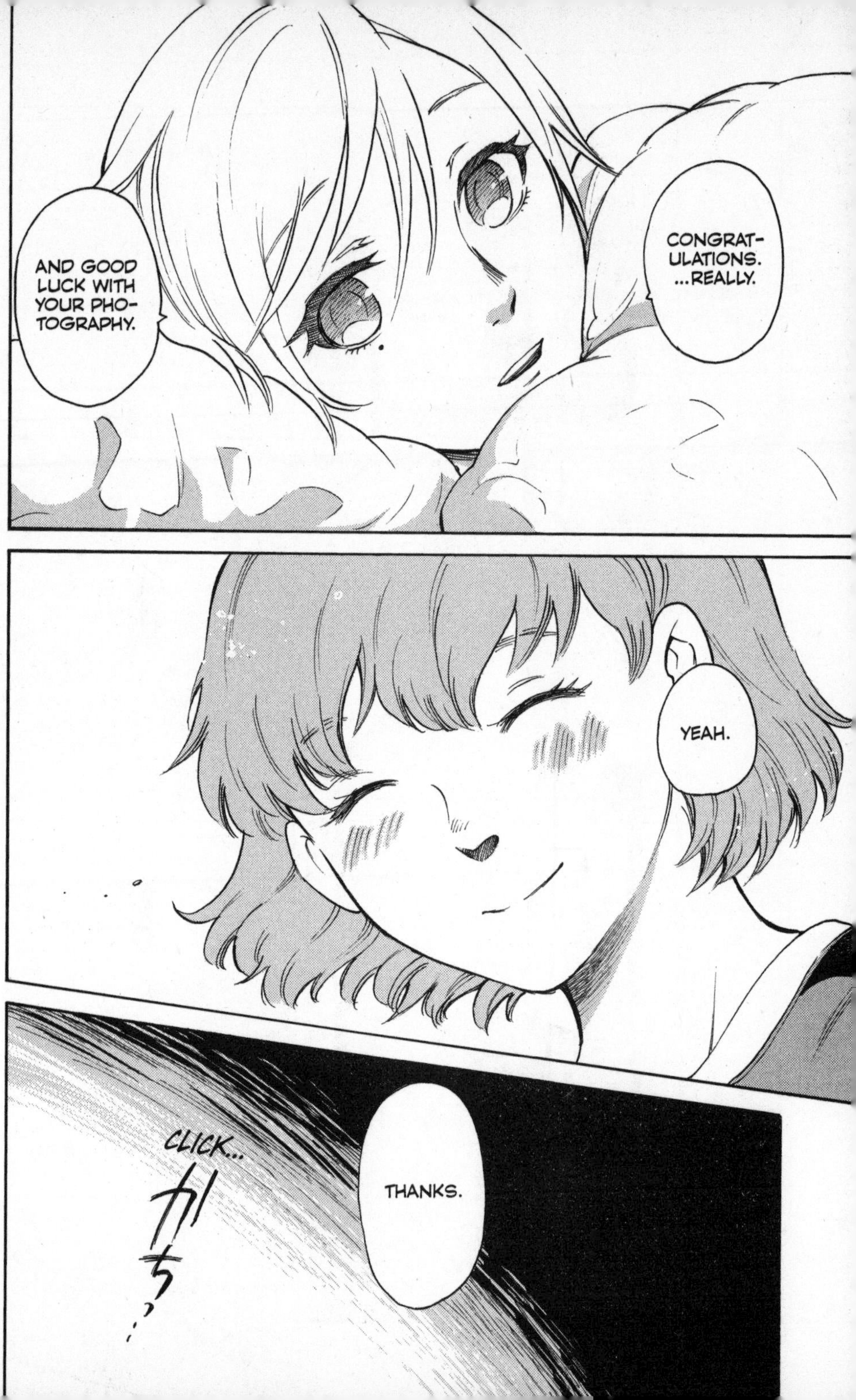
CONGRAT-ULATIONS. ...REALLY.
AND GOOD LUCK WITH YOUR PHO-TOGRAPHY.
YEAH.
THANKS.
CLICK...
カチッ

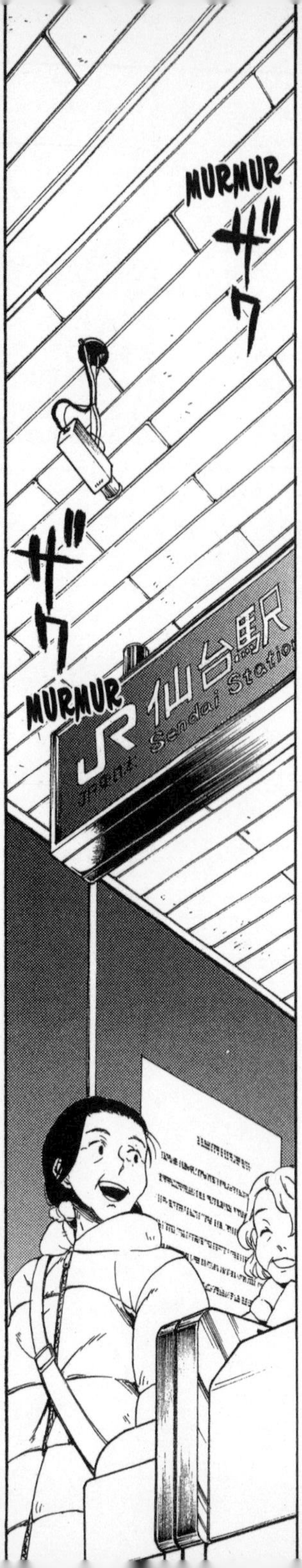
MURMUR
ザワ
ザワ
MURMUR
JR 仙台駅
Sendai Station

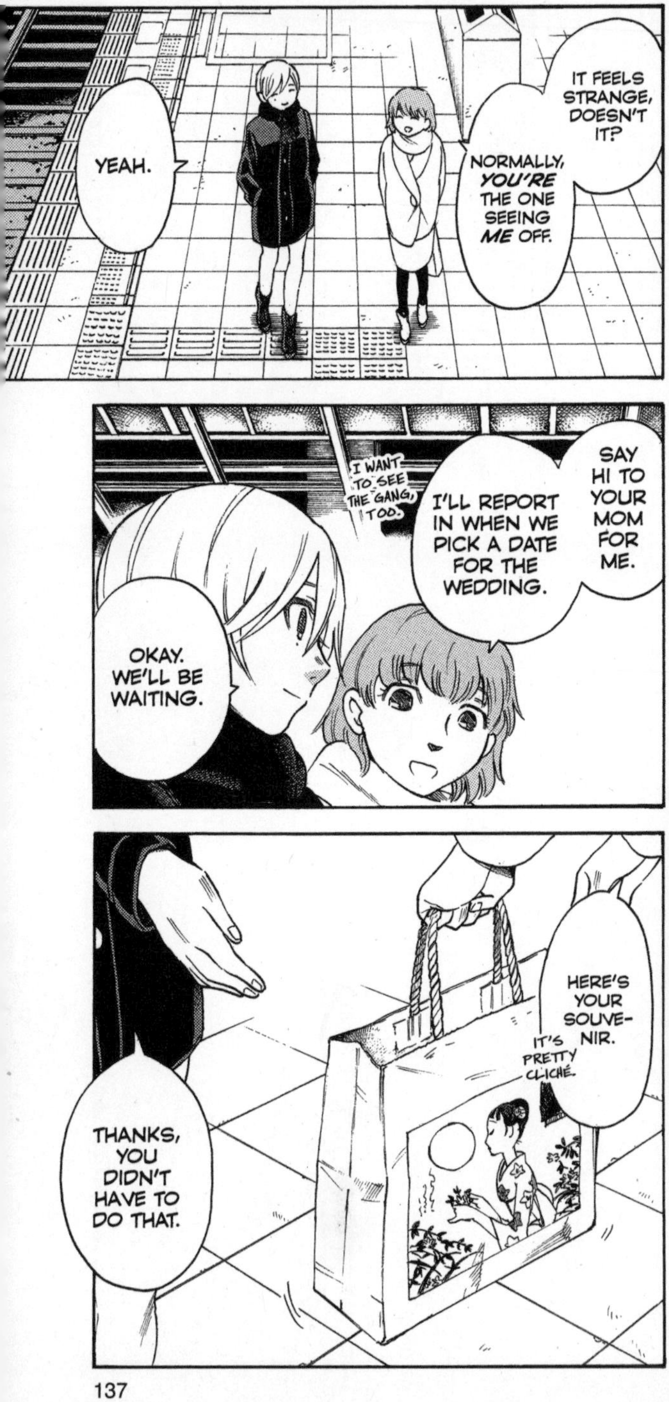
IT FEELS STRANGE, DOESN'T IT?
NORMALLY, *YOU'RE* THE ONE SEEING *ME* OFF.
YEAH.
SAY HI TO YOUR MOM FOR ME.
I'LL REPORT IN WHEN WE PICK A DATE FOR THE WEDDING.
I WANT TO SEE THE GANG, TOO.
OKAY. WE'LL BE WAITING.
HERE'S YOUR SOUVE-NIR.
IT'S PRETTY CLICHÉ.
THANKS, YOU DIDN'T HAVE TO DO THAT.

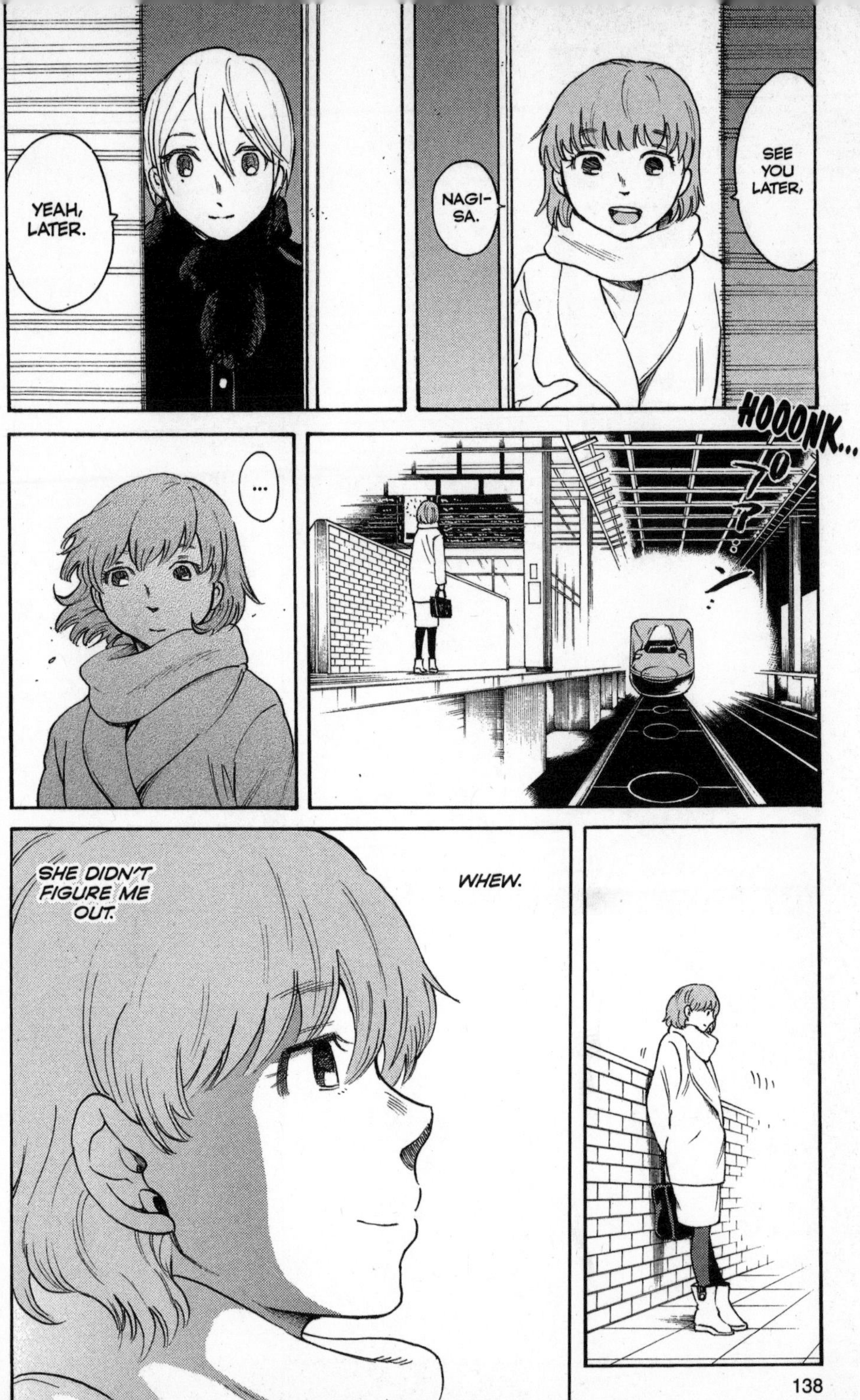
SEE YOU LATER,
NAGI-SA.
YEAH, LATER.
HOOONK...
...
WHEW.
SHE DIDN'T FIGURE ME OUT.

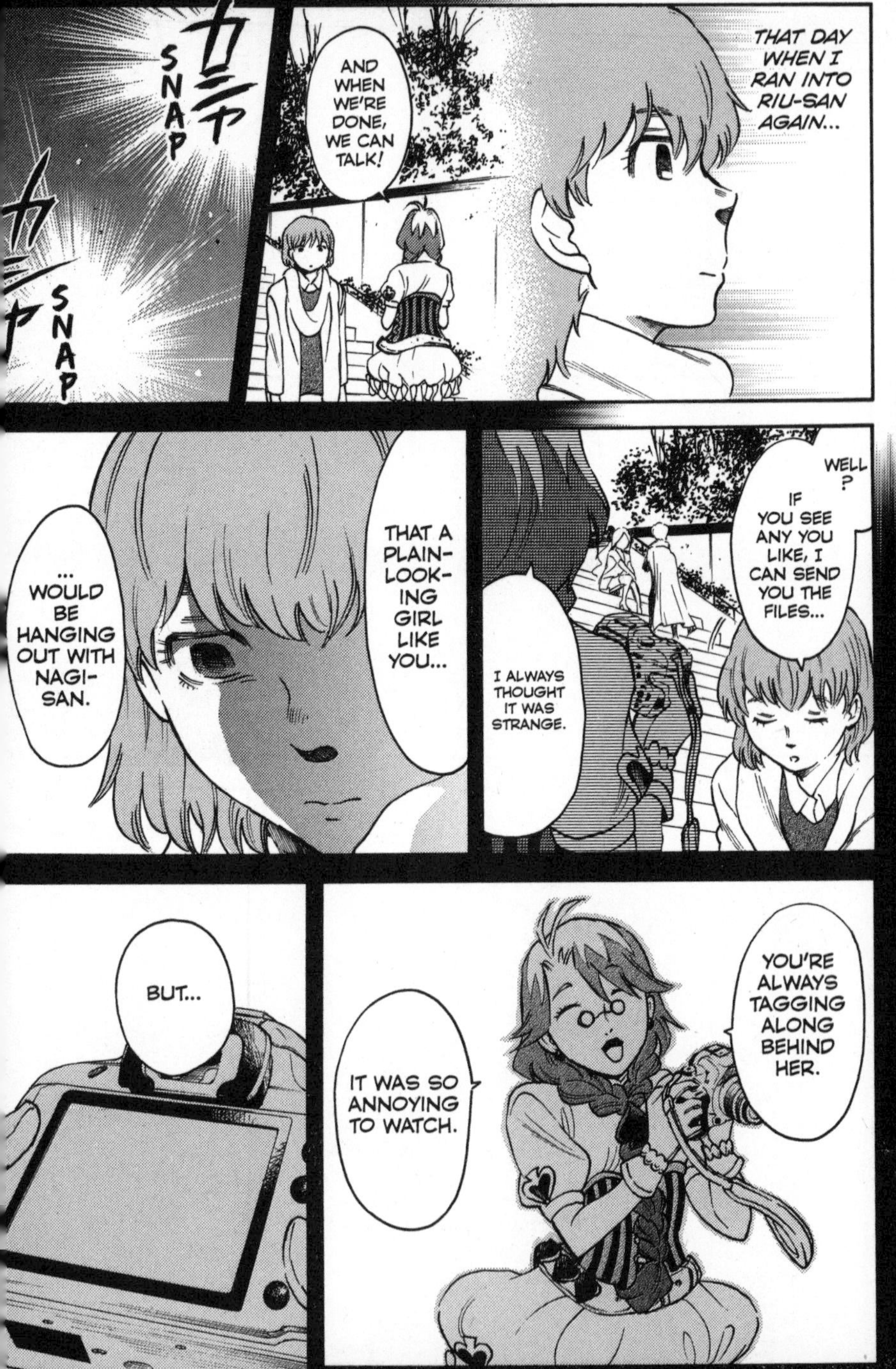
THAT DAY WHEN I RAN INTO RIU-SAN AGAIN...
AND WHEN WE'RE DONE, WE CAN TALK!
SNAP
SNAP
WELL?
IF YOU SEE ANY YOU LIKE, I CAN SEND YOU THE FILES...
I ALWAYS THOUGHT IT WAS STRANGE.
THAT A PLAIN-LOOKING GIRL LIKE YOU...
...WOULD BE HANGING OUT WITH NAGI-SAN.
YOU'RE ALWAYS TAGGING ALONG BEHIND HER.
IT WAS SO ANNOYING TO WATCH.
BUT...

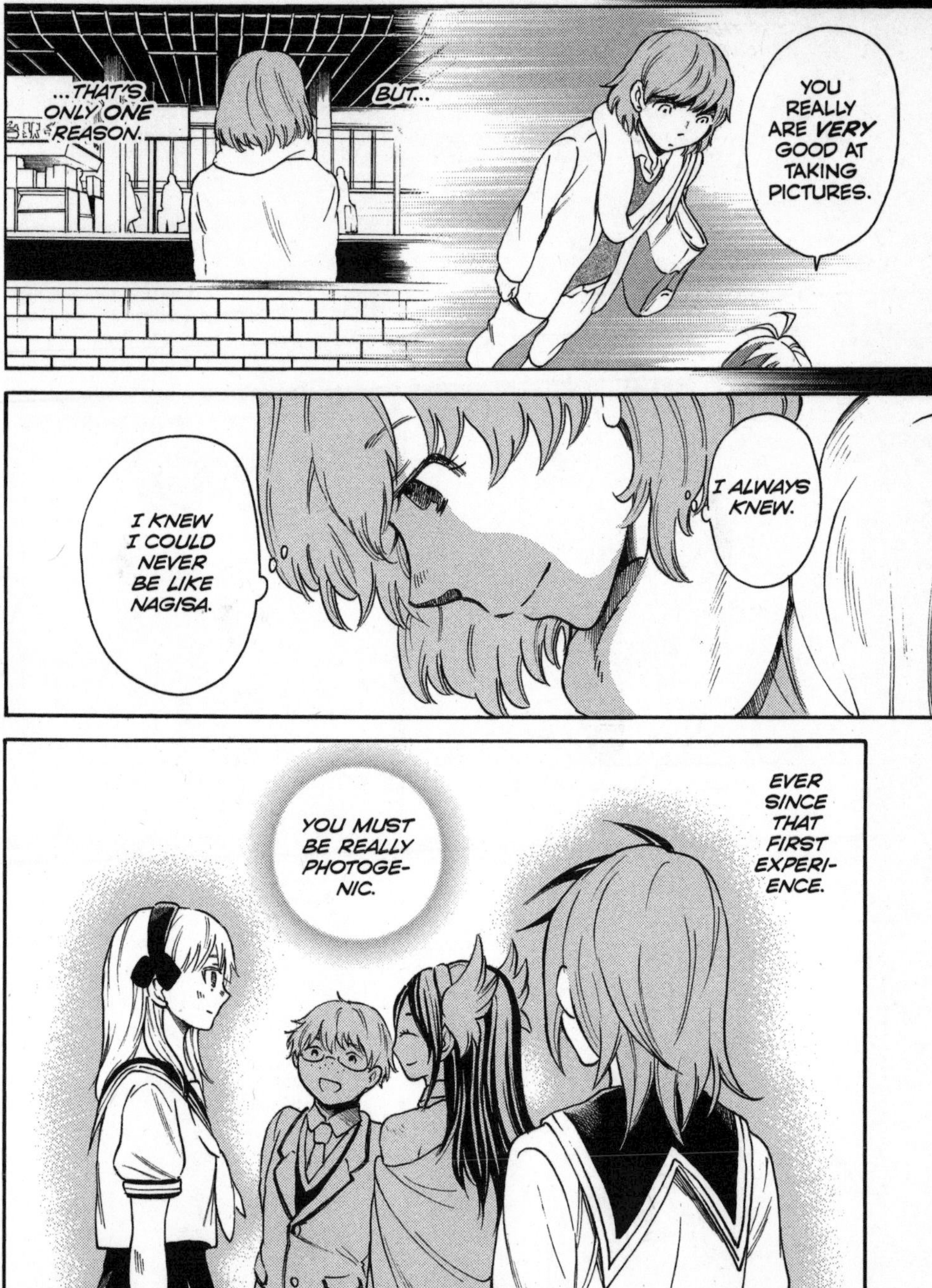
YOU REALLY ARE VERY GOOD AT TAKING PICTURES.
BUT...
...THAT'S ONLY ONE REASON.
I ALWAYS KNEW.
I KNEW I COULD NEVER BE LIKE NAGISA.
EVER SINCE THAT FIRST EXPERI-ENCE.
YOU MUST BE REALLY PHOTOGE-NIC.

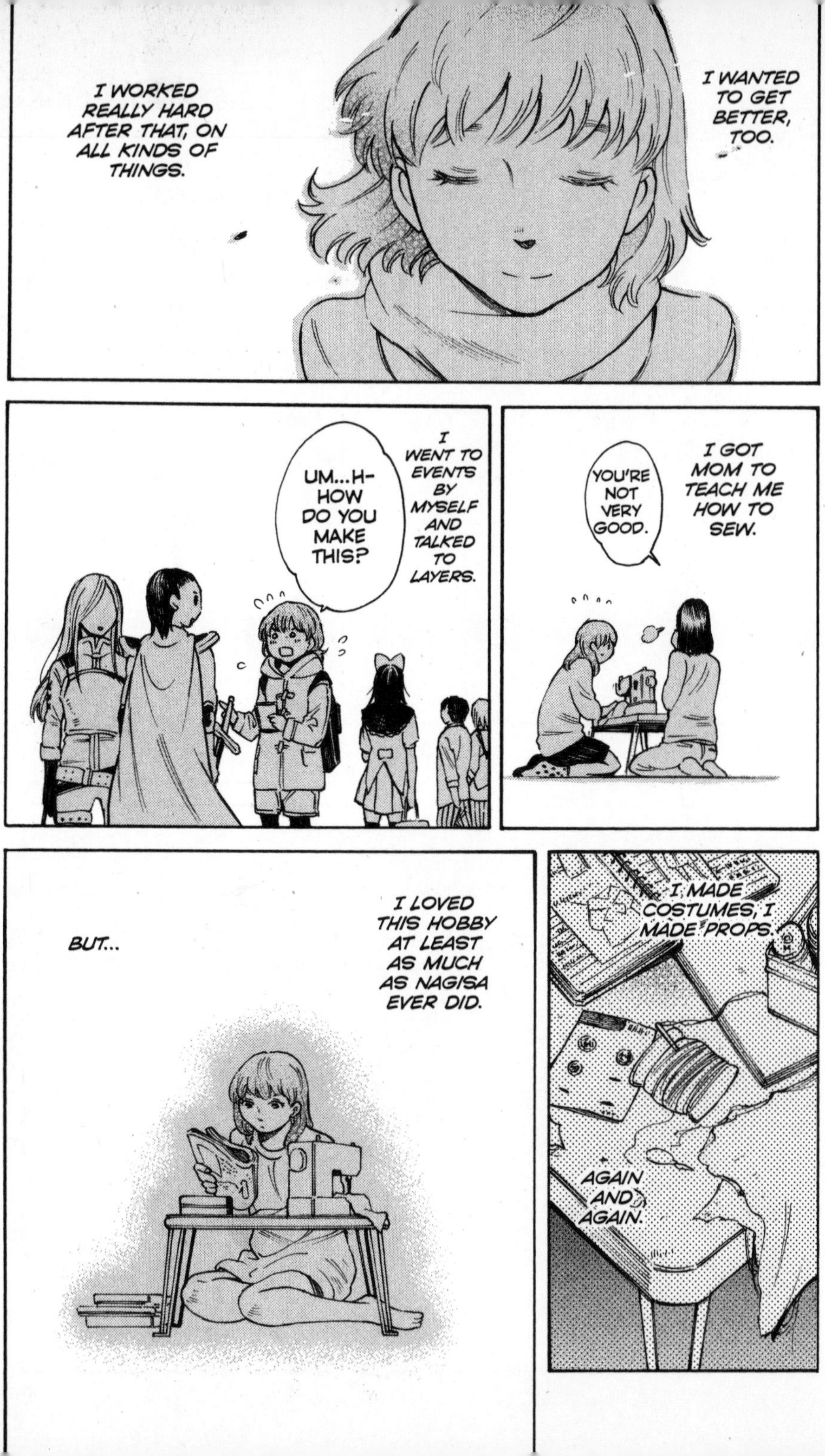
I WANTED TO GET BETTER, TOO.
I WORKED REALLY HARD AFTER THAT, ON ALL KINDS OF THINGS.
I GOT MOM TO TEACH ME HOW TO SEW.
YOU'RE NOT VERY GOOD.
I WENT TO EVENTS BY MYSELF AND TALKED TO LAYERS.
UM...H-HOW DO YOU MAKE THIS?
I MADE COSTUMES, I MADE PROPS.
AGAIN AND AGAIN.
I LOVED THIS HOBBY AT LEAST AS MUCH AS NAGISA EVER DID.
BUT...

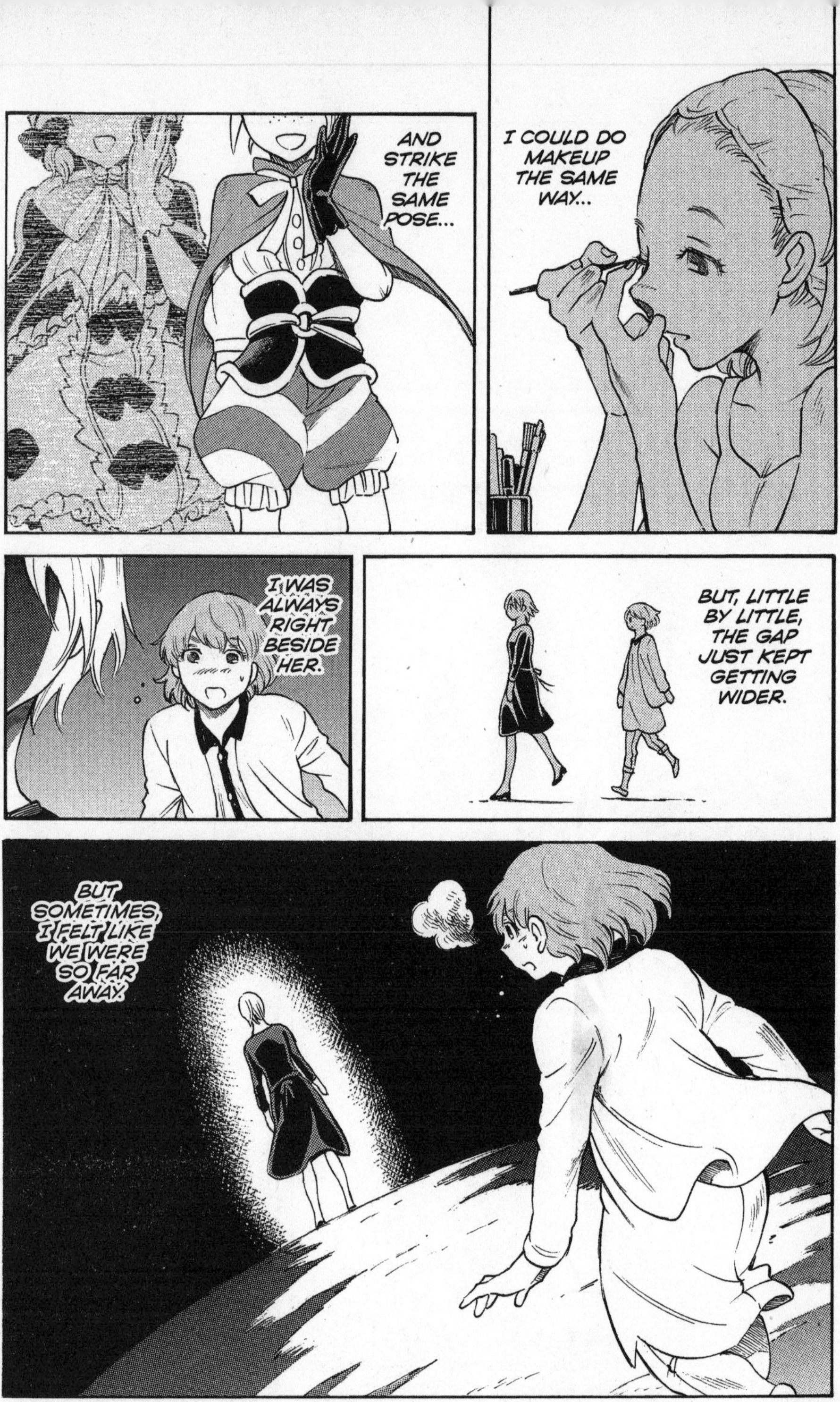
I COULD DO MAKEUP THE SAME WAY...
AND STRIKE THE SAME POSE...
BUT, LITTLE BY LITTLE, THE GAP JUST KEPT GETTING WIDER.
I WAS ALWAYS RIGHT BESIDE HER.
BUT SOMETIMES, I FELT LIKE WE WERE SO FAR AWAY.

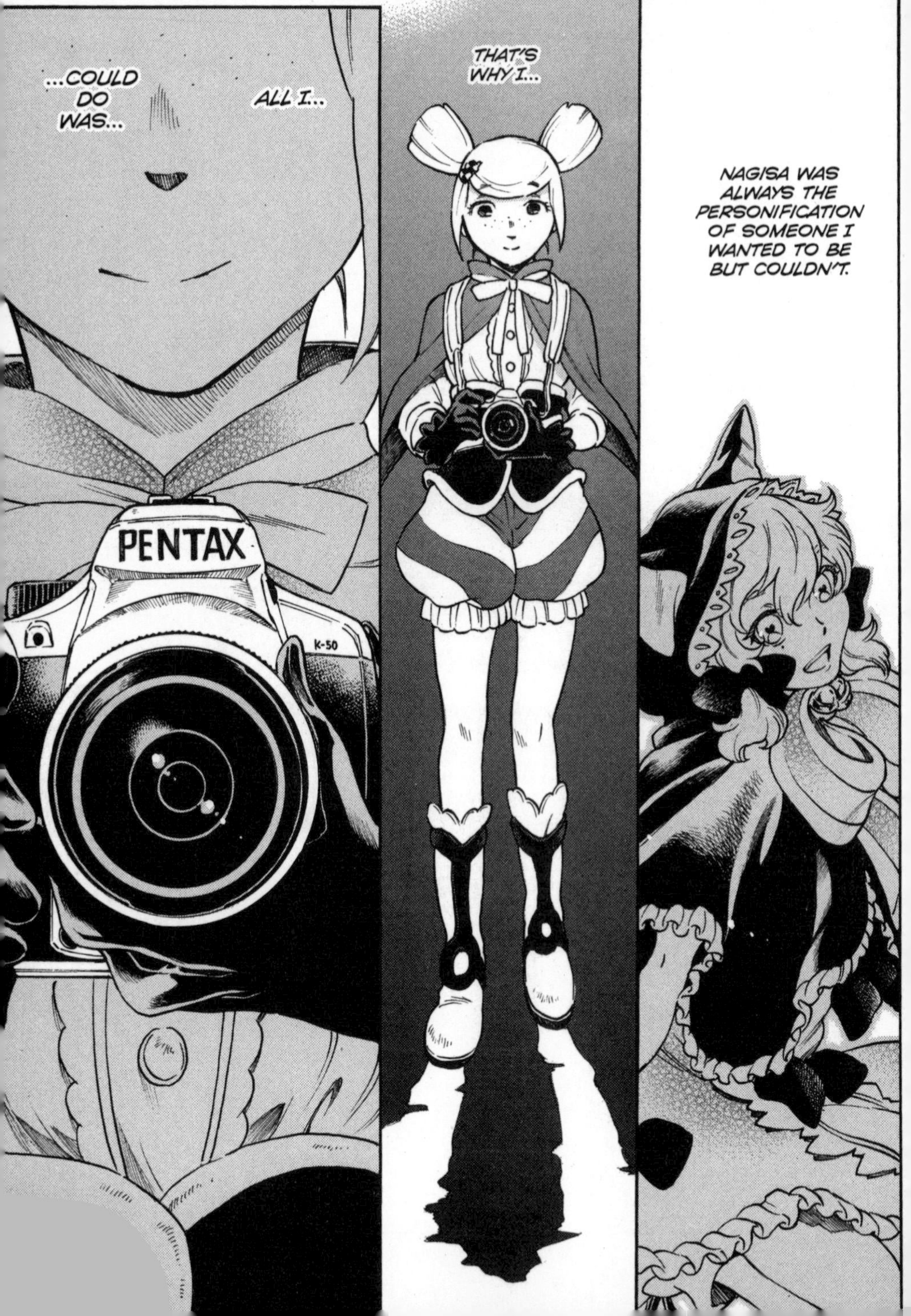
NAGISA WAS ALWAYS THE PERSONIFICATION OF SOMEONE I WANTED TO BE BUT COULDN'T.
THAT'S WHY I...
ALL I...
...COULD DO WAS...
PENTAX
K-50

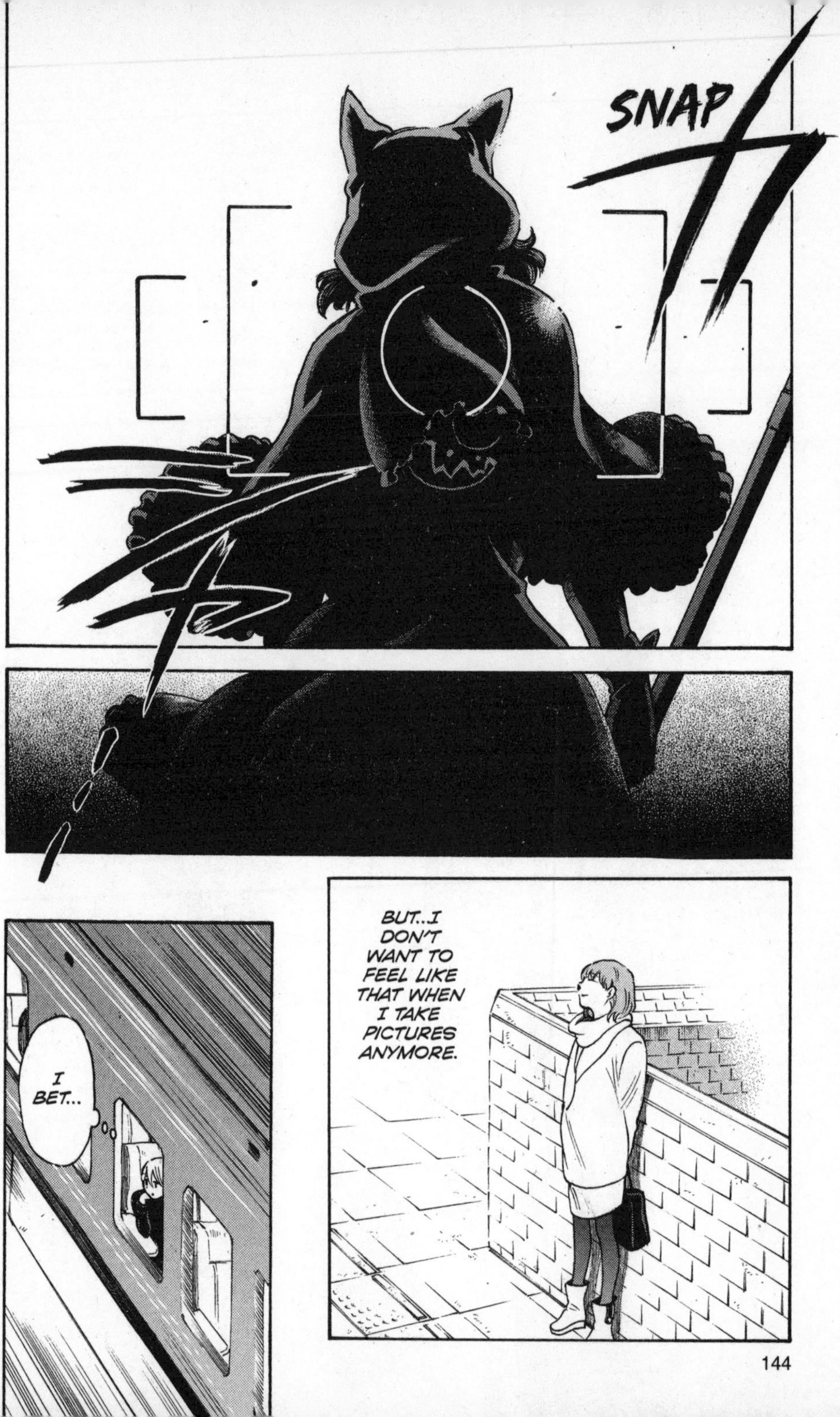
SNAP
BUT...I DON'T WANT TO FEEL LIKE THAT WHEN I TAKE PICTURES ANYMORE.
I BET...

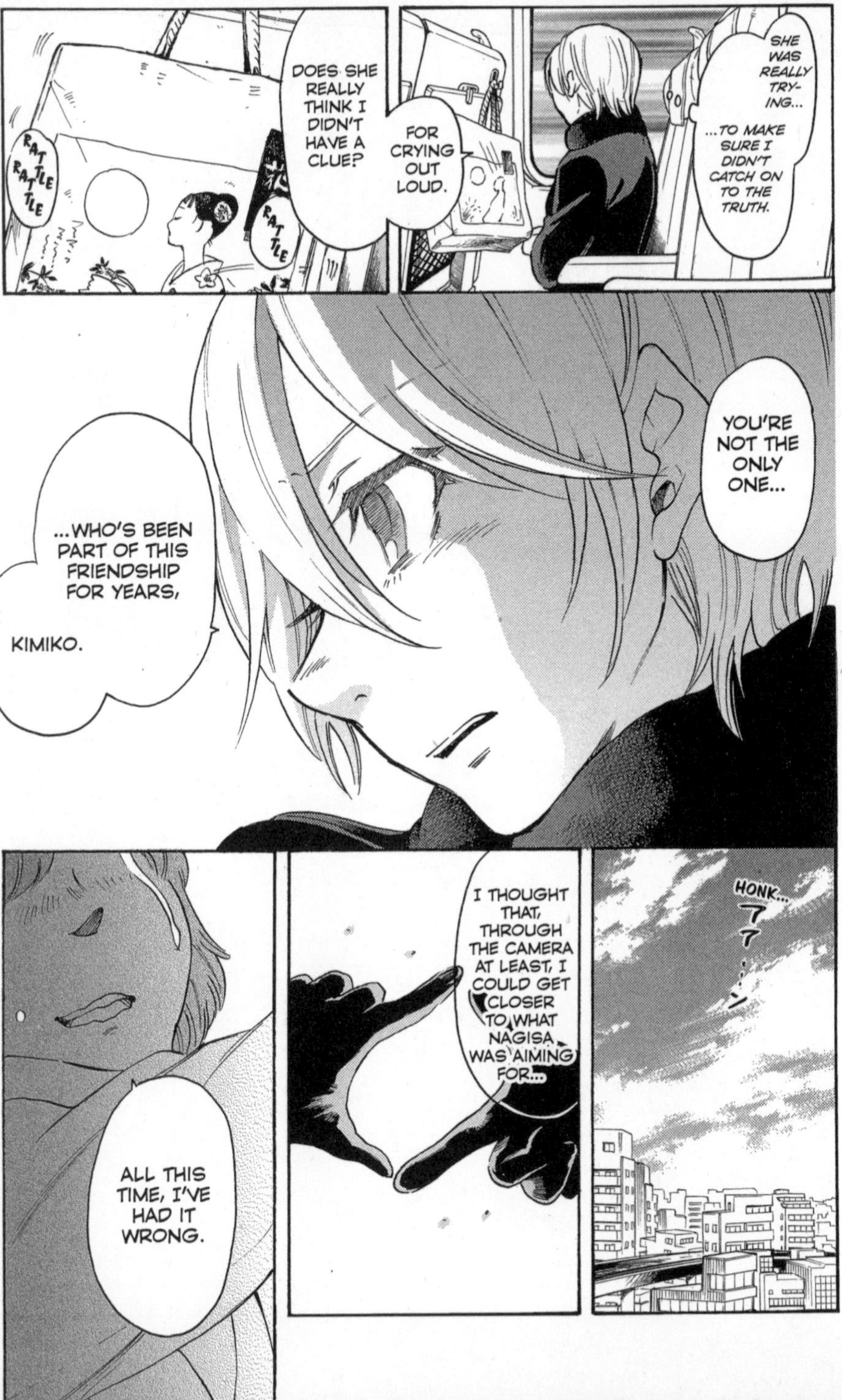
SHE WAS REALLY TRY-ING...
...TO MAKE SURE I DIDN'T CATCH ON TO THE TRUTH.
FOR CRYING OUT LOUD.
DOES SHE REALLY THINK I DIDN'T HAVE A CLUE?
RATTLE
RATTLE RATTLE
YOU'RE NOT THE ONLY ONE...
...WHO'S BEEN PART OF THIS FRIENDSHIP FOR YEARS,
KIMIKO.
HONK...
I THOUGHT THAT, THROUGH THE CAMERA AT LEAST, I COULD GET CLOSER TO WHAT NAGISA WAS AIMING FOR...
ALL THIS TIME, I'VE HAD IT WRONG.

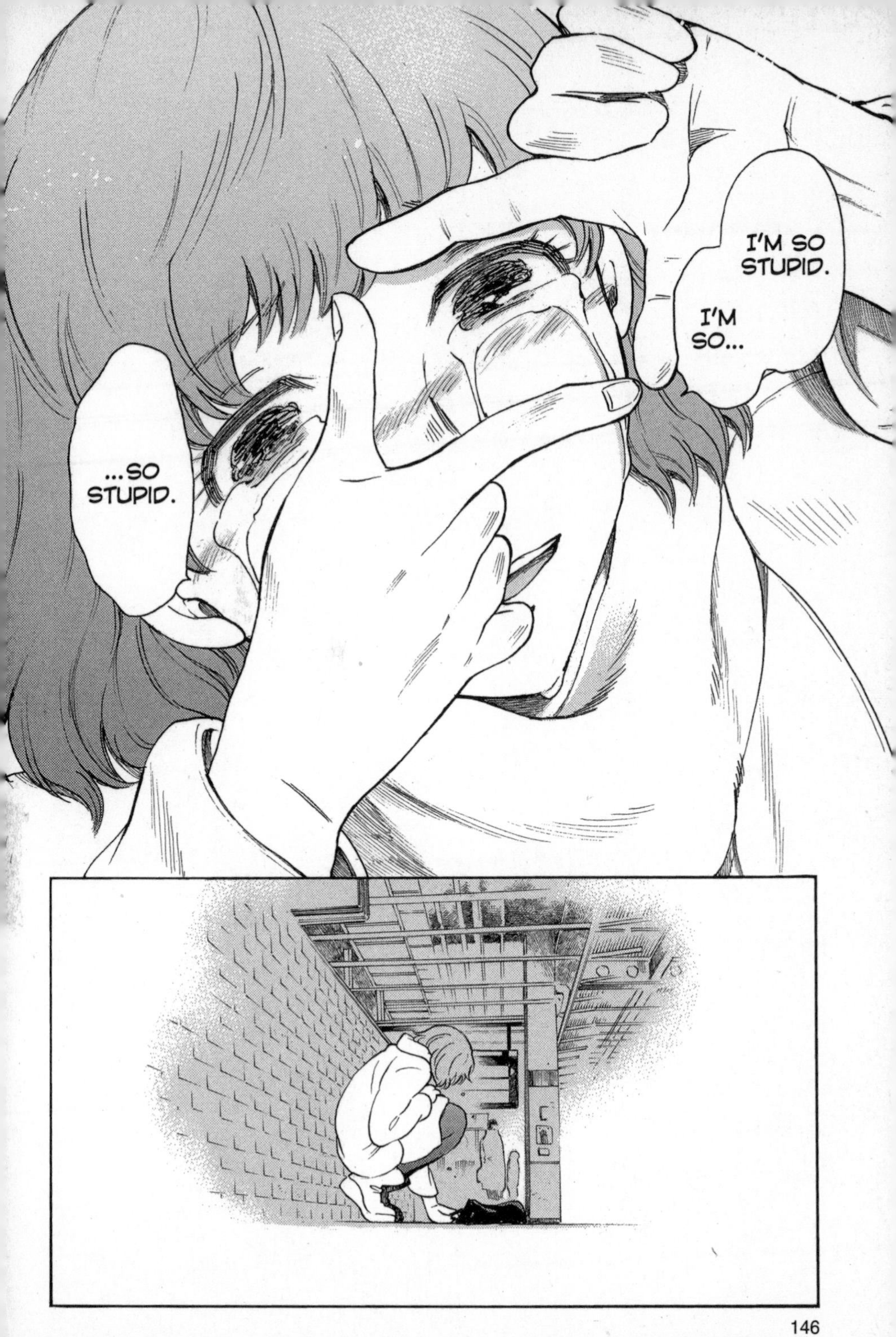
I'M SO STUPID.
I'M SO...
...SO STUPID.

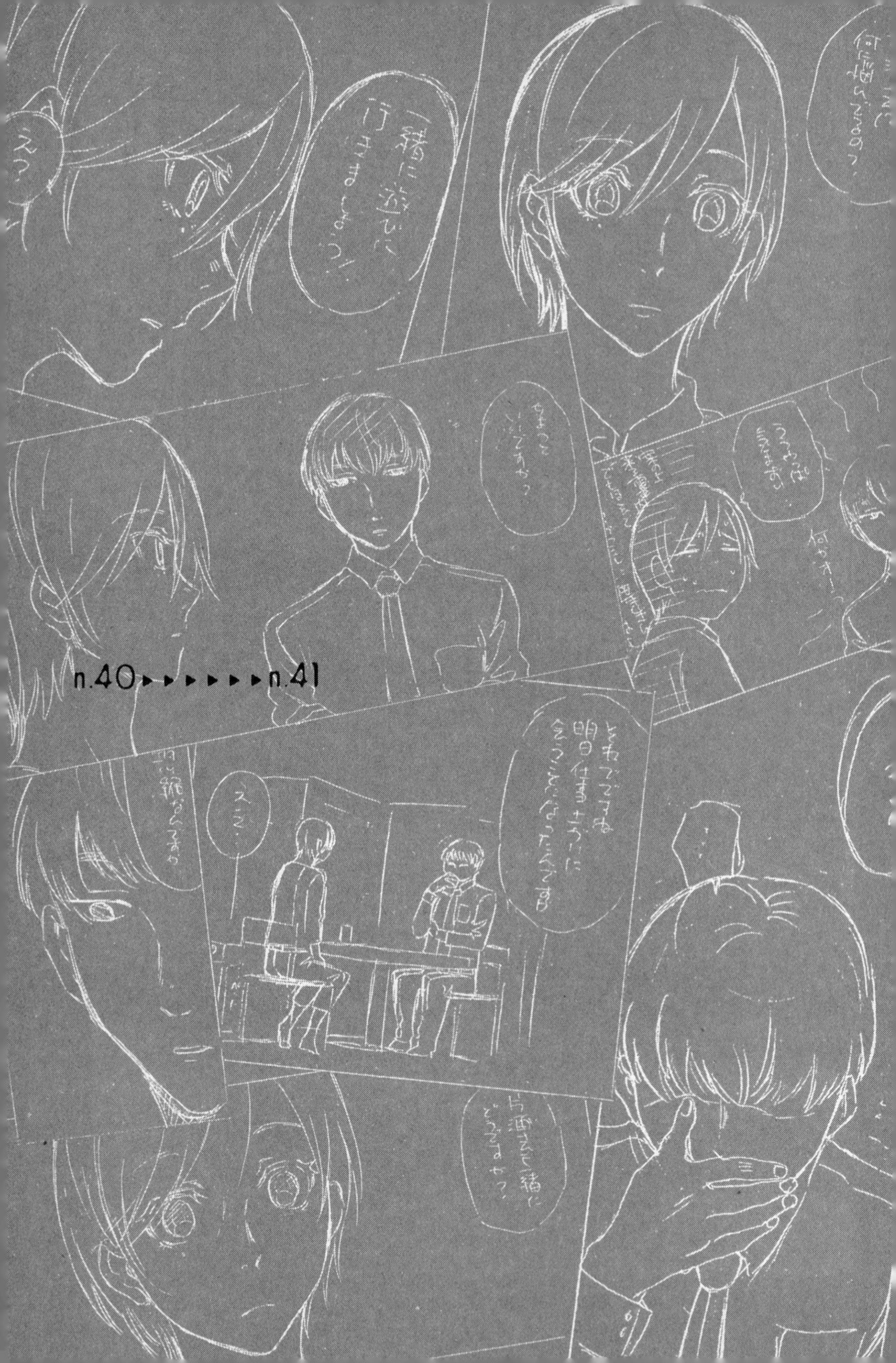
えっ?
ええ…
n.40▸▸▸▸▸▸▸▸n.41

- MATSUSHIMA AQUARIUM -

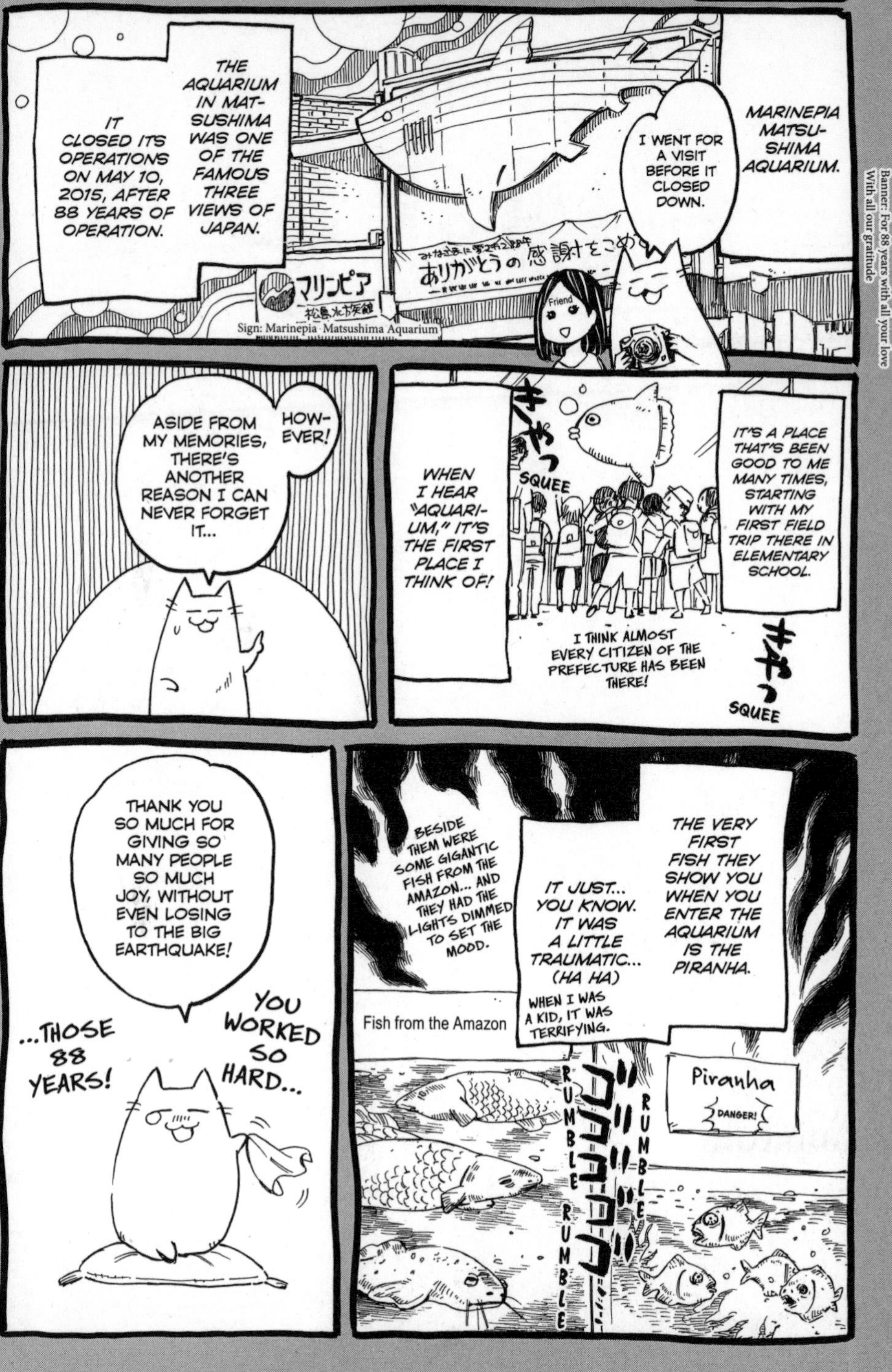
MARINEPIA MATSUSHIMA AQUARIUM.
I WENT FOR A VISIT BEFORE IT CLOSED DOWN.
THE AQUARIUM IN MATSUSHIMA WAS ONE OF THE FAMOUS THREE VIEWS OF JAPAN.
IT CLOSED ITS OPERATIONS ON MAY 10, 2015, AFTER 88 YEARS OF OPERATION.
Banner: For 88 years with all your love With all our gratitude
Sign: Marinepia · Matsushima Aquarium
Friend
IT'S A PLACE THAT'S BEEN GOOD TO ME MANY TIMES, STARTING WITH MY FIRST FIELD TRIP THERE IN ELEMENTARY SCHOOL.
SQUEE
WHEN I HEAR "AQUARIUM," IT'S THE FIRST PLACE I THINK OF!
I THINK ALMOST EVERY CITIZEN OF THE PREFECTURE HAS BEEN THERE!
SQUEE
HOW-EVER!
ASIDE FROM MY MEMORIES, THERE'S ANOTHER REASON I CAN NEVER FORGET IT...
THE VERY FIRST FISH THEY SHOW YOU WHEN YOU ENTER THE AQUARIUM IS THE PIRANHA.
IT JUST... YOU KNOW. IT WAS A LITTLE TRAUMATIC... (HA HA)
WHEN I WAS A KID, IT WAS TERRIFYING.
BESIDE THEM WERE SOME GIGANTIC FISH FROM THE AMAZON... AND THEY HAD THE LIGHTS DIMMED TO SET THE MOOD.
Fish from the Amazon
Piranha
DANGER!
RUMBLE
RUMBLE
RUMBLE
RUMBLE
THANK YOU SO MUCH FOR GIVING SO MANY PEOPLE SO MUCH JOY, WITHOUT EVEN LOSING TO THE BIG EARTHQUAKE!
YOU WORKED SO HARD...
...THOSE 88 YEARS!

HONK...
n.41
Complex age
DID I DO THE RIGHT THING?
I THINK I'M MORE SUITED TO TAKING PICTURES.
YOU SENSED AN END TO YOUR DAYS AS A COSPLAYER,
AND PICKED UP THE CAMERA INSTEAD.

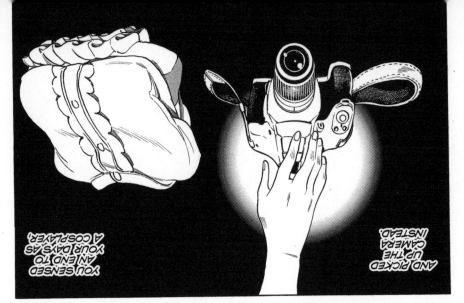

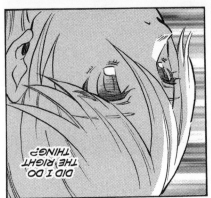

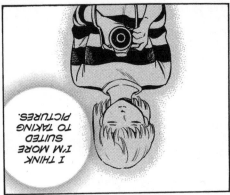

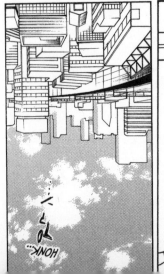

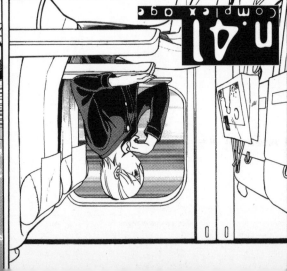

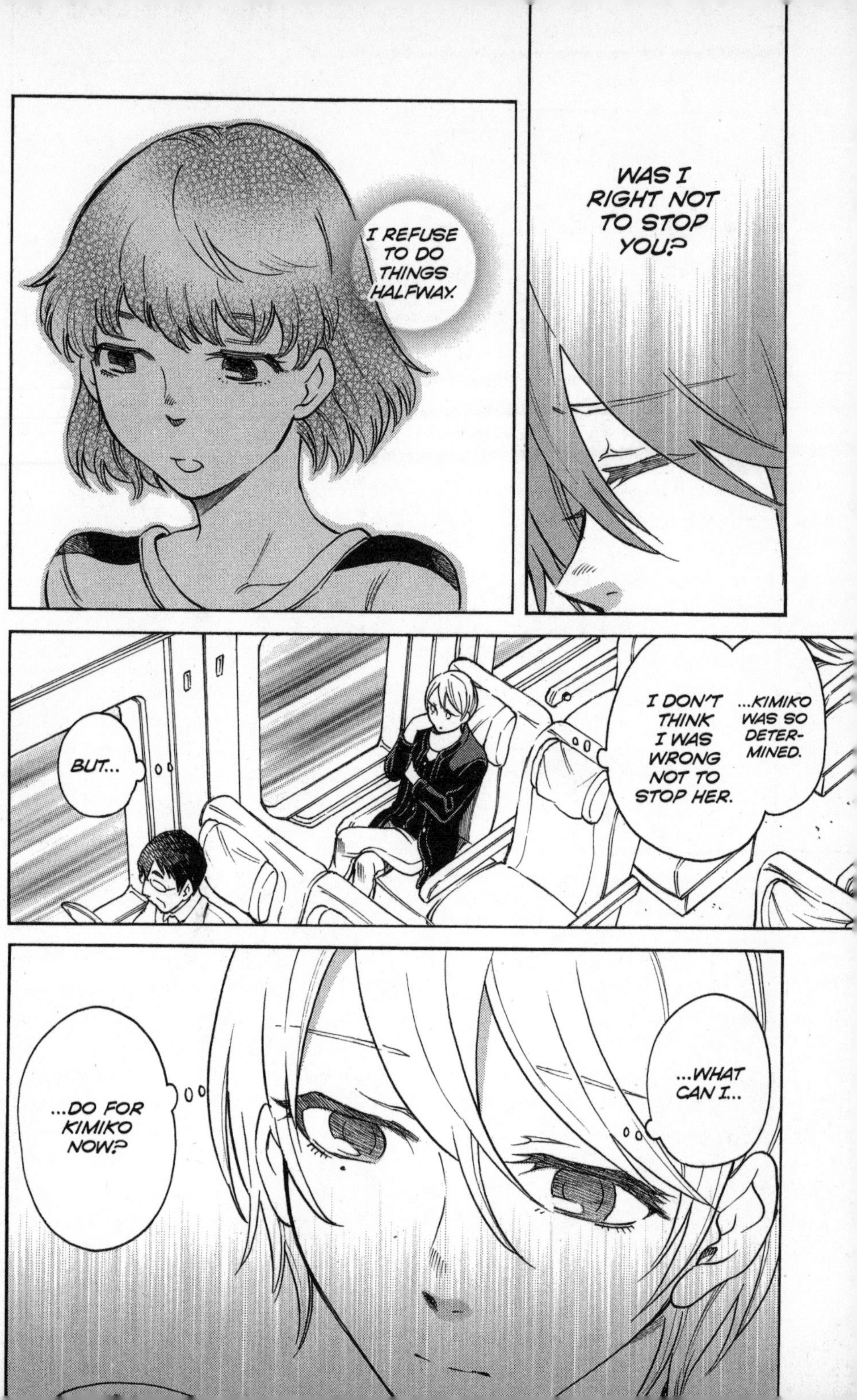
WAS I RIGHT NOT TO STOP YOU?
I REFUSE TO DO THINGS HALFWAY.
...KIMIKO WAS SO DETER-MINED.
I DON'T THINK I WAS WRONG NOT TO STOP HER.
BUT...
...WHAT CAN I...
...DO FOR KIMIKO NOW?

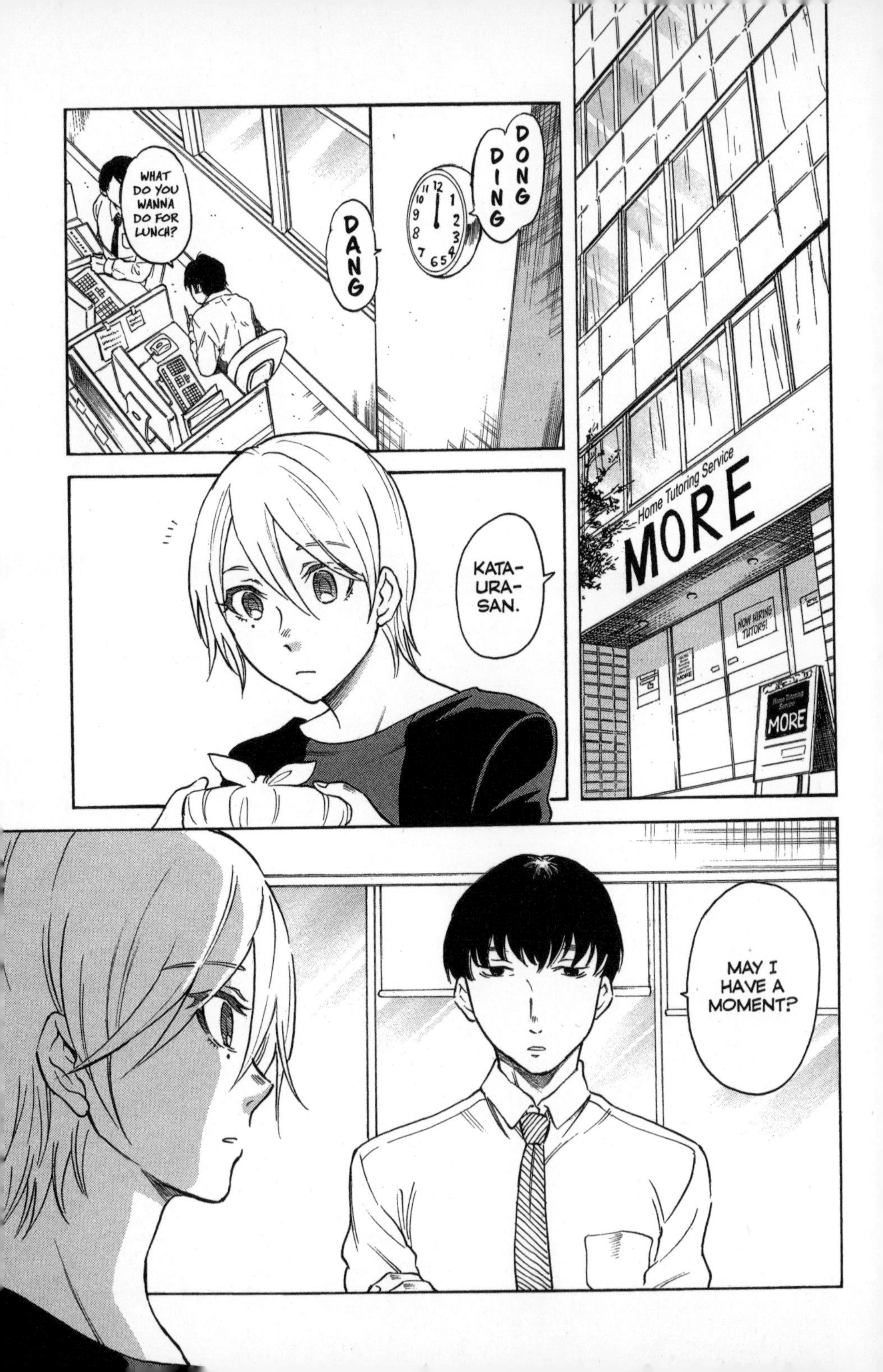
Home Tutoring Service
MORE
NOW HIRING TUTORS!
MORE
DING DONG
DANG
WHAT DO YOU WANNA DO FOR LUNCH?
KATA-URA-SAN.
MAY I HAVE A MOMENT?

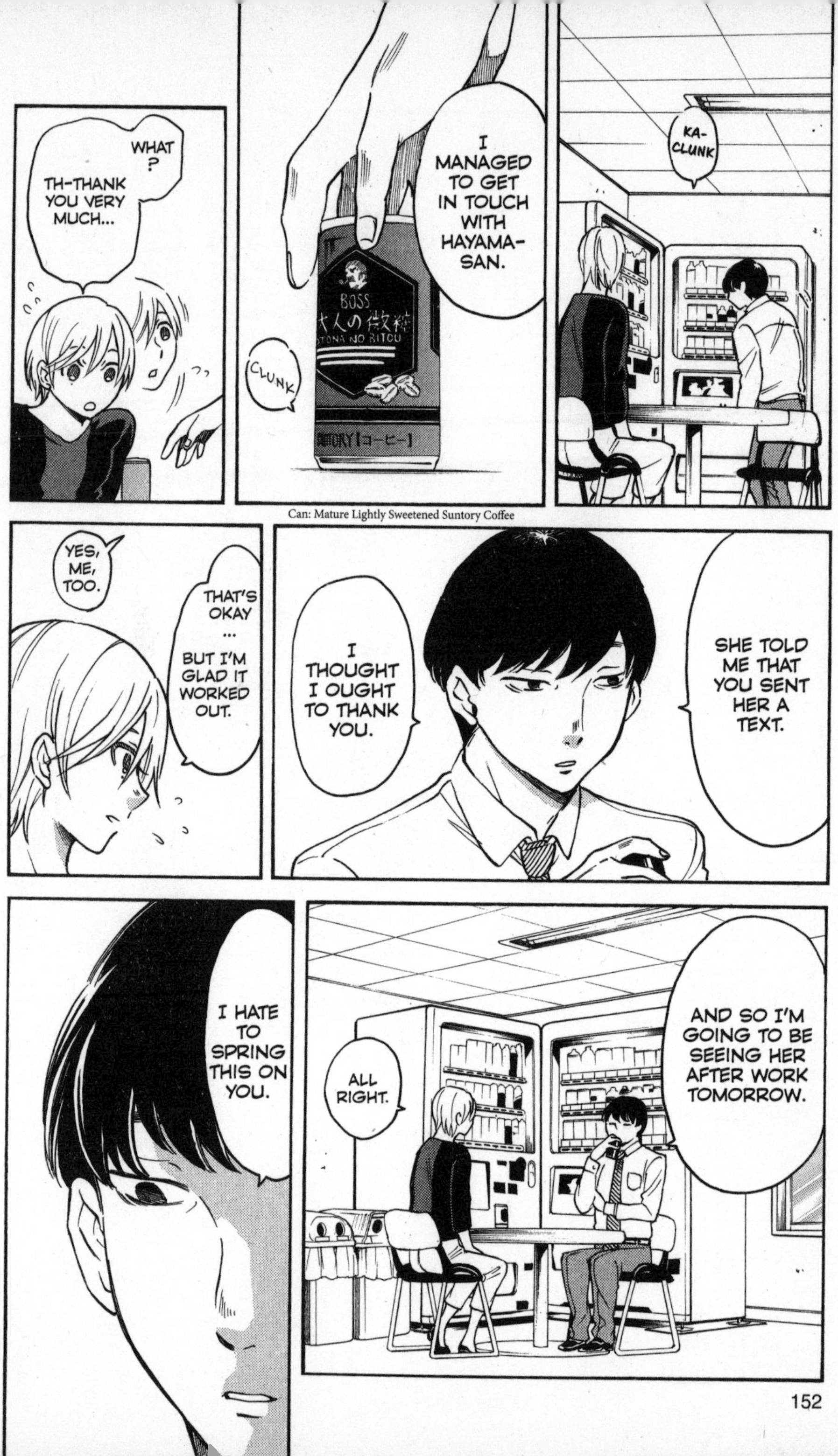
KA-CLUNK
I MANAGED TO GET IN TOUCH WITH HAYAMA-SAN.
CLUNK
BOSS
WHAT?
TH-THANK YOU VERY MUCH...
SHE TOLD ME THAT YOU SENT HER A TEXT.
I THOUGHT I OUGHT TO THANK YOU.
THAT'S OKAY... BUT I'M GLAD IT WORKED OUT.
YES, ME, TOO.
AND SO I'M GOING TO BE SEEING HER AFTER WORK TOMORROW.
ALL RIGHT.
I HATE TO SPRING THIS ON YOU.
Can: Mature Lightly Sweetened Suntory Coffee

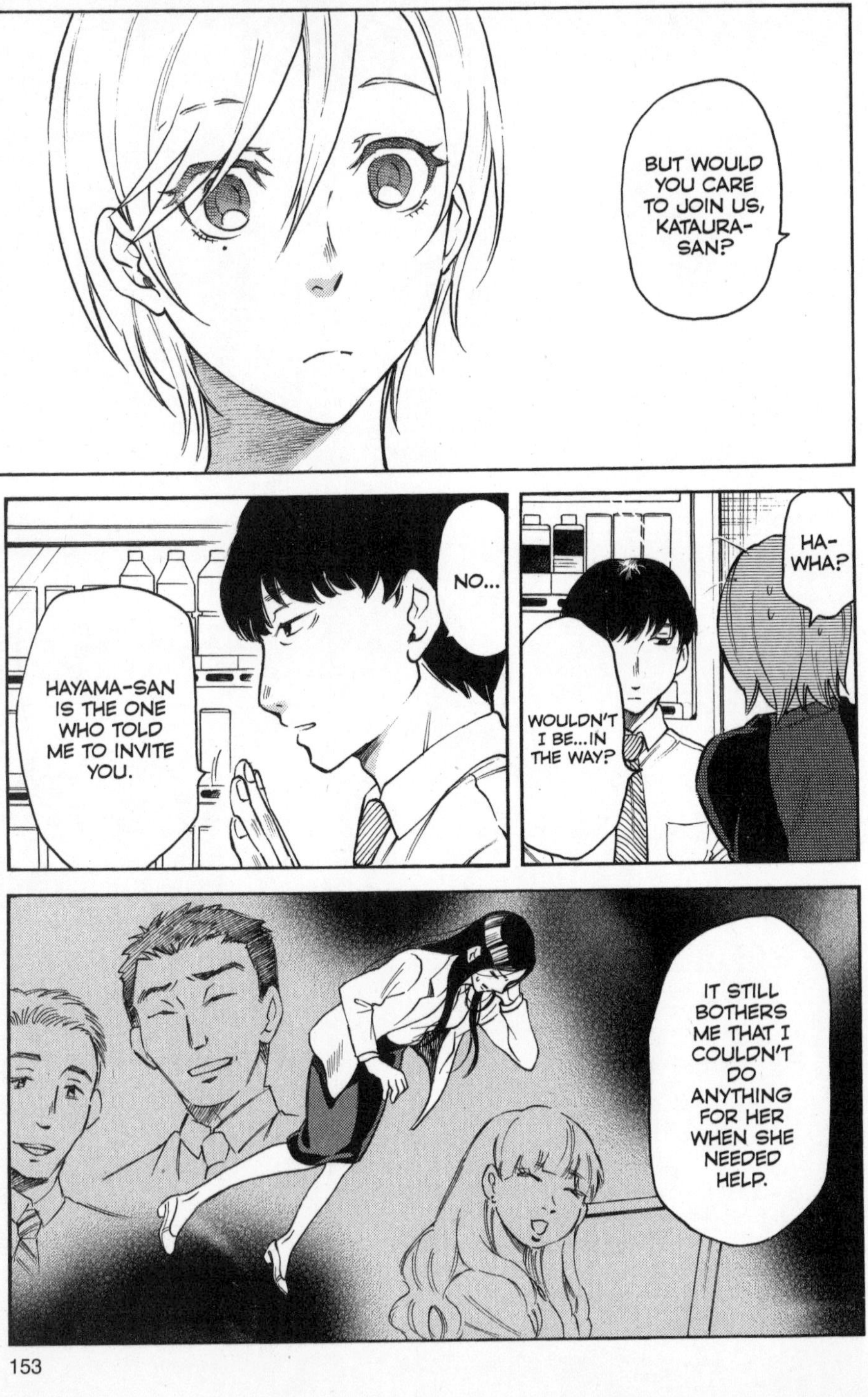
BUT WOULD YOU CARE TO JOIN US, KATAURA-SAN?
HA-WHA?
WOULDN'T I BE...IN THE WAY?
NO...
HAYAMA-SAN IS THE ONE WHO TOLD ME TO INVITE YOU.
IT STILL BOTHERS ME THAT I COULDN'T DO ANYTHING FOR HER WHEN SHE NEEDED HELP.

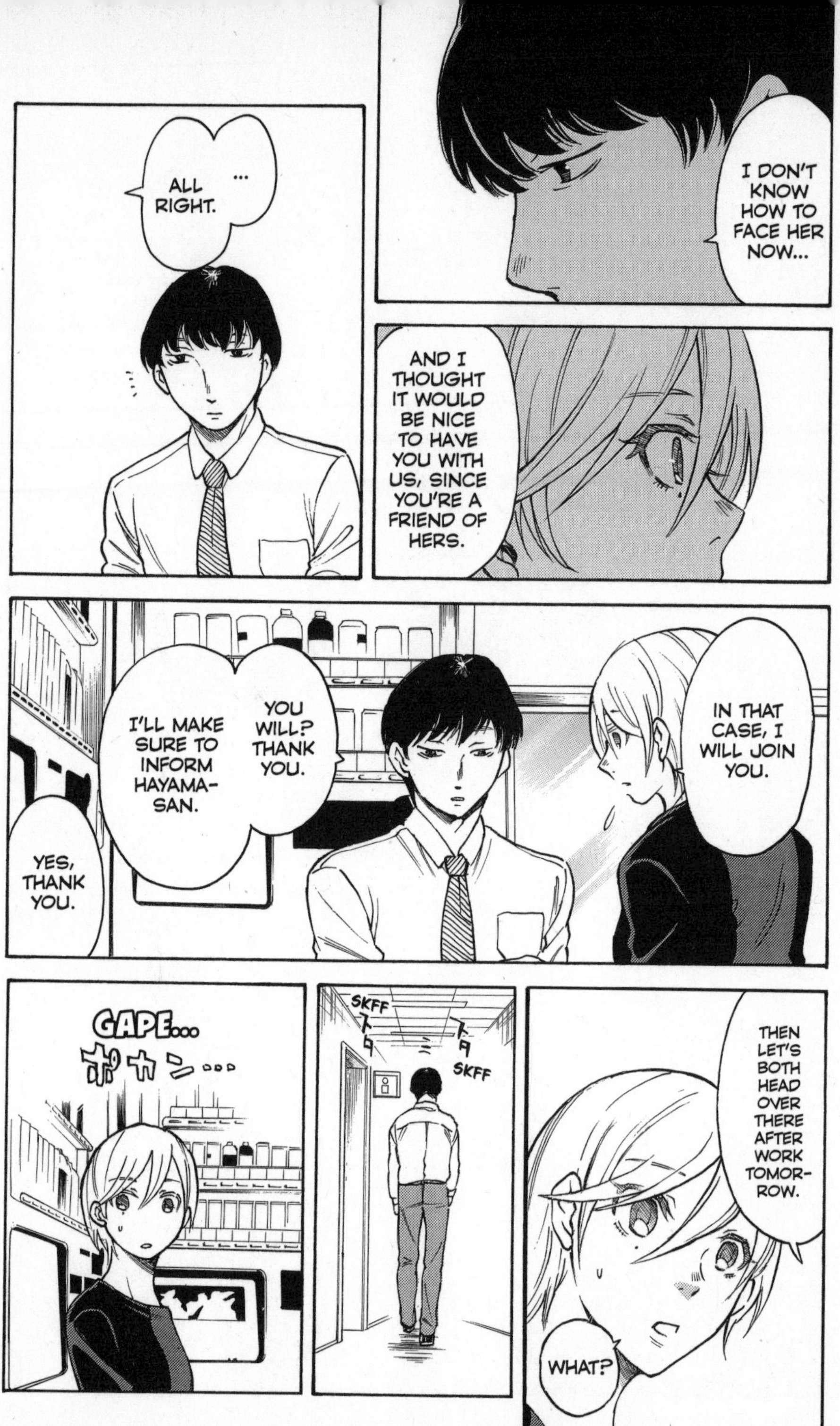
I DON'T KNOW HOW TO FACE HER NOW...
AND I THOUGHT IT WOULD BE NICE TO HAVE YOU WITH US, SINCE YOU'RE A FRIEND OF HERS.
...
ALL RIGHT.
IN THAT CASE, I WILL JOIN YOU.
YOU WILL? THANK YOU.
I'LL MAKE SURE TO INFORM HAYAMA-SAN.
YES, THANK YOU.
THEN LET'S BOTH HEAD OVER THERE AFTER WORK TOMOR-ROW.
WHAT?
SKFF
SKFF
GAPE...
ポカン...

The next night
万々々
2F↑
居酒屋
万々々
Man-man-man.
I SEE WE'RE HERE A LITTLE EARLY.
YES.
MURMUR
MURMUR
...
AND AS EXPECTED, HE BARELY SAID A WORD ON THE TRAIN OVER HERE... HURRY UP, HAYAMA-SAN!
NNGH... THIS IS AWK-WARD.
NOT MAKING EYE CONTACT ...
...BUT RADIATING AN AURA.
SORRY TO KEEP YOU WAITING!
Sign: Izakaya Man-Man-Man

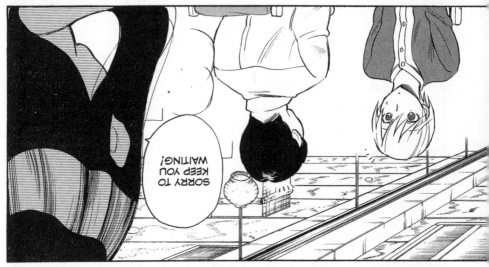

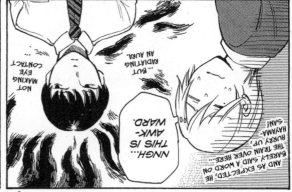

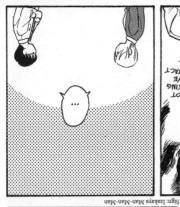

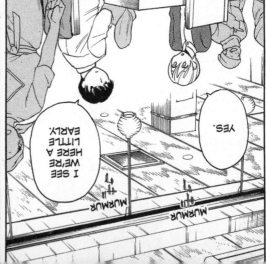

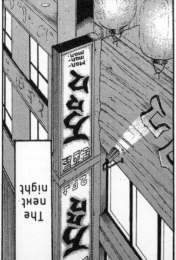

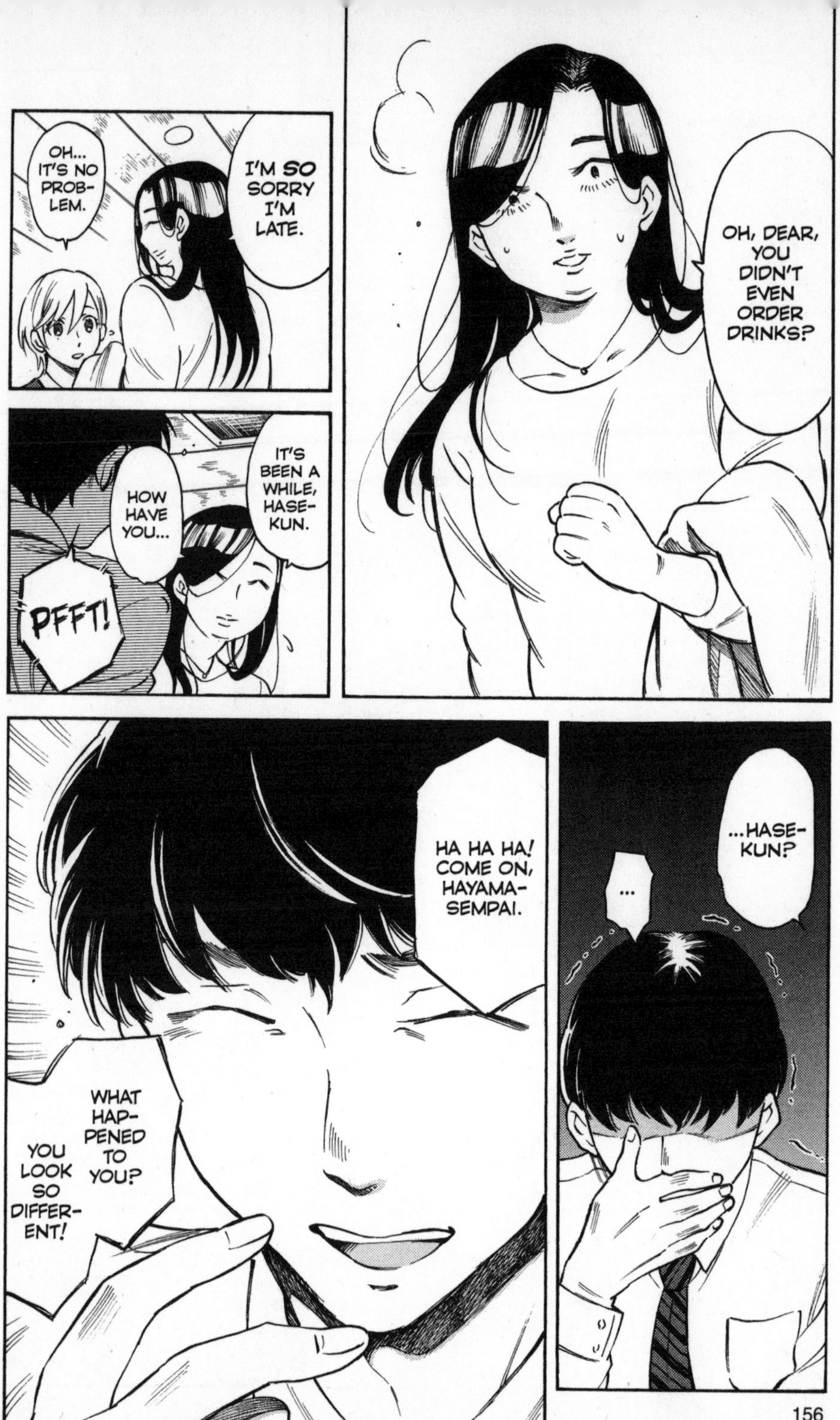
OH, DEAR, YOU DIDN'T EVEN ORDER DRINKS?
I'M SO SORRY I'M LATE.
OH... IT'S NO PROBLEM.
IT'S BEEN A WHILE, HASE-KUN.
HOW HAVE YOU...
PFFT!
...HASE-KUN?
...
HA HA HA! COME ON, HAYAMA-SEMPAI.
WHAT HAPPENED TO YOU?
YOU LOOK SO DIFFERENT!

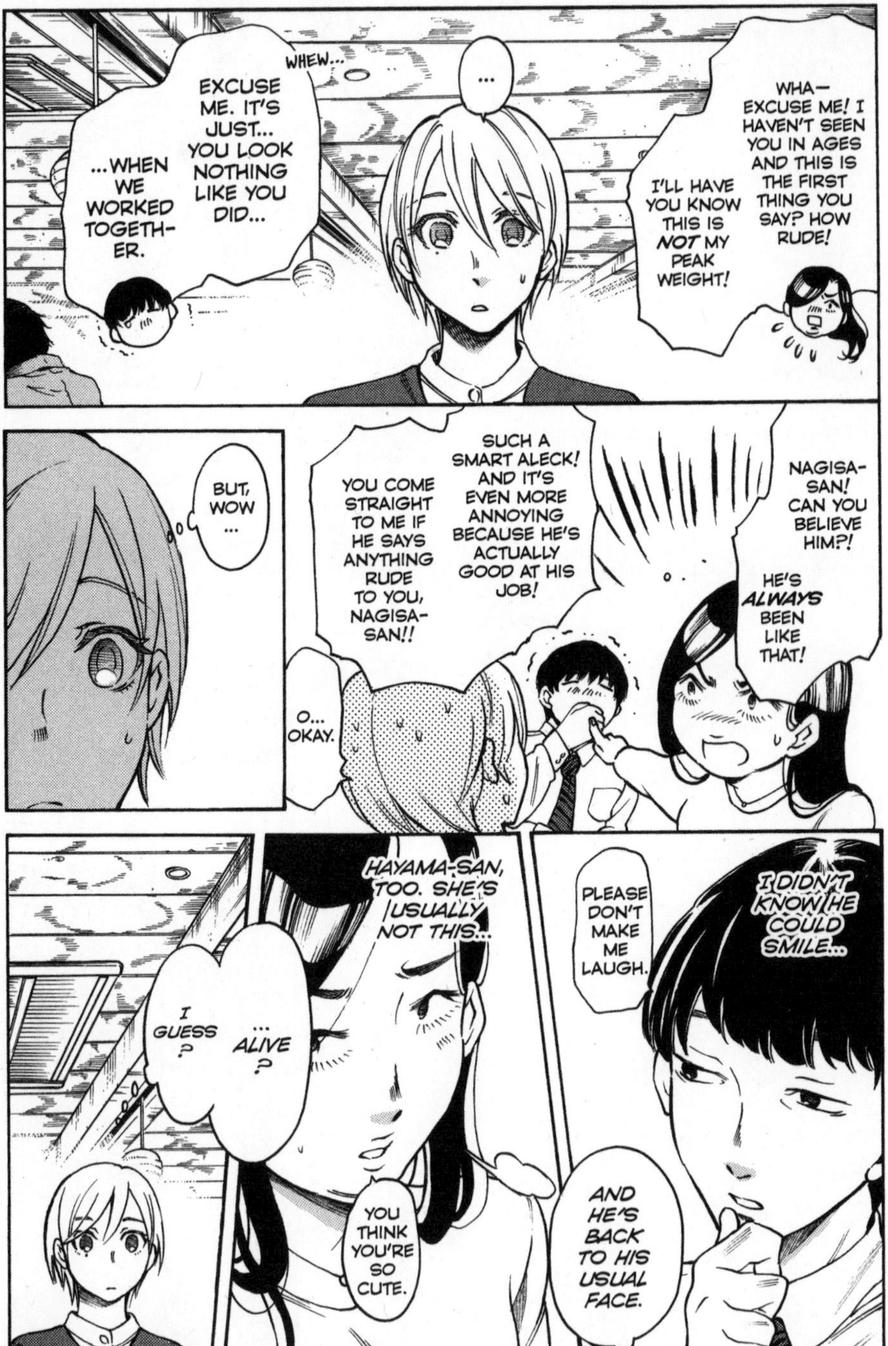
WHA— EXCUSE ME! I HAVEN'T SEEN YOU IN AGES AND THIS IS THE FIRST THING YOU SAY? HOW RUDE!
I'LL HAVE YOU KNOW THIS IS NOT MY PEAK WEIGHT!
...
WHEW...
EXCUSE ME. IT'S JUST... YOU LOOK NOTHING LIKE YOU DID...
...WHEN WE WORKED TOGETH-ER.
NAGISA-SAN! CAN YOU BELIEVE HIM?!
HE'S ALWAYS BEEN LIKE THAT!
SUCH A SMART ALECK! AND IT'S EVEN MORE ANNOYING BECAUSE HE'S ACTUALLY GOOD AT HIS JOB!
YOU COME STRAIGHT TO ME IF HE SAYS ANYTHING RUDE TO YOU, NAGISA-SAN!!
O... OKAY.
BUT, WOW ...
I DIDN'T KNOW HE COULD SMILE...
PLEASE DON'T MAKE ME LAUGH.
AND HE'S BACK TO HIS USUAL FACE.
HAYAMA-SAN, TOO. SHE'S USUALLY NOT THIS...
YOU THINK YOU'RE SO CUTE.
... ALIVE?
I GUESS?

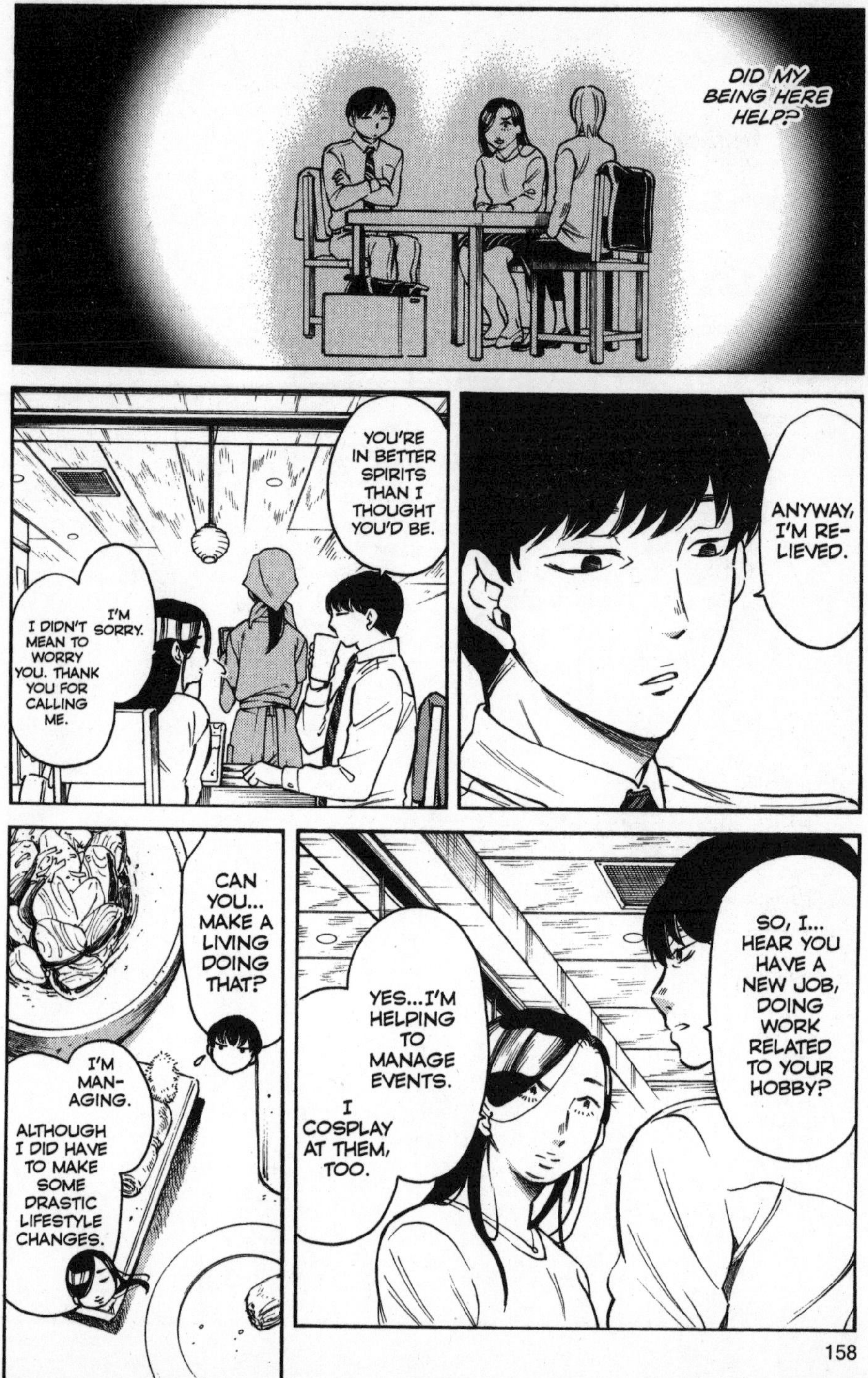
DID MY BEING HERE HELP?
ANYWAY, I'M RE-LIEVED.
YOU'RE IN BETTER SPIRITS THAN I THOUGHT YOU'D BE.
I'M SORRY.
I DIDN'T MEAN TO WORRY YOU. THANK YOU FOR CALLING ME.
SO, I... HEAR YOU HAVE A NEW JOB, DOING WORK RELATED TO YOUR HOBBY?
YES...I'M HELPING TO MANAGE EVENTS.
I COSPLAY AT THEM, TOO.
CAN YOU... MAKE A LIVING DOING THAT?
I'M MAN-AGING.
ALTHOUGH I DID HAVE TO MAKE SOME DRASTIC LIFESTYLE CHANGES.

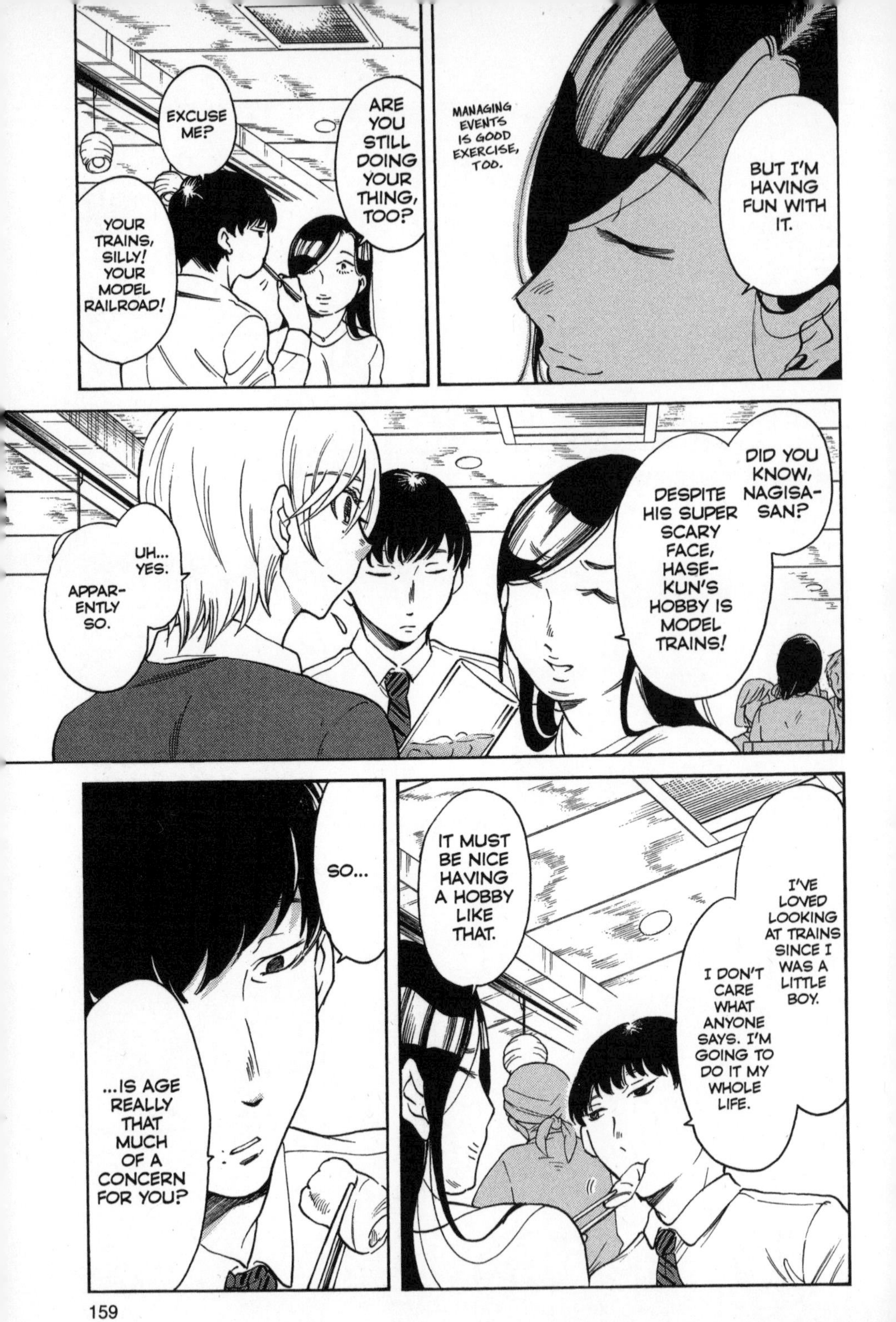
BUT I'M HAVING FUN WITH IT.
MANAGING EVENTS IS GOOD EXERCISE, TOO.
ARE YOU STILL DOING YOUR THING, TOO?
EXCUSE ME?
YOUR TRAINS, SILLY! YOUR MODEL RAILROAD!
DID YOU KNOW, NAGISA-SAN?
DESPITE HIS SUPER SCARY FACE, HASE-KUN'S HOBBY IS MODEL TRAINS!
UH... YES.
APPAR-ENTLY SO.
I'VE LOVED LOOKING AT TRAINS SINCE I WAS A LITTLE BOY.
I DON'T CARE WHAT ANYONE SAYS. I'M GOING TO DO IT MY WHOLE LIFE.
IT MUST BE NICE HAVING A HOBBY LIKE THAT.
SO...
...IS AGE REALLY THAT MUCH OF A CONCERN FOR YOU?

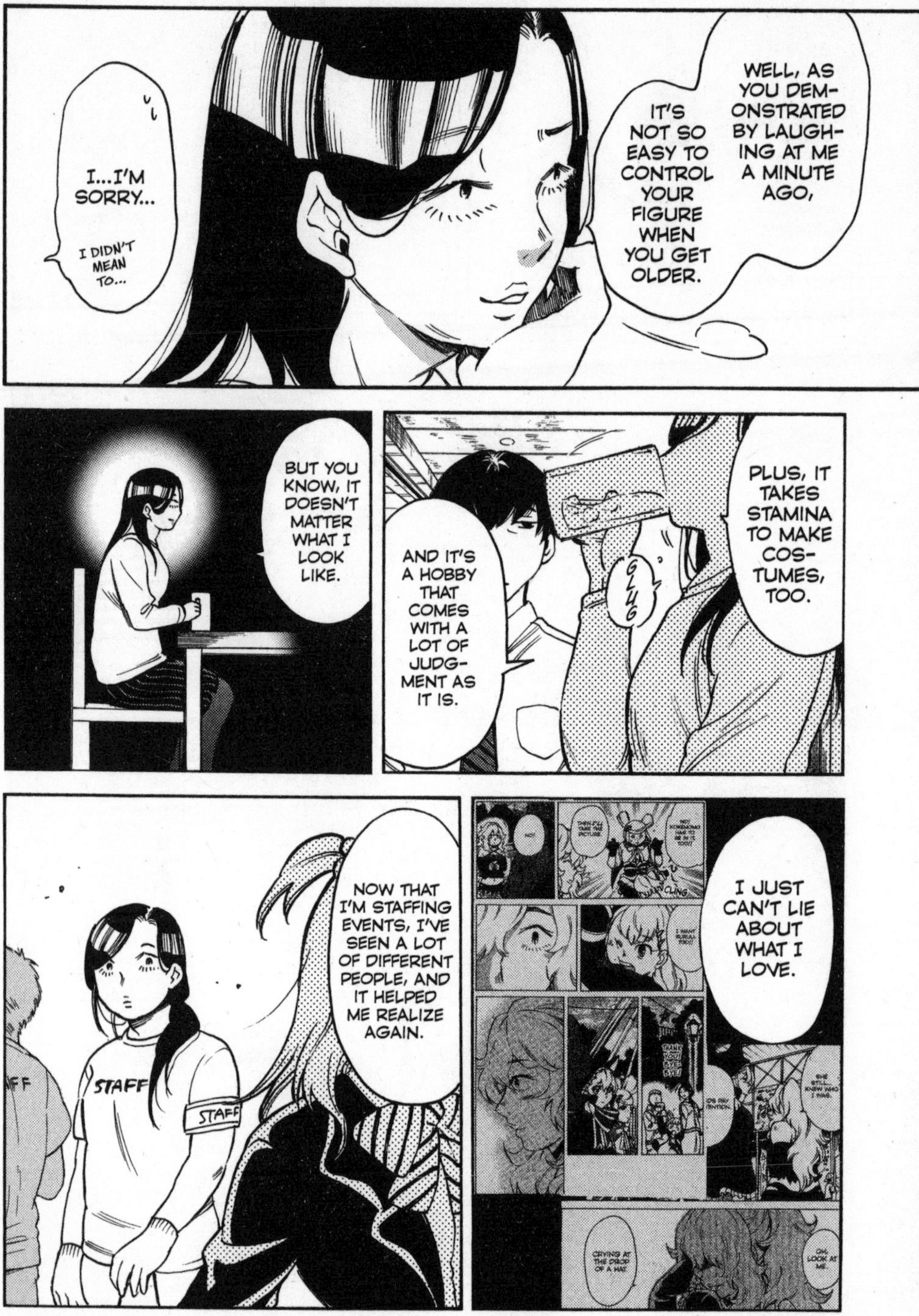
WELL, AS YOU DEMONSTRATED BY LAUGHING AT ME A MINUTE AGO,
IT'S NOT SO EASY TO CONTROL YOUR FIGURE WHEN YOU GET OLDER.
I...I'M SORRY...
I DIDN'T MEAN TO...
PLUS, IT TAKES STAMINA TO MAKE COSTUMES, TOO.
GLUG
AND IT'S A HOBBY THAT COMES WITH A LOT OF JUDGMENT AS IT IS.
BUT YOU KNOW, IT DOESN'T MATTER WHAT I LOOK LIKE.
I JUST CAN'T LIE ABOUT WHAT I LOVE.
NOW THAT I'M STAFFING EVENTS, I'VE SEEN A LOT OF DIFFERENT PEOPLE, AND IT HELPED ME REALIZE AGAIN.
STAFF
STAFF

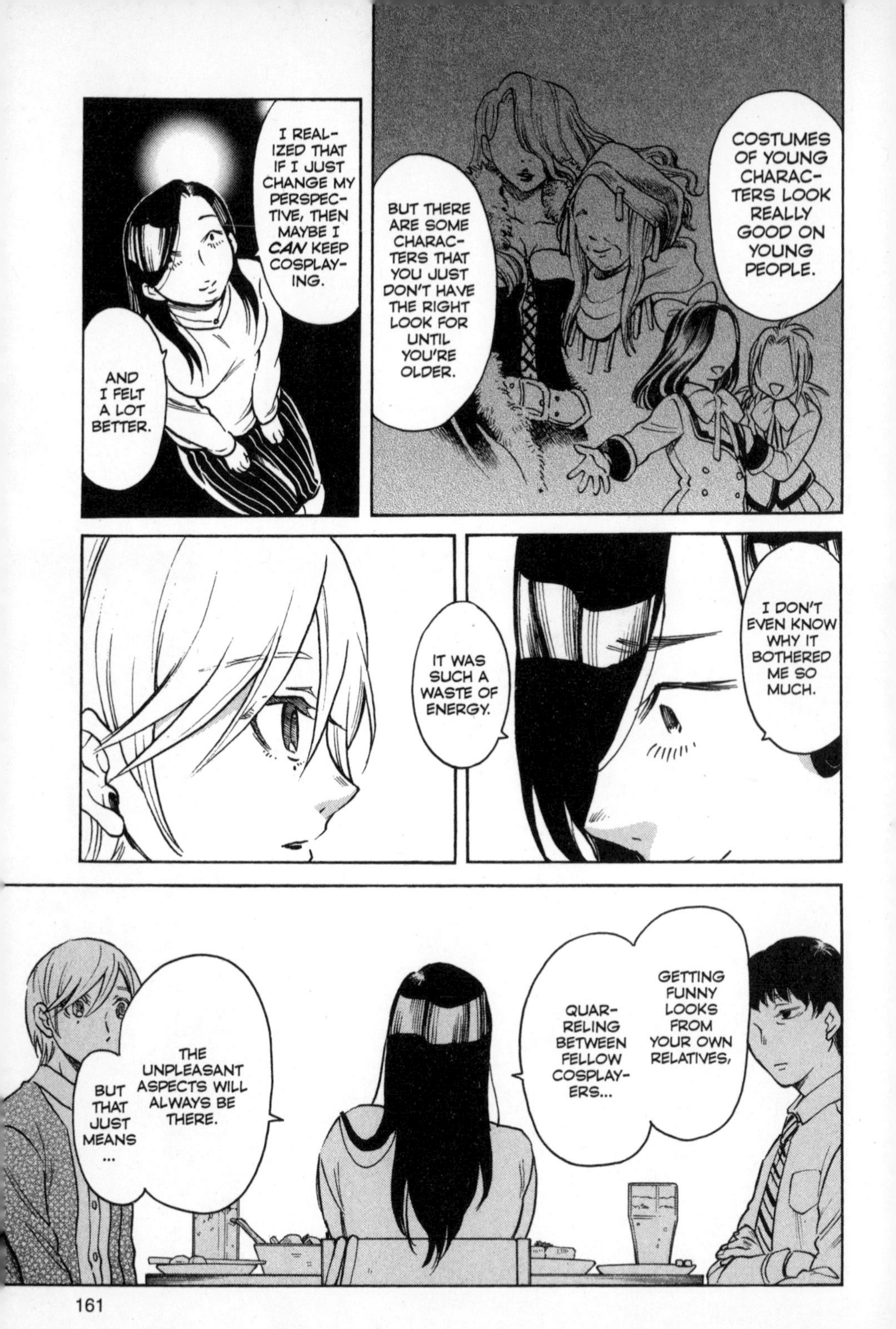
COSTUMES OF YOUNG CHARACTERS LOOK REALLY GOOD ON YOUNG PEOPLE.
BUT THERE ARE SOME CHARACTERS THAT YOU JUST DON'T HAVE THE RIGHT LOOK FOR UNTIL YOU'RE OLDER.
I REALIZED THAT IF I JUST CHANGE MY PERSPECTIVE, THEN MAYBE I *CAN* KEEP COSPLAYING.
AND I FELT A LOT BETTER.
I DON'T EVEN KNOW WHY IT BOTHERED ME SO MUCH.
IT WAS SUCH A WASTE OF ENERGY.
GETTING FUNNY LOOKS FROM YOUR OWN RELATIVES,
QUARRELING BETWEEN FELLOW COSPLAYERS...
THE UNPLEASANT ASPECTS WILL ALWAYS BE THERE.
BUT THAT JUST MEANS ...

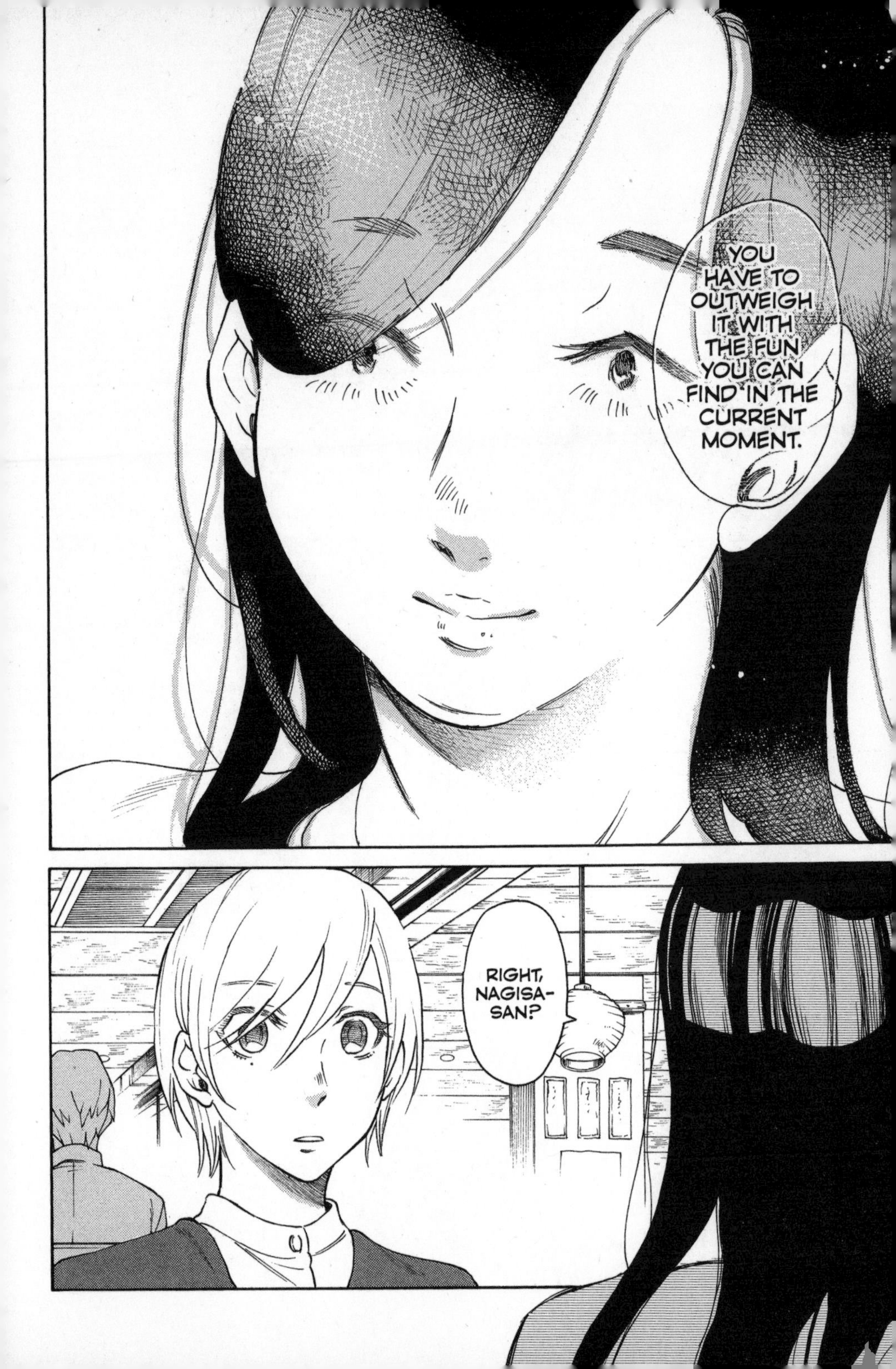
YOU HAVE TO OUTWEIGH IT WITH THE FUN YOU CAN FIND IN THE CURRENT MOMENT.
RIGHT, NAGISA-SAN?

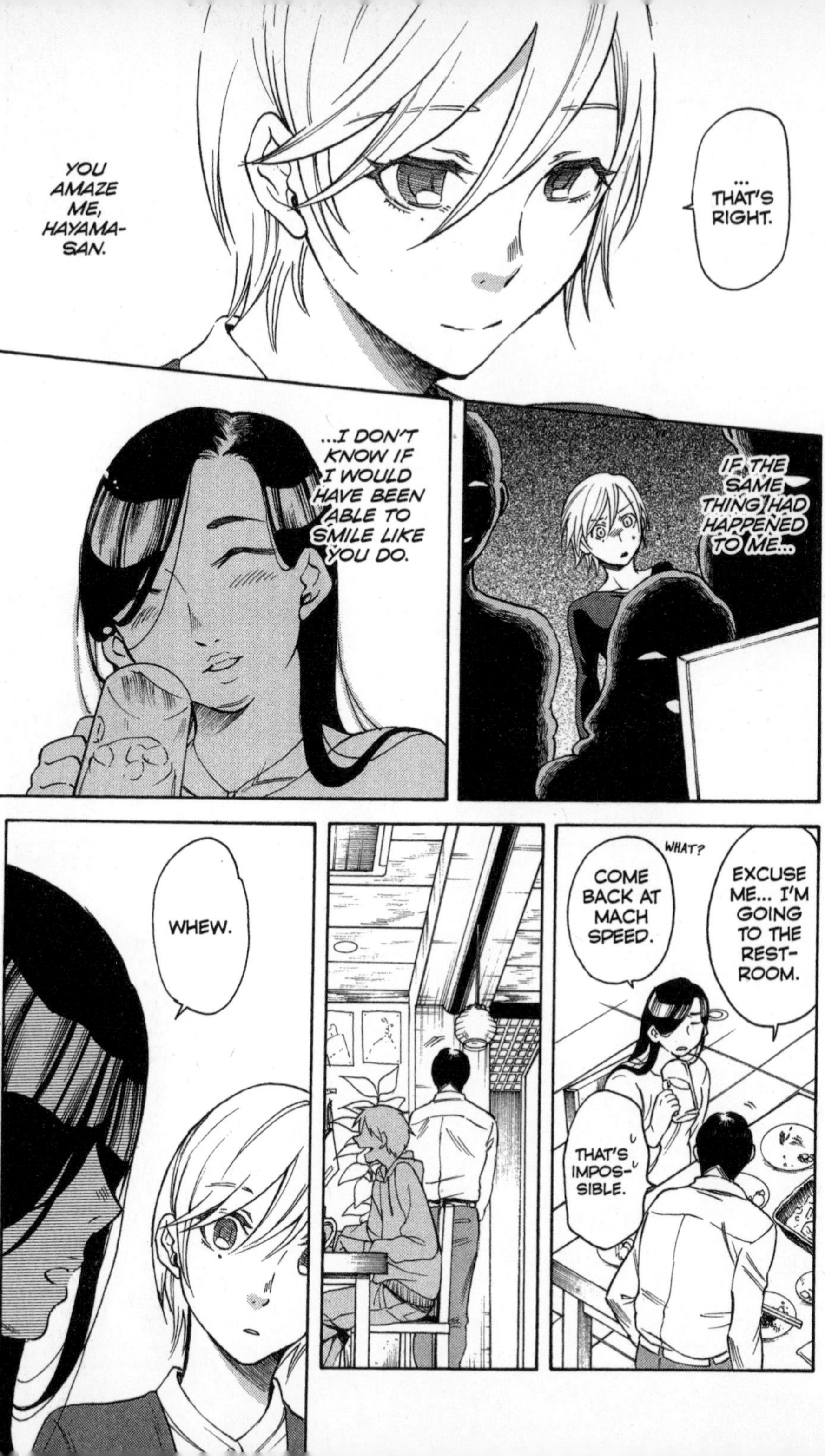
...THAT'S RIGHT.
YOU AMAZE ME, HAYAMA-SAN.
IF THE SAME THING HAD HAPPENED TO ME...
...I DON'T KNOW IF I WOULD HAVE BEEN ABLE TO SMILE LIKE YOU DO.
EXCUSE ME... I'M GOING TO THE REST-ROOM.
WHAT?
COME BACK AT MACH SPEED.
THAT'S IMPOS-SIBLE.
WHEW.

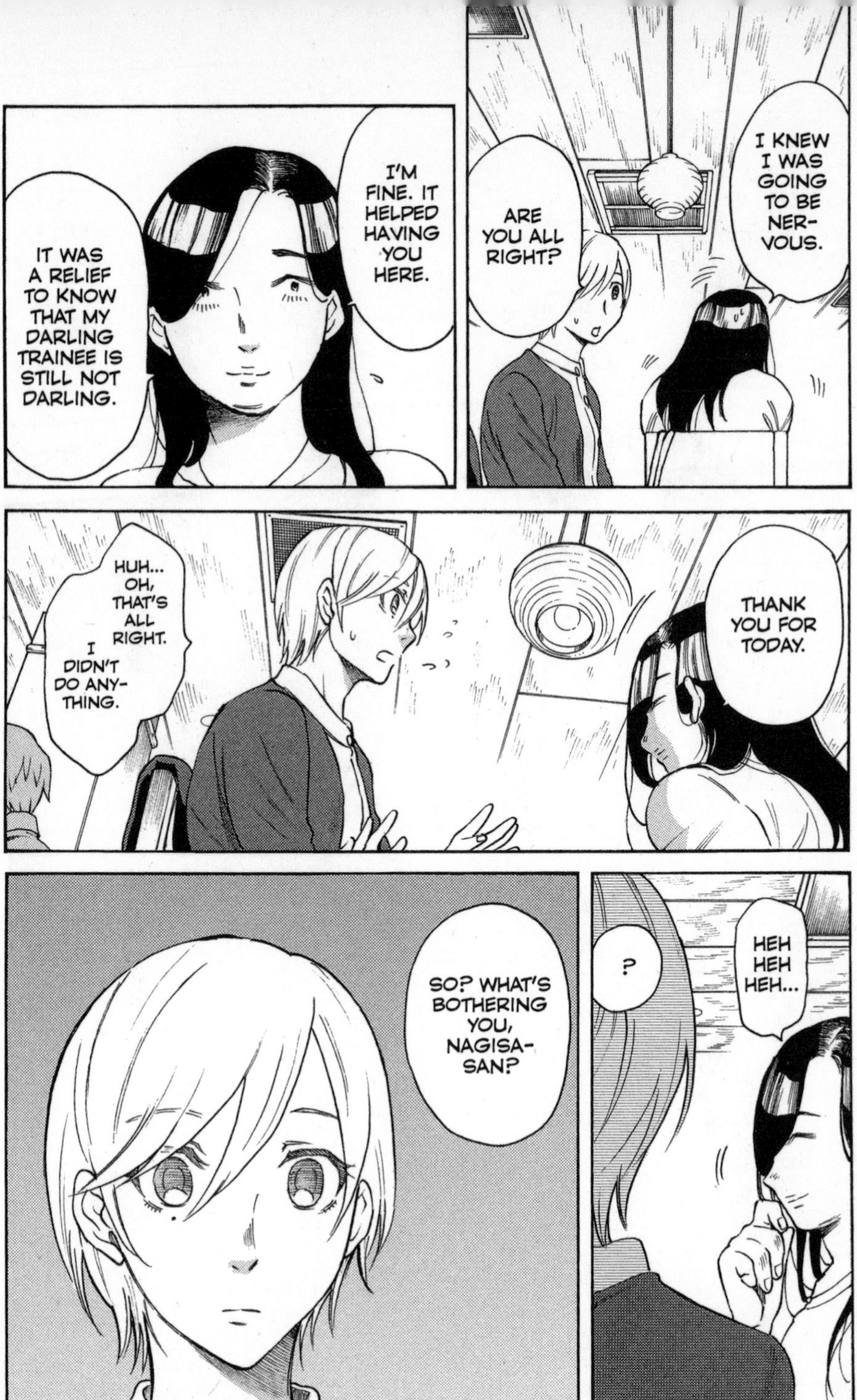
I KNEW I WAS GOING TO BE NER-VOUS.
ARE YOU ALL RIGHT?
I'M FINE. IT HELPED HAVING YOU HERE.
IT WAS A RELIEF TO KNOW THAT MY DARLING TRAINEE IS STILL NOT DARLING.
THANK YOU FOR TODAY.
HUH... OH, THAT'S ALL RIGHT.
I DIDN'T DO ANY-THING.
HEH HEH HEH...
?
SO? WHAT'S BOTHERING YOU, NAGISA-SAN?

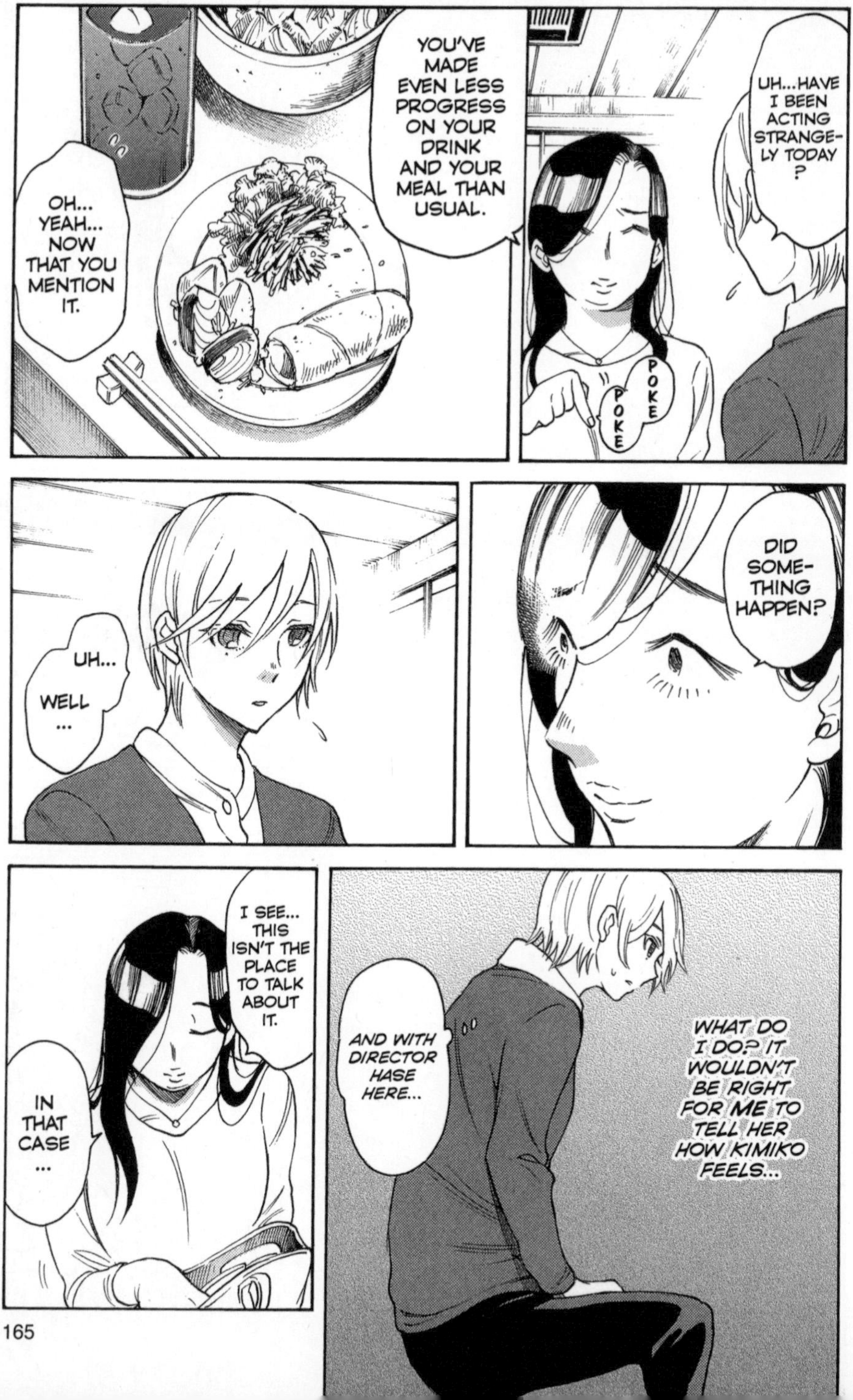
UH...HAVE I BEEN ACTING STRANGE-LY TODAY ?
POKE POKE
YOU'VE MADE EVEN LESS PROGRESS ON YOUR DRINK AND YOUR MEAL THAN USUAL.
OH... YEAH... NOW THAT YOU MENTION IT.
DID SOME-THING HAPPEN?
UH... WELL ...
WHAT DO I DO? IT WOULDN'T BE RIGHT FOR ME TO TELL HER HOW KIMIKO FEELS...
AND WITH DIRECTOR HASE HERE...
I SEE... THIS ISN'T THE PLACE TO TALK ABOUT IT.
IN THAT CASE ...

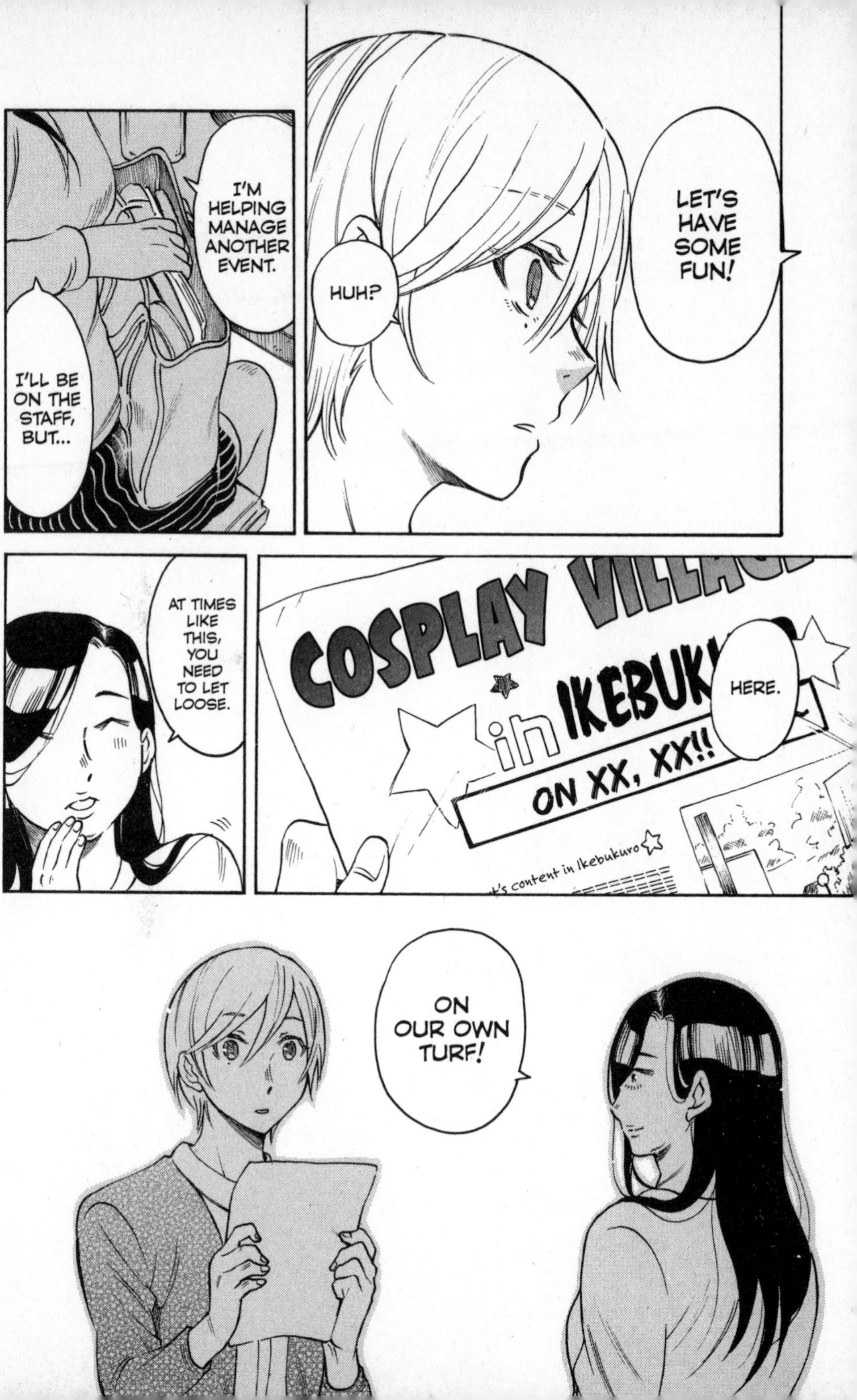
LET'S HAVE SOME FUN!
HUH?
I'M HELPING MANAGE ANOTHER EVENT.
I'LL BE ON THE STAFF, BUT...
COSPLAY
in IKEBUK
ON XX, XX!!
t's content in Ikebukuro
HERE.
AT TIMES LIKE THIS, YOU NEED TO LET LOOSE.
ON OUR OWN TURF!

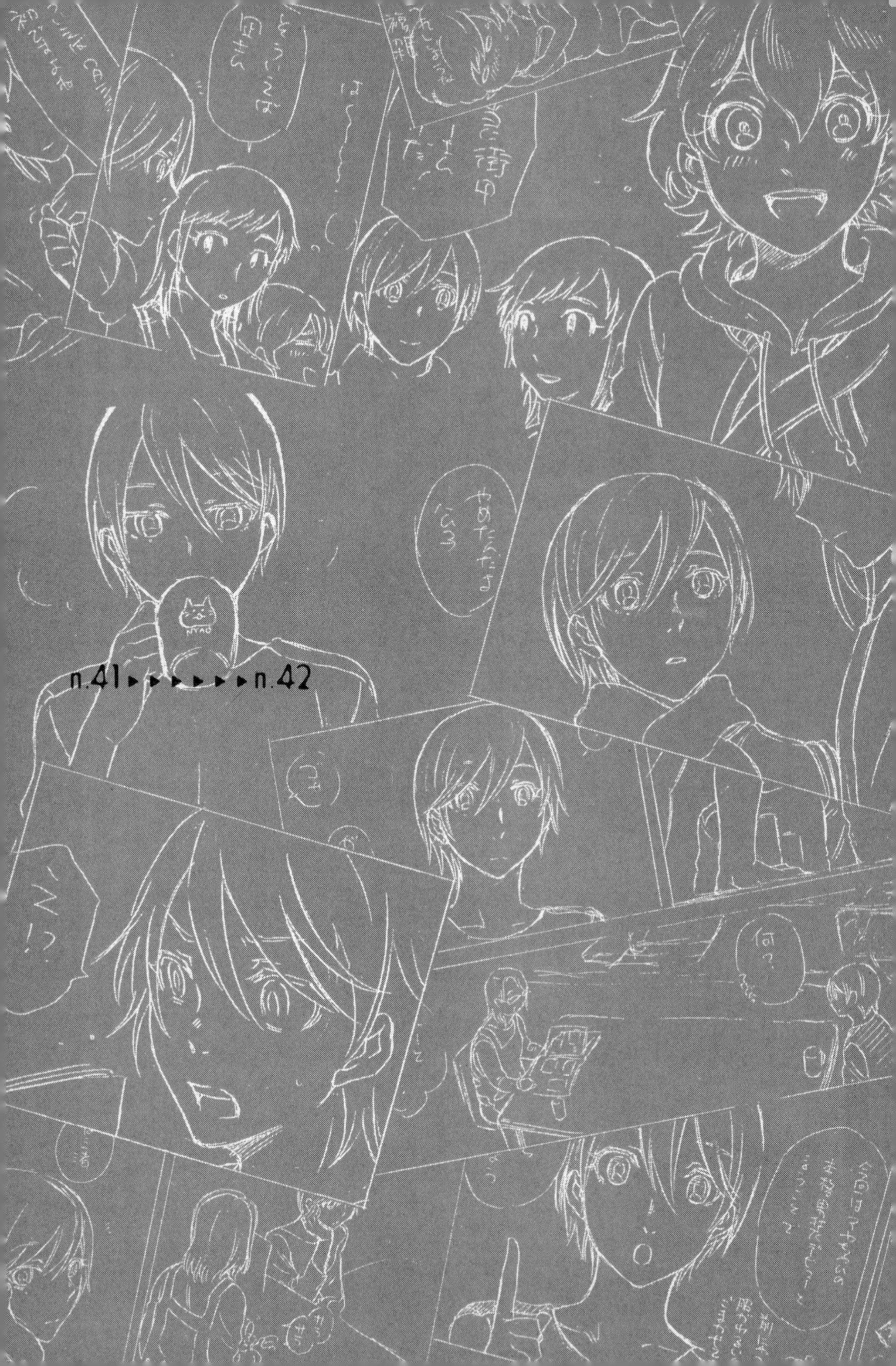
n.41▸▸▸▸▸▸▸n.42

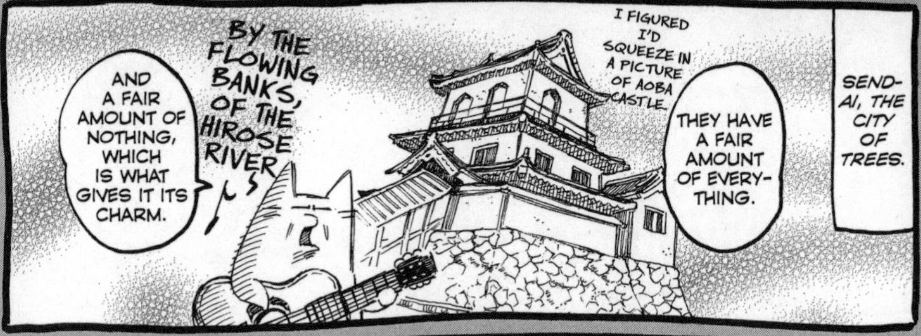
SEND-AI, THE CITY OF TREES.
THEY HAVE A FAIR AMOUNT OF EVERY-THING.
I FIGURED I'D SQUEEZE IN A PICTURE OF AOBA CASTLE.
BY THE FLOWING BANKS, OF THE HIROSE RIVER
AND A FAIR AMOUNT OF NOTHING, WHICH IS WHAT GIVES IT ITS CHARM.

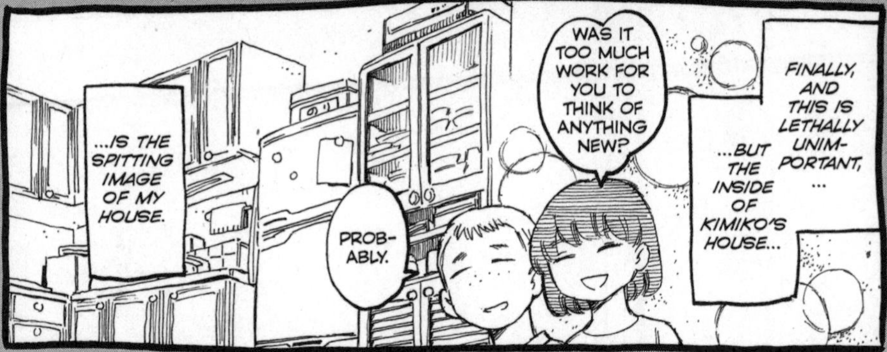
FINALLY, AND THIS IS LETHALLY UNIM-PORTANT, ...
...BUT THE INSIDE OF KIMIKO'S HOUSE...
WAS IT TOO MUCH WORK FOR YOU TO THINK OF ANYTHING NEW?
PROB-ABLY.
...IS THE SPITTING IMAGE OF MY HOUSE.

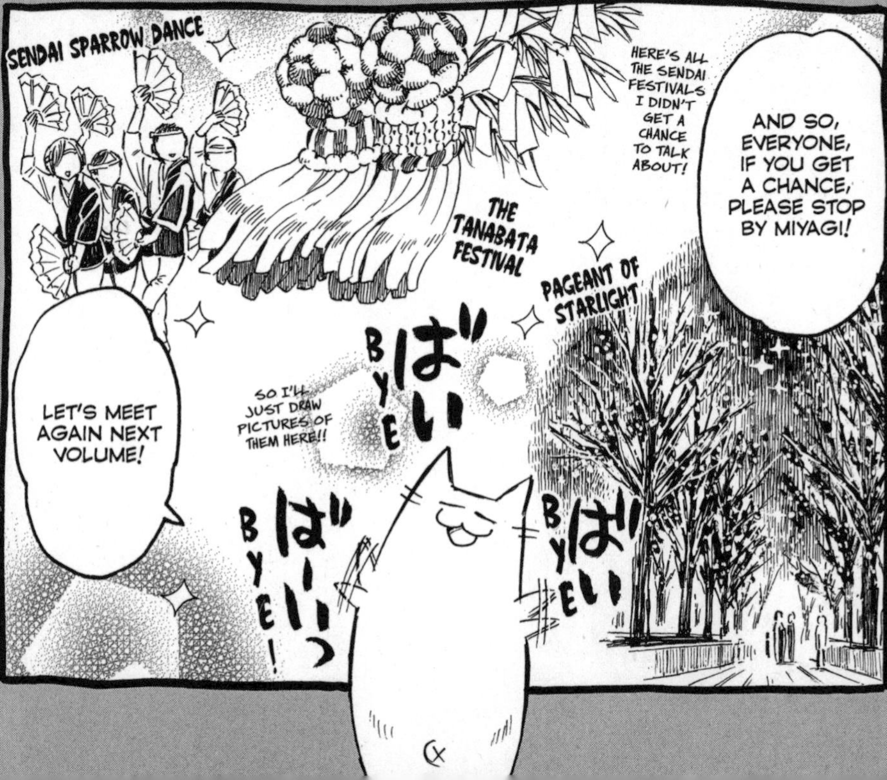
AND SO, EVERYONE, IF YOU GET A CHANCE, PLEASE STOP BY MIYAGI!
HERE'S ALL THE SENDAI FESTIVALS I DIDN'T GET A CHANCE TO TALK ABOUT!
SO I'LL JUST DRAW PICTURES OF THEM HERE!!
SENDAI SPARROW DANCE
THE TANABATA FESTIVAL
PAGEANT OF STARLIGHT
LET'S MEET AGAIN NEXT VOLUME!
ばい BYE
ばい BYE
ばーいっ BYE!

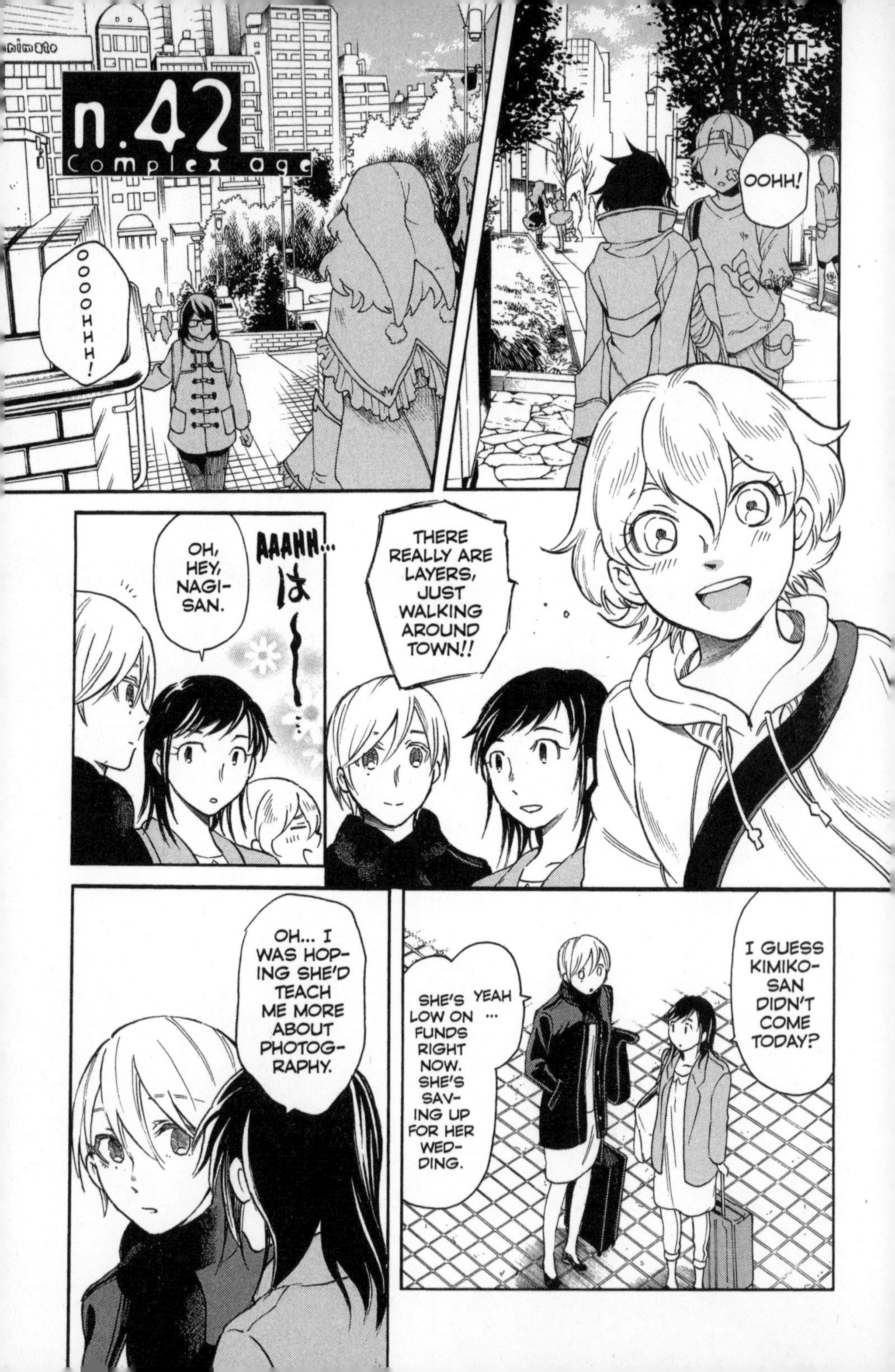
OOHH!
n.42
Complex age
OOOOHHH!
THERE REALLY ARE LAYERS, JUST WALKING AROUND TOWN!!
OH, HEY, NAGI-SAN.
AAAHH... は～…
I GUESS KIMIKO-SAN DIDN'T COME TODAY?
YEAH ... SHE'S LOW ON FUNDS RIGHT NOW. SHE'S SAV-ING UP FOR HER WED-DING.
OH... I WAS HOP-ING SHE'D TEACH ME MORE ABOUT PHOTOG-RAPHY.

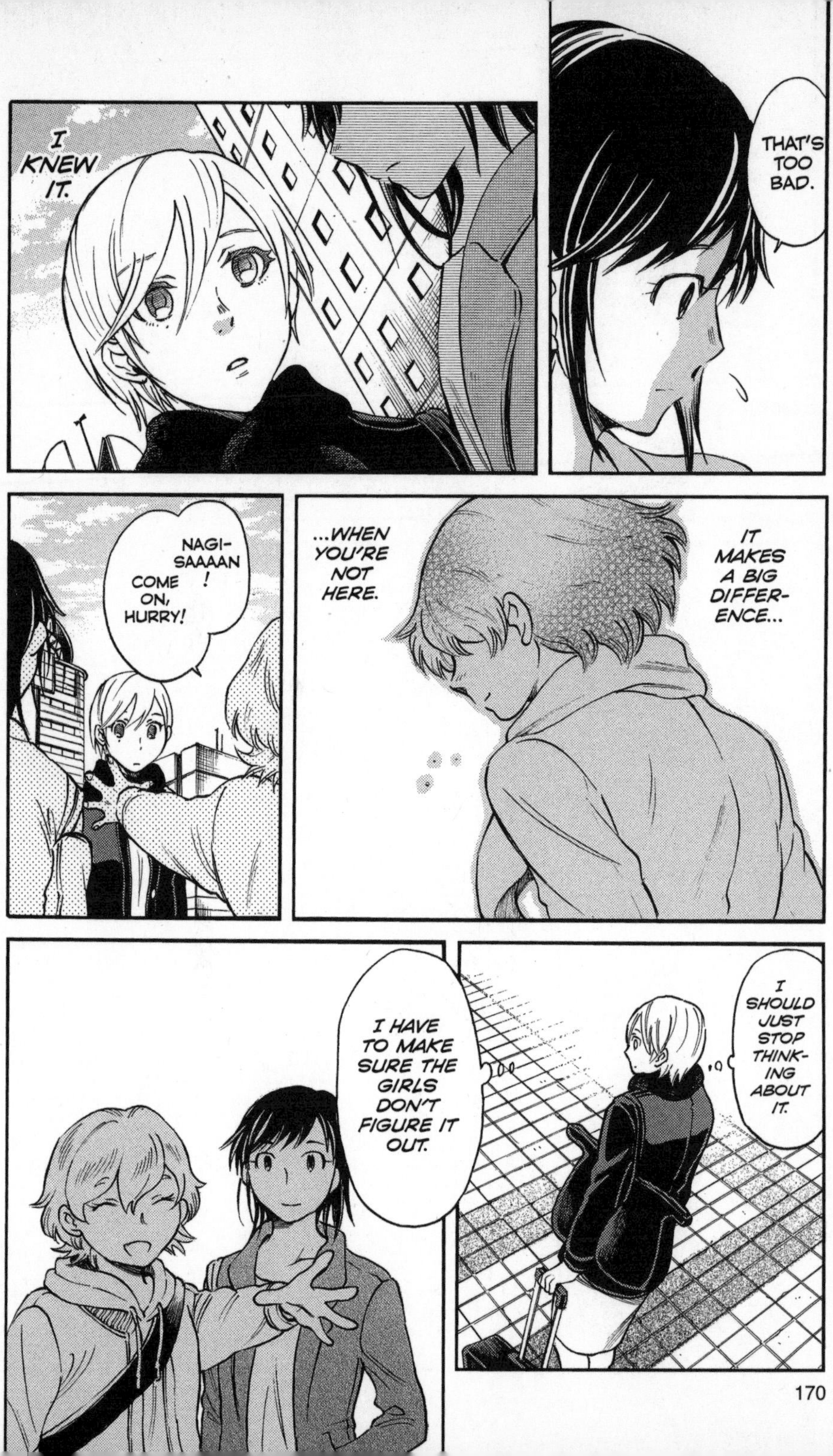
THAT'S TOO BAD.
I KNEW IT.
IT MAKES A BIG DIFFERENCE...
...WHEN YOU'RE NOT HERE.
NAGI-SAAAAN!
COME ON, HURRY!
I SHOULD JUST STOP THINKING ABOUT IT.
I HAVE TO MAKE SURE THE GIRLS DON'T FIGURE IT OUT.

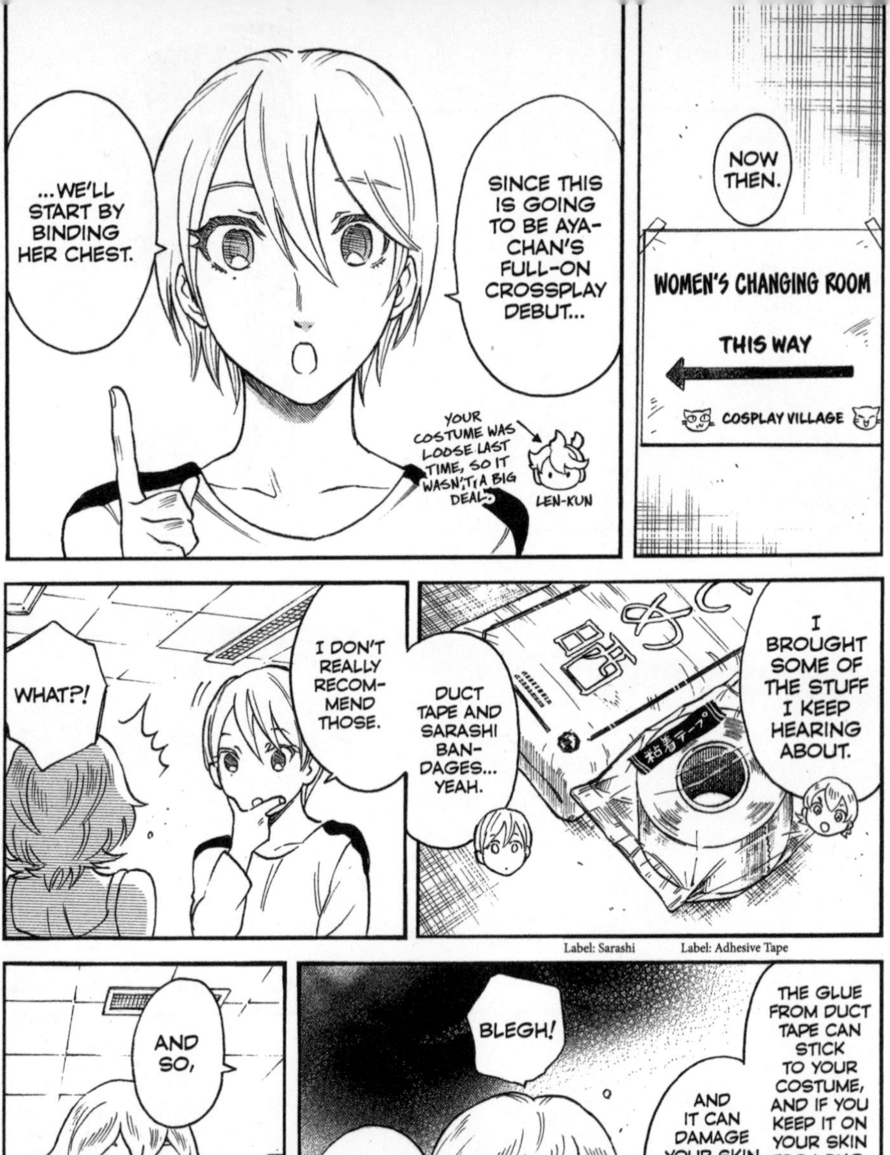
NOW THEN.
WOMEN'S CHANGING ROOM
THIS WAY
COSPLAY VILLAGE
SINCE THIS IS GOING TO BE AYA-CHAN'S FULL-ON CROSSPLAY DEBUT...
YOUR COSTUME WAS LOOSE LAST TIME, SO IT WASN'T A BIG DEAL.
LEN-KUN
...WE'LL START BY BINDING HER CHEST.
I BROUGHT SOME OF THE STUFF I KEEP HEARING ABOUT.
粘着テープ
DUCT TAPE AND SARASHI BAN-DAGES... YEAH.
I DON'T REALLY RECOM-MEND THOSE.
WHAT?!
THE GLUE FROM DUCT TAPE CAN STICK TO YOUR COSTUME, AND IF YOU KEEP IT ON YOUR SKIN TOO LONG, IT CAN GIVE YOU A RASH.
AND IT CAN DAMAGE YOUR SKIN WHEN YOU PEEL IT OFF.
AND THEN YOU HAVE TO THROW IT OUT EVERY TIME YOU'RE DONE.
BLEGH!
SARASHI BAN-DAGES ARE HARD TO PUT ON YOURSELF IF YOU'RE NOT USED TO THEM.
AND SO,
RUMMAGE
RUMMAGE

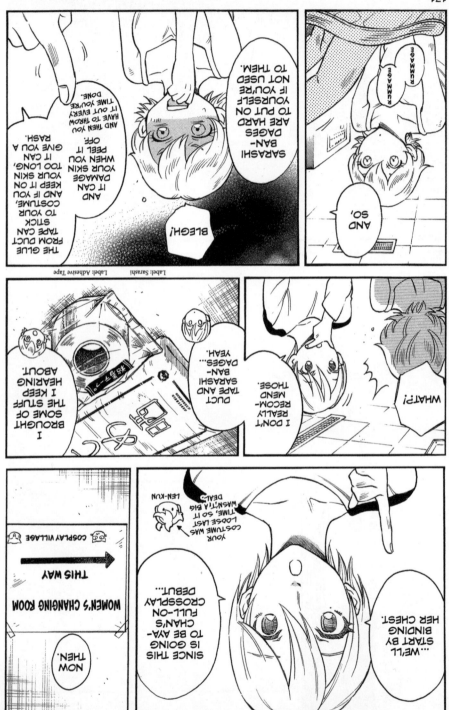

Label: Sarashi Label: Adhesive Tape

HOW ABOUT THIS?
ビローン
SPROING
IS THIS...
A SUP-PORT BELT OR SOME-THING?
YES!
IT ATTACHES WITH VELCRO, SO IT'S EASY TO ADJUST.
AND SOME OF THEM ARE MADE WITH MESH FABRIC, SO YOU CAN USE THEM TO KEEP FROM SWEATING ON YOUR COSTUME.
FIRST WRAP IT ABOVE YOUR BREASTS.
THEN LOWER IT INTO POSITION.
AND IF YOU'RE WORRIED ABOUT THE COST, YOU CAN GET THEM AT THE 100 YEN STORE.
USE TWO FOR EXTRA FLATTENING.
THERE ARE ALL KINDS OF OTHER THINGS YOU COULD DO, LIKE CUT OFF THE TOP PART OF A PAIR OF PANTYHOSE.
THIS PART.
IF YOU ALREADY HAVE A PAIR WITH A RUN, YOU MIGHT AS WELL TRY IT!
OTHER METHODS
B HOLDER
SPRA
NABE SHIRT, ETC.
WHEN DECIDING WHAT TO USE, IT'S GOOD TO CONSIDER THE TIME OF YEAR AND HOW MUCH YOU'RE GOING TO WANT TO MOVE AROUND THAT DAY.
HOW DOES IT FEEL?
I CAN STILL BREATHE ...

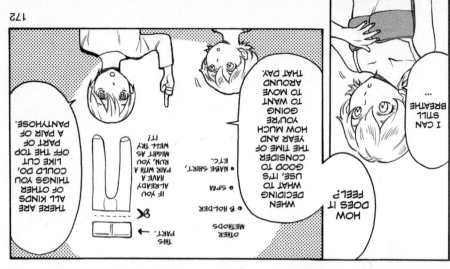

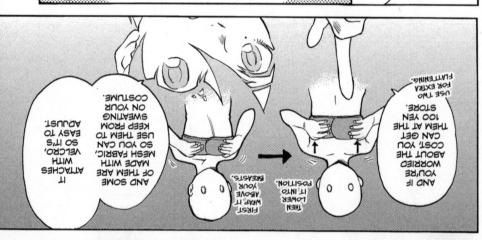

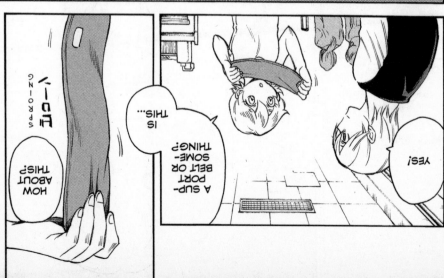

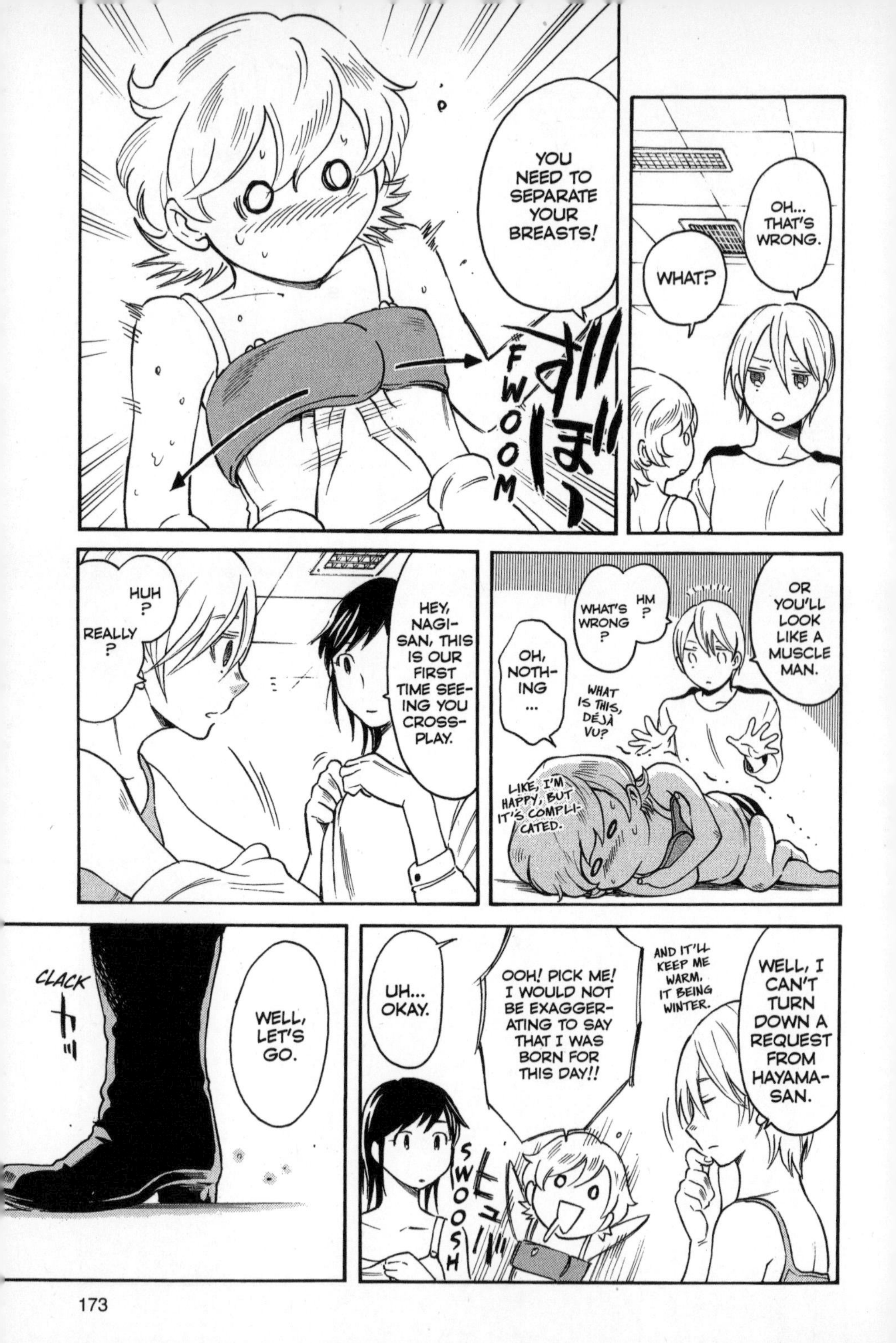
OH... THAT'S WRONG.
WHAT?
YOU NEED TO SEPARATE YOUR BREASTS!
FWOOM
OR YOU'LL LOOK LIKE A MUSCLE MAN.
HM? WHAT'S WRONG?
OH, NOTHING...
WHAT IS THIS, DÉJÀ VU?
LIKE, I'M HAPPY, BUT IT'S COMPLICATED.
HEY, NAGI-SAN, THIS IS OUR FIRST TIME SEEING YOU CROSSPLAY.
HUH? REALLY?
WELL, I CAN'T TURN DOWN A REQUEST FROM HAYAMA-SAN.
AND IT'LL KEEP ME WARM, IT BEING WINTER.
OOH! PICK ME! I WOULD NOT BE EXAGGERATING TO SAY THAT I WAS BORN FOR THIS DAY!!
UH... OKAY.
SWOOSH
WELL, LET'S GO.
CLACK

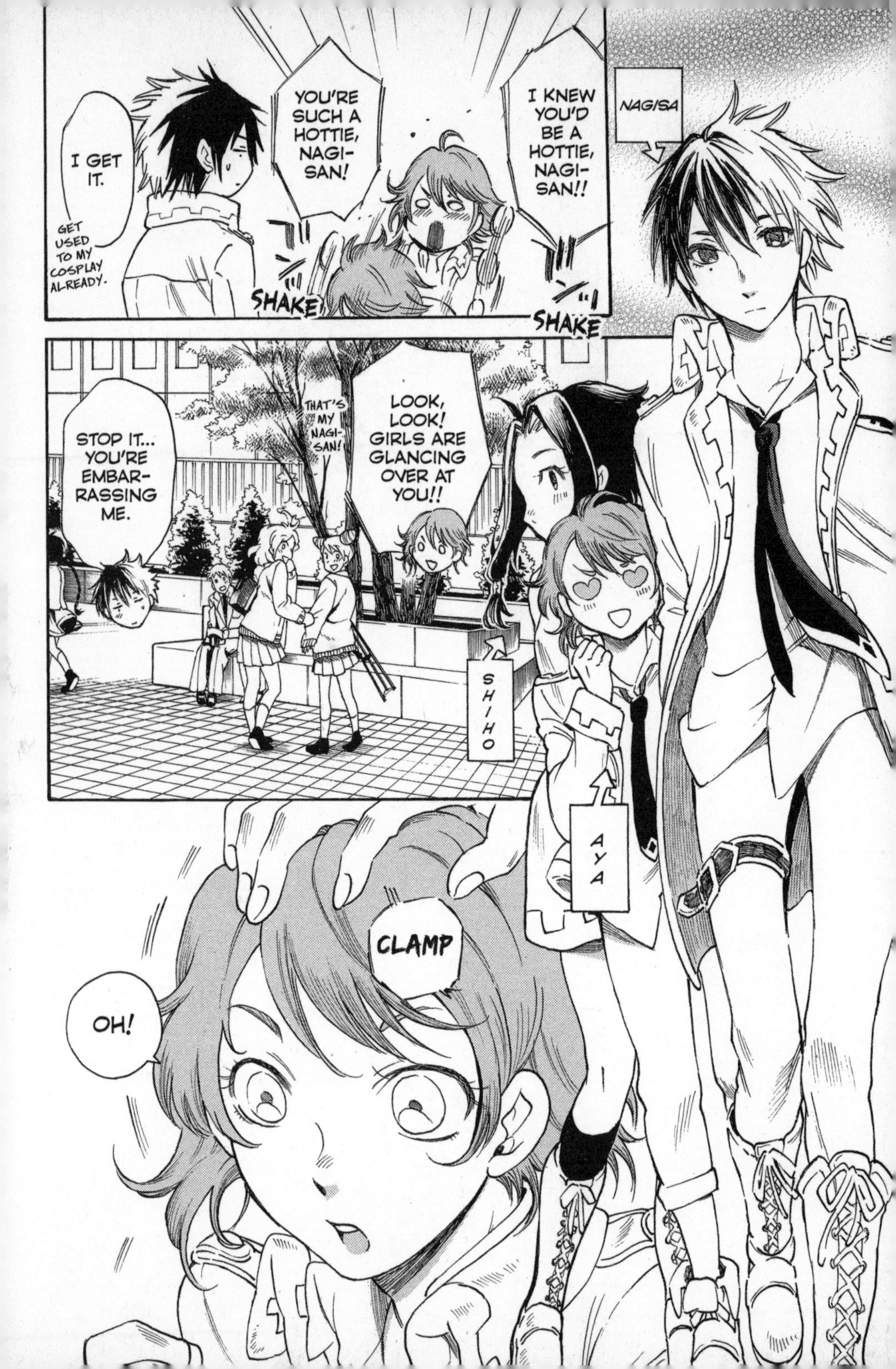
NAGISA
I KNEW YOU'D BE A HOTTIE, NAGI-SAN!!
SHAKE
YOU'RE SUCH A HOTTIE, NAGI-SAN!
SHAKE
I GET IT.
GET USED TO MY COSPLAY ALREADY.
LOOK, LOOK! GIRLS ARE GLANCING OVER AT YOU!!
THAT'S MY NAGI-SAN!
STOP IT... YOU'RE EMBAR-RASSING ME.
SHIHO
AYA
CLAMP
OH!

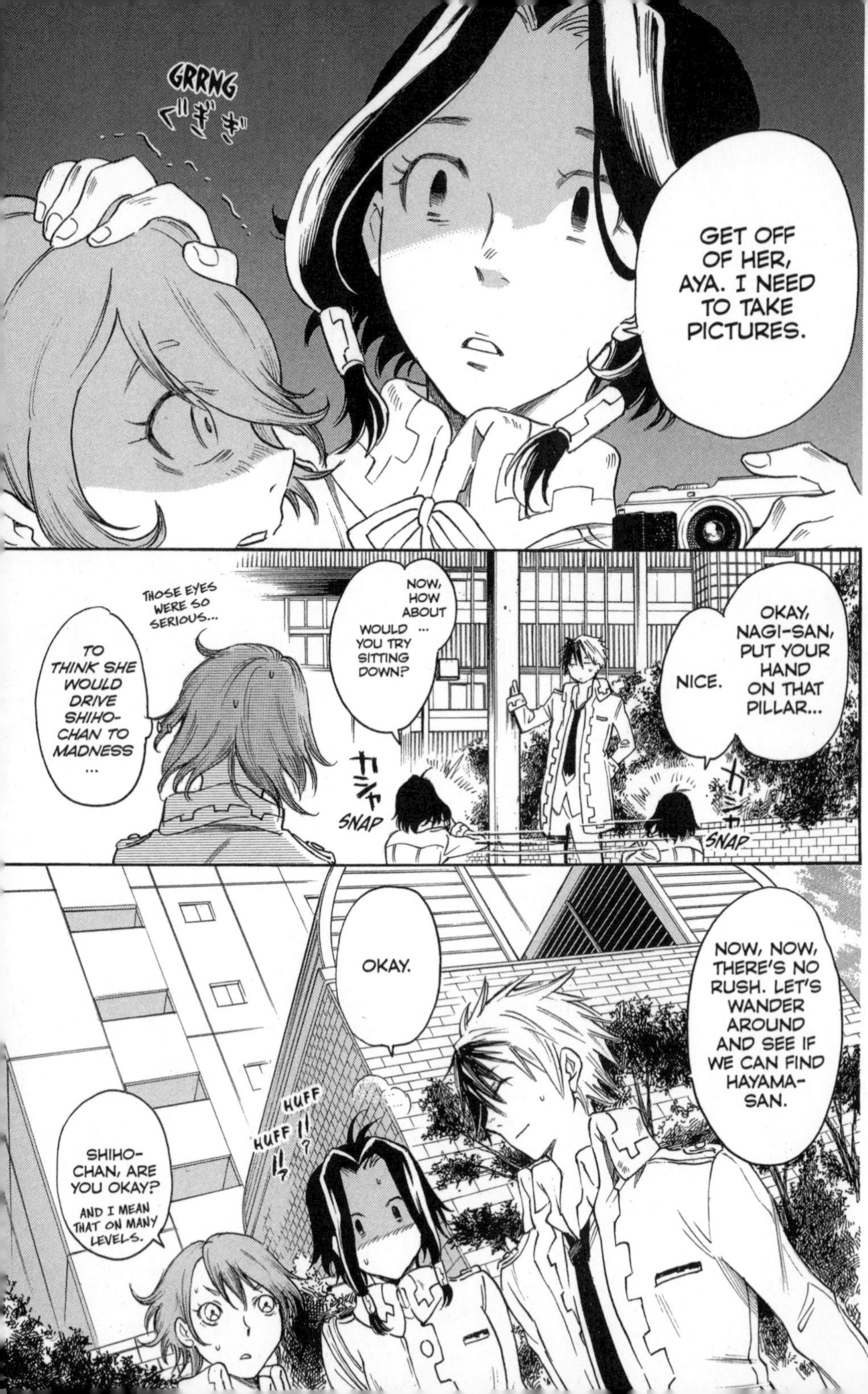
GET OFF OF HER, AYA. I NEED TO TAKE PICTURES.
GRRNG
OKAY, NAGI-SAN, PUT YOUR HAND ON THAT PILLAR...
NICE.
SNAP
NOW, HOW ABOUT ... WOULD YOU TRY SITTING DOWN?
SNAP
THOSE EYES WERE SO SERIOUS...
TO THINK SHE WOULD DRIVE SHIHO-CHAN TO MADNESS ...
NOW, NOW, THERE'S NO RUSH. LET'S WANDER AROUND AND SEE IF WE CAN FIND HAYAMA-SAN.
OKAY.
HUFF HUFF !!?
SHIHO-CHAN, ARE YOU OKAY?
AND I MEAN THAT ON MANY LEVELS.

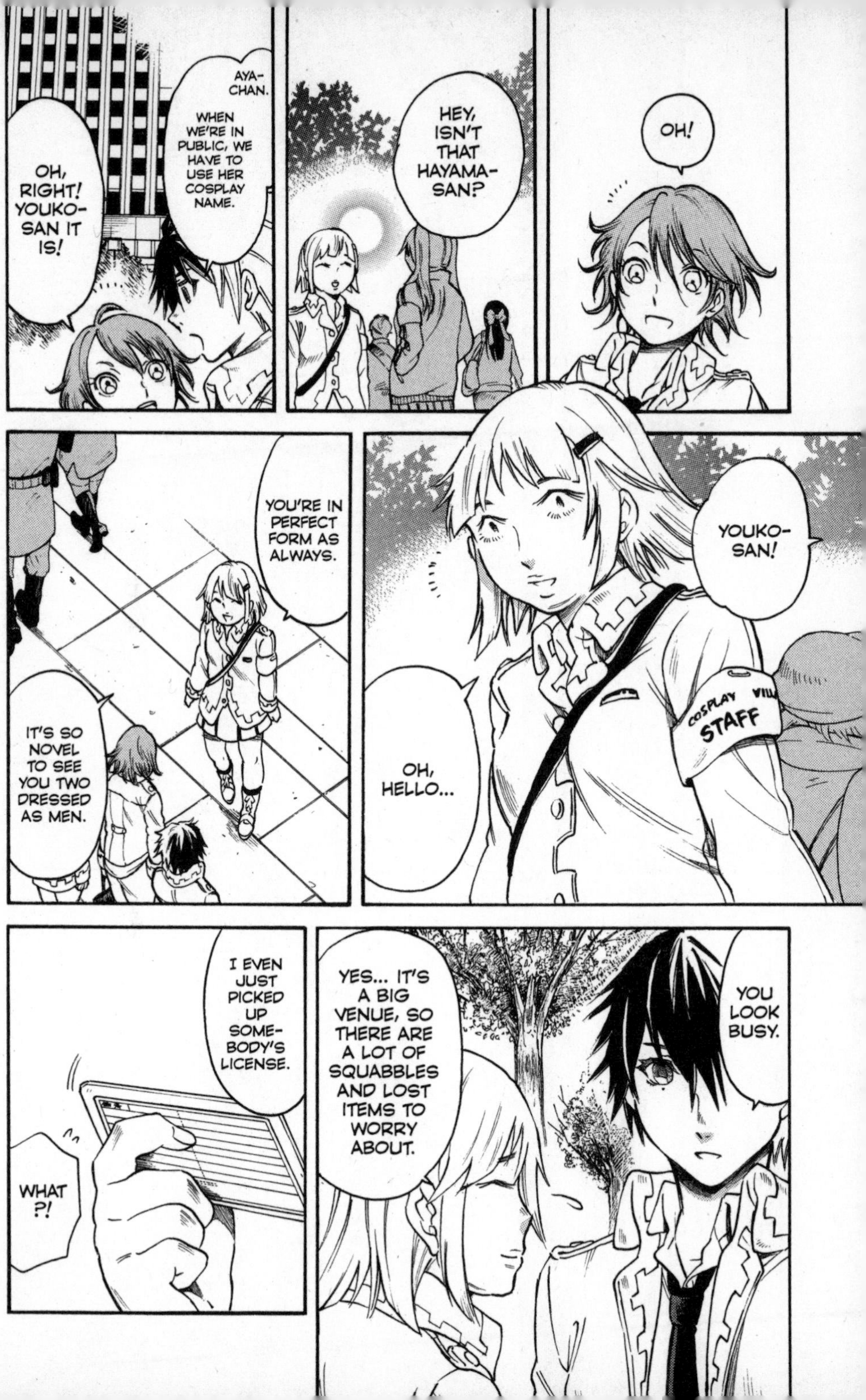
OH!
HEY, ISN'T THAT HAYAMA-SAN?
AYA-CHAN.
WHEN WE'RE IN PUBLIC, WE HAVE TO USE HER COSPLAY NAME.
OH, RIGHT! YOUKO-SAN IT IS!
YOUKO-SAN!
COSPLAY VILL
STAFF
OH, HELLO...
YOU'RE IN PERFECT FORM AS ALWAYS.
IT'S SO NOVEL TO SEE YOU TWO DRESSED AS MEN.
YOU LOOK BUSY.
YES... IT'S A BIG VENUE, SO THERE ARE A LOT OF SQUABBLES AND LOST ITEMS TO WORRY ABOUT.
I EVEN JUST PICKED UP SOME-BODY'S LICENSE.
WHAT ?!

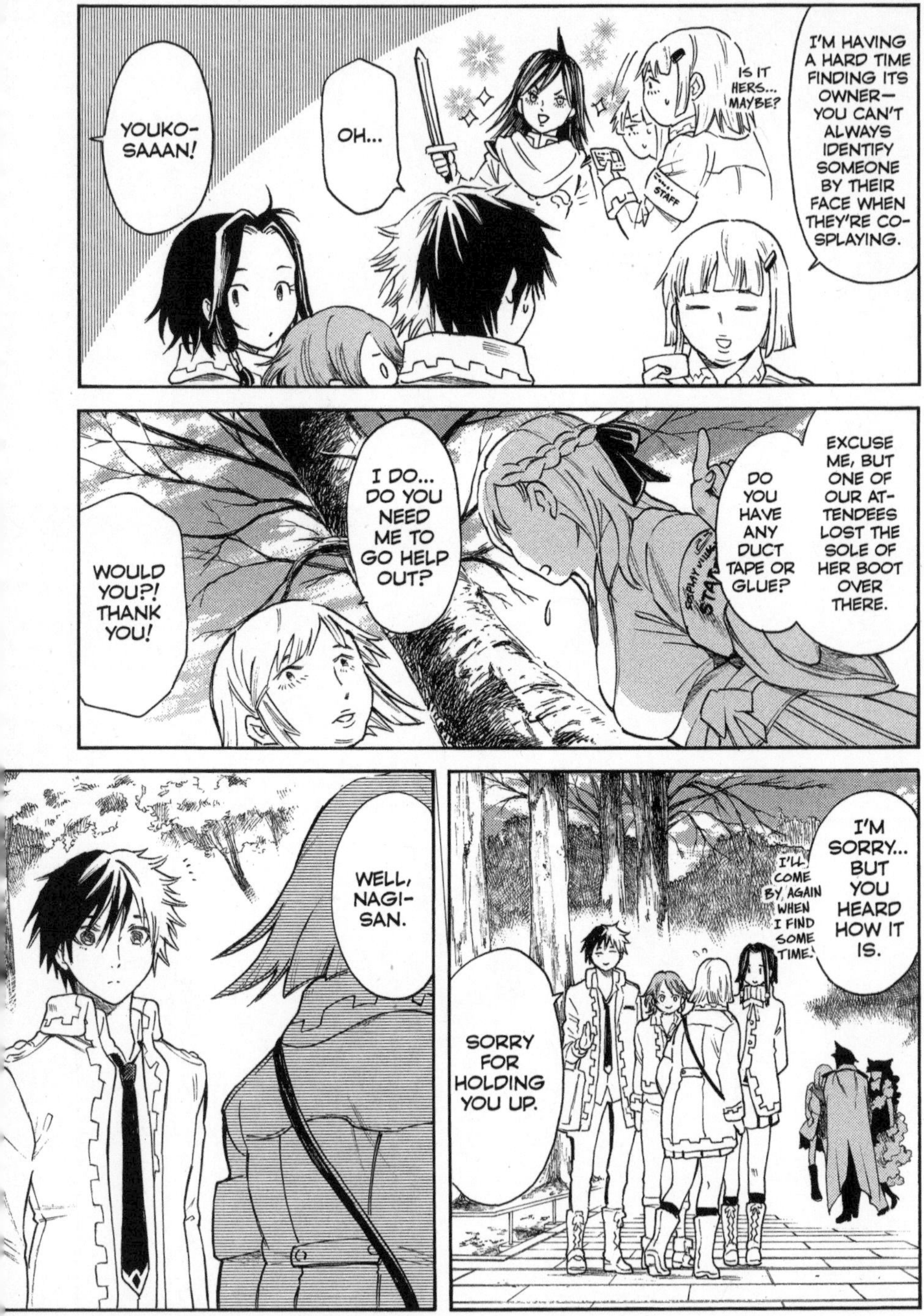
I'M HAVING A HARD TIME FINDING ITS OWNER—YOU CAN'T ALWAYS IDENTIFY SOMEONE BY THEIR FACE WHEN THEY'RE CO-SPLAYING.
IS IT HERS... MAYBE?
STAFF
OH...
YOUKO-SAAAN!
EXCUSE ME, BUT ONE OF OUR AT-TENDEES LOST THE SOLE OF HER BOOT OVER THERE.
DO YOU HAVE ANY DUCT TAPE OR GLUE?
I DO... DO YOU NEED ME TO GO HELP OUT?
WOULD YOU?! THANK YOU!
I'M SORRY... BUT YOU HEARD HOW IT IS.
I'LL COME BY AGAIN WHEN I FIND SOME TIME.
SORRY FOR HOLDING YOU UP.
WELL, NAGI-SAN.

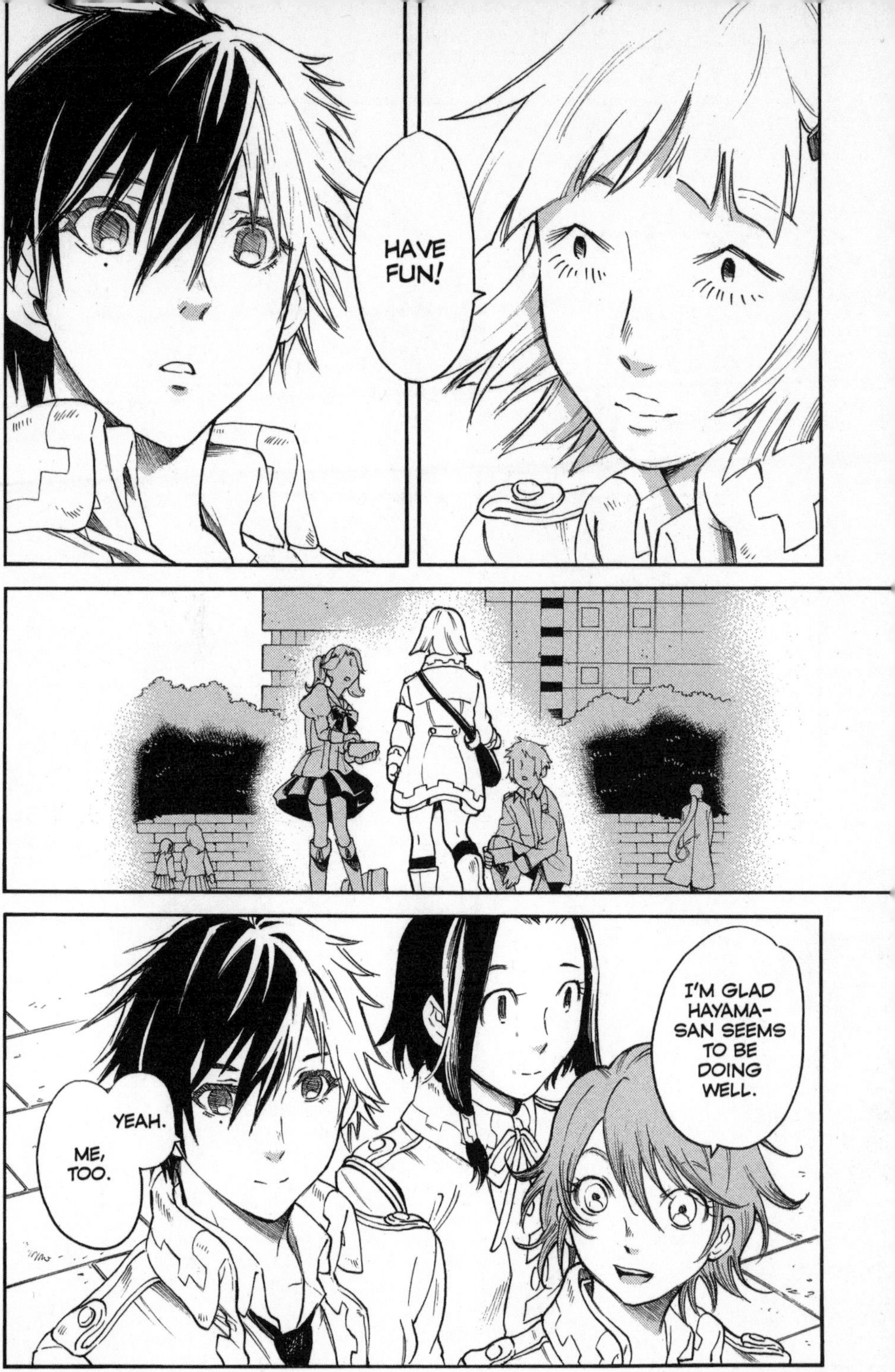
HAVE FUN!
I'M GLAD HAYAMA-SAN SEEMS TO BE DOING WELL.
YEAH.
ME, TOO.

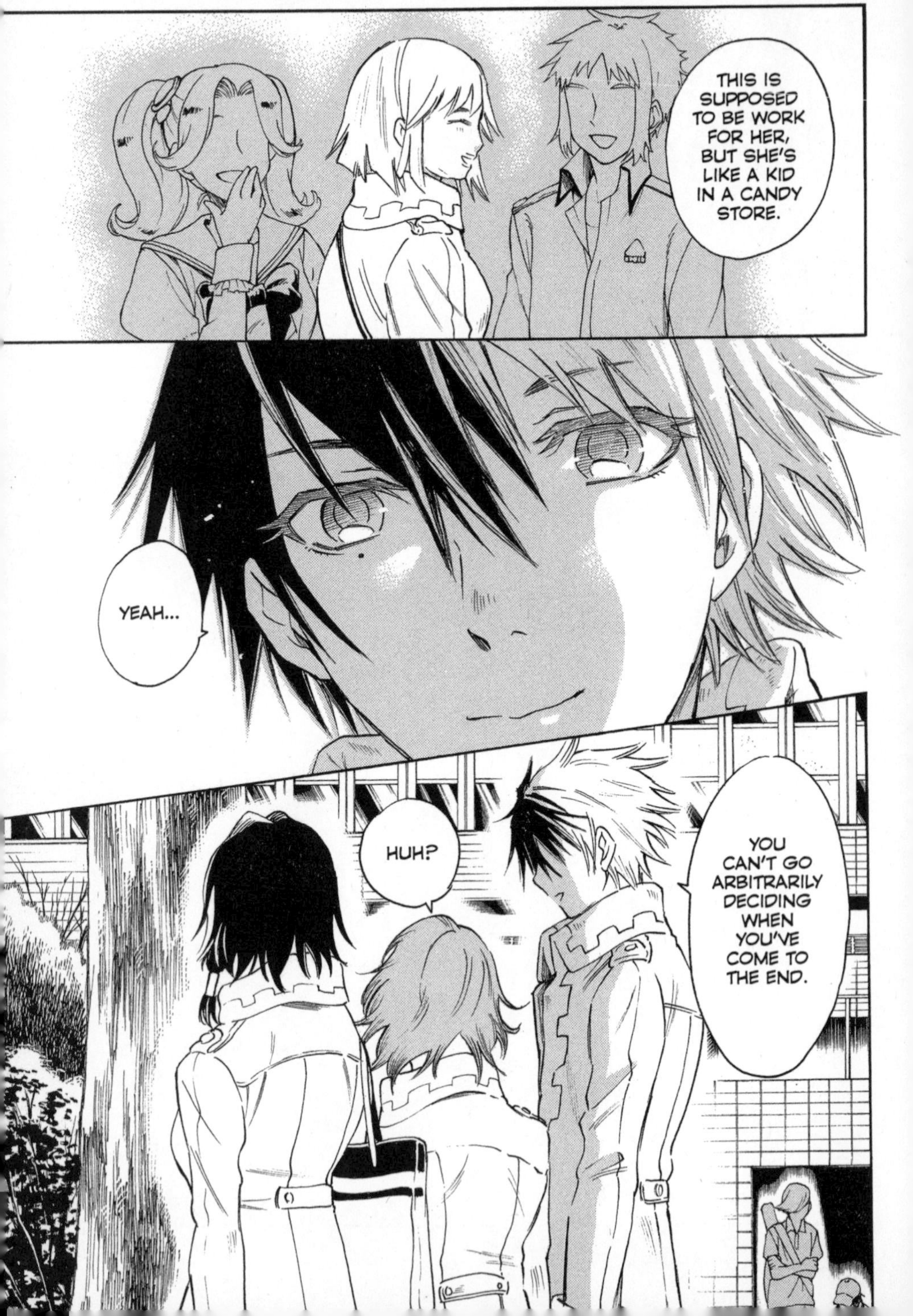
THIS IS SUPPOSED TO BE WORK FOR HER, BUT SHE'S LIKE A KID IN A CANDY STORE.
YEAH...
YOU CAN'T GO ARBITRARILY DECIDING WHEN YOU'VE COME TO THE END.
HUH?

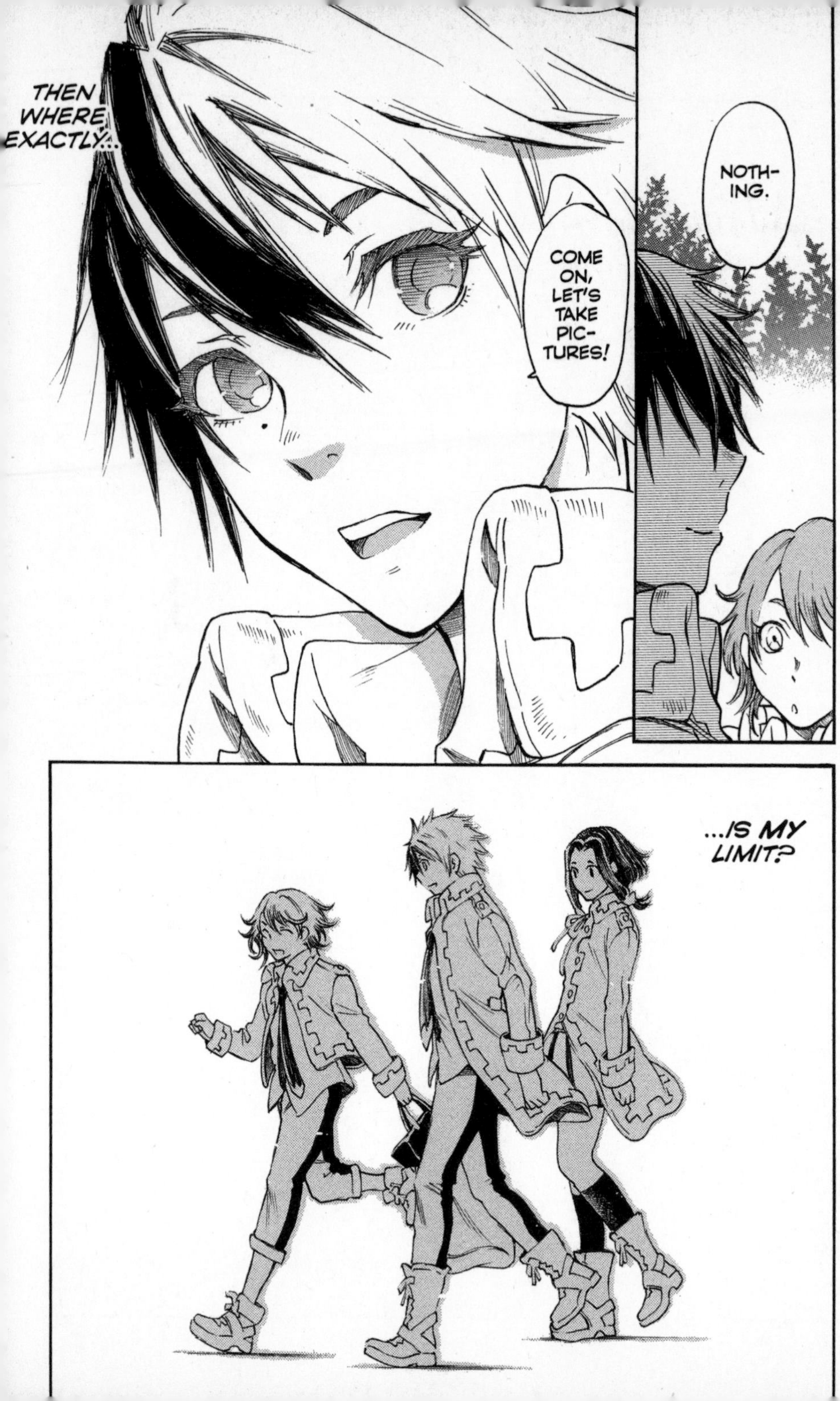
NOTH-ING.
COME ON, LET'S TAKE PIC-TURES!
THEN WHERE EXACTLY...
...IS MY LIMIT?

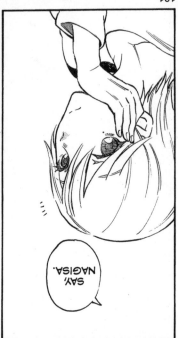

SAY, NAGISA.

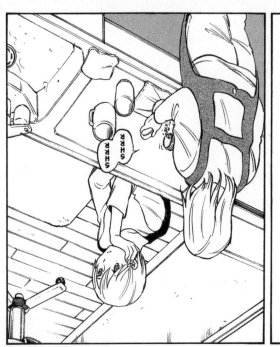

SHRR
SHRR

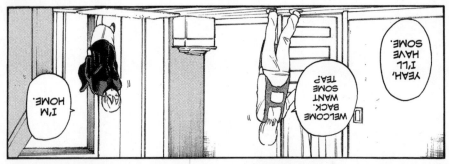

I'M HOME.

WELCOME
BACK.
WANT
SOME
TEA?

YEAH,
I'LL
HAVE
SOME.

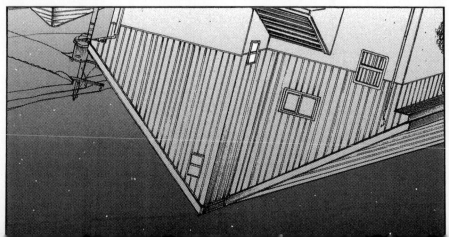

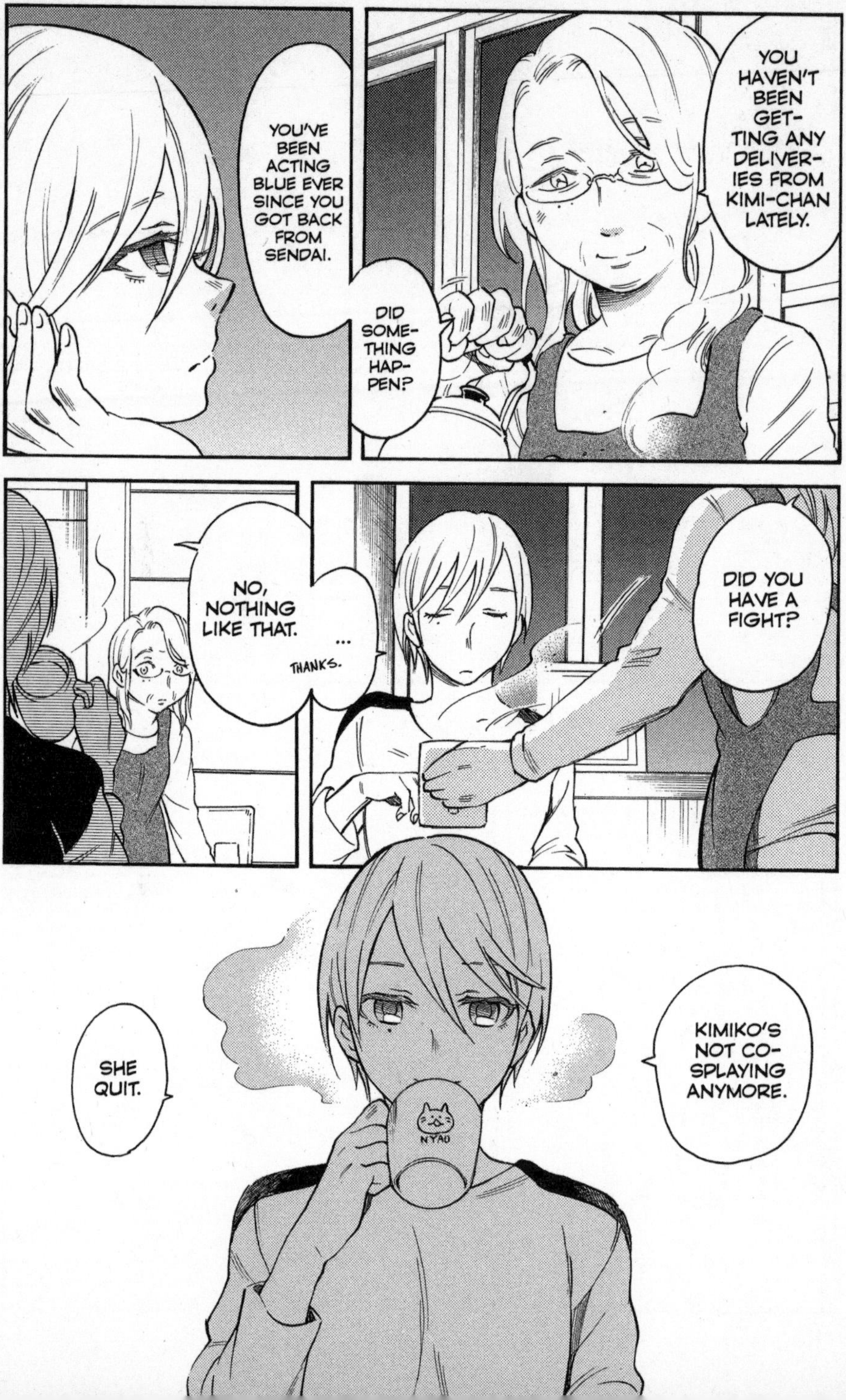
YOU HAVEN'T BEEN GETTING ANY DELIVERIES FROM KIMI-CHAN LATELY.
DID SOMETHING HAPPEN?
YOU'VE BEEN ACTING BLUE EVER SINCE YOU GOT BACK FROM SENDAI.
DID YOU HAVE A FIGHT?
NO, NOTHING LIKE THAT.
... THANKS.
NYAO
KIMIKO'S NOT CO-SPLAYING ANYMORE.
SHE QUIT.

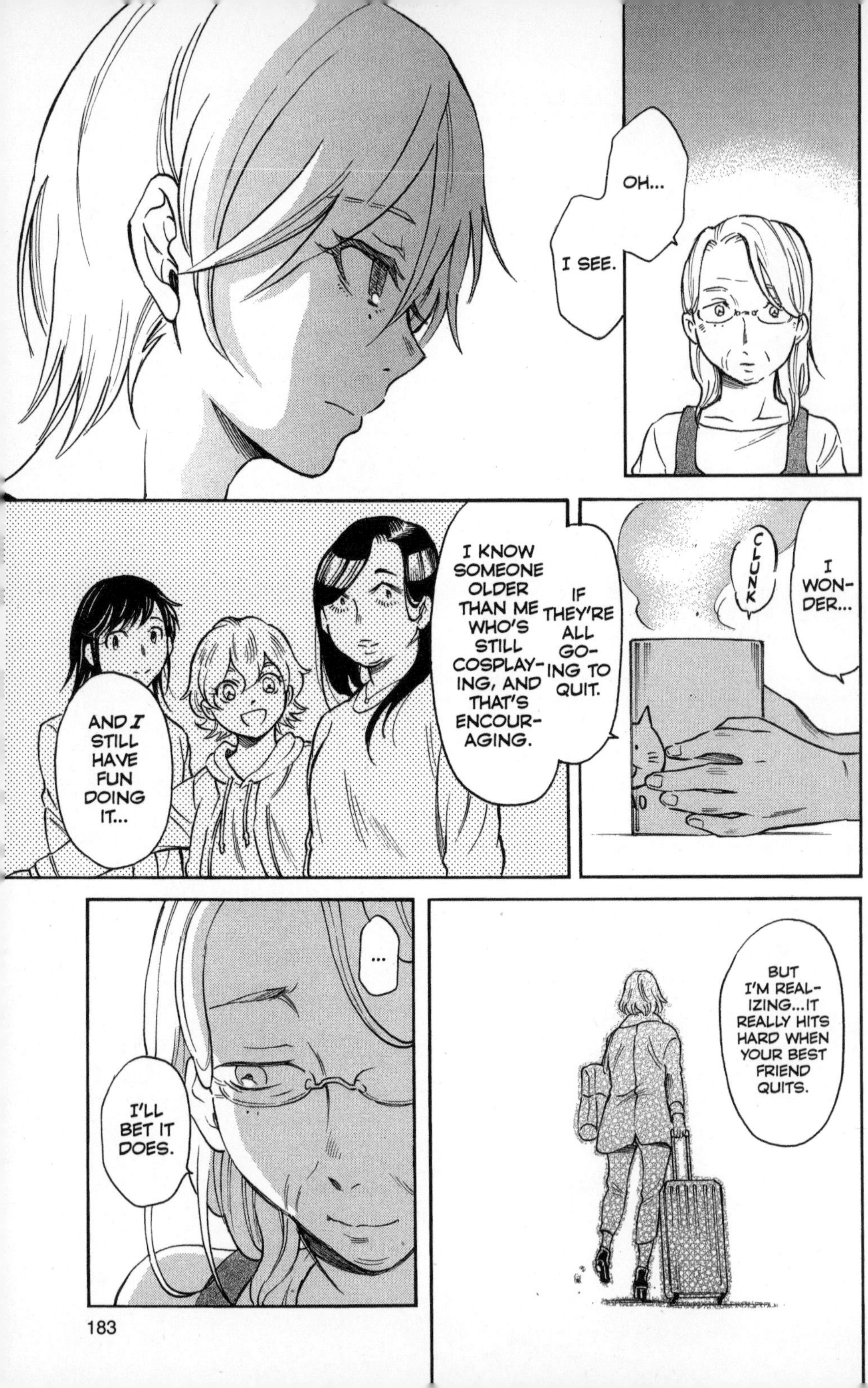
OH...
I SEE.
I WONDER...
CLUNK
I KNOW SOMEONE OLDER THAN ME WHO'S STILL COSPLAYING, AND THAT'S ENCOURAGING.
IF THEY'RE ALL GOING TO QUIT.
AND *I* STILL HAVE FUN DOING IT...
BUT I'M REALIZING...IT REALLY HITS HARD WHEN YOUR BEST FRIEND QUITS.
...
I'LL BET IT DOES.

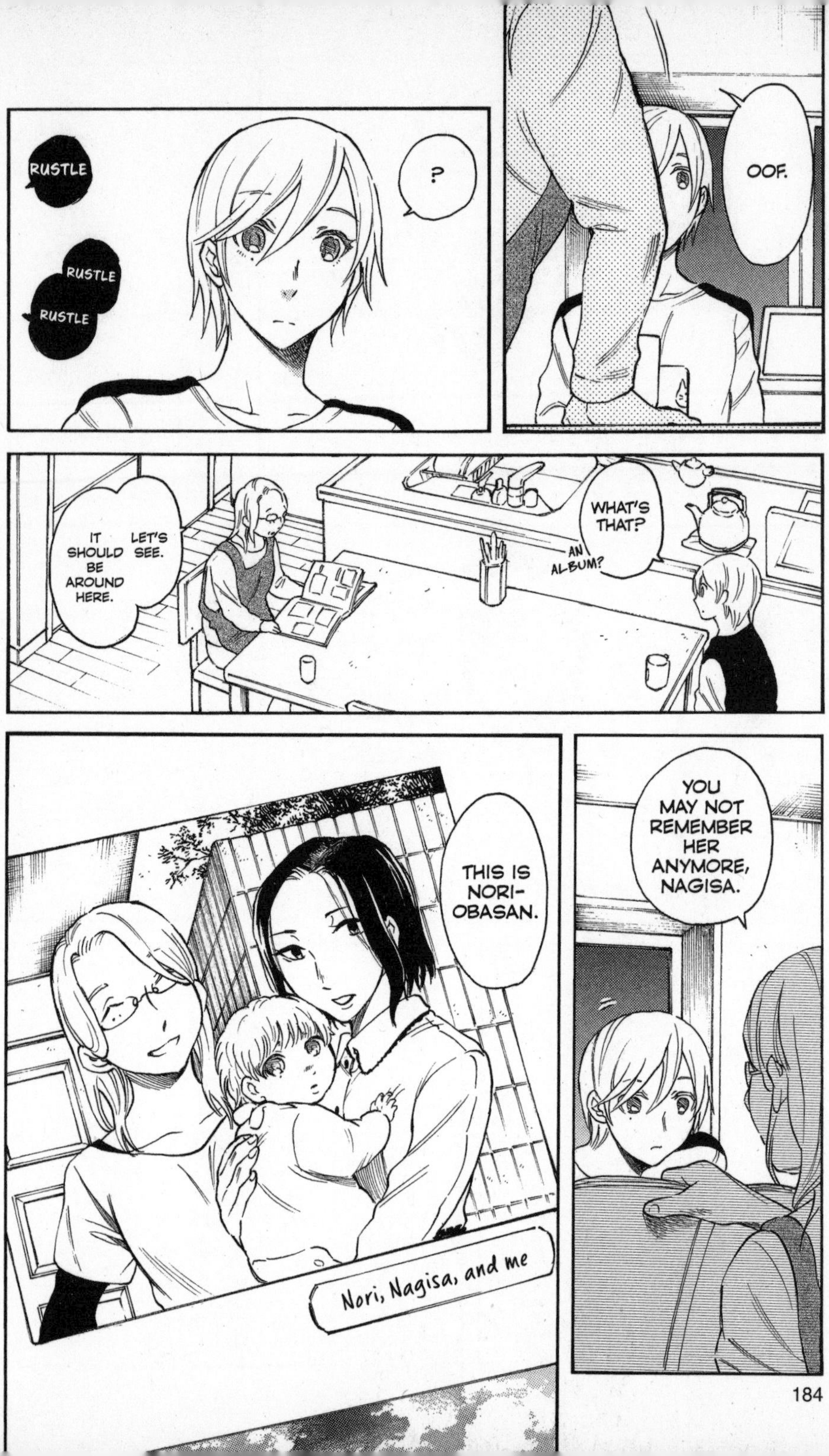
OOF.
?
RUSTLE
RUSTLE
RUSTLE
WHAT'S THAT?
AN ALBUM?
LET'S SEE.
IT SHOULD BE AROUND HERE.
YOU MAY NOT REMEMBER HER ANYMORE, NAGISA.
THIS IS NORI-OBASAN.
Nori, Nagisa, and me

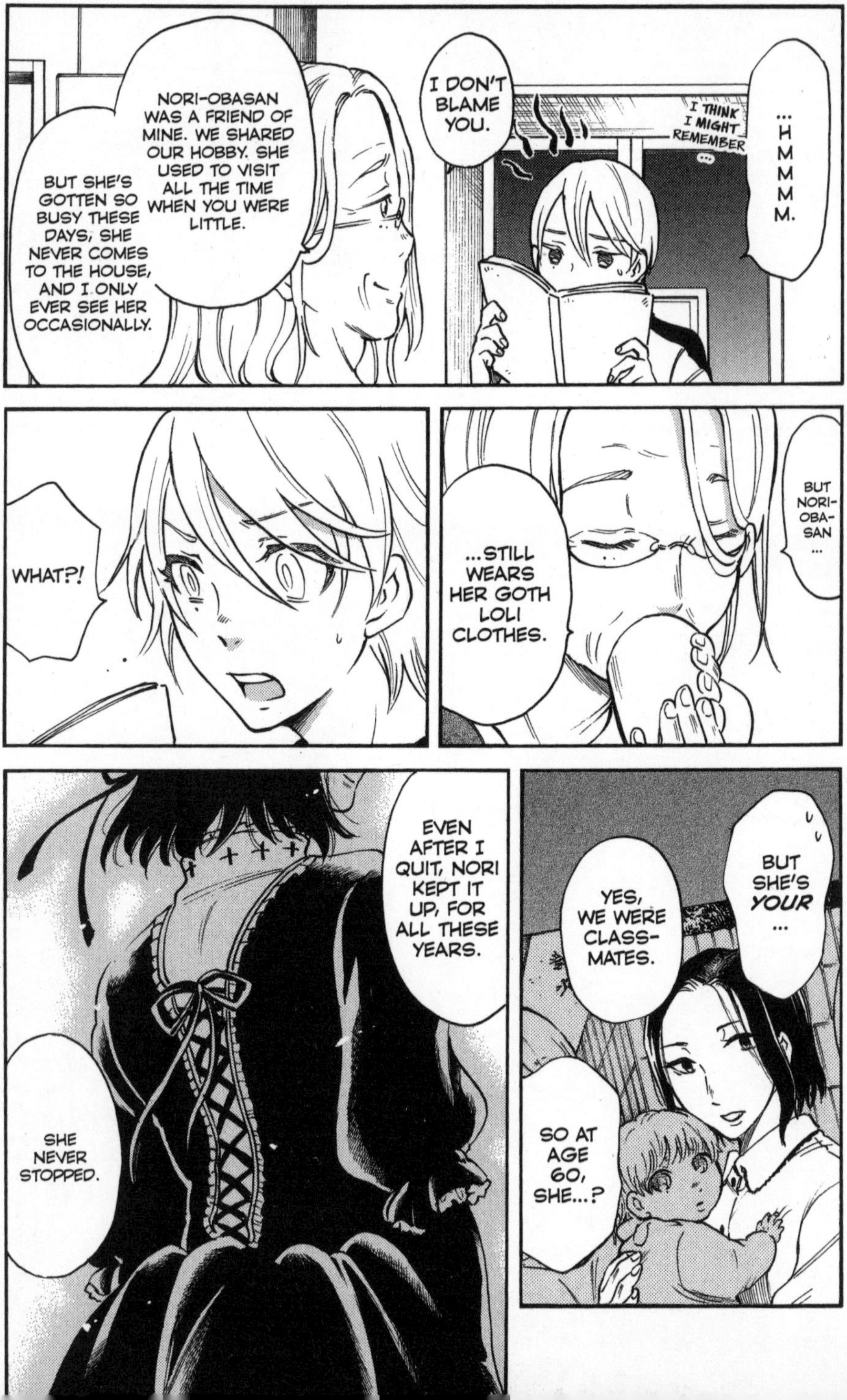
...HMMMM.
I THINK I MIGHT REMEMBER
...
I DON'T BLAME YOU.
NORI-OBASAN WAS A FRIEND OF MINE. WE SHARED OUR HOBBY. SHE USED TO VISIT ALL THE TIME WHEN YOU WERE LITTLE.
BUT SHE'S GOTTEN SO BUSY THESE DAYS, SHE NEVER COMES TO THE HOUSE, AND I ONLY EVER SEE HER OCCASIONALLY.
BUT NORI-OBASAN...
...STILL WEARS HER GOTH LOLI CLOTHES.
WHAT?!
BUT SHE'S *YOUR*...
YES, WE WERE CLASSMATES.
SO AT AGE 60, SHE...?
EVEN AFTER I QUIT, NORI KEPT IT UP, FOR ALL THESE YEARS.
SHE NEVER STOPPED.

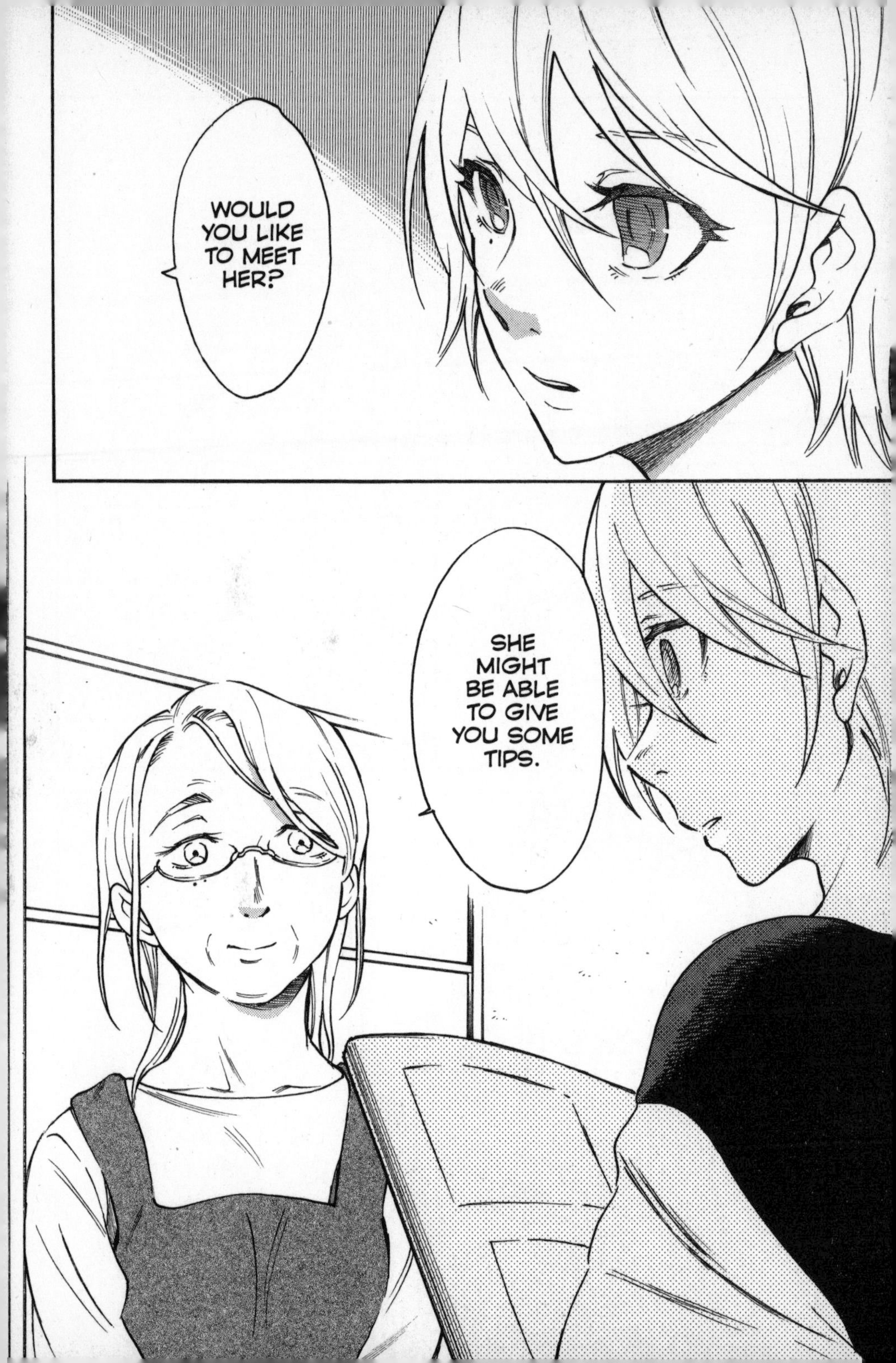
WOULD YOU LIKE TO MEET HER?
SHE MIGHT BE ABLE TO GIVE YOU SOME TIPS.

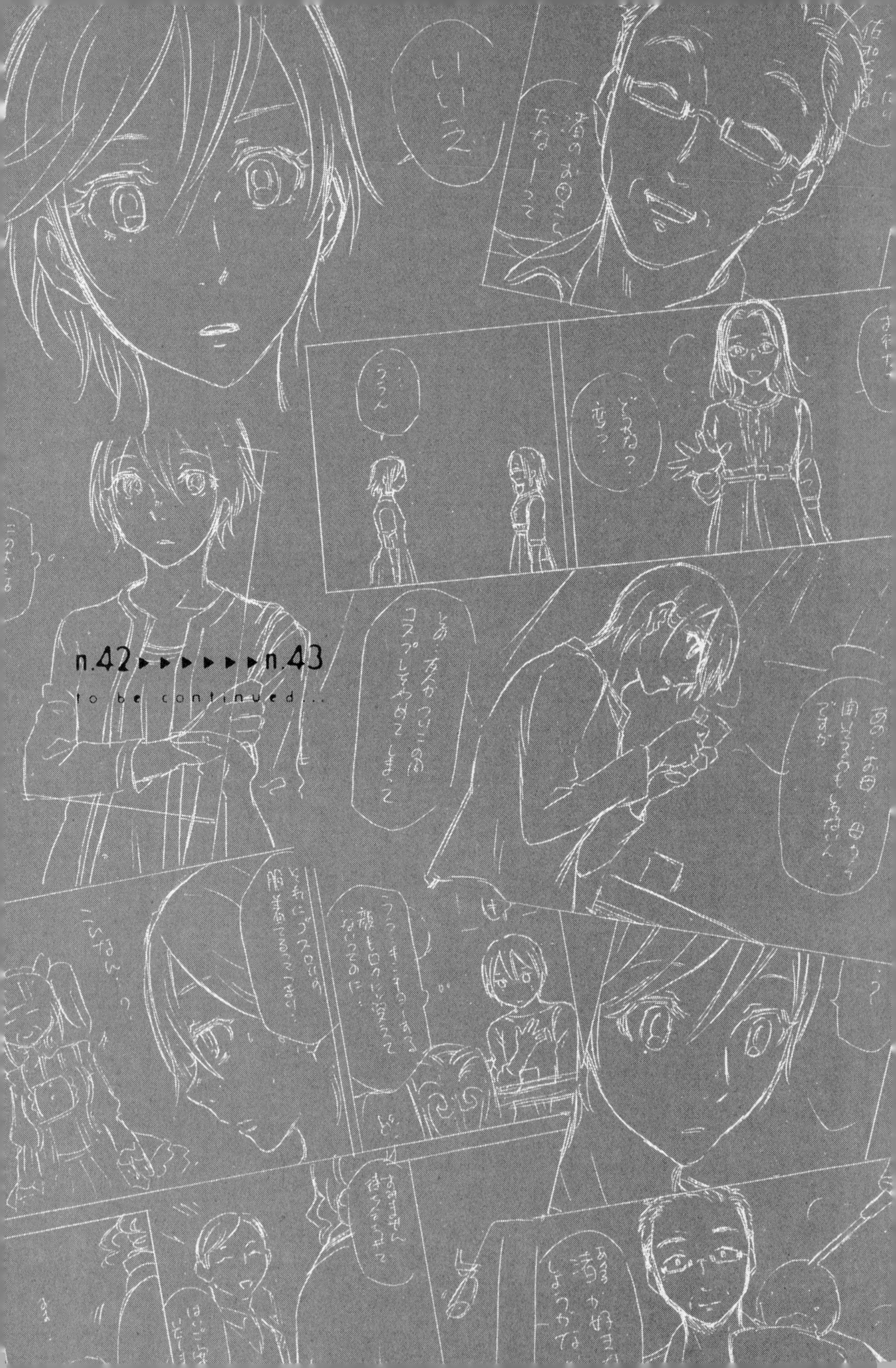
n.42▸▸▸▸▸▸▸▸n.43
to be continued...

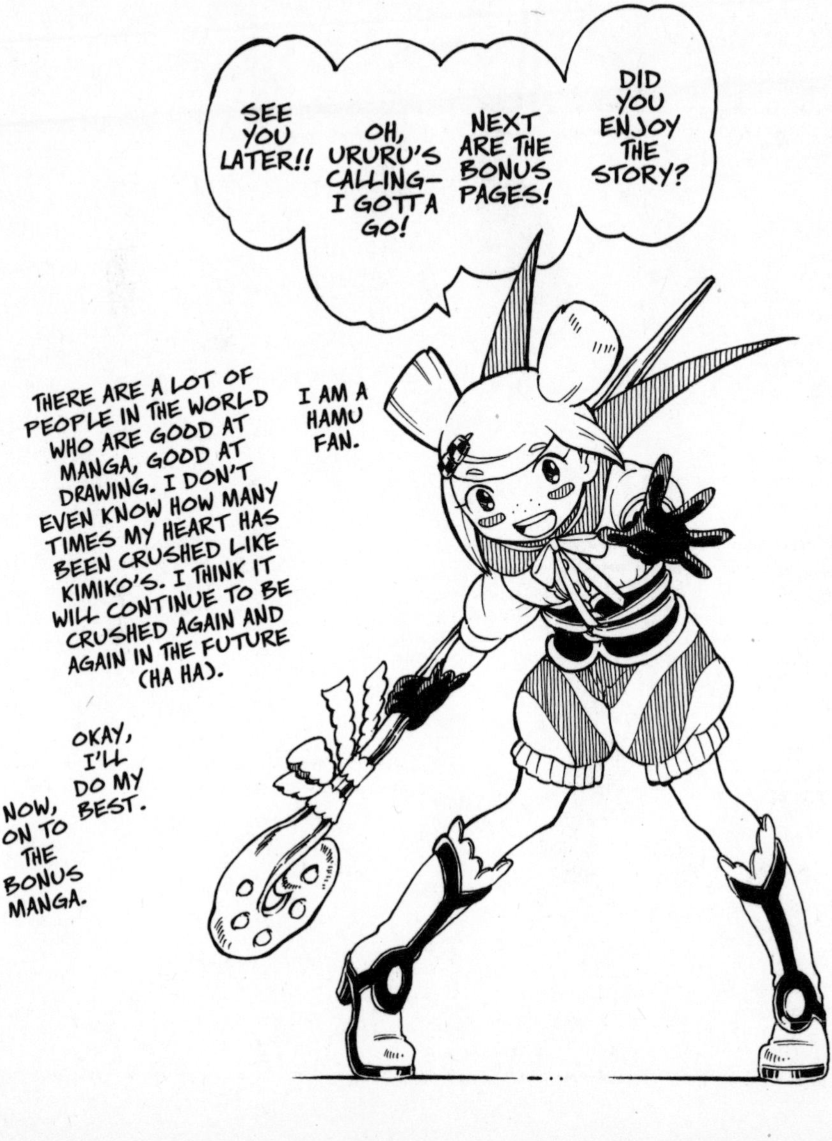
DID YOU ENJOY THE STORY?
NEXT ARE THE BONUS PAGES!
OH, URURU'S CALLING— I GOTTA GO!
SEE YOU LATER!!
I AM A HAMU FAN.
THERE ARE A LOT OF PEOPLE IN THE WORLD WHO ARE GOOD AT MANGA, GOOD AT DRAWING. I DON'T EVEN KNOW HOW MANY TIMES MY HEART HAS BEEN CRUSHED LIKE KIMIKO'S. I THINK IT WILL CONTINUE TO BE CRUSHED AGAIN AND AGAIN IN THE FUTURE (HA HA).
OKAY, I'LL DO MY BEST.
NOW, ON TO THE BONUS MANGA.

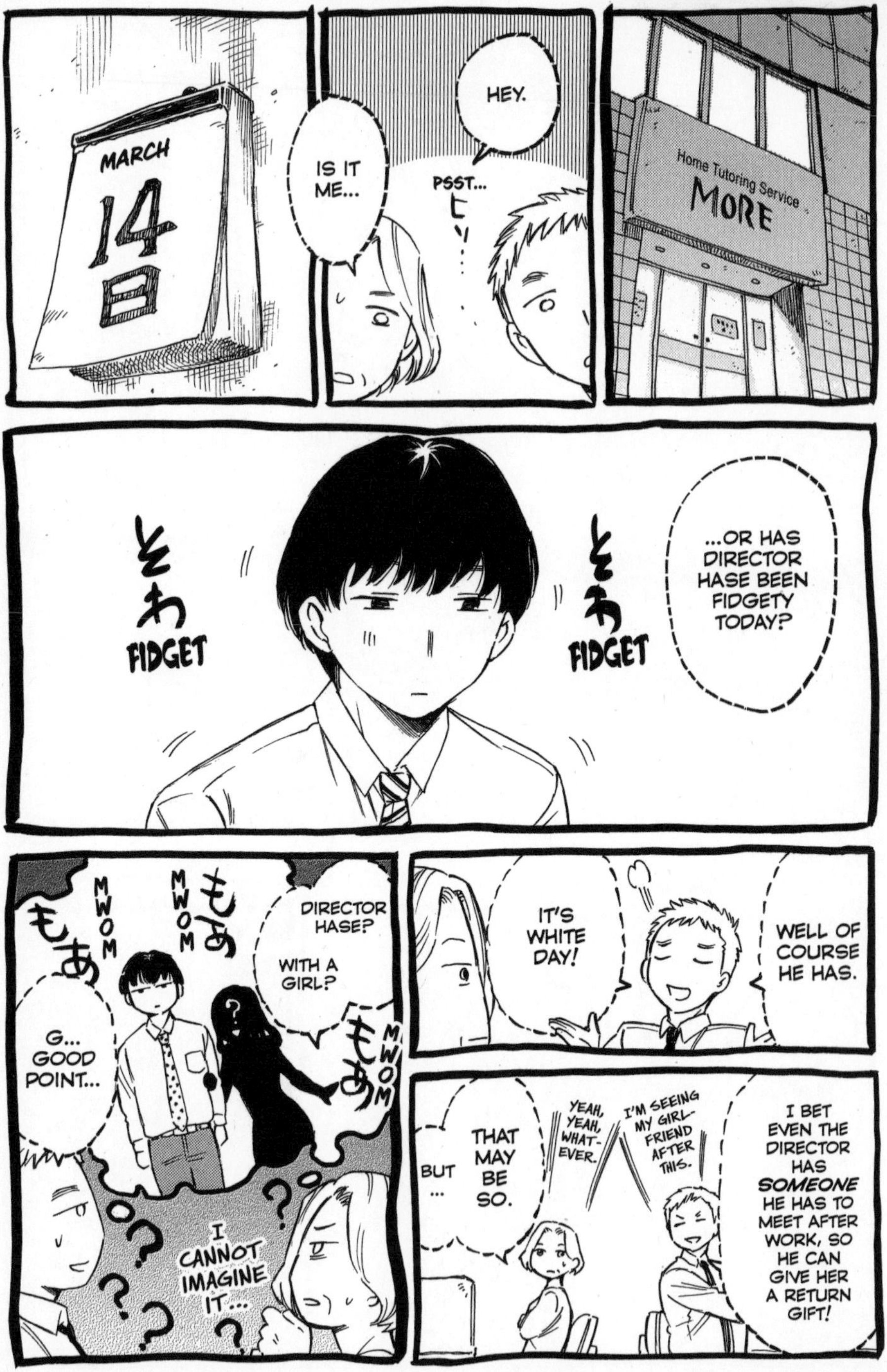
Home Tutoring Service
MORE
HEY.
PSST...
ヒソ...
IS IT ME...
MARCH
14
日
...OR HAS DIRECTOR HASE BEEN FIDGETY TODAY?
そわ FIDGET
そわ FIDGET
WELL OF COURSE HE HAS.
IT'S WHITE DAY!
I BET EVEN THE DIRECTOR HAS *SOMEONE* HE HAS TO MEET AFTER WORK, SO HE CAN GIVE HER A RETURN GIFT!
I'M SEEING MY GIRLFRIEND AFTER THIS.
YEAH, YEAH, WHATEVER.
THAT MAY BE SO.
BUT ...
DIRECTOR HASE?
WITH A GIRL?
もあ MWOM
もあ MWOM
もあ MWOM
G... GOOD POINT...
I CANNOT IMAGINE IT...

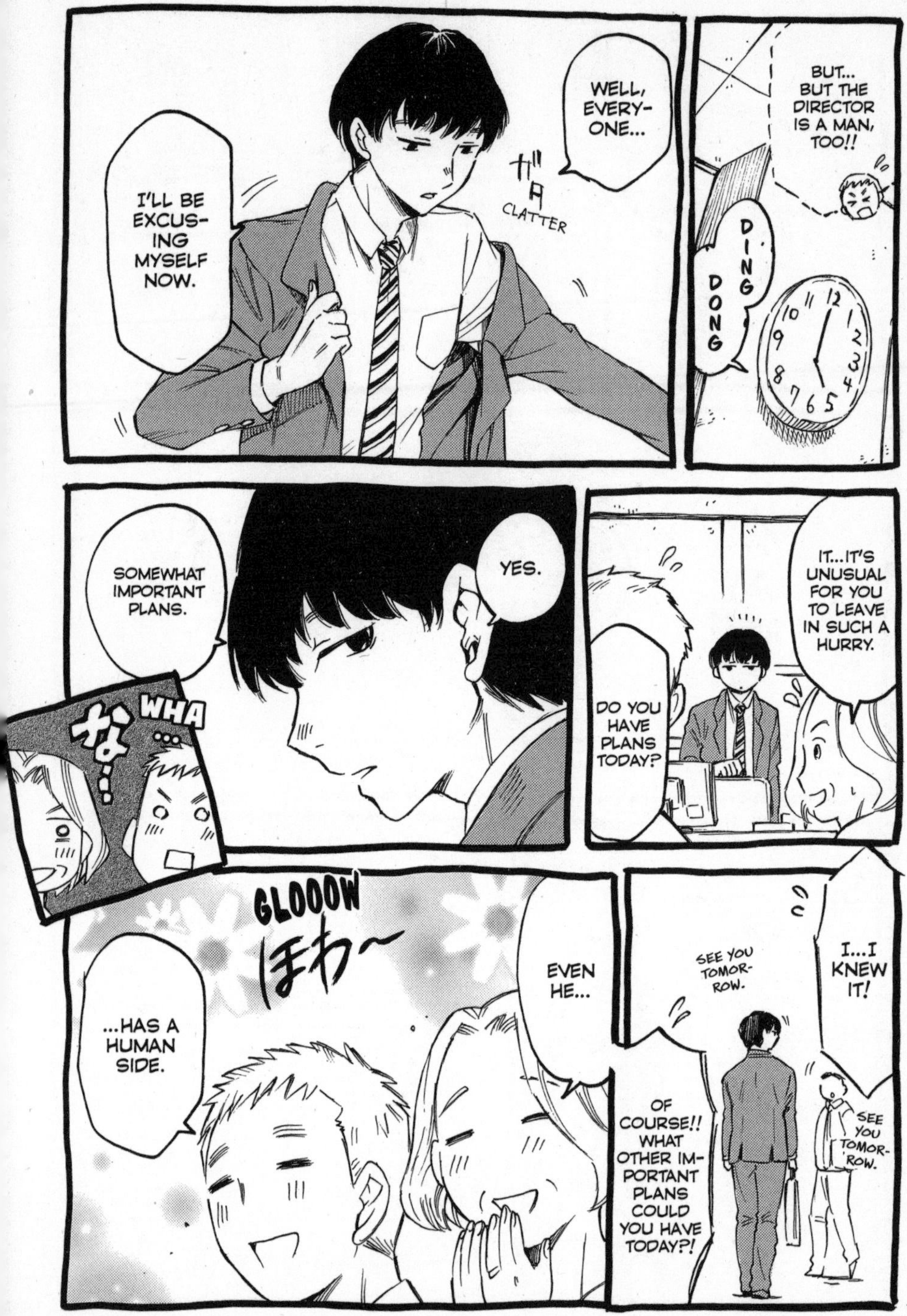
BUT... BUT THE DIRECTOR IS A MAN, TOO!!
DING DONG
WELL, EVERY-ONE...
ガタ CLATTER
I'LL BE EXCUS-ING MYSELF NOW.
IT...IT'S UNUSUAL FOR YOU TO LEAVE IN SUCH A HURRY.
DO YOU HAVE PLANS TODAY?
YES.
SOMEWHAT IMPORTANT PLANS.
な... WHA...
I...I KNEW IT!
SEE YOU TOMOR-ROW.
SEE YOU TOMOR-ROW.
OF COURSE!! WHAT OTHER IM-PORTANT PLANS COULD YOU HAVE TODAY?!
EVEN HE...
ほわ~ GLOOOW
...HAS A HUMAN SIDE.

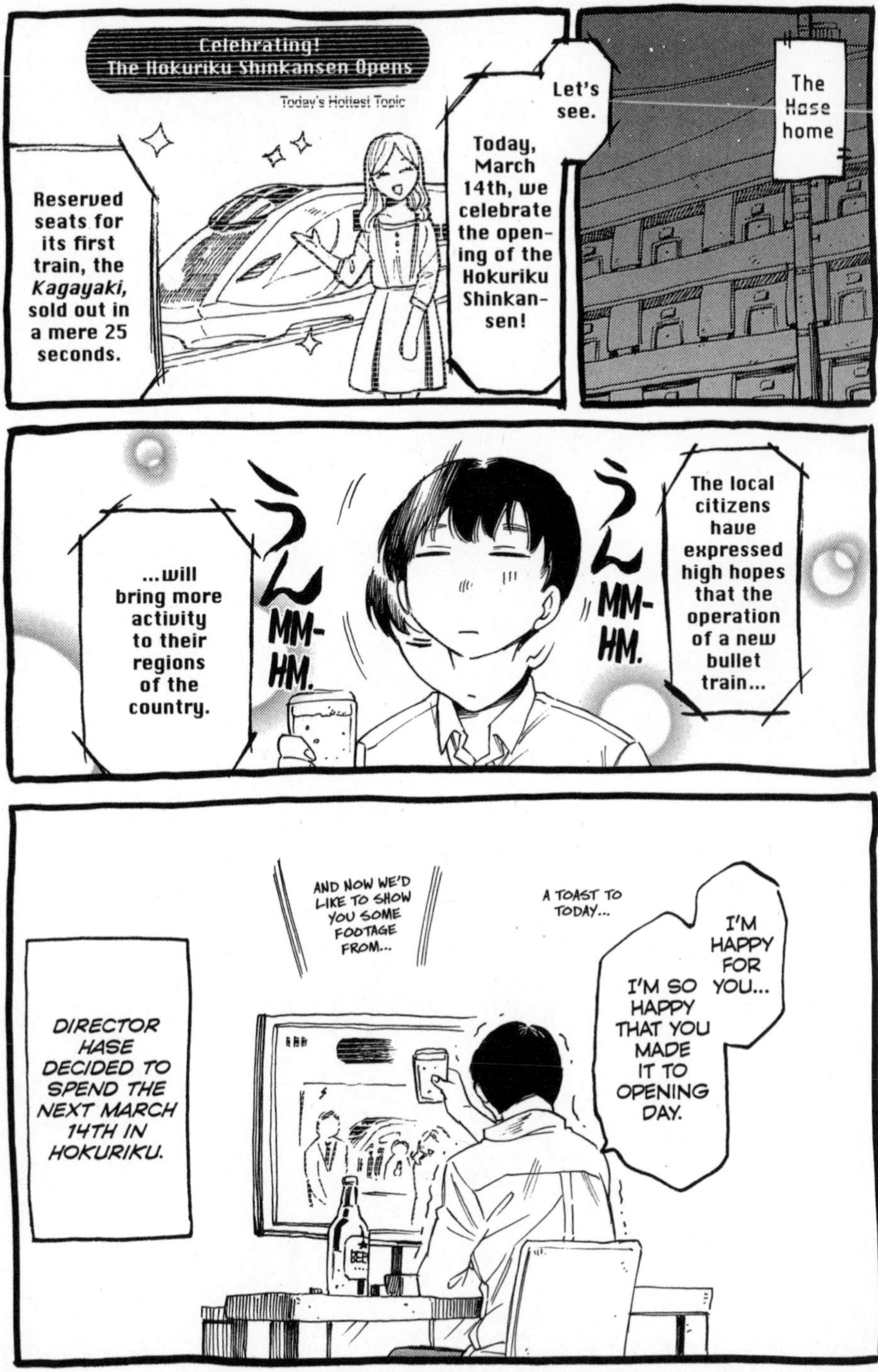
The Hase home
Let's see.
Today, March 14th, we celebrate the opening of the Hokuriku Shinkansen!
Celebrating! The Hokuriku Shinkansen Opens
Today's Hottest Topic
Reserved seats for its first train, the *Kagayaki*, sold out in a mere 25 seconds.
The local citizens have expressed high hopes that the operation of a new bullet train...
うん MM-HM.
うん MM-HM.
...will bring more activity to their regions of the country.
I'M HAPPY FOR YOU...
I'M SO HAPPY THAT YOU MADE IT TO OPENING DAY.
A TOAST TO TODAY...
AND NOW WE'D LIKE TO SHOW YOU SOME FOOTAGE FROM...
DIRECTOR HASE DECIDED TO SPEND THE NEXT MARCH 14TH IN HOKURIKU.

END

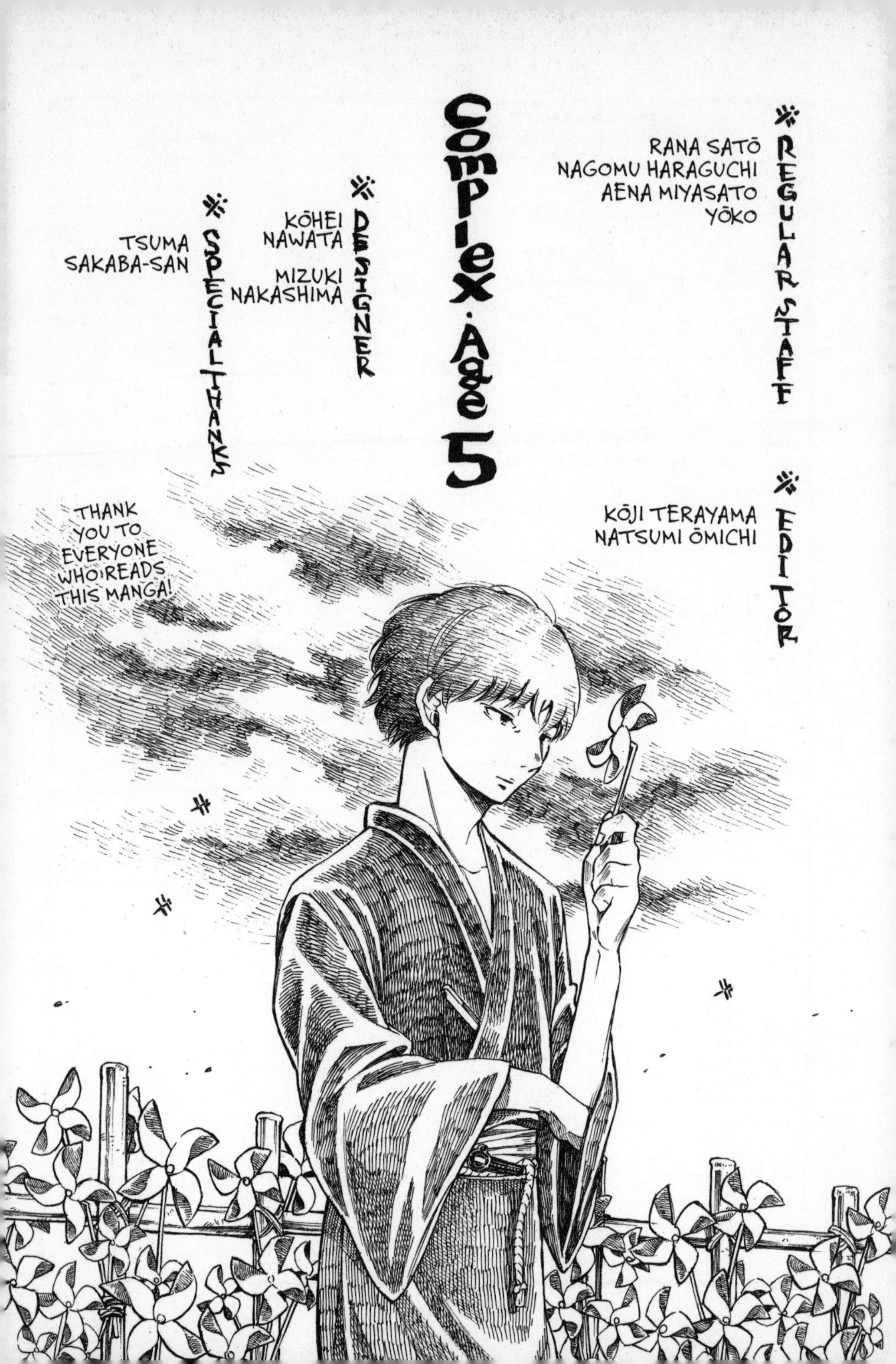
Complex Age 5
※ REGULAR STAFF
RANA SATŌ
NAGOMU HARAGUCHI
AENA MIYASATO
YŌKO
※ EDITOR
KŌJI TERAYAMA
NATSUMI ŌMICHI
※ DESIGNER
KŌHEI NAWATA
MIZUKI NAKASHIMA
※ SPECIAL THANKS
TSUMA SAKABA-SAN
THANK YOU TO EVERYONE WHO READS THIS MANGA!

Cospedia

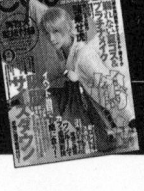

[GLOSSARY OF COSPLAY TERMS]

Supervisor: コスプレイモード COSPLAY MODE

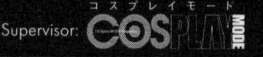

The cosplay magazine that has taken over the reins of *Cosmode* magazine, which ran until spring 2014. It publishes everything related to cosplay, including pinup photos, fan-submitted cosplay photos, and information on costumes, makeup, photography, armor and prop building, and cosplay culture. Released on the 3rd of every even-numbered month. (Published by Famima.com)

that time lapse videos have been posted to the internet showing the formation of the entry line, as well as its organized movement once the doors are opened. It is recommended that first-time Comiket attendees arrive in the afternoon, when it is possible to get into the venue without a wait.

▶ Page 18

"People fall like rubble..."

This is a famous line spoken by Colonel Muska in the Studio Ghibli animated film, *Laputa: Castle in the Sky* (released August 1986), directed by Hayao Miyazaki. He said it with a cackle as he watched the crew of the Air

Cure. The Kamikita Twins, who have done the manga version of the *Precure* series since its first season, are twin sisters who work together on the manga, and established a reputation for quality early on.

▶ Page 15

"But it's gonna be super crowded."

If an attendee arrives on the first train, the average wait time to get into Comiket (see Volume 3: Comiket) is approximately five hours (from the Comiket official website). The act of waiting has become such a famous part of the Comiket experience

n.34

▶ Page 10

The manga of a morning kids' show

The manga based on a television show aimed at children. A few TV channels broadcast children's shows in the morning time slots on Saturdays and Sundays, the most notable of which being the special effects *(tokusatsu)* hero shows (like *Masked Rider* and the *Power Rangers* series) and animated shows like *Pretty*

Costume Set

A store-bought set containing items needed for cosplay. Some sets include not only jackets and skirts, but hair accessories and shoes, as well.

I THINK WE SHOULD GO WITH SOMETHING ...
...WE CAN PUT TOGETHER PRETTY EASILY, LIKE A SCHOOL UNIFORM OR A MAID OUTFIT!
COSTUME SET
SIMPLE!! COSTUME SET
SAILOR SUIT

TOKYU HANDS

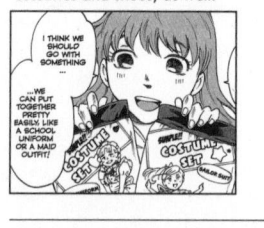

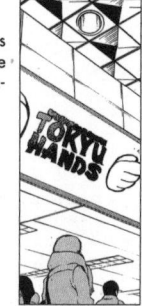

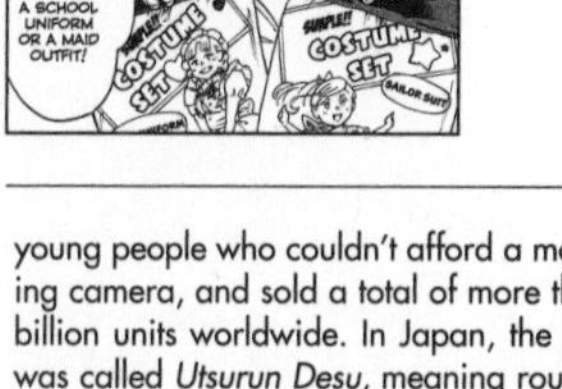

in large cities (see Volume 1: "I'd rather look around for something cheaper. But since I don't have time, then it's nice I can come here."). It has a wide selection of products, mainly focusing on household goods, and they have an especially complete collection of DIY products (short for "do it yourself," DIY refers to doing home projects yourself, as opposed to relying on stores or professionals).

Destroyer Goliath fall to their deaths after he shot it down. The line is frequently used to refer to the crowds at Comiket. Muska's real name is Romuska Palo Ur Laputa, and he is voiced by Minori Terada (Mark Hamill in the most recent English version).

n.35

▶ Page 25

Tokyu Hands

A chain of home improvement centers that can mainly be found

---

young people who couldn't afford a more lasting camera, and sold a total of more than 1.7 billion units worldwide. In Japan, the product was called *Utsurun Desu,* meaning roughly, "It takes pictures." Since the rise of digital cameras and camera phones, production was drastically scaled back in 2012, and as of now, July 2015, only three different types are available for purchase.

THIS SHOULD DO IT.
POCKET HEAT
FUN AND CA
RUSTLE RUSTLE

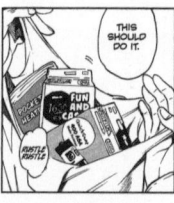

carry not only medicine and makeup, but a wide variety of daily necessities. At their shopping website, a visitor can buy approximately 13,000 different items (as of July 2015).

QuickSnap

The world's first one-time use camera, released by Fuji Film in 1986 (also known as a "disposable camera"). This product was the realization of a desire to allow anyone to easily enjoy photography. It was a big hit, especially among

薬 マツモト キヨシ

"We could color our hair with spray, but..."

By using colored hair spray, a layer can add color to the surface of her hair without dying it all the way through. The color lasts about a day. If the layer uses a wig, she can easily change its color using lacquer spray or Copic markers (see also Volume 1: "You're basically not allowed to bring wax or hairspray into the convention center.")

Matsumoto Kiyoshi

A major drugstore chain. They

▶ Page 27

"I want to make you crossplay..."

"Crossplay" means to cosplay a character of the opposite gender: In Nagisa's case, it means she would dress as a man. Male characters tend to be very tall, so when crossplaying them, some women supplement their height by wearing thick-soled shoes. Female to male (FtM) crossplay requires various other efforts, including wearing shoulder pads to recreate the sturdy build, binding one's chest, and makeup tricks.

▶ Page 33

"Could I make weapons out of cardboard?"

Cosplay props can be made with any material, but the preferred material is lion board (see Volume 3: Lion). Additionally, one can recreate various textures by using such materials as polymer clay, which can be translucent, and wood clay, which made from wood. However, some events have restrictions on the size and types of props that can be brought in, so a layer must be aware.

▶ Page 40

Yamabiko 55

The *Yamabiko* is a limited express train operated by East Japan Railway Company, that runs on the Tōhoku bullet train line from Tokyo Station to Sendai Morioka Station, as well as from Nasushiobara Station/Kōriyama Station to Sendai Station. It's been in operation since the Tōhoku Shinkansen first opened, and the name *Yamabiko* was used for the express train that ran on the Tōhoku main line before the bullet train line opened. It has a relatively large number of stops, not entirely unlike the *Kodama,* which runs on the Tōkaidō Shinkansen.

n.36

▶ Page 58

"Makeup might fool some people, but not me."

Because cosplay makeup is worn to make a layer look like a character, it tends to go on thicker than regular makeup. It is not uncommon for a layer's aversion to heavy makeup to fade with experience, and the layers of her makeup will increase as she cosplays more.

n.37

▶ Page 71

Pocari

Short for Pocari Sweat, the soft drink sold by Otsuka Pharmaceutical Co., Ltd. It has 49 mg of sodium for every 100 mL of water, and stimulates hydration better than water. The anime *Ben-to,* which aired in Japan beginning October 2011, had a partnership with Otsuka Pharmaceutical, and Pocari Sweat appears in the series. It was even the title of episode 11 ("Pocari Sweat 125 kcal").

▶ Page 72

Night Event

A cosplay event held during the nighttime hours. There are all-night events restricted to people 18 and older, as well as New Year's events, and it's easy for working people to take time out of their schedules to participate. In addition to cosplay events, there are club events called *Anison* DJ Events where they play *anison* (see Volume 2: *Anison*) all night long.

n.38

▶ Page 85

Hiepita

The name of a gel cooling sheet (the one Jintan had on his head in the first episode of *Anohana: The Flower We Saw That Day* (April 2011 anime)) sold by the Lion Corporation. The water inside the sheet evaporates as it absorbs heat, for a long-lasting cooling effect. In addition to using them to fight the fevers caused by colds and other illnesses, some people use them when studying or focusing on work.

▶ Page 87

TAMIYA

A manufacturer of model kits founded in 1946. Its famous two-star logo features a red star on the left to symbolize passion, and a blue star on the right to symbolize precision. They deal in a wide variety of products, from plastic models and RCs to painting supplies and any other tool you might need to build a model. The company's line of miniature motorized automobiles, the Mini Four-Wheel Drives, enjoyed its first boom from the late 1980s to the early 1990s, and then a second boom in the late 1990s, demonstrating a popularity that crossed generational boundaries, and its total sales numbers have risen to over 175 million cars to the present day.

▶ Page 96

Train Geek (Tetsu)

A train enthusiast (fan of the railways). Originally, they were almost all men, but in recent years, there has been a rise in the number of female fans, known as *Tetsuko* ("Iron Girl," referring to the iron of the tracks). The trends of this hobby are diverse and sundry, including the *Noritetsu* (Riding Tetsu), who lust for experiencing the railroad and its train stations; the *Toritetsu* (Photo Tetsu), who love to photograph the cars; and the *Ototetsu* (Sound Tetsu), who are nuts about recording the in-train announcements and the departure melodies played at the various train stations in Japan.

N-Gauge

A train model that is scaled 1/140-1/160 that runs on a 9 mm wide track. Its name comes from its gauge (the distance between the two rails) being nine (N) millimeters. An electric current runs through the metal rails, and the wheels conduct that electricity to the train's motor, thus allowing the model to move. By hooking it up to a controller, one can create a realistic simulation, complete with switchable points. In addition to building the model itself, many enthusiasts also create a landscape (diorama) for the tracks, and there are even competitions where they are judged on their degree of perfection.

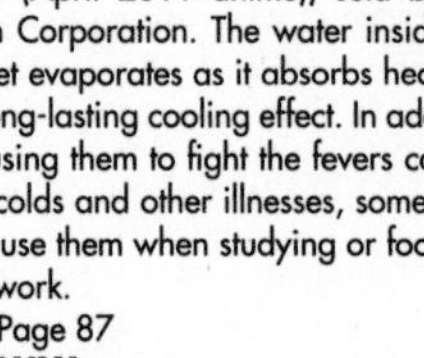

n.39

▶ Page 109

"The snow is so smooth."

Smooth, dry snow (powder snow) falls in cold, dry weather. Because Sendai is on the Pacific Ocean side of Japan, it gets less snow than areas on the Sea of Japan side, but when the seasonal winds cross the Ōu Mountains, they make the air drier and colder, so sometimes powder snow will fall.

n.40

▶ Page 129

"The next thing I knew, I had all this equipment."

no hagi, or Thunberg's bushclover. At an event for the *Kannagi* anime, held in Shichigahama the summer of 2009, they printed the anime's heroine Nagi on wrappers for *hagi no tsuki* and *hagi no shirabe* ("clover melody," the chocolate version, also sold by Kashō Sanzen; no longer in production). They renamed them Nagi no Tsuki and Nagi no Shirabe, and distributed them as event swag.

▶ Page 130

"And, well, I have to save up some money for the wedding."

According to *Zexy Wedding Trend Report 2014*, the national average of money spent for a wedding ceremony and reception is 3,337,000 yen, or about $33,370.

▶ Page 137

Hagi no tsuki

Meaning "clover moon," a dumpling-style confection that consists of sponge cake with a custard cream filling, sold by Kashō Sanzen since 1979. It is the most standard of standard souvenirs from Miyagi. It was named after the official flower of Miyagi Prefecture, the *Miyagi*

▶ Page 143

PENTAX K-50

An entry model (beginners' camera) SLR camera sold since July 2013 by

Tripod, memory card, bag maintenance equipment, etc.—even the most basic use of an SLR camera can require a lot of equipment. Additionally, lenses come in various interchangeable types, including the wide-angle lens (to take pictures of a wide landscape), the zoom lens (to take pictures of faraway objects), and the fixed-focus lens (for more natural pictures). If the photographer uses different lenses for different scenes, her pictures will come out even better.

Howl's Moving Castle (animated feature film by Studio Ghibli). The September 2011 issue of *Cosplay Mode* even had a feature on how to use makeup to create shadows and wrinkles to make a layer look older.

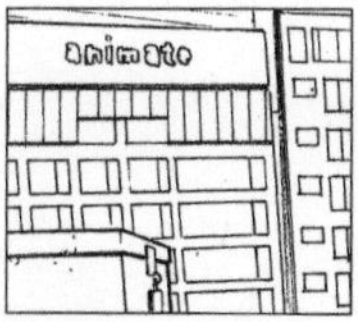

n.42

▶ Page 169

Animate

A chain store that specializes in anime, game,

tographers are a relatively small group.

n.41

▶ Page 161

"But there are some characters that you just don't have the right look for until you're older."

There are many characters who are still appealing despite their older ages, including Balsa from *Moribito: Guardian of the Spirit* (light novels by Nahoko Uehashi, also has an anime), Enya the Hag from *Jojo's Bizarre Adventure* (original manga by Hirohiko Araki), and the old lady version of Sophie from

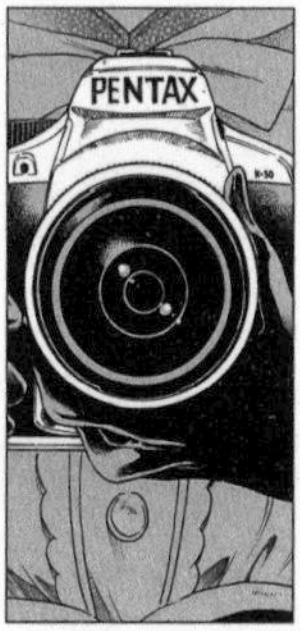
PENTAX

Ricoh Imaging Company. It is the only entry model that is rainproof and dustproof, making it very cost effective. Compared to Canon and Nikon users, Pentax pho-

chest-binding, but also for when warriors commit seppuku, or simply as underwear. The downside to using sarashi includes the difficulty of wrapping them around oneself and the ease with which they slide out of position.

▶ Page 172

Mesh fabric

Fabric woven or knit in a lattice style. Because it breathes very well, it is an especially popular material in athletics and active scenes, as well as during hot summer months.

Pantyhose

Long, thin socks. Hose is used to dress

use of the outdoors. They also attract many non-layer spectators.

▶ Page 171

Chest binding

This something done in FtM crossplay (a woman cosplaying a male character) to prevent the layer's chest from standing out. This is recommended for FtM crossplay regardless of the layer's chest size. Because it becomes difficult to breathe when the chest is bound too tightly, a layer must always take care not to overdo it. When a layer can't get her chest flat enough, she may also pad her belly.

Sarashi bandages

Narrow bandages made of bleached cotton. They have been used for centuries, not only for

and manga merchandise, run by Animate Ltd. It has more than 130 stores across Japan (as of July 2015). Its Animate-only goods enjoy immense popularity.

"There really are layers, just walking around town!!"

Some cosplay events are held with the city's cooperation. Layers can use designated shops while still in costume, and there might be stages set up throughout town—these events make good

COMPLEX AGE VOLUME SIX (FINAL VOLUME!) ON SALE FALL 2017!

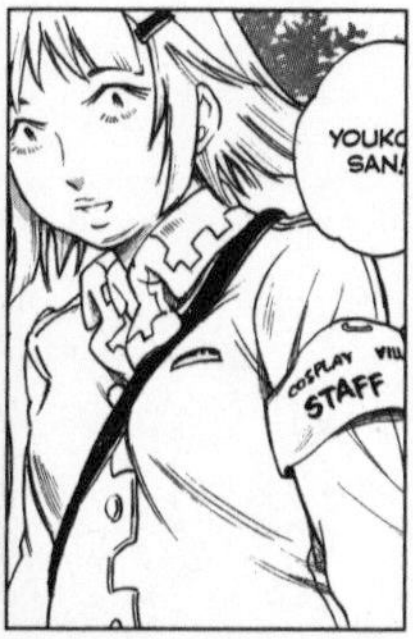
STAFF

specifically to bind the chest. Spra is short for "sports bra." Because they were made with sports in mind, they not only keep the breasts in place, but have high absorbency for sweat. The term "nabe shirt" comes from the fact that they were worn by *onabe*, women who desired to looked more masculine, and the tank top style is the most popular.

▶ Page 176

Armband

Many event staffers wear armbands to help attendees distinguish them from the general attendees. If the event is large enough, sometimes staffers will be provided with a staff jacket.

up one's legs, to stave off cold, and to accentuate the beautiful contours of one's legs through the elasticity of the netting. They are differentiated from tights by denier, a unit measuring fiber thickness in fabrics. Stockings have fewer than 30 deniers, and tights have more than 30.

B holder, spra, nabe shirt

Each of these is an item used to prevent the breasts from jiggling and to flatten the chest. The B holder, or bust holder, was made

Translation Notes

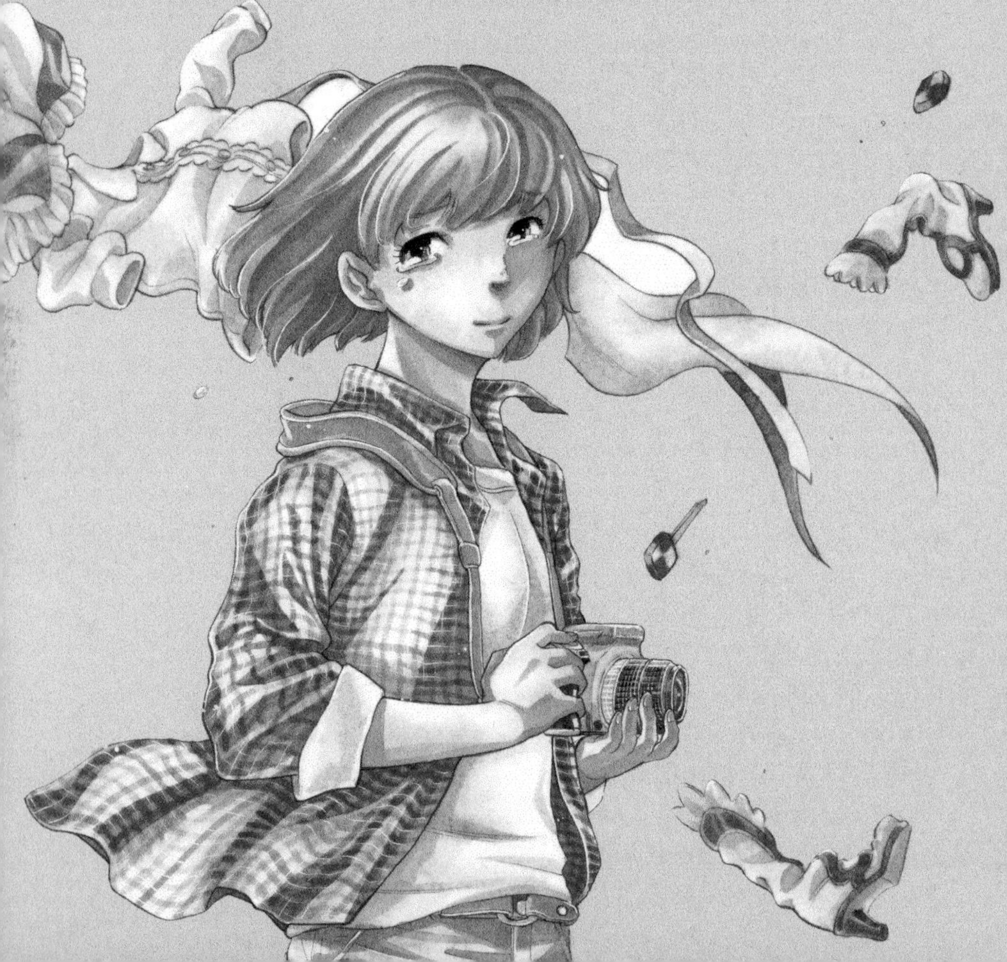

PAGE 17

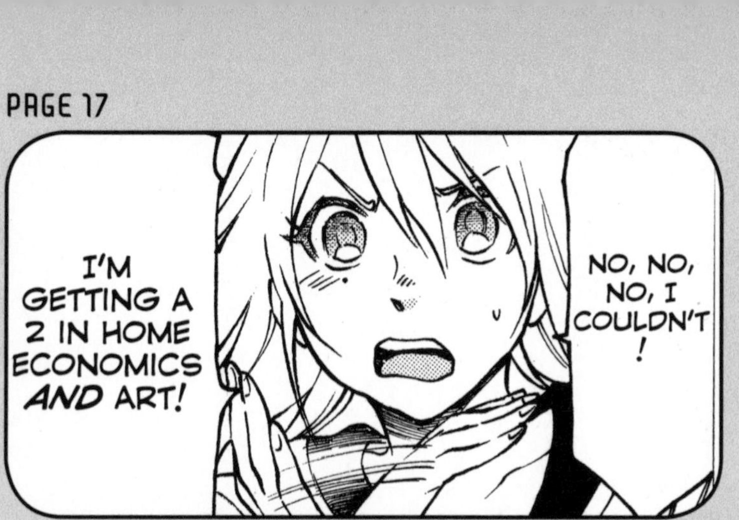
NO, NO, NO, I COULDN'T!
I'M GETTING A 2 IN HOME ECONOMICS AND ART!

GETTING A 2 IN HOME ECONOMICS AND ART

In Japan, it is common for schools to grade students using numbers instead of letters. The top grade (an A) is 5, and the bottom is 1. Since home economics is where they teach sewing, and cosplay requires some artistic ability, it is understandable that Nagisa would have misgivings about her ability to make costumes.

PAGE 44

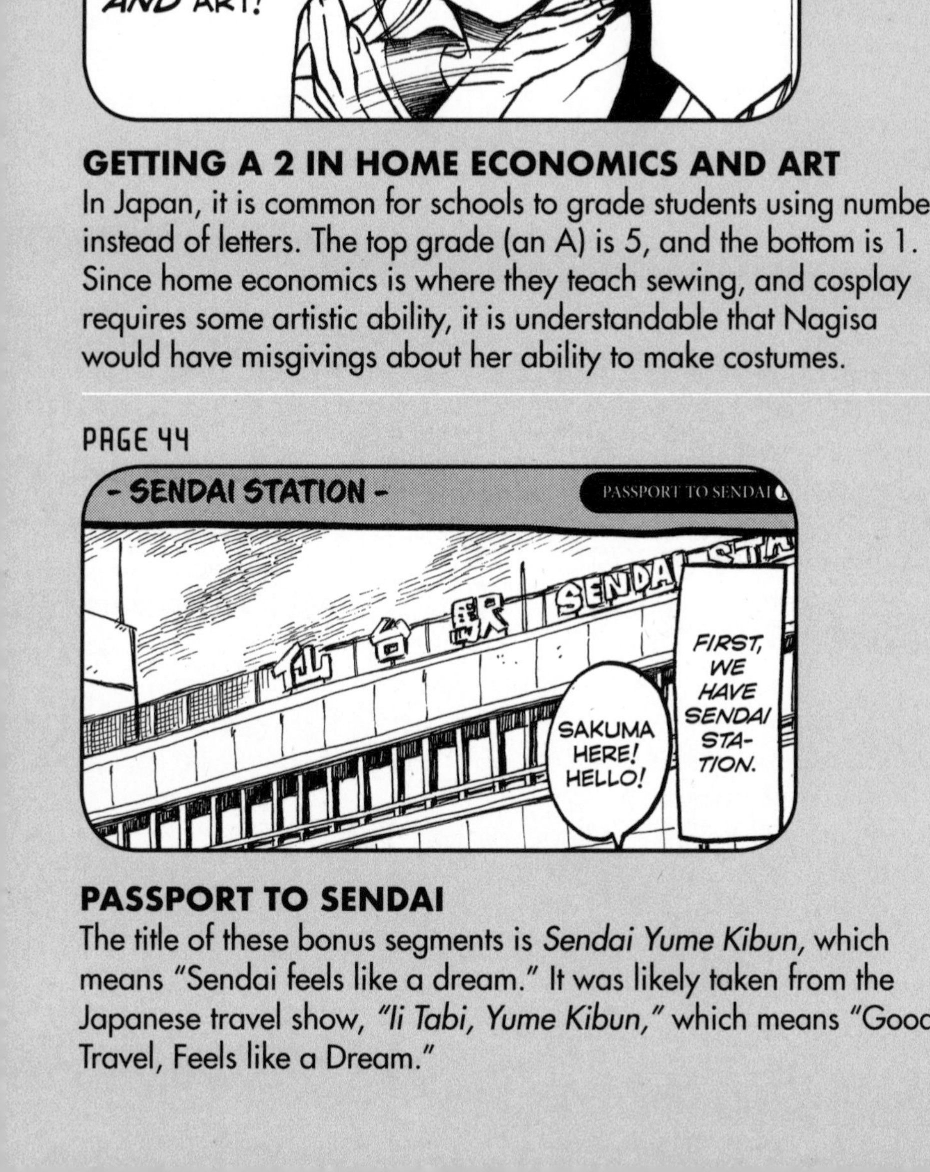
- SENDAI STATION -
PASSPORT TO SENDAI
仙台駅
SENDAI
FIRST, WE HAVE SENDAI STA-TION.
SAKUMA HERE! HELLO!

PASSPORT TO SENDAI

The title of these bonus segments is *Sendai Yume Kibun,* which means "Sendai feels like a dream." It was likely taken from the Japanese travel show, *"Ii Tabi, Yume Kibun,"* which means "Good Travel, Feels like a Dream."

PAGE 44

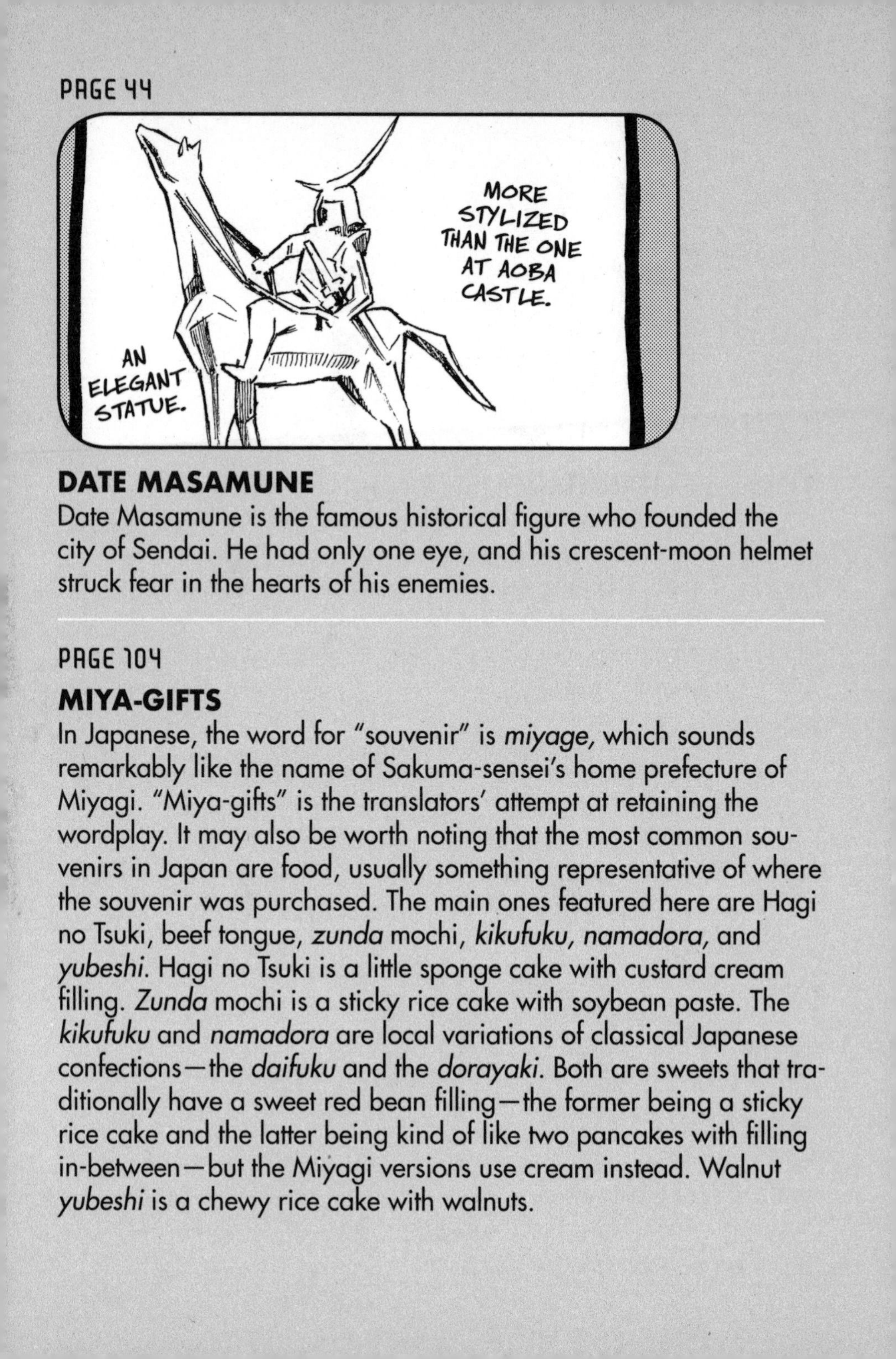
MORE STYLIZED THAN THE ONE AT AOBA CASTLE.
AN ELEGANT STATUE.

DATE MASAMUNE

Date Masamune is the famous historical figure who founded the city of Sendai. He had only one eye, and his crescent-moon helmet struck fear in the hearts of his enemies.

PAGE 104

MIYA-GIFTS

In Japanese, the word for "souvenir" is *miyage,* which sounds remarkably like the name of Sakuma-sensei's home prefecture of Miyagi. "Miya-gifts" is the translators' attempt at retaining the wordplay. It may also be worth noting that the most common souvenirs in Japan are food, usually something representative of where the souvenir was purchased. The main ones featured here are Hagi no Tsuki, beef tongue, *zunda* mochi, *kikufuku, namadora,* and *yubeshi*. Hagi no Tsuki is a little sponge cake with custard cream filling. *Zunda* mochi is a sticky rice cake with soybean paste. The *kikufuku* and *namadora* are local variations of classical Japanese confections—the *daifuku* and the *dorayaki*. Both are sweets that traditionally have a sweet red bean filling—the former being a sticky rice cake and the latter being kind of like two pancakes with filling in-between—but the Miyagi versions use cream instead. Walnut *yubeshi* is a chewy rice cake with walnuts.

PAGE 113

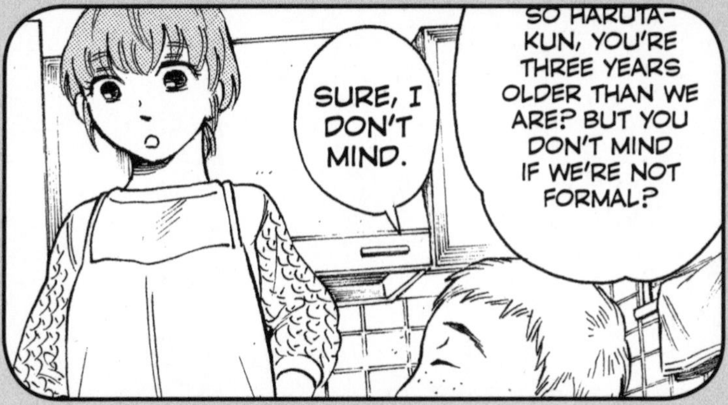
SO HARUTA-KUN, YOU'RE THREE YEARS OLDER THAN WE ARE? BUT YOU DON'T MIND IF WE'RE NOT FORMAL?
SURE, I DON'T MIND.

YOU DON'T MIND IF WE'RE NOT FORMAL

A more exact translation of Nagisa's question would be, "You don't mind if we use plain speech?" The Japanese language has different forms of speech that vary in levels of politeness. Generally, when speaking to someone who is older or otherwise above the speaker in a hierarchy, the one doing the talking would use more polite language, but not everyone is strict about formalities. Nagisa has noted that Kimiko does not use polite speech with her future husband and has followed suit, but remembers her manners and asks Haruta's permission, just to be sure.

PAGE 114

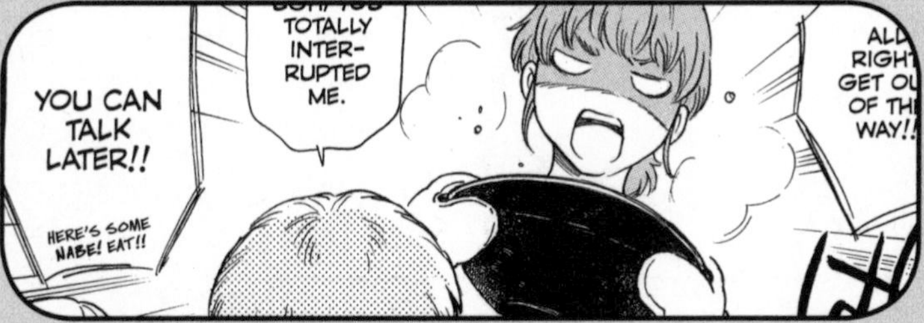
TOTALLY INTER-RUPTED ME.
YOU CAN TALK LATER!!
HERE'S SOME NABE! EAT!!

NABE

Nabe literally means "pot," and is short for *nabemono*, or "things in a pot." As seen in the picture, various ingredients have been cooked in this pot, and the diners are free to serve themselves whatever they want from within.

PAGE 168

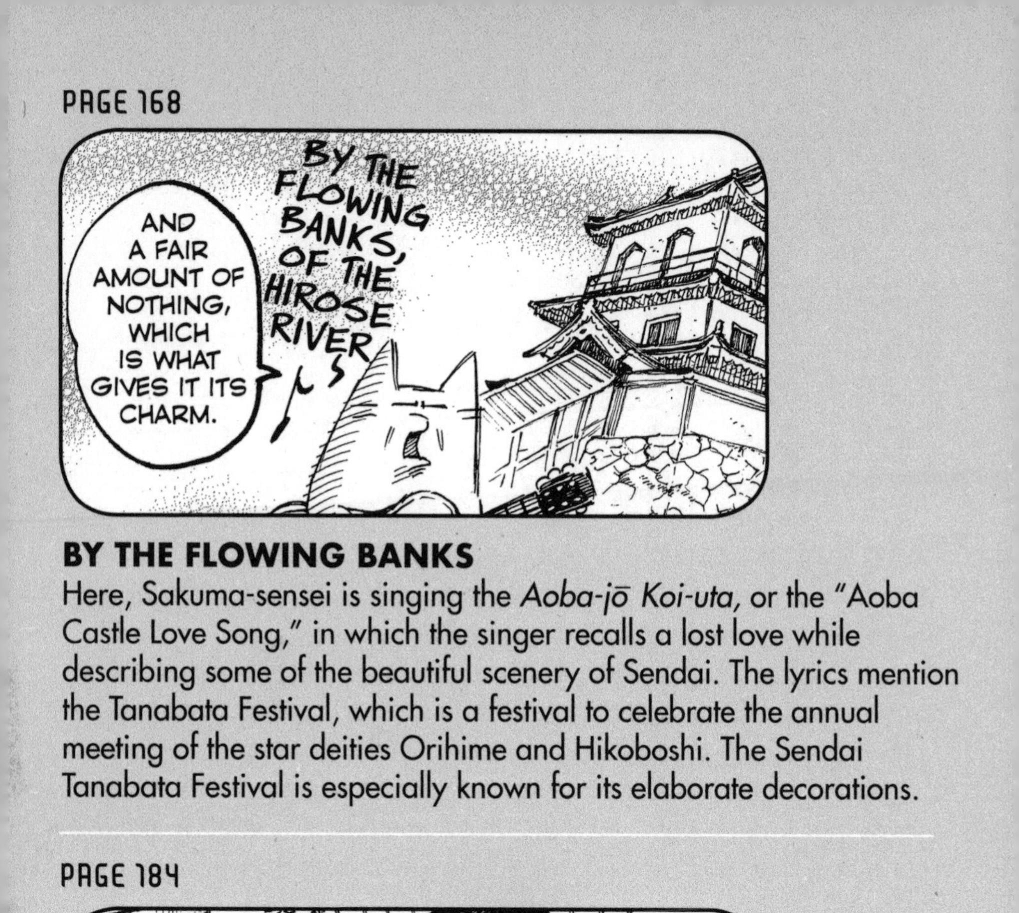
BY THE FLOWING BANKS, OF THE HIROSE RIVER
AND A FAIR AMOUNT OF NOTHING, WHICH IS WHAT GIVES IT ITS CHARM.

BY THE FLOWING BANKS

Here, Sakuma-sensei is singing the *Aoba-jō Koi-uta,* or the "Aoba Castle Love Song," in which the singer recalls a lost love while describing some of the beautiful scenery of Sendai. The lyrics mention the Tanabata Festival, which is a festival to celebrate the annual meeting of the star deities Orihime and Hikoboshi. The Sendai Tanabata Festival is especially known for its elaborate decorations.

PAGE 184

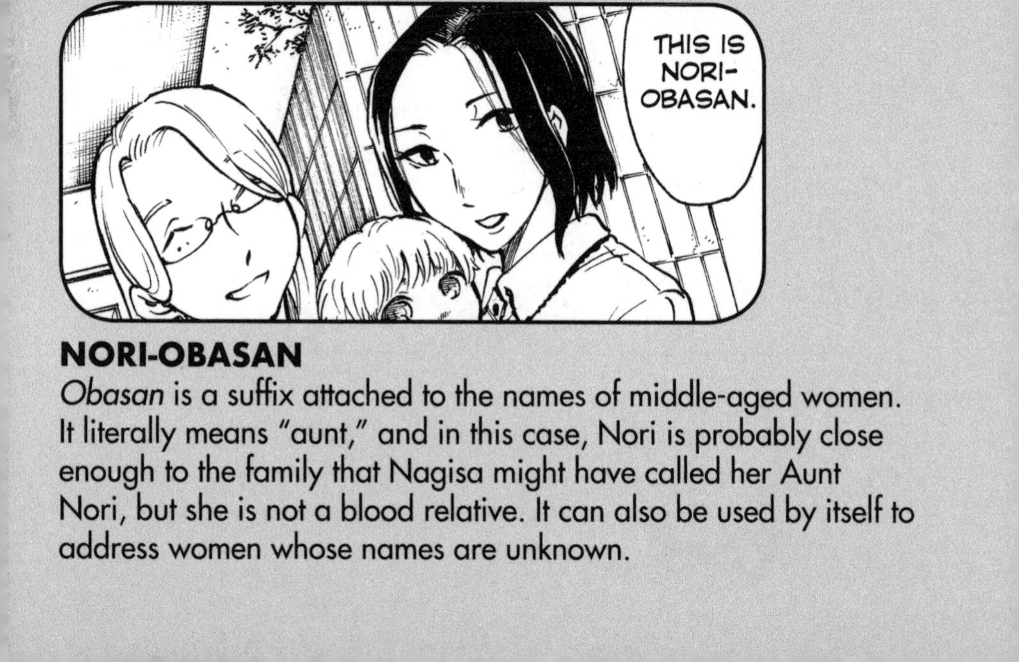
THIS IS NORI-OBASAN.

NORI-OBASAN

Obasan is a suffix attached to the names of middle-aged women. It literally means "aunt," and in this case, Nori is probably close enough to the family that Nagisa might have called her Aunt Nori, but she is not a blood relative. It can also be used by itself to address women whose names are unknown.

PAGE 189

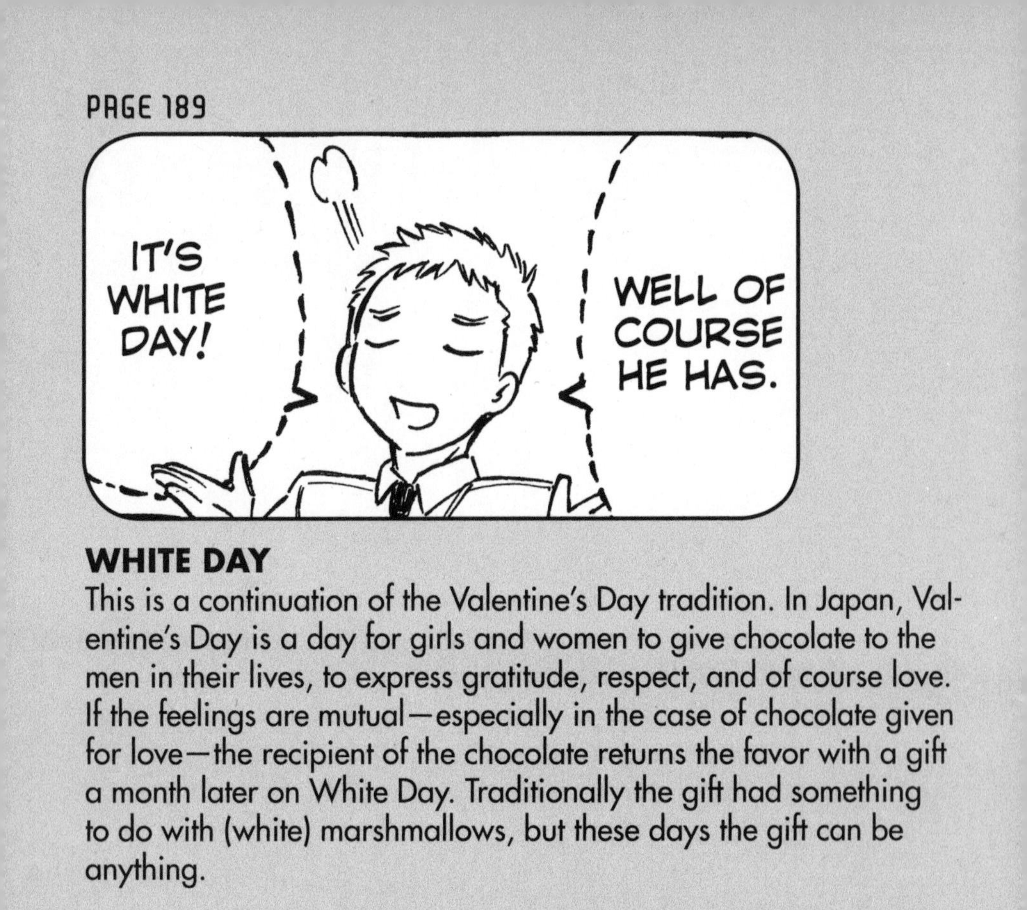
WELL OF COURSE HE HAS.
IT'S WHITE DAY!

WHITE DAY

This is a continuation of the Valentine's Day tradition. In Japan, Valentine's Day is a day for girls and women to give chocolate to the men in their lives, to express gratitude, respect, and of course love. If the feelings are mutual—especially in the case of chocolate given for love—the recipient of the chocolate returns the favor with a gift a month later on White Day. Traditionally the gift had something to do with (white) marshmallows, but these days the gift can be anything.

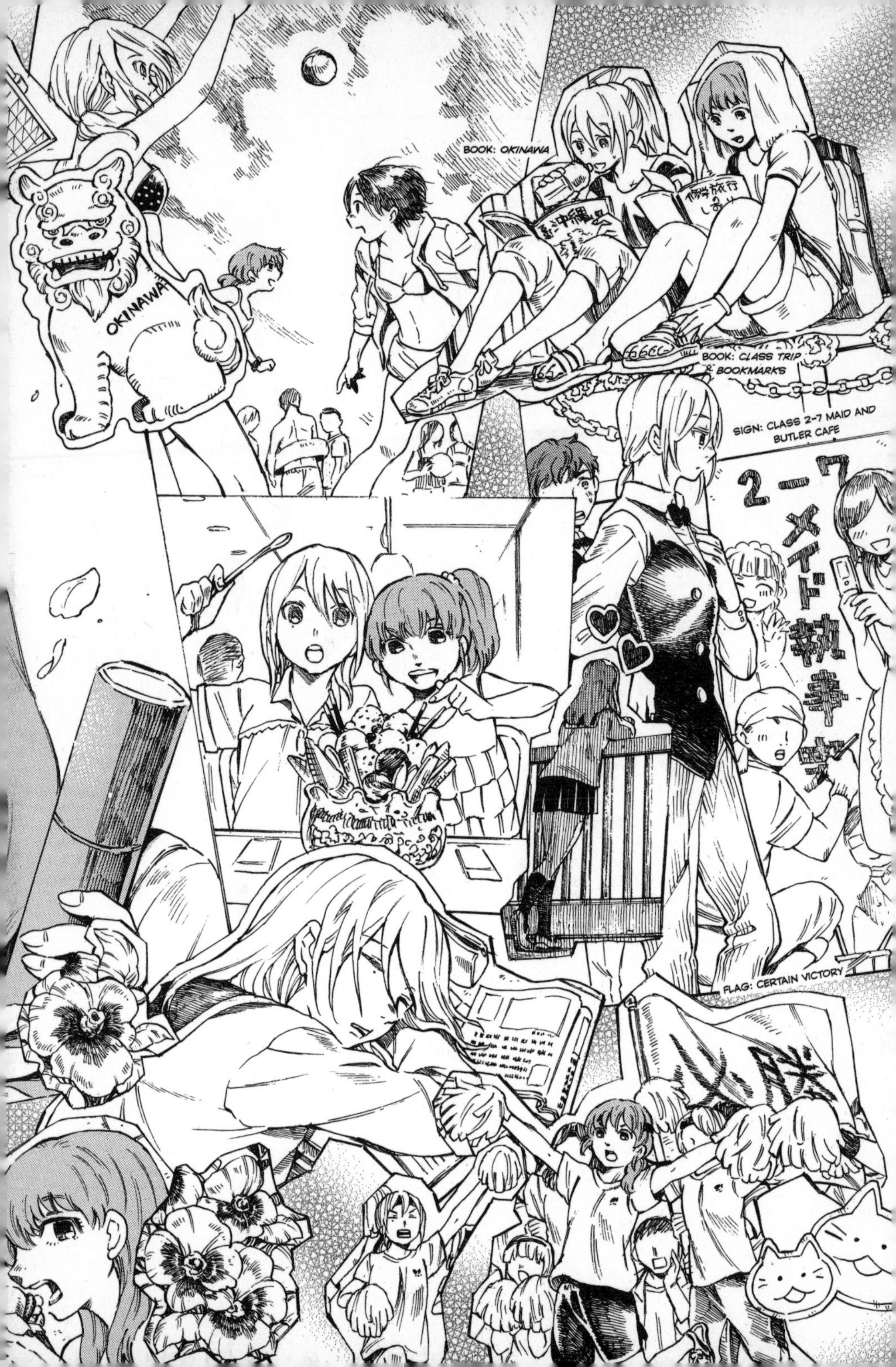
BOOK: OKINAWA
修学旅行 しおり
BOOK: CLASS TRIP BOOKMARKS
OKINAWA
SIGN: CLASS 2-7 MAID AND BUTLER CAFE
2-7 メイド執事
FLAG: CERTAIN VICTORY

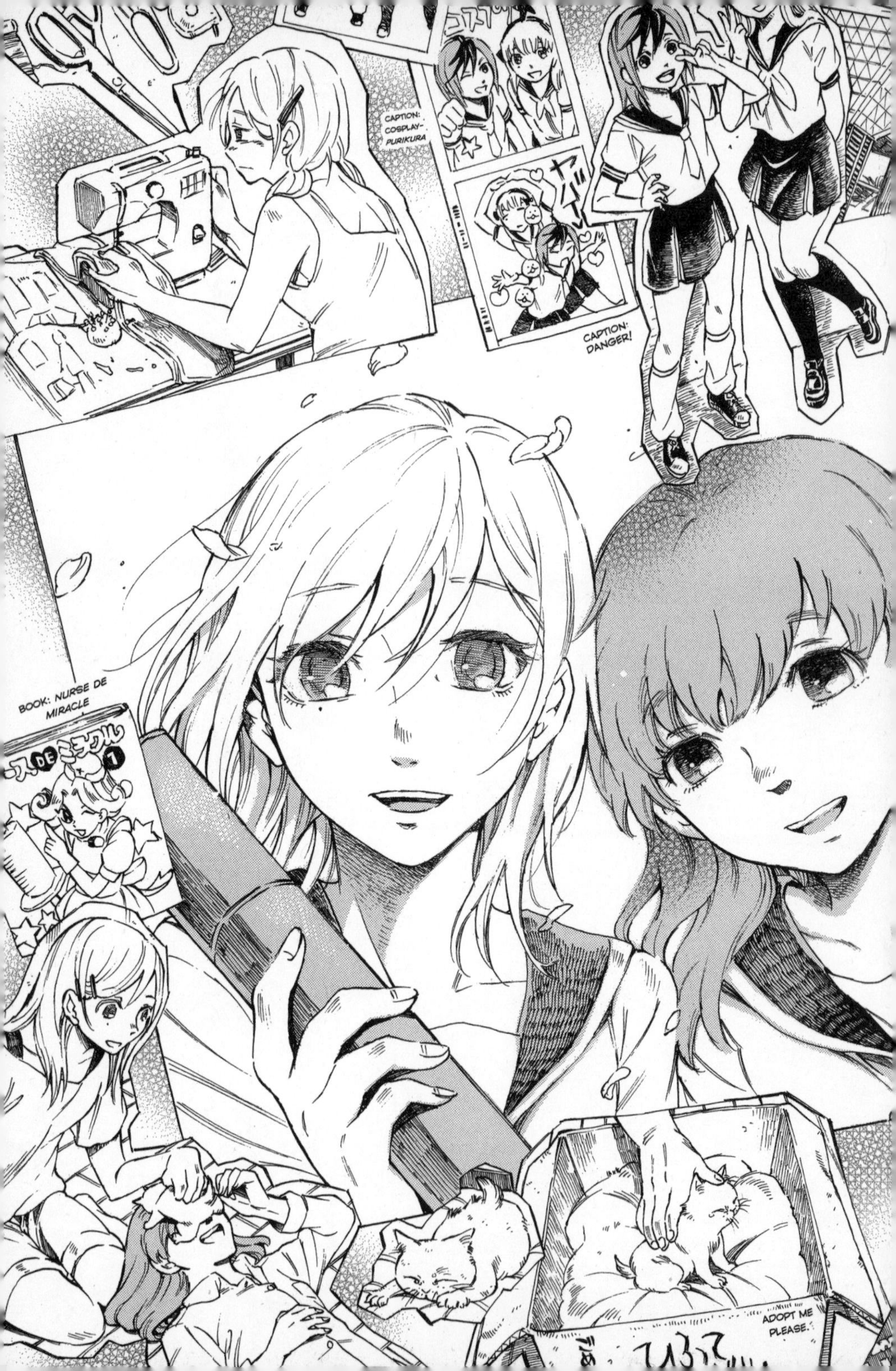
CAPTION: COSPLAY-PURIKURA
CAPTION: DANGER!
BOOK: NURSE DE MIRACLE
ADOPT ME PLEASE.

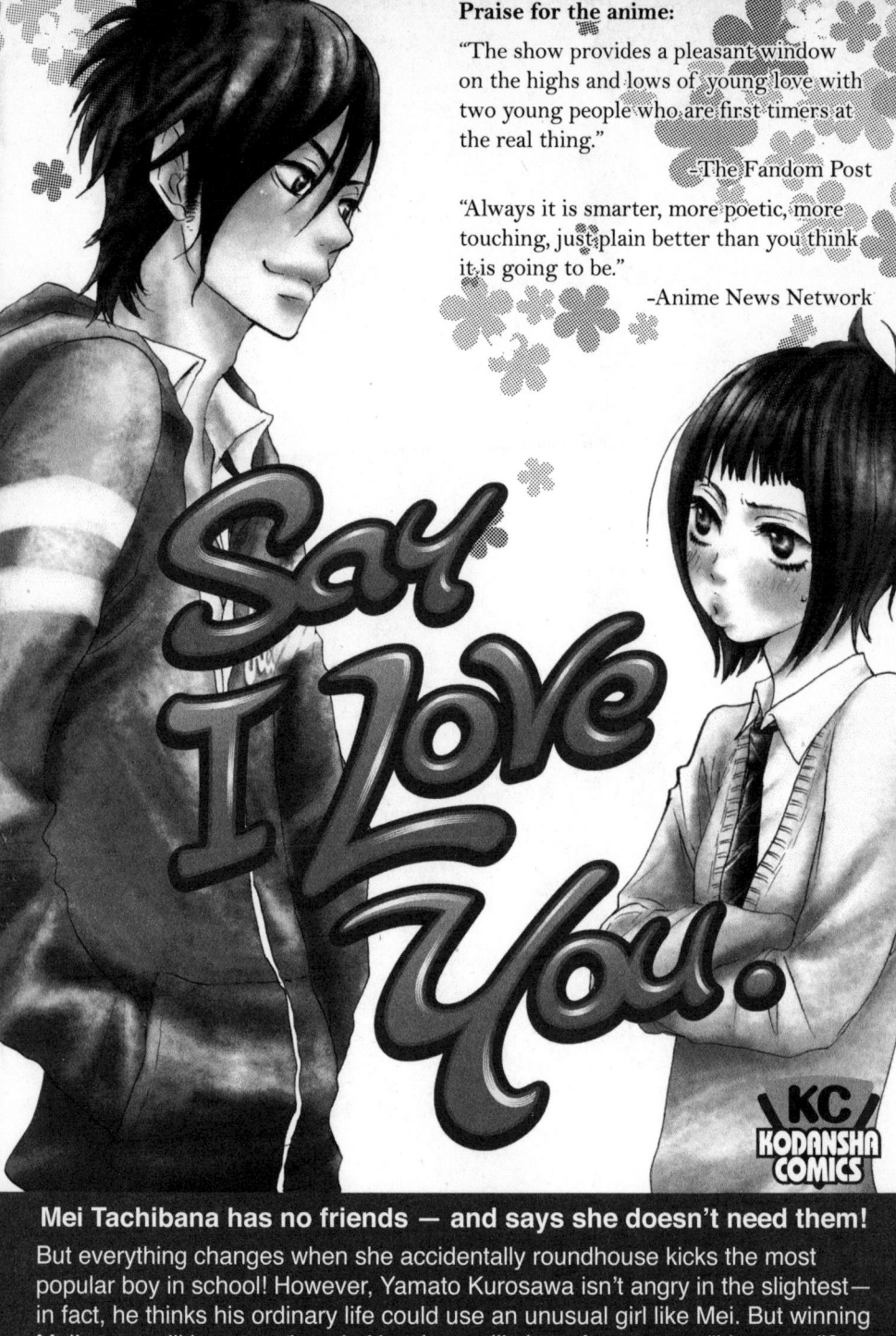

SAY I LOVE YOU.

KC
KODANSHA
COMICS

Mei Tachibana has no friends — and says she doesn't need them!
But everything changes when she accidentally roundhouse kicks the most popular boy in school! However, Yamato Kurosawa isn't angry in the slightest— in fact, he thinks his ordinary life could use an unusual girl like Mei. But winning Mei's trust will be a tough task. How long will she refuse to say, "I love you"?

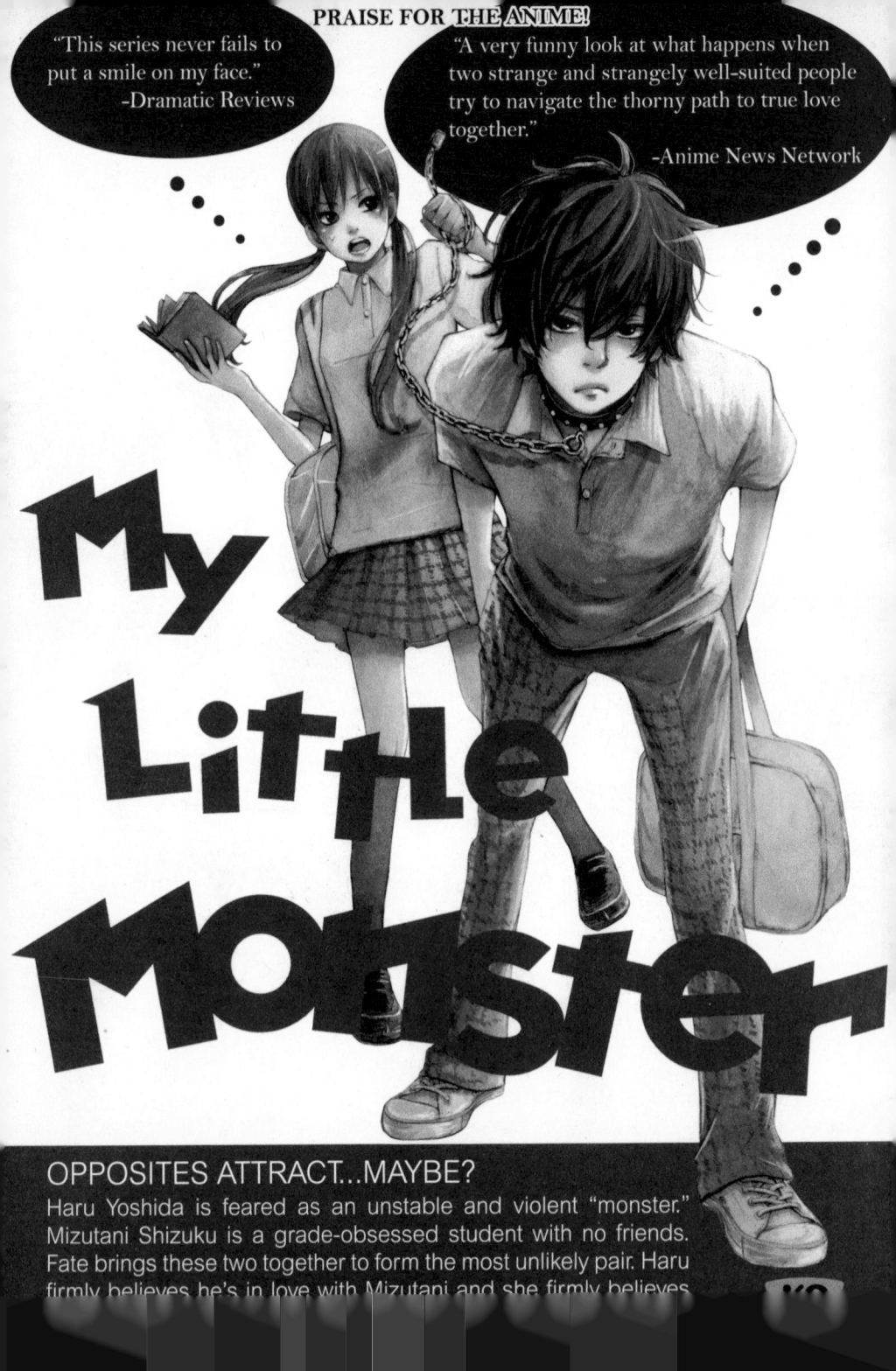

My Little Monster

OPPOSITES ATTRACT...MAYBE?

Haru Yoshida is feared as an unstable and violent "monster." Mizutani Shizuku is a grade-obsessed student with no friends. Fate brings these two together to form the most unlikely pair. Haru firmly believes he's in love with Mizutani and she firmly believes

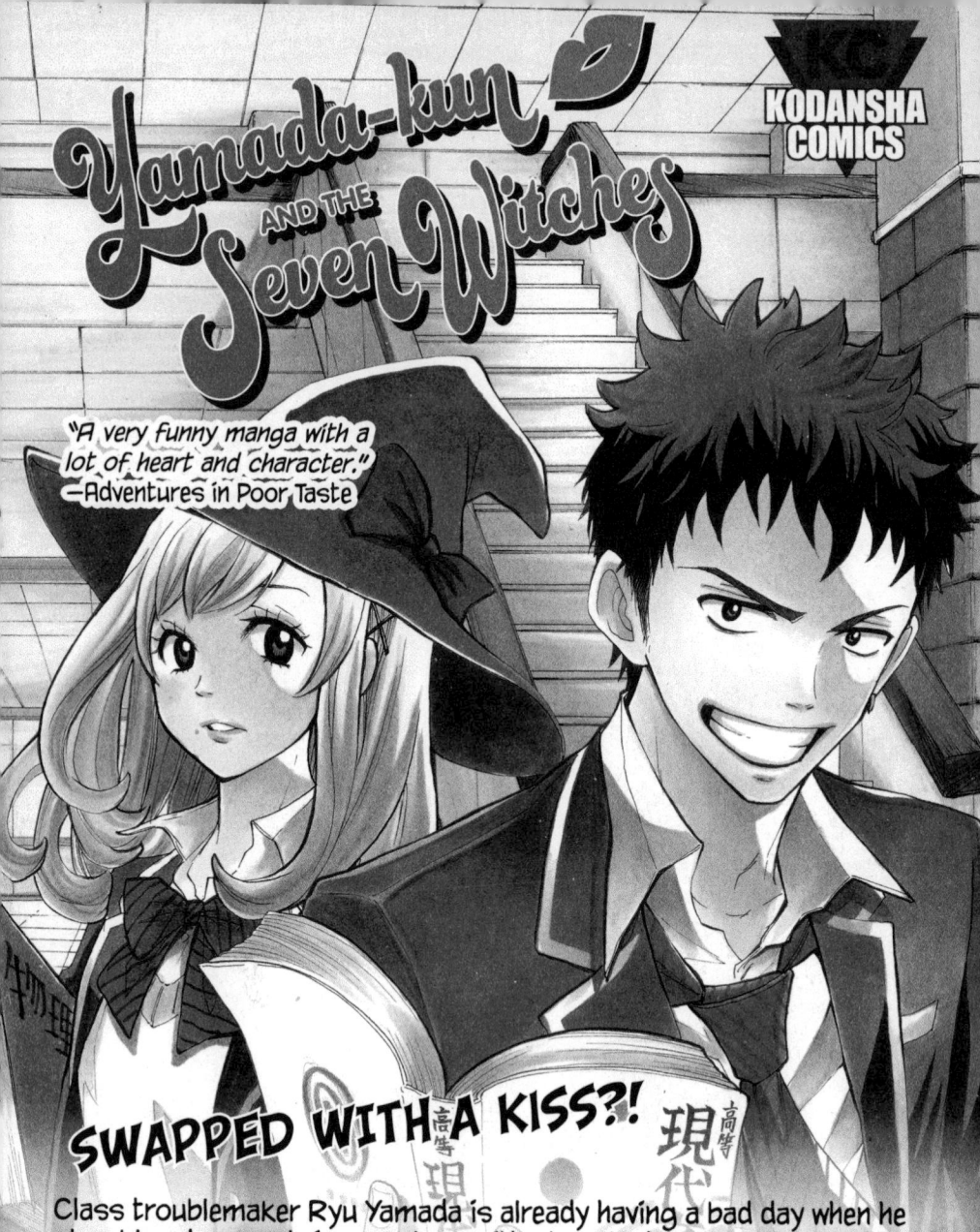

SWAPPED WITH A KISS?!

Class troublemaker Ryu Yamada is already having a bad day when he stumbles down a staircase along with star student Urara Shiraishi. When he wakes up, he realizes they have switched bodies—and that Ryu has the power to trade places with anyone just by kissing them! Ryu and Urara take full advantage of the situation to improve their lives, but with such an oddly amazing power, just how long will they be able to keep their secret under wraps?

Available now in print and digitally!

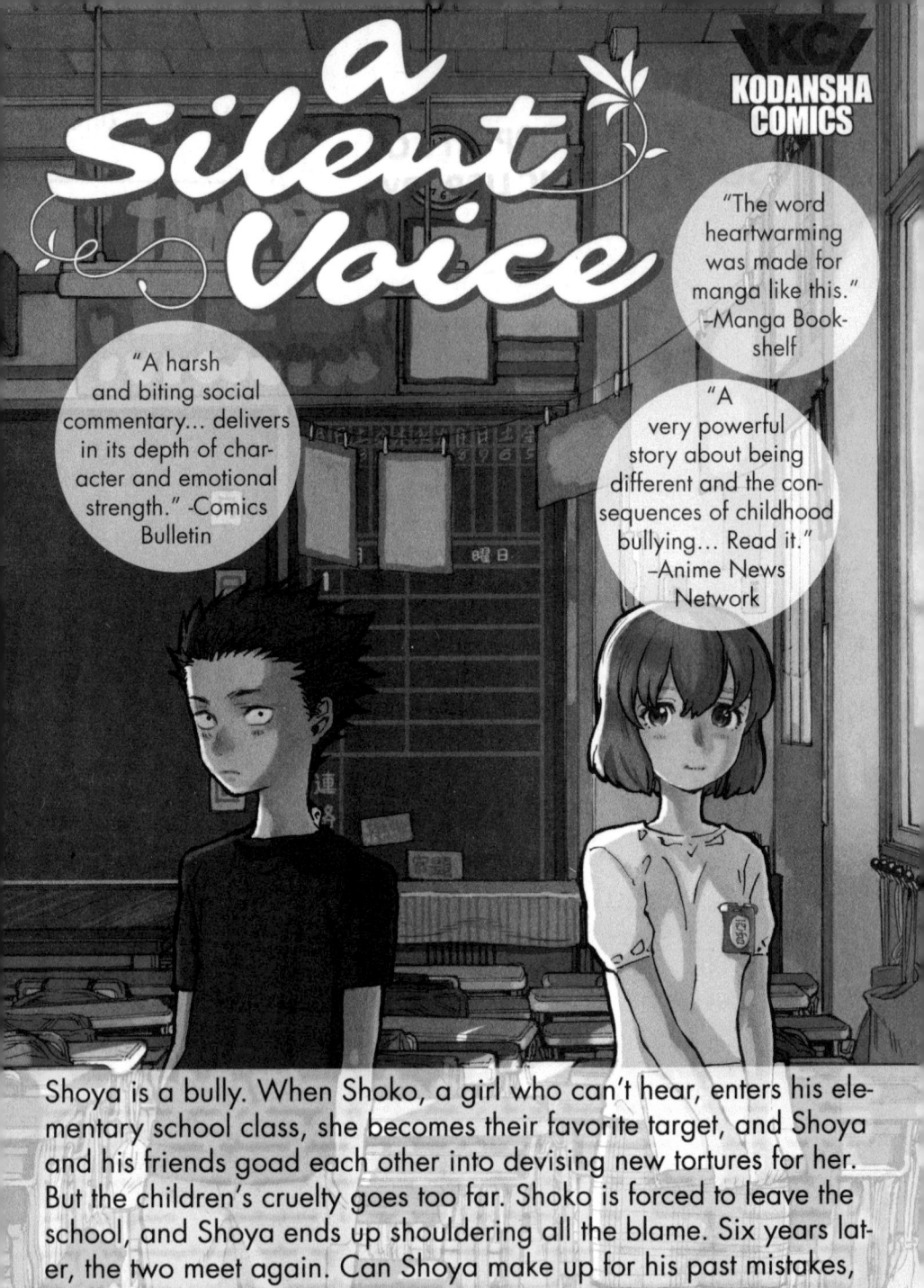

a Silent Voice

"The word heartwarming was made for manga like this." –Manga Bookshelf

"A harsh and biting social commentary... delivers in its depth of character and emotional strength." -Comics Bulletin

"A very powerful story about being different and the consequences of childhood bullying... Read it." –Anime News Network

Shoya is a bully. When Shoko, a girl who can't hear, enters his elementary school class, she becomes their favorite target, and Shoya and his friends goad each other into devising new tortures for her. But the children's cruelty goes too far. Shoko is forced to leave the school, and Shoya ends up shouldering all the blame. Six years later, the two meet again. Can Shoya make up for his past mistakes, or is it too late?

Available now in print and digitally!

Complex Age volume 5 is a work of fiction. Names, characters, places, and incidents are the products of the author's imagination or are used fictitiously. Any resemblance to actual events, locales, or persons, living or dead, is entirely coincidental.

A Kodansha Comics Trade Paperback Original.

Published in the United States by Kodansha Comics,
an imprint of Kodansha USA Publishing, LLC, New York.

Publication rights for this English edition arranged through Kodansha Ltd.,
Tokyo.

First published in Japan in 2015 by Kodansha Ltd., Tokyo, as Complex
Age volume 5.

ISBN 978-1-63236-428-9

Printed in the United States of America.

www.kodanshacomics.com

9 8 7 6 5 4 3 2 1

Translation: Alethea Nibley & Athena Nibley
Lettering: AndWorld Design
Editing: Lauren Scanlan
Kodansha Comics edition cover design: Phil Balsman